The Abortion Market

THE ABORTION MARKET

Buying and Selling Access in the Era Before Roe

KATHERINE J. PARKIN

PENN

University of Pennsylvania Press
Philadelphia

Published by
University of Pennsylvania Press
Philadelphia, Pennsylvania 19104-4112, USA
www.pennpress.org

EU Authorized Representative:
Easy Access System Europe - Mustamäe tee 50, 10621 Tallinn, Estonia,
gpsr.requests@easproject.com

Printed in the United States of America
on acid-free paper

10 9 8 7 6 5 4 3 2 1

A Cataloging-in-Publication record for this book
is available from the Library of Congress.
Hardcover ISBN 978-1-5128-2820-7
eBook ISBN 978-1-5128-2821-4

To Julie Berebitsky,
who fiercely supported and defended free and unimpeded access to legal and safe abortion services for all women (1962–2023)

CONTENTS

PREFACE

WE KNOW THAT ABORTION has always existed. In the United States, its history has centered principally on the vital stories of women and the courts in the twentieth century. After coming across an ad for a 1972 New York state "abortion directory," offering telephone numbers, addresses, and costs for providers, I began examining the market forces that shaped abortion provision in the decade before *Roe*, as an estimated one million women a year sought abortions. I was surprised to find that men dominated almost every aspect of selling abortions.

The evidence I discovered in the archives revealed men's elusive role. Between the sporadic legalization of therapeutic abortions in the 1960s and *Roe* in 1973, a burgeoning trade, made up of profit-driven hospitals and male doctors, entrepreneurial brokers, and compassionate providers, exploded into the open. An unexpected but welcome outcome of this industry was that in the era when abortion remained illegal, it delivered better, safer abortions for less money to more women. As I researched the abortion market before *Roe*, one of my most disconcerting discoveries was that ideologues committed to population control and eugenics played a central role in advancing legalization and access to abortion. Eugenicists in the mid-twentieth century who desired "good offspring" had allied comfortably with those who wanted to limit the population in general, not just fearful of the "wrong" people, but also committed to stopping *over*population. While proponents of both ideologies at first disapproved of abortion, by the late 1960s, many came to see the advantage of abortion access for all women to achieve the movements' end goals. As feminists advanced the language of individual choice, some men—like eugenicist and National Association for the Repeal of

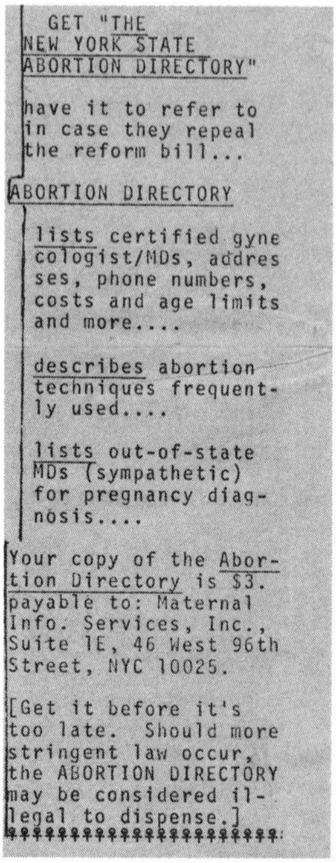

GET "THE NEW YORK STATE ABORTION DIRECTORY"

have it to refer to in case they repeal the reform bill...

ABORTION DIRECTORY

lists certified gynecologist/MDs, addresses, phone numbers, costs and age limits and more....

describes abortion techniques frequently used....

lists out-of-state MDs (sympathetic) for pregnancy diagnosis....

Your copy of the Abortion Directory is $3. payable to: Maternal Info. Services, Inc., Suite 1E, 46 West 96th Street, NYC 10025.

[Get it before it's too late. Should more stringent law occur, the ABORTION DIRECTORY may be considered illegal to dispense.]

FIGURE 1. This ad for a New York abortion directory appeared in the short-lived newspaper *Working Mother* in 1971–1972. The clear, direct advertising for information helped people access a legal abortion in New York State. Smith College Special Collections, Northampton, Massachusetts.

Abortion Laws (NARAL) co-founder Garrett Hardin—could not abide letting women choose to have children. Others, like population control advocate and NARAL co-founder Lawrence Lader, remained committed to abortion access as a means to depress the population, and as the organization turned toward feminism, he too left, going on to advocate for the first US approval of mifepristone (then called RU-486).[1]

The discovery that stalwart feminist organizations like the National Abortion Rights Action League, Planned Parenthood, and the Guttmacher Institute sprang from eugenicists and population control ideologues was disconcerting. Yet, over the subsequent fifty years, these abortion rights organizations renounced this abhorrent ideology and chose new leadership and missions centered on personal autonomy, reproductive justice for all, and the right to health care. By confronting this history, we can understand how population control motivated key financiers to make abortion access part of the national discourse and increasingly to make abortions available. We also learn that without this funding from these ideologues, the United States would not have secured the right to legal abortions. Like the third co-founder of NARAL, Dr. Lonny Myers, early abortion activists were not motivated by women's personal liberty, but instead mobilized for population control. Understanding the degree to which men and women of wealth, power, and pseudoscientific fixations shaped the evolving abortion market in the twentieth century lets us appreciate all the more the feminists who, in reframing the vital case for abortion access, eventually won an American majority to a better vision: a human being's fundamental right to control their own body and their own life.

Introduction

PREGNANT WOMEN TRAVELED from across the country and around the world to the small, rural, southwest community of Grove, Oklahoma. They relied on word-of-mouth networks to find a doctor who performed inexpensive abortions in a free-standing clinic. Dr. William Jennings Bryan Henrie started providing medical care in Grove in 1938 after moving to Oklahoma. He initially claimed to have done five thousand abortions across his twenty-four-year career. While many community members had been aware that Henrie did abortions in his unlicensed clinic, probably few could believe the scale of his operation, with a reported income of $2 million. He eventually confessed to even more shocking numbers: twenty thousand abortions and $8 million in profit.[1]

As his clinic grew, Henrie poured his profits back into the business. In 1952, he expanded and renovated a two-story brick building, accommodating an estimated seventy-five beds. In a town of fewer than a thousand people, the clinic's size relied on continued external demand. The doctor delivered 1,250 babies across his career, but abortion was the growth area in his professional practice. Between 1957 and 1962, his last five years in practice, he reportedly did a thousand abortions a year.[2]

How did this country doctor, traveling his rural county, caring for sick patients, and getting paid in chickens, land on abortion as his calling? Henrie argued that women had a right to an abortion and that the only crime, including the case that sent him to prison, was in denying him the ability to care for his patients. In an unpublished manuscript, Henrie contended that abortions allowed women and men to continue on with their lives and ensured that all children were wanted. He was proud of his role in helping people accept abortion as a fact of life, without shame. Henrie also claimed financial value in his work providing abortions, asserting that he saved his county and state tremendous amounts of money in helping women not have indigent and unwanted children. After he lost his medical license, Henrie took an increased interest in pushing the courts and legislatures to legalize abortion, including attending the Society for Humane Abortion's Conference on Abortion and Human Rights in 1966 and the 1969 founding meeting of the National Association for the Repeal of Abortion Laws (NARAL; later the National Abortion Rights Action League). He also underlined the importance of abortion in countering overpopulation.[3]

The national scarcity of providers for the illegal procedure guaranteed reputable doctors a consumer base that was willing to travel thousands of miles to get an abortion. The stability of the Henrie clinic, in a brick building downtown, also assured women that they did not need to worry that the provider would disappear or relocate his business, which was a risk women took in traveling long distances, especially to clinics in Puerto Rico and Mexico. Its size also ensured that women could be seen and attended to without an appointment, as telephone communication risked exposure and was another cost. Desperate people could confidently invest in the trek, hours and days by car, plane, and bus to a rural, agricultural area in the northeast corner of Oklahoma, because they could be confident that the doctor would see them and that the abortion cost would be relatively low.

According to one nurse who worked with him in 1955, Henrie charged the same fees for an abortion or a delivery, $25 if the woman went home or $75 if she stayed the night. From religious leaders to the flight attendants who greeted Henrie by name in a New York airport, the reliability and affordability of an abortion by Henrie spread through word-of-mouth networks that brought thousands upon thousands of people to Grove. His son remembered, "Pastors, priests, ministers all sent patients to dad. The network was basically through word of mouth. I had a friend

FIGURE 2. Dr. William Jennings Bryan Henrie delivered 1,250 babies across his career, but abortion was the growth area of his professional practice. In this 1962 photo he is heralded at a picnic attended by hundreds of residents in Grove, Oklahoma, before he is sent to prison. Author's collection.

of mine who was at a party in California and she was asked 'where are you from?' When she responded Grove, Oklahoma, they looked at her and said, 'Oh, abortion capital of the world.'"[4] Before legalization, Henrie typified illegal providers in the United States: a medical doctor who operated as a singular provider.[5]

The community served an important role in protecting Dr. Henrie's medical practice, because they relied on him for affordable medical care and employment opportunities. As one woman said to his son in 2003, "If it hadn't been for your dad, we would have starved to death." Henrie provided jobs, not just in his clinic, but in the town. One man interviewed while Henrie was in prison said, "This is a small town. He

[Henrie] brought a lot of business." As satirist Paul Krassner noted of Henrie's better-known Pennsylvania counterpart, Dr. Robert Douglas Spencer, providing abortions was "not merely tolerated; the community depended on it—the hotel, the restaurant, the dress shop—all thrived on the extra business that came from his out-of-town patients." The community benefited by keeping Henrie in business and did not expose or prosecute him.[6]

Dr. Henrie, by offering abortions in a rural area and balancing his profits with generosity and desperately needed general medical care, threaded the abortion needle. He prospered by meeting the nearly insatiable demand of a national and international consumer base of girls and women seeking abortions. Women found the money, traveled long distances, subjected themselves to providers they did not know, and returned home after the abortion. When women and men needed to find someone to do an abortion, networks sprang into action and produced phone numbers for rumored providers like Henrie, hoping that the care would be good and financially within reach. Each community with an abortion provider thought that they were "the abortion capital"—and effectively they were, for that network. From Charleston, South Carolina, to Rapid City, South Dakota, from Grove, Oklahoma, to Ashland, Pennsylvania, abortion providers rose up to meet the incredible demand emanating from single and married women of all faiths, all ages, all races, and all classes. An estimated one million women sought abortions each year.[7]

Those thousands of women who sought abortions from Dr. Henrie comprised one small piece of a massive consumer market, the buying and selling of abortions, in the decade before the Supreme Court decision *Roe v. Wade* made abortion legal nationally.[8] Women marshaling their financial resources drove the expansion of the market, but it did not accord them power in their consumer role. Instead, those women usually paid exorbitant prices for poor treatment. Men seeking to profit and women seeking to buy abortion procedures were essential to the creation of the abortion market. Business operators in this illegal industry, based on a publicly denounced clientele, profited from abortion's identification as a woman's shameful action rather than a medically warranted and socially valued procedure. Medical doctors who stepped into the void could make millions of dollars providing illegal abortions. Henrie and Spencer, who operated above board, treated women with respect, and did not overcharge, developed a lucrative business model based on volume.

Millions of women bought illegal abortions between 1962 and 1972, joined by relatively minuscule numbers of women who had legal abortions sanctioned as therapeutic, and followed by hundreds of thousands of women who bought legal ones in New York starting in 1970. In every capacity, abortion was dominated by men, including the lawyers and doctors who brought legal cases; the entrepreneurs who sought to profit; the legislators and doctors who advocated for the laws and policies governing the procedure; and those who advanced abortion to limit population growth. These men had no interest in women's rights or women's bodily autonomy generally, and never worked for abortion rights to empower women or secure reproductive justice. More often, men hindered women's agency and access by making abortions more costly, not only by profiting from referral information and the procedure, but also by insisting that abortions be approved by and performed by doctors and in hospitals. Even the most minimal reform of abortion laws demanded that women demean themselves by falsely claiming to be mentally unwell and paying exorbitant sums for those claims to be rubber-stamped by psychiatrists, and then paying more doctors and the hospital for the therapeutic abortion. Even when these cruel requirements were met, men approved only a negligible number of therapeutic procedures between 1962 and 1972.

Advocates hoped that the reform approach, modifying existing abortion laws and allowing therapeutic abortions, would improve and expand abortion access. Unwittingly, permitting abortions only to "preserve the mental or physical health of the mother or in cases of rape or incest," and then allowing the procedure only "in licensed hospitals," instead *reduced* the number of women receiving legal care by medical professionals. In 1965, only about eight thousand women (in a country of about 70 million women of childbearing age) who sought therapeutic abortions in the United States got approved. Therefore, those funding and leading the reform effort shifted their resources to repealing all the laws that controlled abortions.

With public support for abortion access limited only and very reluctantly to women whose pregnancies endangered their health, the medical profession remained recalcitrant. Even as some doctors confronted more and more patients with injuries and deaths from botched abortion attempts, the medical profession persisted in refusing to provide or support abortions, even for medically agreed-upon conditions. With the traditional medical structure shirking the role, male providers and entrepreneurs moved into the vacuum to profit from the incredible demand.

This book seeks to understand the consumer experience, with an estimated one million abortions bought each year. In the early 1960s, illegal abortions cost hundreds or thousands of dollars, with $1,000 a commonly referenced going rate and a good estimate of the average cost. To consider the potential profit, charging $1,000 for an illegal abortion in 1962 was the equivalent of paying about $10,000 sixty-two years later. With few indirect costs, illegal abortions attracted the interest of men who sought to capitalize on this consistently booming market. Women, with limited information and time to address their unwanted pregnancies, had to pay dearly for information and access. Even confirming the pregnancy took much more time and money, with the first at-home pregnancy tests not yet available. Before *Roe*, women had to pay for a doctor or clinic visit, as well as the pregnancy test, and await the results. Illegal providers preferred to do abortions at the eighth week of pregnancy or earlier; certainly ten or twelve weeks was an upper limit for most, and the later the pregnancy, the more expensive and difficult it was to find someone to do the procedure. For every unwanted pregnancy, timely information was of the essence.[9]

Most women seeking abortions were effectively poor relative to abortion's exorbitant cost. A teenager living at home, working a pink-collar part-time or seasonal job, could not easily finance an abortion. A college student who had a job to pay tuition and living expenses did not have a way to quickly come up with the doctor's fee plus transportation costs for an abortion. A married couple with several children did not have a lot of give in a household budget already committed to a mortgage, food, and transportation. Even when economic competition helped drive the 1971 cost of the procedure down to $150 in New York City, many women still faced a struggle to pay the cost on top of travel expenses. Without a competitive market, prices did not drop as precipitously or as fast anywhere else.[10]

Of course, women in absolute poverty faced these challenges at a tremendous disadvantage. Attorneys seeking plaintiffs for abortion test cases *Roe v. Wade* (Texas) and *Doe v. Bolton* (Georgia) knew they had to find poor white women in difficult circumstances, because if women could afford an abortion, they would no longer be pregnant and be able to serve as plaintiffs. It was precisely because poor women lacked resources that they elicited the question from Justices Thurgood Marshall and William O. Douglas, "Did existing abortion restrictions deny 'equal protection by discriminating against the poor?'" For those advancing abortion rights in the courts and in popular opinion, using Black women as test cases risked not generating empathy or, worse, engendering vilification.[11]

In addition to facing a lack of empathy or outright racism, girls and women of color seeking abortions faced additional obstacles. They had the economic burden of paying for the procedure and the necessary travel, but also lacked fruitful connections to medical doctors and financial lenders, as well as access to better-paying jobs. Those in the business of referrals and doing abortions readily noted that white, middle- and upper-class women comprised most of their market. Black women across the country could not find affordable providers for legal abortions, most especially for therapeutic abortions, which went almost exclusively to white women. Some Black providers tried to help and profit by offering reduced rates to Black girls and women.[12]

What this reveals, in its absence, is that those motivated to support abortion rights to limit the population or to profit did not generally target abortion access to people of color. Some overpopulation adherents publicly stated that it was white, middle-class women driving their population concerns by wreaking more havoc on the planet, consuming many more resources than poorer families. Therefore, they principally targeted abortion information in the United States to white women, rather than only singling out Black or Puerto Rican women rhetorically or in practice.[13]

Eugenicists and population control adherents also realized by the 1960s that overt racism was counterproductive to their goal of achieving a reduction in unwanted children. Wary of the claim some Black men made that abortions were a genocide on African Americans, individuals and organizations generally parsed their rhetoric more carefully than in decades past. And many shielded themselves against the accusation of racism by actively incorporating a defense of women of color into their abortion arguments. Planned Parenthood-World Population lawyer and population control supporter Harriet Pilpel charged in 1970 that without abortion law reforms, Black and Puerto Rican women faced discrimination and increased risk of death due to illegal abortions. Pilpel also bemoaned that abortion-related deaths occurred disproportionately in women of color, with Puerto Rican women making up 23 percent and Black women 56 percent of the dead. Legal scholar Mary Ziegler found that abortion rights groups embraced the language of "choice" and asserted respect and support for whatever choices women of color would make regarding abortion. They did so even as they continued their coercive and manipulative efforts to compel sterilizations, birth control, and abortions among women of color.[14]

By the early 1970s, about two-thirds of Americans feared population growth, and this anxiety, along with shifting legal ideas about constitutional rights and rights to privacy, as well as a building assertion of women's rights, converged in growing support for abortion access. This study explores all the ways that people bought and sold abortion access, as well as the ways the marketing of abortion shaped public discourse around the procedure. While many looking to the past have focused on the efforts of a few exceptional, heroic women supporting women's abortion access, this account analyzes the stunning amount of money poured into laying the groundwork for that access, including its ultimate legalization with *Roe v. Wade*.

Population control ideologues invested money in abortion to help women *control population growth*. Each year an estimated one million girls and women bought illegal abortions from coast to coast. Abortion supporters realized, therefore, that unlike with earlier birth control efforts, they did not need to invest in door-to-door proselytizing by paid emissaries; American women were not only already seeking out abortions, they were also paying through the nose for them. Putting money into abortion access for those women was seen as an excellent return on investment. Moreover, by shielding their eugenic purpose from view, population control advocates were able to invest in legitimizing scientific studies to persuade political leaders to shape government policy to help pay for the rest.[15]

Chapter 1 considers how, starting in the 1960s, population control proponents funded the discourse that laid the foundation for social acceptance and eventual legal footing for abortion. Individuals and foundations strategized that, in addition to funding population studies and demographic reports, they could fund research on maternal deaths caused by illegal abortions, the safety of legal abortions, and the lack of psychological harm that abortions created. With this expanded focus, they could shift the conversation from viewing abortion as bad and dangerous to promoting legal abortion to save and improve lives. Population financiers also paid in full for the legalization of abortion, from early efforts that laid the groundwork, like the formation of NARAL, all the way to *Roe v. Wade*; the money flowed directly from and through the population movement. From targeting state legislatures and courts to the Supreme Court, the money came from eugenicist men like Hugh Moore and Joseph Sunnen, and the movement advanced arguments centered on everything but reproductive justice and women's rights. While most of the effort and funds helped shepherd normalization and legalization, there were also some instances in which benefactors sought to reduce costs to drive the abortion business. This chapter considers how eugenics and fears of overpopulation drove funding for the three intertwined efforts, laying the foundation, fighting legal battles, and encouraging abortion business.

Whether they found a legal abortion or an illegal one, an estimated one million girls and women a year faced the crushing need to find an immense amount of money in short order. Chapter 2 examines how people acquired the necessary funds in the fastest, most private way possible. Exploring loans, funds, and other strategies discloses the motivations of funders. It also reveals the strength of a massive consumer market. With the potential for a $1 billion annual market (one million abortions at $1,000 each), capitalists and entrepreneurs vied to get into the market and supported legalization to perpetuate its growth.[16]

A new business was born in July 1970 with the legalization of abortion in New York. With virtually no restrictions or regulations, businessmen nationally did everything from setting up phone banks to charge money for referral information to securing kickbacks from doctors and hospitals, and even chartering planes to deliver women to abortion providers. These efforts were aided by those who bought and sold advertising and abortions, and these men are the subject of Chapter 3. From small towns to big cities, and especially on college and university campuses, advertisers made media buys in newspapers and magazines across the country. For people seeking abortion access, this catered approach delivered exactly what consumers needed: a phone number to unlock it all. This chapter showcases how businesses and consumers fully understood selecting an abortion to be like any other service bought on the open market, with legalization enabling new consumer protections and analysis, including a review in *Consumer Reports*.

Many of the entrepreneurs marketed directly to college students, and Chapter 4 analyzes the unique and lucrative college campus setting, filled with large numbers of young women experiencing unexpected pregnancies and the subsequent desperation to find and pay for an abortion. The growing expectation that colleges and universities should be attentive to the needs of their students—male and female, rich and poor—transformed institutional approaches to medical care and the administrative responses to the open discourse surrounding abortion. Tracing the shift from policing sexuality to empowering women, this analysis of abortion on college campuses before *Roe* offers an important window to examine changing ideas about and legal responses to abortion discourse and access. Starting in 1970, students demanded abortion information and access, and organized when they found both came at a cost that was both steep and discriminatory, especially to the poorest among them.

Chapter 5 argues that before *Roe*, legal and medical restrictions forced women to pay significant sums to travel for abortions. The desire for distance and the desperate need for access led thousands of women to fly to Japan, Puerto Rico, and England, and to travel south to Mexico. For those women who stayed stateside, more affordable access emerged and eased their travel burden. As abortion providers opened for business, out-of-state women flocked to regional centers like Kansas, California, and Washington, D.C., and entrepreneurs across the country developed opportunities to profit.

The final chapter is focused on New York as the center of the abortion market in the years immediately before *Roe*. It considers the suburbs of New York City and upstate New York as destinations for both providers and women seeking to buy abortions, and then analyzes New York City, the "abortion capital of the world" between 1970 and 1972. The city provided hundreds of thousands of legal abortions in the time between state-level legalization and the passage of *Roe*, and this chapter analyzes how legalization transformed the economics of abortion in the city, especially for hospitals (private and public), clinics, and individual doctors. At first, abortions could be performed legally in private doctors' offices, but objections led to new restrictions, and subsequently abortions could be done only in sanctioned clinics and hospitals. Entrepreneurs scrambled to open private clinics to profit from the needs of out-of-state women—who would eventually comprise about 60 percent of all abortion consumers in New York. The clinics realized staggering profits—with one clinic worker describing it as "like Monopoly money," piled high in a back room. In addition to all the ways abortions were sold, the chapter also analyzes how consumers learned where to buy them in New York.[17]

This study concludes that the abortion market was a powerful economic force in American life between 1962 and 1972. By the fall of 1970, if people were looking to get an abortion, they could rely on word-of-mouth networks, and some needed only to check their local newspaper, pick up a copy of *Seventeen* or *Playboy*, or look up an abortion provider under "A" in the phone book. While many have imagined that securing an abortion before *Roe* was best understood as a hidden, woman-only experience, this history reveals the extent to which businesses and businessmen selling abortions shaped the experience of buying abortions for millions of women.

1

Solving the Population Crisis

A HISTORY OF THE ABORTION market in the decade before *Roe* must consider the role population control played in driving financial investment in every aspect of abortion access. Wealthy financiers used newspapers and magazines as open forums where Americans could learn about abortion and funded the reform and legalization battles. Rich men (and a few women) advanced abortion as a favored solution to *over*population, an imagined problem they considered to be a dire threat. Across the twentieth century, population control leaders invested a tremendous amount of money in developing and distributing birth control. As innovation and scientific advances made abortion a demonstrably safe option, the movement embraced abortion in the arsenal of weapons they used to fight the imagined war against population growth. Instead of prioritizing a woman's personal choice, they funded abortion access because it aligned perfectly with the goal of people voluntarily limiting their reproduction. The population control movement and their eugenic allies were at the heart of the effort to legalize abortion, with financial resources and cultivated scholarly and political networks. While the term "eugenics" might conjure an image of people who aimed to lower the reproduction rates of *certain groups* of people, the movements explicitly underlined the rhetoric of population control for all.

As early as 1916, Margaret Sanger argued that a looming threat of overpopulation threatened the country's peace and stability. The coast-to-coast newspaper coverage of overpopulation, starting during the First World War, escalated to hundreds of articles by the 1920s. Alarmists warned of a population crisis, particularly "among the least desirable." Sanger and others encouraged the United States to accept birth control (illegal for many into the 1970s) to help "uneducated" and "foreigner" groups who persisted in having large numbers of children. As historian Matthew Connelly notes of the early twentieth century, "Initially eugenics was the more mainstream movement, so birth control advocates" used it to build support. Eugenicists and population control adherents did not infiltrate the birth control movement or the later abortion movement; instead, those seeking support for family planning relied on leadership, funding, and ideology from eugenic and population control–focused individuals and foundations.[1]

As scientific advances led to greater life expectancy worldwide, the potential for exponential population growth aligned perfectly with fears of global starvation and increased militarism fueled by the struggle for food, creating a manufactured crisis of global *over*population. Following two world wars, business and government leaders amped up this fear of more war and conflict, first laid out by Sanger in 1916. While activists, historians, and critics have charted Sanger's ideological fealty to women's rights and eugenics, Sanger and those she worked with at Planned Parenthood also shared a long-standing commitment to population control.[2]

In fact, while we might imagine Sanger as the singular leader of the birth control movement that resulted in the feminist organization Planned Parenthood, the history of the movement and the organization is markedly more complex. The men heading and funding Planned Parenthood (and its various iterations) first forced the name change (against Sanger's objection) in 1942 from the Birth Control Federation of America and then drove Sanger out of leadership completely by the end of the 1950s. From changes in name and leadership to barring Sanger "from mentioning family planning in public appearances," the population control movement wanted to save family planning from the taint of being a "women's issue."[3]

Eugenicist William Vogt, whose 1948 *Road to Survival* gave birth to "apocalyptic environmentalism" decrying both consumer culture and overpopulation, served as the president of Planned Parenthood for eleven years, starting in 1951. Vogt and his male colleagues wanted to control reproduction to reduce the global population, and, as part of a "reformed eugenics," embraced the language of population control. None of the Planned Parenthood leadership considered family planning a women's rights issue, including one of the few women who publicly represented the organization, attorney and eugenicist Harriet Pilpel. Instead, her writings in the *Atlantic* and the *New York Times* and speeches to conferences all underlined fears about population control. Indeed, the first few editions of Planned Parenthood's *Medical Handbook*, published between 1962 and 1971, consistently described overpopulation concerns and stated organizational aims including stimulating scientific research about the eugenic implications of human fertility. There was nary a word about women's rights or reproductive justice for the poor. Pilpel also served as legal counsel for the Human Betterment Association, later renamed the Association for Voluntary Sterilization (AVS), and argued in the *Atlantic* in 1969 that "voluntary abortion should be infinitely preferred to compulsory sterilization or compulsory birth control, and that may well be the choice."[4]

The World Population Emergency Campaign (WPEC) was founded in 1960 by Hugh Moore and General William H. Draper Jr. "for the purpose of alerting Americans to the danger of the 'world population explosion' and raising money for international birth control programs." The WPEC attracted wealthy, connected people. The organization officially joined forces with Planned Parenthood as the PP-WPEC in 1963. For ten years, starting in 1964 and under the leadership of Dr. Alan Guttmacher, the organization was Planned Parenthood-World Population, dropping "Emergency Campaign" and leaving their alliance and commitment to population control clear to all.[5]

Backed by research reports, books, articles, and conference proceedings that substantiated a "population crisis," environmental groups clamored for a national and global reduction in population for the good of the planet. In the years preceding *Roe*, the environmental movement's popularity dramatically outpaced that of the women's movement and was vitally important in shaping attitudes toward abortion in this era. For example, in 1971 the Zero Population Growth (ZPG) group had twice as many members (30,000) as the National Organization for Women (NOW). The Sierra Club, a decades-old environmental organization, claims that its membership surpassed a hundred thousand that same year. In part, the popularity of these environmental groups, the adoption of "apocalyptic" fears about population size, and support for abortion stemmed from biologists Paul Ehrlich and Ann Ehrlich's 1969 book, *The Population Bomb.* The authors offered a full-throated endorsement of abortion access, calling it "a highly effective weapon" against overpopulation.[6]

The presumed existence of *over*population was an ideal focus for a burgeoning university network of researchers like the Ehrlichs, in fields ranging from anthropology to zoology. Philanthropists and foundations funded a whole host of shell committees, councils, scholarly journals, academic positions and departments, and government programs to facilitate the study of birth control and abortion. They used considerable financial means to shape the thinking and practices of everyday people through seemingly reputable, scholarly works.[7]

In 2012, Supreme Court Justice Ruth Bader Ginsburg described the period preceding the historic *Roe v. Wade* decision. She remembered, "'At the time, there was a concern about too many people inhabiting our planet. There was an organization called Zero Population Growth.' She continued, 'In the press, there were articles about the danger of crowding our planet. So there was at the time of *Roe v. Wade* considerable concern about overpopulation.'" Against the backdrop of a narrative of choice, the right to privacy, and the heroic experiences of the Jane collective in Chicago, Ginsburg illuminated a powerful undercurrent running through the abortion activism of the 1960s and early 1970s leading up to the *Roe* decision. A belief in overpopulation fueled a financial commitment to the birth control and abortion rights movements to help stem the tide. Indeed, anyone reading the paper or watching television between 1962 and 1972 would have been familiar with the argument that overpopulation was plaguing the world.[8]

Historical distance from these origins, however, distorts our understanding. From the vantage point of the late twentieth and early twenty-first centuries, historical assessments held that righteous public activism and courageous leadership secured legal abortion, informed by legal scholars about the ins and outs of a handful of cases (*Griswold*, *Doe*), especially *Roe*. But as Ginsburg remembered it, overpopulation informed the popular consciousness of Americans and did so with everything from pamphlets, newspaper and magazine coverage, and best-selling books to a presidential commission and foreign-aid funding. The discourse and the paid effort to put it front and center had the effect of normalizing population control language and concepts in ways that proved vital to the acceptance of abortion. Funded by a commitment to population control, abortion appeared in a television sitcom plot, as a topic on morning talk shows, and in skywriting over the Super Bowl.[9]

While the goal of abortion access ostensibly married the feminist aims of the growing women's movement and the control sought by population crisis groups (such as Planned Parenthood), it did not generally align the movements. At points they did join forces, with some in the population control groups grudgingly including the language of rights as a distasteful necessity, and some feminists conceding to include population concerns, including NOW in 1970. NOW president Wilma Scott Heide led the organization to form partnerships with several population control organizations, including the Population Council and ZPG, and "asserted that women's rights and overpopulation were inextricably linked." Although there was resistance, significant feminist leaders in the abortion effort also embraced population concerns outright.[10]

Betty Friedan's revolutionary feminist manifesto *The Feminine Mystique* charged that the "problem that has no name" helped cause "the population explosion." Seven years later, in calling on college students to join a general strike on August 26, 1970, the fiftieth anniversary of women getting the vote, she added to the more expected feminist claims, "Ecology also puts a moral demand on women to limit their families to counteract overpopulation." California abortion rights leader Patricia Maginnis's growing realization of "the horror of overpopulation" not only motivated her desire to have an abortion, but also led her to radical abortion activism. The analysis of Maginnis and her allies Rowena Gurner and Lana Clarke Phelan as leading feminists for abortion ignored the women's long-standing motivation to control the population, as well as their funding from and alliance with leading eugenicists, Cordelia Scaife May and Garrett Hardin. In 1970, Maginnis's referral and activist group Society for Humane Abortion (SHA) brought on Richard Bowers as its executive director, after he co-founded ZPG with Paul Ehrlich. In his final report before stepping down from ZPG and moving to SHA, he asserted that without complete abortion access, voluntarism would not work to stem the rising birth rate. Moreover, he anticipated that achieving "family limitation" would not be possible without its being "enforced by criminal law sanctions."[11]

In the span of just a decade, attitudes of Americans on abortion, including those actively involved in population control and the birth control movement, moved to acceptance. Compromises, strategies, and alliances shifted with the social and political headwinds, with once radical and moderate categories blurred and evolving. What once seemed crass and ill-advised (Hugh Moore's 1954 pamphlet *The Population Bomb Is Everyone's Baby*) gave rise to best-selling books, appearances on late-night talk shows, established organizations, government policy, and presidential speeches.[12]

Men in command of fortunes borne of Dixie Cups, automotive parts, and oil opened their checkbooks to ensure that eugenic and population control ideologies suffused the abortion rights movement. Illuminating how this ideological sell transpired reveals men's central role in securing legalized abortion. Wealthy women also proved to be staunch supporters, often serving as a 1960s and 1970s "mink brigade," holding meetings out of their apartments at the Dakota in New York City, and enshrined on boards of abortion rights organizations.[13]

While abortion law scholar Mary Ziegler concluded in 2009 that "the abortion reform and population control movements remained distinct before *Roe*," in fact the movements were so completely intertwined as to be indistinct. The wealthy, seeking to control the country's population, extended their influence to the highest reaches of the federal government, including social agencies, legislators, and presidents. Instead of evolving independently, population control infused the abortion reform and repeal movements from start to finish, ultimately securing *Roe*.[14]

Instead of crude caricatures or readily-seized-upon vile language that condemned groups of people, American eugenicists in the 1960s and early 1970s subverted ideals of scientific research and intellectual inquiry to their aims. Individuals and organizations advanced birth control, sterilization, and abortion to control population growth with "crypto-eugenics" and steered clear of the damning language of "imbeciles" and "the unfit" that could have exposed their ideology.[15] Across the twentieth century, historian Wendy Kline found that eugenically motivated messaging appeared in popular magazines, on the radio, and on television without generating "any negative, Nazi-based connotations." Dating back to the 1930s and stretching into the 1970s, for example, eugenicist Paul Popenoe used marital counseling as a pretext to advance his "positive eugenics" aim of encouraging increased reproduction only among what he deemed desirable people. It may seem like an oxymoron to see the words positive and eugenics together—outrageous, even. However, historians have adopted this terminology to capture another way that eugenics operated in American ideology. Rather than the readily identifiable distasteful historical terminology of the early twentieth century, such as sterilizing the "feebleminded" and controlling the "unfit," advanced by the "negative eugenicists," the "positive eugenicists" in the later decades of the twentieth century sought to encourage the reproduction of only those deemed "good."[16]

One way later eugenic adherents achieved social acceptance (and escaped detection) was to adapt to more socially palatable language. They built on the success of eugenicist Frederick Osborn, who noted in 1968 that "eugenic goals are most likely to be attained under a name other than eugenics." Historians use words like "mundane" and "ordinariness" to describe the pervasiveness of eugenics in American culture, with one noting that it "gave scientific authority to social fears and moral panics" and defining it as a "'modern' way of talking about social problems." Medical and scientific figures embraced eugenic ideology and shrouded it in neutral, scientific language.[17]

Another significant aspect of the relationship between later eugenics and abortion is that while legal scholars emphasize how eugenics came "to describe the use of law to prevent the births of persons with physical, mental, or moral defects," the social, cultural, and political use of the ideology was applied in broader and softer, nonlegal ways. Looking back to the 1910s, 1920s, and 1930s, when the majority of states embraced eugenics ideology to pass laws that allowed them to forcibly sterilize "unfit" people, it is tempting to believe that the ideology was overturned through law. Instead, it was absorbed into policies and programs that helped ensure that unwanted children did not burden parents or society. These efforts did sometimes home in on poor communities, including especially African Americans, Mexican Americans, and Native Americans, but publicly supporters maintained that the effort was to end poverty, not to eliminate people. The rationale, they claimed, was to use abortion to save both individuals and society from the burden of unwanted children that led to poverty, rather than eliminating people based on "defects." Moreover, at home and abroad, supporters of eugenic ideals discovered after the Second World War that forced sterilization risked an association with the Nazis. Groups instead turned their public relations machines to the new language of individual rights and population policy. By the 1960s, eugenicists realized that they could invest in abortion access to get people to seek out abortions themselves, and as they rebranded themselves, they found success in ensuring the availability of voluntary sterilization, something that white men increasingly wanted, too.[18]

Of course, not all who advanced abortion rights were motivated by population control and not all who advanced population control embraced eugenic ideology. Many who believed that controlling one's body and having a right to privacy were paramount supported abortion rights. Many who believed that the planet could not sustain the growing population favored limiting their own reproduction and ensuring access to affordable birth control and abortions. But within this milieu were identifiable eugenics figures who advanced eugenic ideals in their writings or were members of eugenics-focused groups like the American Eugenics Society. Rebranded individuals and organizations in this pre-*Roe* era are not off the hook. Despite new language and rationales, people and organizations continued to be fueled by the same beliefs. Organizations that welcomed individuals with professed eugenic ideology into membership and leadership had a set of shared values. An organization not wanting to be associated with the Nazis is not a rejection of eugenic beliefs, but just an effort (guided by a public relations firm) to shape the public's perception.[19]

Ultimately, financial brokers poured millions of dollars into three streams of interwoven actions to facilitate abortion acceptability. The first and most fundamental effort was to normalize abortion in the public's eye and to position it as the answer to the urgent problem of overpopulation. The second effort was advancing legal concepts and establishing legal standing for abortion by financially bringing and backing legal cases. Finally, individuals and organizations promoting population control prioritized investing in making abortion as affordable and accessible as possible.

Funding Abortion Discourse

Some population control influence peddlers controlled the mediums they used to disseminate abortion information, achieving both horizontal and vertical control of their messaging. By financing creators and advertisers to reach the larger public, prominent newspaper and magazine owners invariably got invited into the leadership of abortion organizations. These men were politically savvy and financially successful. One leading figure was Frederick Osborn, a decorated soldier sought out by President Franklin Delano Roosevelt to lead the military's morale division in the Second World War. He went on to lead the Population Council, generating data and strategies to turn the public and legislatures to population control, all to achieve eugenic ends.[20]

Newspaper publishers like Edward W. Scripps and Harry Chandler laid the rhetorical groundwork for overpopulation and eugenics concerns. Their papers supplied plentiful coverage of eugenics, with columns by reporters like Fred Hogue (from 1935–1941) and doctors like Dr. Lawrence Lamb (1960s and 1970s), as well as multipart stories on abortion. The Scripps Foundation for Research in Population Problems at Miami University (Ohio, 1922) researched eugenics, overpopulation, and abortion and shared its findings with the broader public in newspaper and magazine articles. Investing financially in the research and reporting for these concerns provided the validating power of visibility so often denied to those seeking to secure progressive goals (such as workers' rights, civil rights, and women's rights) and helped make eugenics, overpopulation, and abortion a part of the discourse.[21]

In the 1960s and 1970s, individuals, offices, and clinics all contributed research studies to sell the belief that legal, accessible abortion could remedy overpopulation. Under cover of academic legitimacy, these eugenicists surveyed the scene and tried to advance abortion access. Charles Westoff, at the Office of Population Research at Princeton University, was a longstanding member of the American Eugenics Society and a professor of sociology and demography who wrote extensively on fertility, reproduction, and contraception. Another abortion supporter was eugenicist and genetic researcher Victor McKusick at Johns Hopkins University. On the West Coast, institutions had similar investments in scholarship and academic centers, especially by Fred Bixby's foundation, which hired eugenicist Judith Blake as a population chair at the University of California, Los Angeles (UCLA). She requested that the Gallup company add abortion questions to its polls, the responses to which she analyzed along with those from the National Fertility Study, gathered by Westoff.[22]

Positive articles about Planned Parenthood began to appear in *Parents* magazine in 1942 and by 1965 made the case for abortion to be legalized, drawing on Planned Parenthood president Alan Guttmacher's support. The owner of the magazine, George Hecht, openly supported abortion and population control and in 1970 and 1971 showcased overpopulation in twenty articles and ads.[23] The magazine contained a surprising amount of content devoted to limiting reproduction, including articles by eugenicists and population control advocates. It advanced the population threat to its two million subscribers, joined by hundreds of articles in other popular periodicals, like *Time* and *Life*. The leadership of Hearst Media also used its stable of mainstream magazines, from *Seventeen* to *Good Housekeeping*, to promote ideas about overpopulation and abortion. Everyday people, women and men, were exposed to these ideas, not just scientists or theorists writing in obscure journals.[24]

Eugenicist Hugh Moore helped normalize the language and the concept in his bombastic pamphlet *The Population Bomb Is Everybody's Baby,* and then with the executive director of the Sierra Club he helped biologists Paul and Anne Ehrlich publish *The Population Bomb* in 1968 to depict dangers about overpopulation in apocalyptic terms. The paperback landed Paul Ehrlich on the *Tonight Show* more than twenty times, an interview with *Playboy,* and went on to sell millions of copies. Even more important than book sales, it sold the concept of overpopulation. The groundwork laid by Hecht, Moore, and others prepared the public and government officials to accept the dire messaging and to act on it, including through growing acceptance of legal abortion.[25]

Convinced that the fate of the planet hung in the balance, wealthy believers raised more than $100,000 in 1972 to produce the "Population, the U.S. Problem, the World Crisis" supplement to the *New York Times.* The insert called for population stabilization and a eugenic shift in America's focus from quantity to quality. It also focused on the "serious problem of unwanted fertility" and characterized controlling one's own reproduction as inherently American, noting, "Making it easier to avoid unwanted childbearing will make a substantial contribution to the lives of the people involved as well as slowing growth—and in any case, it is consistent with American values and desirable on that ground." Indeed, the report claimed that enacting its recommended policies would "promote desirable social conditions by increasing opportunities to exercise freedom of choice." In this light, the movement applauded access to birth control and abortion as inherently patriotic.[26]

For these proponents, reproductive choice was not intended as a feminist aim. It was part of the rebranding to sell Americans on these new methods of birth control as individual choices that would also benefit one's life, family, community, and country. Appealing to influential policymakers and philanthropists, the *New York Times* supplement showcased its recommendations, including an explicit call to "Liberalize access to abortion services." The commission also called to "Extend and improve the delivery of health services related to fertility." Hugh Moore and Ruth Proskauer Smith used a public relations firm in 1962 to sanitize their eugenicism and rebrand their movement as embodying "reproductive choice." They transformed the Association for Voluntary Sterilization (AVS) in 1964, taking it from an "old eugenics lobby" to a seemingly innocuous organization, with Alan Guttmacher chairing its medical and scientific committees and Lawrence Lader serving on the executive committee. Lader later remembered that he "put a two-child resolution through AVS," and the organization, through "public and private financing mechanisms," helped advance voluntary sterilization and abortion.[27]

Science magazine laid the groundwork for the population control campaign, offering policymakers and adherents the language, evidence, and platform they needed to support abortion access. In 1967, the magazine published sociologist and eugenicist Kingsley Davis, for example, who argued, with the prima facie existence of overpopulation, that leaving reproduction up to choice would not limit the population. Davis further objected to abortion being illegal and deprioritized, because of abortion's vital role in ensuring population control. Legislators placed his article into the testimony of the Congressional Record that same year as they met to consider the population crisis. In 1969, biologist Garrett Hardin followed up in *Science* with his "Tragedy of the Commons" parable, concluding, "Freedom to breed is intolerable." Other magazines followed suit, with men dominating the discourse in the pages of newspapers and magazines. The one exception to the male voices was anthropologist Margaret Mead, who addressed overpopulation in fourteen articles in her monthly *Redbook* column. *Redbook* also published stories about limiting family size, with Mead characterizing overpopulation in 1969 as "The Crisis of Our Overcrowded World."[28]

Many authors who feared overpopulation endeavored to popularize it in their fields and legitimize the concept with professional publications and presentations. Financial leaders of the eugenics movement funded data and published studies, including supporting Robert Weisbord, a historian at Brown University, and Lee Rainwater, a sociologist at Harvard University, who researched race and class concerns governing reproduction. Not only did these academics shape and influence their fields and the thinking of the period, but they also continued their reach into the twenty-first century, with contemporary scholars unwittingly relying on outright eugenicists like Donald Bogue and Charles

Westoff. The shifting name of both the American Eugenics Society and its journal offered some cover, but the 1974 mailing list for the journal *Social Biology* still revealed dozens of academics in the United States and around the world, as well as known eugenicists, like Harry Shapiro at the American Museum of Natural History. Members of the American Eugenics Society who subscribed to the journal included Virginia Apgar (inventor of a medical evaluation score for newborns) and geneticist Victor Musick.[29]

The author who best married support for abortion and controlling overpopulation, however, was Lawrence Lader. From his comfortable perch in Manhattan, with a network of wealthy Harvard activists and media connections, he played a significant and heretofore hidden role in shaping public opinion on population control. Lader advanced his certainty that the world's population size and projected growth was a crisis and offered cautionary tales designed to make population control a self-evident and necessary goal.[30]

Lader and his partnership with wealthy eugenic population control proselytizer Hugh Moore helped ensure success in promoting population control, eugenic ideology, and abortion. While he appeared on AVS letterhead as a member of the organization's executive committee and included his role as executive director of the Hugh Moore Fund in an early resume, he carefully massaged his public image. Building on Betty Friedan's belief that the "problem that has no name" helped cause "the population explosion," Lader argued in his book *Abortion* (1966) that providing American women with the means for financial upward mobility and creative outlets, something other than marriage and motherhood as life goals, would help reduce the nation's fertility. He also asserted that, in addition to focused policies, abortion was a vital tool to help control the population.[31]

Historical accounts regularly suggested that Lader's involvement in the abortion movement stemmed from writing his 1955 biography of Margaret Sanger, despite her personal stated opposition to abortion. Lader affirmed, "I was her disciple," and credited her with introducing him to the "population problem." In chronicling his motivations, observers ignored Lader's 1971 biography of Hugh Moore, *Breeding Ourselves to Death*, in which he not only fawned over a key financier of population

FIGURE 3. Population control motivated NARAL co-founder Lawrence Lader's abortion rights leadership. He authored *Breeding Ourselves to Death*, a 1971 biography of Hugh Moore, a wealthy funder of the population control movement.

control and abortion, but also included photographs and mini biographies of Moore's comrades and acolytes in the overpopulation movement. The only biography missing was of Lader himself.[32]

Lader was silent on his motivations for leading an abortion campaign, but his activism suggests that he was motivated by eugenics, which morphed publicly into support for population control. Former

Redbook publisher Sey Chassler, who met Lader in the 1940s, pointedly commented in a 1995 story, "Larry never seemed interested in the rest of the women's movement, the equal rights amendment, child care and so forth." Lader publicly told only one story to explain his interest in abortion, when he introduced his 1971 "Guide to Abortion Laws." He recalled "going to the airport with a friend who was putting his terrified girlfriend on a flight to Cuba for an abortion. Imagine going to Cuba for that! She was right to be terrified." In this story, Lader put himself at a twice-removed distance—a friend of a friend—an observer. Even as he positioned himself as central to the abortion narrative, including doing hundreds of abortion referrals, he asserted no origin story. Save Chassler, no one reflected on what motivated Lader's singular focus and devotion to liberalizing abortion laws and helping women get abortions.[33]

Lader shared Margaret Sanger's and Hugh Moore's belief that the world was *Breeding Ourselves to Death* and the cover featured the quotation, "This book is published as a historical record and with the hope that the methods and techniques employed by the Hugh Moore Fund may be of use to the growing army of devoted men and women now engaged in the struggle to control the greatest menace of our time." Critics later vilified Sanger for her eugenic beliefs, but her adoring biographer escaped scrutiny for his unwavering focus on population control and his leadership in the eugenicist organizations the AVS and the Association for the Study of Abortion (ASA). As executive director of NARAL, in April 1970 Lader drafted "A Platform on Population," with the first statement decrying the "population explosion" that "threatens the stability and fabric of U.S. Society." In addition to demanding that all city and state hospitals provide free abortions to the poor and affordable ones to everyone else, Lader asserted, "Population control must now become a state responsibility. The 'stop at two' campaign hitherto fostered by private agencies, must become a public policy of the state, and promoted as a patriotic goal." Lader's belief in the threat of overpopulation fueled his abortion leadership, and he leaned toward government control never a woman's right to choose.[34]

When evidence of the doom and gloom forecasts failed to materialize and support for abortion was believed to be secured in *Roe*, support for the population "crisis" waned and most organization leaders faded away. Wealthy male leaders ensured the movement's legacy, however, by shaping the historical record. Population control foundations funded oral histories of population control advocates at the Schlesinger Library at Harvard University (Rockefeller Foundation) and the Neilson Library at Smith College (William and Flora Hewlett Foundation). The Hewlett Foundation also "slightly laundered" its funding of oral history interviews through the Physicians for Reproductive Health and Choice, which then "generously donated" the collection to Columbia University. These oral histories captured the reflections of not just the visible actors, but also those who bankrolled "family planning," compiled the data, created and headed organizations, and wrote the studies.[35]

Lader guaranteed that his own legacy would be upheld by funding the Lawrence Lader Lectureship on Family Planning and Reproductive Rights at the Harvard Medical School Center for Bioethics, which erroneously claimed on the lecture website in 2023 that Betty Friedan called Lader the "father of abortion rights." He also donated his papers to the New York Public Library, as well as to the Schlesinger Library at Harvard, where he did a short interview. Although *Breeding Ourselves* publicity described Lader as a "crusader in the population field," no posthumous coverage of him offers any sense of how central eugenics and population control were to his abortion work.[36]

In February 1969, Lader gathered his population control funders and abortion advocates together and created a national umbrella organization to advocate for abortion law repeal. In forming the organization, Lader instructed his bevy of financial supporters to direct their largesse to NARAL to give abortion a stage with national reach. Although the Chicago program (held at the luxurious Drake Hotel) was subtitled "Modification or Repeal," there was no question that the repeal advocates would win the day. Lader gave himself the last word as he chaired the last session, "Repeal NOW! Goals of the National Association for the Repeal of Abortion Laws." The title and description made clear the intent: "The afternoon session will be concerned with the formation of a national group." The efforts to reform abortion laws had not increased access and Lader helped push supporters of abortion rights to fully embrace and fund repealing all the archaic abortion laws.[37]

While we imagine NARAL and Planned Parenthood as women's organizations, governed by feminism, before *Roe* they were neither. Of those present at the founding of NARAL, at least nine of the fifty-six individual sponsors and speakers had been or were members of the American Eugenics Society. The three founding members of NARAL, Garrett Hardin, Dr. Lonny Myers of Chicago, and Lader, along with many of those who sponsored and attended the NARAL conference, shared a commitment to population control. One of the most notable population control advocates, Estelle Griswold, had taken her challenge for access to birth control all the way to the Supreme Court with Dr. Lee Buxton, while he served on the board of directors for the American Eugenics Society. She professed that the case should have probably assumed his name, but Griswold and Planned Parenthood provided feminist cover for those looking back.[38]

Although NOW under Betty Friedan's leadership publicly affirmed its support for legalized abortion in January 1968 and co-sponsored the 1969 NARAL conference, one of the conference organizers, Dr. Bernard Nathanson, claimed that NOW president Betty Friedan was only on the program to give a nod to feminism. In her speech at the conference, she proclaimed, "The right of woman to control her reproductive process must be established as a basic and valuable human civil right not to be denied or abridged by the state." However, Friedan's motion that NARAL should support the "right of a woman to decide when to have or not have children" did not elicit even a second, to allow for discussion, reflecting the movement's continued rejection of embracing abortion as a women's choice. This unwillingness to even discuss reproductive justice for women reflects NARAL's early eugenic and population control history. As had been the earlier pattern with birth control and family planning, men and women prioritizing population control dominated the new abortion organization and told its history.[39]

In a recorded appearance decades later, Lader regretted that, even though NARAL secretary Conni Bille considered him "a master of the media" and "uniquely positioned" to communicate, there were no reporters, cameras, or video of the conference. Without the visuals, he claimed, it was hard to tell the story. However, Lader could not guarantee that he would move the organization to abandon the failed reform route and take up abortion law repeal. Co-founder Myers described the last day as a "disaster" filled with "infighting." More likely, Lader wanted to control the narrative and had a tight hold over the early leadership of the new organization. In July 1969, he mailed new members a single-slate ballot with his handpicked candidates for the board's executive committee.[40]

NARAL gave voice to abortion rights discourse in public debates, granting public support to those already active in the fight. Shaping media discourse was not unique. It was a tried-and-true strategy for population control and eugenics adherents, and with Lader's leadership the abortion repeal movement embraced it as well. The group unified already-established abortion activists and organizations, and by 1970 it had signed on more, including the feminist Redstockings and the United Auto Workers. In a 1972 ad, the organization claimed the endorsement of ZPG and the Sierra Club, along with religious and medical groups. While Lader encouraged a perception of the group as national, with vice presidents in California and Chicago, the group's first executive committee looked much more like an elite, New York organization. He argued that emphasizing New York was appropriate because it was the first legislative fight and it best accommodated the New York–heavy board, as they held meetings sponsored by board member and eugenicist Beatrice McClintock at the glamorous Colony Club. Those with deep pockets (or pocketbooks) and the profitable abortion market helped give rise to legalization.[41]

Funding the Legal Fight

In 1962, the American Law Institute (ALI), a national, nonpartisan legal organization, created a model abortion reform law that shaped abortion laws across the country in the 1960s. There are two key aspects of ALI's seemingly neutral review and policy process, however, that have escaped scrutiny. First, like all legal endeavors, the abortion reform effort was funded—and the funding came from the Rockefeller Foundation. The funding ensured a smoother path for the national legal fights for abortion. And second, obstetrician and gynecologist Dr. Alan Guttmacher and his twin brother Manfred Guttmacher, a forensic psychiatrist, helped draft ALI's 1962 legal model for abortion. Back in 1956, Alan had complained in an opinion piece in the *Eugenics Quarterly* that ALI had neglected to include eugenic considerations, but he planned to redress that and include a stipulation for the health of the mother. As described by leading abortion rights attorney Harriet Pilpel, ALI wrote laws that "permitted abortion not only to save the life of the woman but also to preserve her mental and physical health, in cases of rape and incest, and to avoid the birth of defective offspring." The inclusion of "defective offspring" reflected the age-old eugenic goals of "fit" children.[42]

Supporters hoped that reforming abortion laws to allow for therapeutic abortions would expand access to them. In practice, hospitals interpreted the reformed laws very narrowly. The laws permitting legal, therapeutic abortions did not open the floodgates of women who were already seeking illegal abortions. Permitting abortions only to "preserve the mental or physical health of the mother or in cases of rape or incest," and then, in that small number, only allowing them to be performed "in licensed hospitals," dramatically reduced the number of women permitted to have abortions. In a 1965 *New York Times* article, Lader reflected that in New York City, for example, the number of therapeutic abortions had declined by two-thirds compared to 1945. The therapeutic abortion laws conceivably offered more discretion, but hospitals embraced stingy, restrictive abortion review committees and a set minuscule number of abortions the hospital would do each month, which made abortions harder to obtain than before. Some commentators reported that "it was easier to obtain an abortion in a state that criminalized all abortions than it was in a reform state," and with the continued impediment, hundreds of thousands of women continued to get illegal abortions. From the Beilensen Bill in California (which opened the door to exceptions for therapeutic abortions) to the Abramowicz case in New York (made moot when the legislature legalized abortion in the spring of 1970), advocates tried to move forward the legal and social acceptance of abortion.[43]

Doctors and lawyers brought court cases centered on illegal abortions to repeal antiquated abortion laws. Publicity generated from trials in California (Dr. Leon Belous), Maryland (Dr. Milan Vuitch),

Minnesota (Dr. Jane Hodgson), Oklahoma (Dr. Bryan Henrie), and other cases across the country helped to raise awareness of the doctors who tried to confront unjust laws, but support from medical colleagues and professional organizations was muted. The most famous and consequential cases ultimately concerned pregnant plaintiffs, not doctors, such as *Roe v. Wade*, a Texas-based effort and a companion case to Georgia's *Doe v. Bolton*, which contended that laws restricting abortion access were unconstitutional.[44]

Joseph Sunnen of St. Louis, Missouri, almost single-handedly funded the yearslong legal fight for abortion, including all of the legal cases upon which *Roe* rested, as well as *Roe* itself. He made his fortune in mechanical parts and a lucrative birth control foam (Emko) and used his wealth to advance abortion rights to ensure population control. The Sunnen Foundation in partnership with Roy Lucas and his James Madison Center for Constitutional Law Institute (JMC) funded every significant legal abortion action between 1968 and 1972. Living in the same three-story building that housed the institute and reporting that the institute had a bank balance of negative $800 and that he had not been paid in a month, Lucas fawned in one 1970 letter, "If one individual is to be credited with having made the abortion movement in the courts successful, it is Joseph Sunnen through his willingness to support the Institute." Sunnen paid for legal fees, copies of filing materials, a law library, and the staff and attorneys who coordinated and tried cases before fifty different judges in nine states, all while having briefs used in nearly twenty more states. Lucas was also not the only recipient of the Sunnen largesse. Reflecting on NARAL's achievements, Lader told Sunnen in April 1970 it was his "support that was largely responsible," suggesting Sunnen had provided the bulk of the $24,000 NARAL spent its first year.[45]

Lucas and Morris Dees used Dees's million-dollar fortune to co-found the JMC. Then, in 1968, Lucas wrote "Federal Constitutional Limitations on the Enforcement and Administration of State Abortion Statutes" for the *North Carolina Law Review*, which defined his career trajectory. By December 1970, Lucas asserted that "over a dozen courts have recognized the constitutional right of a woman to control her own fertility" and claimed that his institute was "handling most of these cases." He asserted himself as "one of the nation's foremost experts on the legal aspects of abortion" and frequently iced out other attorneys—nearly including Sarah Weddington.[46]

Lucas also sought out other funders, like the American Civil Liberties Union (ACLU), Planned Parenthood of New York, the ASA, and the Playboy Foundation. Before the institute could establish its tax-free status, John D. Rockefeller III funneled his donations through the United Methodist Church, which had the added advantage of looking like an additional donor. To foundations and colleagues alike, Lucas proclaimed himself the best bet to secure abortion victories in the courts. To a major funder, he explained that the "ACLU relies on local attorneys in private practice to do these cases on a part-time basis. Nine times out of ten the local counsel have insufficient training to handle a major federal case with any degree of professional competence." Of course, if cases reached the US Supreme Court, they were "nearly always lost." He proudly suggested that only he had the "thorough preparation, research, and understanding of the legal, medical, and sociological facets of the problem." Touting coverage in *Time*, the *New York Times*, and the *Washington Post*, Lucas challenged, cajoled, and begged for financial support to keep his legal fight for abortion alive.[47]

Lucas also used Sunnen's support to solicit other funders. Sarah Weddington expressed appreciation that the wealthy philanthropist Thomas Cabot contributed $15,000 to cover the cost of printing most of the briefs for *Roe*. Overpopulation zealots funded abortion law reform at the research stage, the litigation stage, and eventually the legislative stage, with the end goal not of benefitting women, but of curbing population growth. Lucas established himself as the chief fundraiser and attorney for the abortion rights legal effort. While one observer believed that Lucas was "enterprising and charming enough to convince several wealthy women to fund him," it was a much broader and deeper-funded operation, and from the records, the funders were almost entirely wealthy white men and their foundations.[48]

In 1971, amid his multitude of legal cases, Lucas endeavored to create a prospectus to reposition himself with a new Population Law Institute. Population control may have always been the motivation. Lucas would likely also have been aware that the abortion fight might be winding down, with the Supreme Court willing to hear *Roe v. Wade* and *Doe v. Bolton* and his institute in dire financial straits. Sarah Weddington eventually joined the JMC advisory board and later served on the Population Council's board.[49]

In addition to establishing legal precedents, abortion reform supporters recognized the need to finance the necessary histories for legal briefs. The two most significant works establishing the legal understanding of abortion were funded by population control adherents. Hugh Moore and the Unitarian Association helped finance and publish Lawrence Lader's book *Abortion* in 1966. Lader's work was cited in Lucas's pioneering article and eventually by the Supreme Court's *Roe* decision seven times. The court also relied on law professor Cyril Means's historically focused article, "The Phoenix of Abortional Freedom." The ASA funded the research for Means's article, which "paid dividends when the Supreme Court cited the article in support of its ruling Roe v. Wade," and gave Lucas a grant "to prepare a model trial brief that could be used to test the abortion laws of any state." The ASA's money came principally from their "perennial major donor Cordelia Scaife May," a wealthy overpopulation zealot. Being co-founded by Dr. Guttmacher and Dr. Robert E. Hall, who was a vocal, visible abortion rights leader, cloaked the organization and the movement to get legal abortions with a staid, scholarly, medical imprimatur. The association never publicly revealed its financial origins. While eugenicists may have felt at home, this scholarly cover may have led some individuals to unwittingly join the board of directors in 1973 and 1974. Lawyers Ruth Bader Ginsberg and Eleanor Jackson Piel were both present at the ASA board meeting where May's role was disclosed.[50]

Funding Abortion Access

In addition to laying the social and legal groundwork for abortion access, funders tried to offset the exorbitant costs and limited availability of abortions. Confronting practical impediments, like high costs and the small number of trained doctors committed to providing abortions, necessitated funding abortion access itself. Many of the larger foundations with millions in assets, like the Rockefeller Foundation, saw their role as establishing the academic, medical, and governmental framework for abortion, and limited their financial support to studies and organizations. It fell then to some smaller foundations to use their financial might to underwrite direct access to abortions. While some provided financial support by volunteering their services, which enabled free referrals and reduced charges at clinics, foundations played the largest role in lowering costs when they provided the funds to enable clinics to reduce fees.

Joseph Sunnen's foundation, so central to the legal fights waged by Roy Lucas, also funded reproductive control and abortion access in a multitude of other ways. Preceding his heavy focus on abortion, Sunnen developed, marketed, and dispensed Emko, a birth control foam, globally, including in Puerto Rico, Japan, and the United States. He started in the early 1950s, and by 1972 was sending millions of free samples to women around the world. Emko products brought in millions in profits that he poured back into population control.[51]

Newspaper reporting reveals that Sunnen also funded an abortion group run by Planned Parenthood-World Population. In 1971, he and California philanthropist Prynce Hopkins each put forward $43,000 to fund the San Francisco Center for Legal Abortion and help cover expenses. Through their largesse, the men helped lower the cost of an abortion in California by about half, to $300. With 150 clients anticipated per month, the more affordable clinic helped contribute to the 78 percent increase of the abortions performed in 1970, with the state overall reporting 116,749 abortions in 1971.[52]

Similarly, at the for-profit Women's Medical Center in New York City, created to facilitate abortions in New York City after legalization, three philanthropists contributed $75,000 to buy a building and others made donations of medical equipment and furniture, while volunteers assisted with the intake of patients. The net effect of these financial efforts enabled the clinic to open quickly with low operating costs, charging only $75 per abortion. Donations of cash and stocks, goods, and in-kind services enabled abortion clinics to lower their costs, which not only served women of more limited means, but also drove down costs in all clinics. While the philanthropists behind the Women's Medical Center were not identified, the long-standing practice of including benefactors on the board of directors suggests that they were socialite Beatrice Kellogg McClintock, Stewart Mott, and Ruth Proskauer Smith. This is further supported by Bernard Nathanson's accounting; he noted that McClintock, Mott, and Smith invested a "large sum of money" into the women's clinic. The investment did not pay off in a traditional sense but paid larger dividends in helping the clinic lower costs and increase abortions. The property also housed Sarah (and later Ron) Weddington across the summer of 1971 as they worked to prepare the *Roe v. Wade* case for the Supreme Court.[53]

Looking beyond traditional funding sources and direct efforts to lower the costs of abortions, it is revealing to consider the reach of a grant or a fellowship for abortions. The Cleveland-based Brush Foundation, led by Dorothy Brush (close friends with Margaret Sanger) and her father-in-law, Charles Francis Brush, was small, with a stated purpose that was both pro-eugenics and pro–population control. In the fall of 1971, the foundation made two grants in support of abortion. The first was awarded to a joint venture between the Cleveland Planned Parenthood and the Cleveland Problem Pregnancy Counseling Service to provide a free abortion referral service for pregnant women in the Cleveland area, which allowed these two not-for-profit groups to reach more women and compete with businesses that charged for referral services.[54]

The second awardee even more explicitly aligned with the foundation's pro-eugenics ideology. The foundation committed $18,000 to Dr. Bruce Ferguson, who sought support for a one-year fellowship to pursue population control with the Navajo in New Mexico and Arizona. Ferguson set out three objectives in his application: develop a population control curriculum focused on nursing students at the Navajo Community College; plan and implement primary health care services, training Navajo personnel; and "Further clinical training in methods and techniques of population control." Ferguson's description of the Navajo population laid out his case:

> Situated on a vast reservation in Arizona and New Mexico and constituting the largest American Indian tribe, the Navajos suffer

> many of the problems of foreign underdeveloped countries, including low per-capita income, high infant mortality (49 per 1000 live births), protein and calorie malnutrition, very rapid population growth rates (crude birth rate of 38 per 1000 population and net growth of over three per cent per year), slow rate of economic development, and generally inadequate health care (especially in remote areas).[55]

He indicated that the "applicant would work in birth control clinics, perform abortions and sterilizations (both male and female), and gain expertise in the techniques, indications and contraindications." His aims were clear and specific.

In a revised proposal, Ferguson called for funding to enable him to spend two half days in the pregnancy termination clinic, one half day in the postpartum and family planning clinics, and one half day in the vasectomy clinic. He also tried providing some historical context for the distrust he faced:

> As with many developing nations and ethnic minorities, the Navajos are generally critical of family planning efforts. During the Thirties, a major problem of sheep overgrazing on the reservation was met by a government program of forcible stock reduction without adequate understanding of the problem by the Navajos, and a great deal of bitterness was generated. Many Navajos view family planning programs as a new "stock reduction."[56]

The board members of the pro-eugenics foundation were undoubtedly familiar with Garrett Hardin's "Tragedy of the Commons," which called for removing life-sustaining resources to keep populations down, be they sheep or people. The Navajo community saw the parallel clearly.

Navajo communities generally opposed abortion more than other family planning services. Still, Ferguson reported on abortions performed at the therapeutic abortion clinic each week and helped to organize a Navajo Planned Parenthood affiliate.[57] By May 1972, Ferguson had completed approximately seventy-five to one hundred abortions and about twenty-five vasectomies. For the foundation, the return on investment was a doctor who would go on to serve as a dedicated abortion provider for decades. A guiding belief in eugenics and population control gave the Brush Foundation every reason to fund Ferguson, who promised to advance population control through not just ideology, but abortion and sterilization as well.[58]

Funding Eugenics

Abortion advocates worked for and with a variety of organizations, like the Human Betterment Association for Voluntary Sterilization (the HBA added "Voluntary Sterilization" to emphasize that they supported individual choice, later dropping "Human Betterment" to disguise their eugenic mission), the Population Council, and Planned Parenthood, sometimes simultaneously. One of the most prolific researchers who helped legitimize the study of legal abortion was Dr. Christopher Tietze. He wrote dozens of birth control and abortion studies, and media coverage frequently cited him as a statistical authority on the safety and effectiveness of birth control and abortion. His early work involved studying birth control with Clarence Gamble and John Rock, which reflected a long-standing quest to find effective birth control. From the rhythm method to the IUD, researchers like Tietze studied methods that worked best for the people his funders believed most needed to control their reproduction. He tested devices and treatments that could prevent pregnancy to determine if women were willing and able to use them successfully. From the Lippes Loop to Emko foam, population control proponents bankrolled his studies, hoping for scientific backing endorsing the effectiveness of their products. When abortion entered the mix, Tietze brought decades of experience and his medical authority to bear. Newspaper reports offer a clear example of the circularity of the money and influence in abortion reporting. Reliant on spokespeople from institutions and organizations funded by population control adherents eager to limit births and frequently staffed by eugenicists who shared the goal of restricting reproduction, reporters blithely interviewed eugenicists like Christopher Tietze and Charles Westoff for articles.[59]

The most significant public figure to advocate for abortion, however, was Alan Guttmacher. Serving as head of Mt. Sinai's ob-gyn department; vice president, director, and long-standing member of the American Eugenics Society; medical director for the Human Betterment Association, and a president of Planned Parenthood-World Population, Guttmacher represented the ideal male medical authority for 1960s Planned Parenthood supporters, who wanted the organization to fund research and access to birth control and abortion. To honor him and spin off the work of research to another body that could fundraise independently based on his credibility, Planned Parenthood created its Center for Family Planning Program Development in 1968 and then renamed it the Guttmacher Institute in 1974. This had the advantage of removing the Planned Parenthood and family planning language from the name, leaving the focus entirely on an "institute." Guttmacher's interviews, publications, and public support of abortion lent tremendous legitimacy and enabled both individual, foundational, and governmental support for the institute's quest to increase safe access to abortion.[60]

Like Guttmacher, some other organizations and foundations with eugenic pasts remain active, with many families (including wives and sons, especially) carrying out the same ideological mission. Just as most women who entered political office after suffrage did so through marriage or their father, so too did women follow men's lead in committing financially to eugenics and population control. Many sons also followed in their fathers' footsteps, striving to fulfill their legacies by directing a foundation, pursuing the same aims, or, in the case of John D. Rockefeller III, evolving from his father's outright eugenics to a more subtle pursuit of eugenics through population control.[61]

Facilitating social acceptance, legal rulings, and access, advocates of population control played a heretofore hidden role in securing abortion rights and access. Along with a myriad of other more familiar actors, population control adherents and eugenicists played a vital role in ensuring abortion availability and legality. From the pages of *Parents* magazine to a remote Navajo reservation, in clinics from San Francisco to New York City, the financial might of these influencers and the scholarly imprimatur of the studies they funded signed on as a silent *amicus curiae* brief to all abortion activity. These individuals and organizations invested money and social capital to encourage abortion with the intent that it would limit the population. The largesse touched every aspect of the buying and selling abortion before *Roe*, up to and including, most significantly, the *Roe* decision itself.

2

Finding the Money

WOMEN PLAYED A CENTRAL consumer role in one of the largest illegal industries in the country, and abortion providers, businesses, and entrepreneurs vied to capture the incredible wealth it generated. The price of an abortion before twelve weeks in this period varied from gratis to about $1,500. There were certainly more expensive ones, and those done for later pregnancies always cost a lot more, requiring more skilled medical intervention, likely hospitalization, and risk. With legalization in New York, prices there for abortions before twelve weeks dropped to about $150 by 1972. To have some context for how much money this was in people's lives, in 1970, the average tuition, room, and board in a public university in the 1970–1971 academic year was $1,287, and a new Volkswagen Beetle cost $1,985. For those profiting, estimates of the market's national value went as high as one billion dollars a year. Abortion financing options both fueled the market and enriched the lenders. There were profit motives to keep abortion illegal and commensurate ones to legalize, all with the shared goal of growing the massive consumer market.[1]

Women who discovered they were pregnant and wanted an abortion needed to acquire the necessary funds in the fastest, most private way possible. Those who did not work full time for pay because they were students, homemakers, or unemployed, or who worked in low-paying pink-collar jobs or were paid less because they were women, generally did not have a lot of money available to them. Turning to friends and family was therefore an immediate and likely response for many. Others found financial support from the man who impregnated them. Those who could not get help in their immediate proximity, however, had to look elsewhere. Efforts to secure funds took time and risked exposure, and most women did not want anyone to know about their intention. Some chose a more expensive option because it came with certainty and privacy. Most did not have the ability to comparison shop. Newspaper coverage of financial options informed the discourse about how to find and pay for more affordable abortions. From banks to loan sharks, lenders profited from women's desperation. College students across the country mobilized their financial might to make money available to students in need, so that even the poorest of students would not have their studies disrupted by an unwanted pregnancy. Finally, with pressure building from those in need, the insurance industry and government aid responded to the demands to include abortion coverage. This chapter explores how women managed the extraordinary financial burden of paying for abortions.[2]

In the late 1960s and early 1970s, most women seeking an abortion faced the unenviable task of quickly and quietly coming up with a very large sum of money. Quite often women only learned the cost of the abortion when they got a referral or spoke to the place doing the procedure. Faced with an immediate and unforgiving deadline, women learned that delaying getting an abortion had dire consequences, particularly as the pregnancy continued. Not only did more complex procedures mean increased costs, but delays could also foreclose on the option of an abortion altogether.[3]

The laws and social mores governing the availability of abortion access helped shape its cost. The abortion itself was usually a woman's biggest expenditure. For women seeking a legal, hospital-approved abortion, the financial costs to secure it included letters from her doctor and from psychiatrists. A medically approved legal, therapeutic abortion depended on a panel of decision-makers appointed by the hospital who weighed the recommendations. In 1965, only eight thousand women (in a country of about 70 million women of childbearing age) who sought therapeutic abortions in the United States received approval. The letters alone proved to be a significant financial burden for most, with each one costing up to $100. Women paid for hundreds of thousands of letters, but hospital boards rejected the overwhelming majority of applicants. Many rejected women then paid for an illegal abortion, and then found themselves in the same hospital, paying again, this time to complete the abortion or treat an infection.[4]

Most women did not even attempt to secure therapeutic abortions, opting instead to locate an illegal provider. The Jane organization, which operated a free counseling and referral service in Chicago (reliant on the phone and an early type of answering machine), asked for donations for the referral and charged "at least $500 to $600" for the abortion. From 1969 to the spring of 1971, women paid steep prices and generated incredible profits for the male providers, who may have earned more than $250,000 a year. Although the Janes eventually took over the abortion procedure and only charged what the women could pay, they needed income to pay women to work for the referral service, to pay for rent, and for supplies to keep the operation going.[5]

Sometimes women had to travel a great distance. The costs to travel by car, taxi, bus, train, and plane piled on top of the medical costs. Some abortion procedures also necessitated staying overnight, which added lodging costs. For some women, the motel room they paid for was the place where they had their abortion. The procedure could also require buying various tests, supplies, medications, and perhaps even a pregnancy test, and patients paid for those as well. Working women also lost wages and students jeopardized their schoolwork seeking out abortions, and some mothers faced added costs of childcare. And finally, through negligence and misfortune, women sometimes had to pay for more than one procedure to terminate a pregnancy. Whatever the process to finally secure an abortion, money was at the center.[6]

This chapter explores the many ways women found money to secure abortions. For most women, finding the money was not their only difficulty. "Even among those who did not need to borrow money, financial transactions were often complicated and time-consuming," according to sociologist Nancy Howell, writing contemporaneously. Women frequently "had to make a trip to a bank to get the necessary large amounts of cash," or to acquire them as traveler's checks, cashier's checks, or money orders. Rolling the money or putting it flat in an envelope, making sure they were "small bills," having money accessible but not appearing to be flush with cash so that the provider increased the price: women faced these considerations while often traveling for the first time to a new neighborhood, city, state, or country. And when it was all over, they had to repay all the people or institutions that had loaned them money.[7]

There was a tremendous range in costs nationally, also shaped by the length of pregnancy and whether or not the procedure was legal. Economic scholar Charlotte Muller reported that in 1970 nationally, the "price of a qualified practitioner's care" for the illegal service averaged about $1,000. In 1971 a reporter estimated the costs for the hundreds of women at the University of Rhode Island (URI) who sought abortions. The article concluded, "It is 'safe to say' that at least a quarter of a million dollars was spent (at an average of $1,000 per co-ed for travel, hotel accommodations, food, doctor's fees, hospital bills, etc.) by URI girls last year for out-of-the-country legal abortions." Most women had to raise hundreds of dollars, regardless of how far along they were, where they lived, and where they had the procedure. Travel, particularly international travel, often dramatically increased a woman's costs. Following legalization in New York and increasing access to legal therapeutic abortions, the Clergy Consultation Service (CCS), population control advocates, and feminist groups led the effort to lower costs, but the procedure and travel costs (including airfare and hotel) continued to be a substantial economic burden.[8]

Close Proximity

Most women contemplating an abortion started searching for funds in their immediate proximity. As they looked around, they started to see everything in terms of economic value that could help them achieve their immediate needs. In Massachusetts, Susan Tracy, a student, orphaned and unable to rely on family, with limited financial support from the man, had to sell off "almost everything I owned. I sold my winter coats.

I sold my books . . . I sold my stereo. I sold my skis. Because the abortion was $600, which in those days was three times my tuition." Women who sought abortions considered this type of short-term economic devastation a good investment of their limited capital.[9]

The heavy financial burden sometimes led to other unusual and desperate acts. Famed lawyer Sarah Weddington, who argued *Roe v. Wade* in the Supreme Court, described a 1969 effort to use a garage sale to raise money for women seeking abortions. At URI, an unnamed student argued that it was "reliably estimated that at least seven hundred and fifty URI co-eds got out-of-state legal abortions this year." These anguished women "were frantically selling their possessions; clothing, books, records, cars, (themselves?), and dope and narcotics as well, in order to obtain the money to fly to London or the Caribbean for a legal abortion." The author even speculated that the "hawking of personal possessions" and "bookstore thievery" "was not confined to the girls alone but rather included their swains." People made tremendous financial sacrifices and liquidated every possible asset in search of cash.[10]

Nationally, the first woman to be arrested, charged, and convicted of having an illegal abortion, Shirley Ann Wheeler, was one such poor woman who could not raise the money in time for an early, safer abortion. It was only when her boyfriend's income tax refund came through that she was able to get an illegal abortion. But the first procedure did not work, and she had to return for a second one. The financial delay in finding the $300 for the first abortion (she was not charged for the second attempt) placed her health in jeopardy and made her vulnerable to scrutiny; Wheeler's delayed ability to get an abortion reflected the same despair felt by so many.[11]

"Kathy D.," an eighteen-year-old woman from a Boston suburb, took two weeks to pull together enough money to buy round-trip bus tickets to New York for herself, her husband, and her brother. But she faced a crisis upon arrival. The doctor's office had only alerted her to their $300 charge, not the additional $275 hospital cost. The trio sold their bus tickets back to Boston, called everyone they knew, donated blood five times ($50), spent the night in Central Park, and still faced a $25 deficit, and the doctor refused to accept a reduced fee. Kathy's husband "was so desperate he waltzed along St. Mark's Place trying to solicit a homosexual." These plights illustrate the lengths couples went to in order to locate funds for abortion, as well as the unexpected obstacles they encountered.[12]

Ascertaining if men would contribute financially also potentially introduced another time-consuming obstacle, as the couple had to agree on how to divide the costs. In one study, the vast majority of the women, single and married, "shared the costs with the man involved in the pregnancy or got him to pay all the costs." When Linda Proctor discovered she was pregnant after a brief relationship, she contacted the man and he sold some of his camera equipment to get her the money she needed for the abortion. Another woman described the man giving her the money and telling her, "Go take care of it." One woman could only borrow half of the needed fee, so she had to ask the man for assistance, which he grudgingly provided.[13]

One obvious potential resource was the couple's parents, but unwed pregnancy and abortion were so stigmatized that few women or men wanted to share their dilemma. Some women did approach their parents, generally their mother, in the quest for money, but most often girls and women tried to scrounge up the money independently. In just 7 percent of the cases in a 1969 study did parents pay part or all of the costs. Not only did the women not want to involve their parents, the men, too, did not want to involve their parents. Sometimes that left them with less money, as in one case in which the man "borrowed some money" from his parents but left the bulk of the expense to his girlfriend. Without other resources, or to preserve their social capital, some people sought out more formal and expensive loans with high interest rates.[14]

Loans and Credit Cards

In the first public reporting on women's abortion testimonials, journalist Susan Brownmiller in 1969 recounted in the *Village Voice* the experience of twelve women who testified before an audience of three hundred spectators. Angry that New York's hearings on abortion included testimony from only one woman (a nun), the feminist action group Redstockings organized a speak-out in a Washington Square church. One woman described her abortion experience: "It only cost $900. I went to a bank and got a vacation loan. I'm still paying it off."[15]

Even when applying for a loan or credit, most women did not reveal that the money was for an abortion. The pretext that the loan was for a vacation or home improvements helped offer social cover for a woman's true purpose in seeking funds. Carol Wall, a married woman in Connecticut with four children, sought out an abortion and took a loan "from our credit union." Traveling to Puerto Rico, she was not even sure how much it would cost and had to fly there; the abortion ended up costing $800. She remembered, "I was to bring it in cash. That was *a lot* of money in 1966." A study of 114 abortion seekers between 1967 and 1969 revealed that forty-eight "couples had to borrow money in order to pay the costs involved." Of those, twelve "borrowed money from a bank or loan company, giving a false reason for the loan."[16]

There were some exceptions, with both borrowers and banks naming the loan's purpose. In September 1972, a large, front-page headline in the *Des Moines Tribune* declared "Bank Loans Help Iowans Get Abortions," with a subheading noting "Most Women Use Loans for Trips to N.Y., California Clinics." The reporter investigated how Iowa women were securing abortions, finding that "Hundreds of Iowa women are forced to borrow money to pay the cost of an abortion" and concluding that "with increasing frequency they're turning to banks and small loan companies to obtain those loans." Ronald Hammerle, a Planned Parenthood executive in Iowa, understood that secrecy was one motive leading women to seek out private loan funds (as opposed to loans from friends and family). Although "small loan company interest rates are higher," he said, "they also ask fewer questions." He recommended women seek bank loans over "collegiate student groups and women's liberation groups" because those funds were often exhausted quickly. Still, the bank requirement that a woman be "at least 19 years old and currently employed, usually for two years on the same job" proved to be a significant barrier to securing loans, with about half of bank applicants being rejected. For those unable to get a loan on their own, having someone cosign their loan was often "easier than trying to dig up the money from somewhere else." And banks were lending for abortions.[17]

Banks and small loan companies all across Iowa lent money for abortions. Moreover, they were lending to women without male intervention to secure loans. Organizations doing abortion referrals and working with banks to help women secure funds demurred from naming the institutions they used to protect lenders from outside pressures. There was a fear that "If word got out . . . the banker here might stop helping the women." The reporter was able to interview one lender, James Motis of King Finance in Des Moines. His small loan company "openly makes loans for abortions," but he believed that "women who come to King for abortion loans 'rarely' admit they want the money for an abortion. 'I think they may just say they need it for a home improvement or to buy clothes.'" Another interview with anonymous officers of the Iowa-Des Moines National Bank, which also offered abortion loans, reported that they had "about two requests a week" for abortion loans.[18]

Nor were these practices unique to Iowa. A 1970 first-person account in the *Appleton Post Crescent* (Wisconsin) recounted how a young woman went to a local loan company to borrow the money the day before she was to drive to Chicago for an illegal abortion. She discovered that they would "only give her a $300 loan company check," instead of the $600 she requested. In addition to having to scramble for the other $300 she needed, the Chicago bank she went to was "hesitant to cash it, and she was questioned closely." She described the experience: "I expected the cops to grab me when I was walking out of the bank for a bad check." Young women handling large sums alone could raise suspicions. In addition to the financial burden, these women had to subject themselves to scrutiny and sometimes still failed to get the money they needed.[19]

While there were undoubtedly pressures on financial institutions to downplay their willingness to loan money for abortions, there were also strong, competing incentives for them to publicize themselves to women seeking abortion loans. For example, what would motivate lenders to speak to a reporter about their business? As Hammerle noted in Iowa in 1972, "bankers in metropolitan Des Moines are beginning to treat abortion loans "'like a medical not a moral' matter," reflecting changing views of abortion across the country. Moreover, participation in news stories served as free publicity to drive business to their doors.

Profit was another motivator. The simple interest on a $500 loan through a bank was about 12 percent, while the small loan companies, such as King Finance, charged 33.47 percent. Just as people were so desperate to borrow the money that they would pay exorbitant interest rates, financial institutions were willing to withstand public scrutiny in the interest of profit. One Iowa woman took a two-year loan for $404; when it was fully repaid, she would have paid off $576 in interest and principal to the bank, for a net profit of $172. Hers was one of only four abortion loans at the bank across the previous six months, but the lender surely hoped to secure more with the news coverage.[20]

Businesses everywhere sought a cooperative relationship with the media. Financial companies fostered a positive, reciprocal relationship by pairing advertising with adjoining newspaper articles, often minimizing any association between their company and untoward subjects. The newspaper coverage of abortion across the country reveals a shift, however, and by January 1970 banks and loan companies placed their ads on pages reporting on abortion positively. In both mainstream and Black newspapers, with featured drawings and an emphasis on "Personal Loans," small loan companies and banks advertised loans to readers thinking about abortion. An article in the Jackson, Mississippi, *Clarion-Ledger* in January 1970 offered a long, detailed history of abortion, including the claim that "there are between 800,000 and a million" abortions annually. The accompanying Jackson Credit Co. advertisement featured a white woman in an office, pen poised, on the phone, with her pussy bow and a bold, all-caps headline: MONEY WHEN YOU NEED IT! Personal Loans." In smaller font it assured, "We're here to help you solve your financial problems. If you need money for any worthwhile purpose, see us." The messaging and the placement were purposeful and clear.[21]

Articles assuring readers of the morality of abortion, such as "Church Abortion Views Soften" (Binghamton, New York) and "Eugenic Abortion Called Ethical" (Cedar Rapids, Iowa) also appeared alongside ads touting personal loans. Never explicitly describing the loans as abortion loans, the ads listed or depicted purchases (kitchen sinks) and activities (vacations) that might require money. A 1971 referral ad by the "National Abortion Council" appeared in the Black daily, the *Los Angeles Sentinel*,

FIGURE 4. This Bank of Madison ad, promising a friendly woman to assist consumers in getting a loan, accompanied a positive article about abortion in the *Capital Times* (Madison, Wisconsin), 13 May 1971.

followed by one from the Family Savings & Loan company, which promised "Money to keep you in the Black." Another 1971 loan ad accompanied a column in the Utah *Helper Journal* about using health insurance for an abortion. The ad explicitly asked, "Have to pay a big medical or dental bill?" In a Madison, Wisconsin, newspaper a bank loan ad appeared below an article on abortion and featured a woman on the phone. The text assured readers, "Meet Dianne Handel. She's attractive, intelligent and enthusiastic about her job in the Bank of Madison Installment Loan Department. When Dianne greets you, you'll see why she is one of the friendliest, most helpful girls we know. She'll direct you to an installment loan officer for individual, professional assistance with an Auto Lovers Auto Loan or any other type of installment loan. Dianne really cares about people." From specific references to medical bills to friendly and helpful women waiting to assist you, banks and loan companies used newspaper ads to encourage borrowers, especially nervous women, to apply for loans to fund abortions.[22]

A few abortion-referral companies and abortion providers recognized the opportunity to profit by offering in-house loans. Since abortion required immediate payment—known as cash-on-the-barrel, pay-before-receiving-service—locally, nationally, and internationally, loans undoubtedly appealed to many desperate women. In one extraordinary instance, Japan Air Lines and the Bank of Tokyo worked in concert to ensure that American women could book a flight to Japan on the national airline and arrange a bank loan to pay for it and an abortion at the same time. The primary cost to get an abortion in Japan was travel, as the procedure could cost as little as $10. In an undated document, the Society for Humane Abortion in California advised that with 10 percent of the $700 paid down, the Bank of Tokyo would finance the remaining $630 "on a 12-to-18 month pay back plan." The society held an account with the Bank of Tokyo, and their passbooks and bank statements between 1966 and 1972 reveal deposits, accrued interest, and large withdrawals. Their undated guide to seeking an abortion in Japan (passport, vaccinations, doctor's info) assured women that the "Bank of Tokyo at the Tokyo airport is open 24 hours a day, so you can change U.S. money there." As part of its effort to reach white Americans and to encourage their loan business, the Bank of Tokyo offered credit to women seeking abortions in Japan.[23]

In another extension of credit, a few clinics in 1970 began to accept credit card payments from their customers. One Rockland County, New York, clinic advertised itself with a laudatory article in the *Bergen Record* (New Jersey), the headline of which proclaimed, "Abortion? Bring Credit Card." Another clinic accepted "a major credit card" and promised that "A patient will be able to pay for her abortion over 12 months." One clinic even had a "package for out-of-towners," which included motel and taxi arrangements, and promoted that it would accept a credit card.

Just like women's surprising ability to get a bank loan without a male cosigner, we might have imagined that women's credit was elusive until Bella Abzug (D-NY) proposed Title VII of the Consumer Credit Protection Act, which addressed the discrimination women experienced

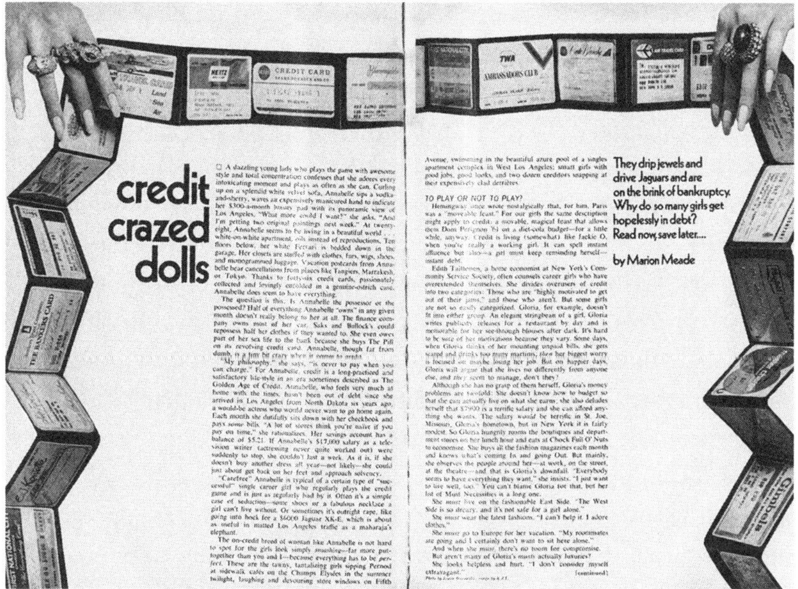

credit crazed dolls

They drip jewels and drive Jaguars and are on the brink of bankruptcy. Why do so many girls get hopelessly in debt? Read now, save later....

by Marion Meade

☐ A dazzling young lady who plays the game with awesome style and total concentration confesses that she adores every intoxicating moment and plays as often as she can. Curling up on a splendid white velvet sofa, Annabelle sips a vodka-and-sherry, waves an expensively manicured hand to indicate her $300-a-month luxury pad with its panoramic view of Los Angeles. "What more could I want?" she asks. "And I'm getting two original paintings next week." At twenty-eight, Annabelle seems to be living in a beautiful world . . . white-on-white apartment, oils instead of reproductions. Ten floors below, her white Ferrari is bedded down in the garage. Her closets are stuffed with clothes, furs, wigs, shoes, and monogrammed luggage. Vacation postcards from Annabelle bear cancellations from places like Tangiers, Marrakesh, or Tokyo. Thanks to forty-six credit cards, passionately collected and lovingly enfolded in a genuine-ostrich case, Annabelle does seem to have everything.

The question is this. Is Annabelle the possessor or the possessed? Half of everything Annabelle "owns" in any given month doesn't really belong to her at all. The finance company owns most of her car. Saks and Bullock's could repossess half her clothes if they wanted to. She even owes part of her sex life to the bank because she buys The Pill on its revolving credit card. Annabelle, though far from dumb, is a tiny bit crazy when it comes to credit.

"My philosophy," she says, "is never to pay when you can charge." For Annabelle, credit is a long-practiced and satisfactory life-style in an era sometimes described as The Golden Age of Credit. Annabelle, who feels very much at home with the times, hasn't been out of debt since she arrived in Los Angeles from North Dakota six years ago, a would-be actress who would never want to go home again. Each month she dutifully sits down with her checkbook and pays *some* bills. "A lot of stores think you're naive if you pay on time," she rationalizes. Her savings account has a balance of $5.21. If Annabelle's $17,000 salary as a television writer (actressing never quite worked out) were suddenly to stop, she couldn't last a week. As it is, if she doesn't buy another dress all year—not likely—she could just about get back on her feet and approach solvency.

"Carefree" Annabelle is typical of a certain type of "successful" single career girl who regularly plays the credit game and is just as regularly had by it. Often it's a simple case of seduction—some shoes or a fabulous necklace a girl can't live without. Or sometimes it's outright rape, like going into hock for a $6000 Jaguar XK-E, which is about as useful in matted Los Angeles traffic as a maharaja's elephant.

The on-credit breed of woman like Annabelle is not hard to spot for the girls look simply *smashing*—far more put-together than you and I—because everything has to be *perfect*. These are the tawny, tantalizing girls sipping Pernod at sidewalk cafés on the Champs Elysées in the summer twilight, laughing and devouring store windows on Fifth Avenue, swimming in the beautiful azure pool of a singles apartment complex in West Los Angeles: smart girls with good jobs, good looks, and two dozen creditors snapping at their expensively clad derrières.

TO PLAY OR NOT TO PLAY?

Hemingway once wrote nostalgically that, for him, Paris was a "moveable feast." For our girls the same description might apply to credit: a movable, magical feast that allows them Dom Pérignon '61 on a diet-cola budget—for a little while, anyway. Credit is living (somewhat) like Jackie O. when you're really a working girl. It can spell instant affluence but also—a girl must keep reminding herself—instant debt.

Edith Taittonen, a home economist at New York's Community Service Society, often counsels career girls who have overextended themselves. She divides overusers of credit into two categories: Those who are "highly motivated to get out of their jams," and those who aren't. But some girls are not so easily categorized. Gloria, for example, doesn't fit into either group. An elegant stringbean of a girl, Gloria writes publicity releases for a restaurant by day and is memorable for her see-through blouses after dark. It's hard to be sure of her motivations because they vary. Some days, when Gloria thinks of her mounting unpaid bills, she gets scared and drinks too many martinis, *then* her biggest worry is focused on maybe losing her job. But on happier days, Gloria will argue that she lives no differently from anyone else, and *they* seem to manage, don't they?

Although she has no grasp of them herself, Gloria's money problems are twofold: She doesn't know how to budget so that she can actually live on what she earns, she also deludes herself that $7900 is a terrific salary and she can afford anything she wants. The salary *would* be terrific in St. Joe, Missouri, Gloria's hometown, but in New York it is fairly modest. So Gloria hungrily roams the boutiques and department stores on her lunch hour and eats at Chock Full O' Nuts to economize. She buys all the fashion magazines each month and knows what's coming In and going Out. But mainly, she observes the people around her—at work, on the street, at the theatre—and that is Gloria's downfall. "Everybody seems to have everything they want," she insists. "I just want to live well, too." You can't blame Gloria for that, but her list of Must Necessities is a long one.

She *must* live on the fashionable East Side. "The West Side is so dreary, and it's not safe for a girl alone."

She *must* wear the latest fashions. "I can't help it. I adore clothes."

She *must* go to Europe for her vacation. "My roommates are going and I certainly don't want to sit here alone."

And when she *must*, there's no room for compromise.

But aren't many of Gloria's musts actually luxuries?

She looks helpless and hurt. "I don't consider myself extravagant."

(continued)

FIGURE 5. This May 1969 article in *Cosmopolitan*, "Credit Crazed Dolls," belies the common assumption that women could not get credit without men's approval before the mid-1970s. Some single women did have access to credit cards, and a few abortion clinics accepted credit to facilitate paying for an abortion.

applying for loans and credit cards. However, for years before the 1974 Equal Credit Opportunity Act, some credit cards were readily available to some women, and to such an extent that *Cosmopolitan* magazine ran a 1969 article describing single women as "Credit Crazed Dolls." The *New York Times* reported in 1970 that BankAmericard and Master Charge each had 30 million cardholders, and within just two years *Woman's Day* advised the 75 million people who had 300 million credit cards what to do "If You Lose a Credit Card." Of course, while some women may have been able to charge it, the credit cards may also have been supplied by partners, husbands, or fathers. Given the history of discrimination exposed by Abzug, it is telling the extent to which banks, loan companies, and credit cards invested in women applying for credit independently to yield large profits from high interest rates.[24]

Excluded from loan and credit contracts with legitimate businesses, some people turned to neighborhood loan sharks. Organized crime profited from this illegal service, lending money at high interest rates. Two economists conservatively estimated in 1968 that Cosa Nostra's control of loan-sharking generated $1 billion to $2 billion dollars in profit, while another maintained in 1969 that it was a $350-million-a-year enterprise. Whatever the true figure, it is clear that millions of desperate people sought out loans, and some of those were to finance abortions.[25] One 1969 study revealed why those who needed money for an abortion would have sought them out, finding, "Not only do loan sharks provide funds to those who cannot secure conventional loans . . . but in many cases, borrowers seek out loan sharks because of the services they offer: secrecy, informal loan procedures, speed, and the regular availability of funds." In wanting to avoid the stigma of either an out-of-wedlock pregnancy or abortion itself, people who needed to pay for an abortion may have specifically sought out these informal, high-interest loans to avoid sitting across the table from a bank representative. One man, lending in a working-class neighborhood in South Philadelphia, reported that the vast majority of his hundred customers were women. They borrowed between $25 and $100, paying it back and borrowing again, relying on the loan shark because it was convenient and "a housewife's only source of credit." The range of activities the loan shark described, from money to go out on Saturday night to paying doctor's bills, certainly make it a likely source of fast, discreet money to pay for an abortion from a local, covert provider.[26]

Another unlikely place where some people found financial support was in church. In the late 1960s, the Southern Presbyterian Church formed the Committee on Therapeutic Abortions (COTA). In its 1970 "Report on Problem Pregnancies and Abortions," the Presbyterian church affirmed the right of a woman, with her doctor's counsel, to get an abortion. After this policy was announced, a leader in a West Virginia congregation purportedly discovered that his daughter had gotten an abortion, assisted by the CCS. He declared, even though he opposed abortion, that he was contributing $50,000 to the COTA to ensure that women got the assistance they needed. The COTA loans did not require means testing. The girls and women receiving the loans did not have to be Presbyterian, they did not have to be from the state issuing the loan, and they did not have to pay it back. Moreover, the church prioritized a "Fly Now Pay Later" program, with loans that covered airfare (generally to New York or California), hospital, hotel bills, and meals. This financial support, as long as the money lasted, meant that women could secure an abortion without delay, lowering both costs and health risks.[27]

A $50,000 gift from the Board of National Ministries of the Presbyterian Church to the Atlanta-area COTA helped about a hundred women. The Atlanta chapter lent out more than half of that money in six months, and the Executive Secretary rejected the charge that this was a new activity: "this is nothing new as the board has been counseling on pregnancies for some time." As the church policy developed, congregations supported the new guidance financially. The 1971 graduating class of St. Andrews Presbyterian College in North Carolina, for example, voted to donate part of their cap and gown rental fees to support COTA, illustrating an unexpected nexus between colleges and churches supporting abortion access. College communities, with large and growing populations in this era, proved to be an important focus for activism, with students pressing administrations and each other to help women get timely abortions so they could stay in college.[28]

"How Do We Repossess on an Abortion?"

In the fall of 1970, college students created their own loan funds to enable women to access safe abortions. Historian Ronald Banks, special assistant to the president of the University of Maine in Orono (UMO), recounted the origins of the Maine students' abortion loan fund. He dated its genesis to a series of lectures by birth control and "abortion crusader" Bill Baird, who traveled the country, appealing to college students to work for increased birth control and abortion access. The first visit by Baird to UMO occurred in April 1969 and elicited front-page coverage in the student newspaper. His speech spoke to the many challenges people faced without abortion access, including thousands of women who resorted to self-abortion and died every year. The students brought

Baird back in September 1969 and then engaged him as a "Distinguished Lecturer" for a third talk in October 1970, when he discussed setting up a "'Stop Population' group or an 'Abortion Freedom League.'"[29]

In addition to Baird's messaging, several significant variables converged at the University of Maine that led the student senate to create an abortion loan fund in December 1970. New York's legalization of abortion with no residency requirement meant that UMO students had a clear destination in mind after July 1, 1970. A student confronted with an unwanted pregnancy knew that a legal abortion was theoretically within reach. However, students also knew that women and men with means could secure legal abortions, while those who could not risked death through self-abortion attempts or a visit to an illegal abortionist.[30]

UMO students also could see that their university was not doing what it could to provide information to students to prevent pregnancies in the first place, even as it faced unprecedented demand from students. Indeed, the university infirmary had "ceased birth control counseling because of the great influx of students seeking information . . . [and] also has discontinued physical examinations for birth control prescriptions and discontinued giving out prescriptions altogether." Financially strapped and unhappy in the role, the university instead encouraged students to seek help at the Family Planning Center in nearby Bangor, but it too was "unable to cope with the great number of people." The university, failing to provide even the most basic reproductive care, pushed students to action.[31]

The UMO president Winthrop Libby heard from many critics who disapproved of the abortion loan fund, including one man who claimed that it would "encourage vice and add oil on the fire" and demanded that the pregnant women "SHOULD BE EXPELLED."[32] Recognition of the students' empathetic motives is recorded throughout president's correspondence in response to the "vehement and virulent" criticism. He believed that this student initiative intended to end women's suffering and did not traffic in shaming women, as past policies had done. So too did Banks's summary of the record reflect that the Student Population Control Committee "did not advertise and claimed that it did not urge girls to seek abortions." The administration defended both the rights of the students and that they were trying to do something compassionate for less fortunate students.[33]

Although some UMO students disagreed with the creation of the fund and contested the right of the student government to form it, the student government reached a compromise with the fifty or so (of approximately seven thousand) students who objected. Objectors could have their seventy-three cents fund the Distinguished Lecture Series. The other modification to the fund came in the form of a name change, officially shifting from the Population Control Fund to the Emergency Loan Fund. Through it all, it was more commonly known as the Abortion Loan Fund, the name that exploded into the public spotlight. A wire service picked up an initial story in the local *Bangor Daily News*, and in small towns and big cities the headlines rang out: “Maine Students Have Abortion Loan Fund” (Nebraska) and “Student Loans to Help Coeds with Abortions” (Arizona). The coverage helped publicize the possibility of other colleges and universities embracing this kind of student legislation.[34]

After only one month, three UMO students had requested money from the fund. About a year and half after its creation, the student paper ran a story headlined, “Abortions in New York: Two Girls Tell Their Stories.” Matter-of-factly, the author described how one sophomore and one junior found themselves pregnant, secured the UMO loan money, and got abortions in New York. While the exposé explained that women who received counseling from the CCS secured lower costs and received help arranging the abortion, like the two featured women, most students who got loans at UMO did not seek counseling from the clergy. Having quick, anonymous access to the needed money and avoiding having to discuss it with a clergyperson seems to have been worth incurring the additional cost and responsibility for all but one of the twenty-five women who had taken an abortion loan to that point.[35]

The UMO loan program remained fairly unique. Only seven other colleges ultimately created and operated abortion loan programs, while a dozen more struggled to move beyond inquiring, proposing, or debating them. A few schools that did manage to create funds on their campuses faced an immediate backlash, forcing them to forgo their efforts.

The College of Charleston, with a student body of just eight hundred, for example, was the second in the nation to draw on student activity fees to create a Student Emergency Loan Fund that could be used to pay for an abortion. The announcement garnered external newspaper coverage in other states that included a statement from the Student Government Association president, who said, "he doesn't think there are many girls at the college who have had abortions. 'But if there is just one person who is forced to go into a back alley to have an abortion and gets hurt, then there is a problem.'" The Charleston college president at first "offered a measured defense of his students saying that 'he would not stand in moral judgment on the possible use of funds for abortions,'" but then forced the student government association to cancel the fund after just one week.[36]

The University of Rhode Island similarly debated a fund and had even more extensive national coverage of it. Given the estimated $1,000 per abortion spent by URI students, some students were determined to secure financial support. After the loan fund, the students planned to call for a "student-run abortion referral agency" and "an on-campus clinic to perform legal abortions." Heartbreakingly, coverage of the abortion loan fund also noted that "Many of these girls were over five months pregnant." While it is possible that the women were immobilized with fear and failed to address their pregnancies earlier, more likely the accounting underlines the importance of women having the resources to determine if they are indeed pregnant and access to financial means to secure an abortion for an unwanted pregnancy as quickly as possible. The URI advocates, however, never managed to get support for a "student activities tax" to fund abortion loans."[37]

At Duke University, following a motion by Bill Kennedy in May 1971, the student government initiated a fund for students to be able to borrow money for an abortion. In an interview, Kennedy remembered that "He and some fellow students had found themselves discussing lack of abortion access during a late-night chat." He had firsthand knowledge, as he and his girlfriend had gotten pregnant and been able to afford an abortion. Believing that there might be a sizable number of the five thousand undergraduate students in need and that everyone should have abortion access, Kennedy requested that the abortion loan fund receive an $8,000 allocation. While the debate in the student legislature was heated at times, the minutes reflect that, "it was stressed that by funding an Abortion Loan Program, a legislator (or other individual) would not necessarily condone the moral aspects of acquiring an abortion." Providing funds on a lending basis would "equalize the opportunity to obtain an abortion for all students." As Kennedy noted, "If you had the dough, you had freedom of choice." The students asserted that supporting the loan "pointed to the responsibility the legislature had taken in acting on basic student needs." On that basis, not only did the legislature "overwhelmingly" approve an allocation of $4,000, but "all presidential candidates endorsed the program" as well.[38]

In the fall of 1971, the Duke student paper reported on the progress. First, in October, a substantial column clarified that the purpose of the fund was to "provide interest-free loans . . . for the indigent person. This is a loan program, not an abortion referral program." The student government records reflect the preparation, including incorporating the fund as a nonprofit organization and opening an account at the local Wachovia Bank. A brief notice on November 10 trumpeted: "ABORTION LOAN: If you are currently enrolled as a Duke university undergraduate and need financial assistance in securing a legal abortion, contact one of the following members of the Abortion Loan Committee." Offering contact information for the six committee members, and assurances of "strictest confidentiality," the committee tried to spread the word.[39]

In his report on the loan usage as the fund chairman, Kennedy noted that four loans had been distributed to Duke undergraduates. He protected their identities and left ambiguous if the loans were being given to women or men, as both were eligible. As with the UMO experience, the program generated tremendous interest and coverage in newspapers around the country. Kennedy noted, for example, that twenty schools nationally requested information, including one neighboring school, the University of North Carolina at Charlotte, one of the few able to offer its own abortion loan program.[40]

Most schools that attempted loan programs met opposition. The College of William & Mary student paper first reported on a proposed Birth Control Service in February 1971, and that alone sparked an incredible furor in the college community. The school administration and two faculty members angrily condemned the newspaper for printing "obscenities," particularly objecting to Student Government Association president Winn Legerton's statement, "Considering the ignorance on this campus about birth control methods . . . and also the number of women who have had abortions this year, we sincerely hope that the information services will prove beneficial." The controversy reignited a few months later with a local newspaper reporting that students were trying to set up an abortion loan fund. There is no evidence that the proposed fund ever reached the level of a formal proposal or debate, but the outrage at even discussing birth control and students having abortions does make it notable.[41]

Much of the pressure against abortion loan funds nationally appears to have come at the level of the college deans or presidents. There were exceptions, and it is possible that loans happened quietly. In one instance at a still all-male Dartmouth, a dean dispensed emergency funds for a sibling's abortion in 1966. Generally, however, the public debates put administrators and students at odds. At the University of Texas–Austin, opposition came from the Board of Regents. The student senate approved an abortion loan fund, and the board responded by stripping 75 percent of its operating budget. In schools that created loan funds, most governing figures and bodies conceded that the students' actions were not illegal and that students had a right to set their own policies. Therefore, university officials that defeated abortion fund efforts generally relied on coercion and threats to funding.[42]

The student effort at the University of Illinois-Chicago Circle campus (UI-CC) stands out because of its unique composition and funding sources. The inspiration to create the Abortion Loan Service (ALS) in November 1971 sprang from a convergence of activists, from student government, the women's movement, and Zero Population Growth (ZPG). Inspired by the UMO fund, program co-founder and student Kathy Mallin (active in women's liberation and the student government) described the twenty thousand urban UI-CC students as "working-class students who find it hard to simply earn enough to survive." Instead of seeking funding from the student government, student founders did independent fundraising and aligned the ALS with the local Planned

Parenthood's abortion referral service. The ALS was both a referral and loan service, and with its formal agreement with Planned Parenthood referred students seeking abortions to Eastside Medical Group (EMG) in New York City.[43]

The most money the ALS program ever reported raising was $1,500, so compared to other schools, especially given its large student population, it was woefully underfunded. About half of their eighteen loans were at the limit of $200, with the rest ranging from $50 to $150; the average loan was $155. The student government funded its advertising, but it depended on donations from faculty and the Chicago Women's Liberation Rock Band, which gave $200. As with all loan programs, the intention was that it would be self-sustaining and that new contributions would allow it to grow and serve more students. Unfortunately, the small amount of money they were able to fundraise meant that the ALS was wholly dependent on students repaying their loans before they could lend out more funds. The group was ultimately stopped in its tracks after just a few months, having lent out all the money. Exacerbating the underfunding, fewer than half of recipients repaid their loan, leaving the program with depleted coffers.[44]

The group's members were aware of the importance of advertising, not just to reach women in need, but also to solicit funds from those moved by their plight. The *Chicago Tribune* reported that the service "advertised by flyers on outdoor bulletin boards and posters in all campus buildings." Coverage in the student paper also proved vital in reaching those in need. Co-founder Diane Ronan noted of the first loan recipients, "The girls we have helped so far include one white, one Chicano, and two black girls. It is a problem that cuts across class and race lines." Co-founder Larry Zawilenski also understood the importance of publicizing their efforts nationally and placed a small announcement in the *ZPG National Reporter* newsletter in February 1972. He explicitly encouraged "Other college chapters, or chapters near colleges interested in setting up such a loan service" to contact him. In his correspondence with Nancy Nist at Minnesota's Carleton College, he suggested that they consider creating "a joint press release to UPI, AP, magazines, etc.," noting, "We have gotten articles in two of Chicago's four daily papers."[45]

FIGURE 6. Ads for the Abortion Loan Service appeared in the *Daily Illini*. This one, from 1972, reflected the unique opportunity that the University of Illinois students on the Chicago Circle campus had to use their health insurance for an abortion. With permission from the *Daily Illini*.

The final aspect of the ALS program that was distinctive was that UI-CC offered students Hospital, Surgical, Medical Insurance that covered the cost of an abortion, up to $200 (if they had conceived while insured). Zawilenski reported that "No other school in the Chicago area has this type of insurance." Moreover, it was confidential, meaning the student held the insurance so neither their parents nor their employers knew how it was being used. Indeed, no other school investigated for this study boasted this kind of coverage. It was a game changer for ALS when they discovered the student insurance covered abortions.[46]

Armed with the knowledge that UI-CC students could effectively guarantee payment through their insurance, Zawilenski tried to broker credit with EMG. The correspondence indicates that the clinic believed that credit should be "reserved for the really needy welfare cases." In arguing for the needs of UI-CC students, Zawilenski noted that their student composition was "quite different from an average university." He offered concrete statistics: "37% receive financial aid" and "two-thirds of the students finance all or a part of their tuition." He concluded, "pregnant girls often find themselves in a precarious financial situation. The Loan Service was established to provide emergency loans to girls with no other source of money." In other words, the women were "really needy welfare cases." The credit Zawilenski sought for UI-CC students was to float them for two to three months, awaiting the insurance payment. He provided the details of the insurance policy, which specified the coverage "up to two hundred dollars for non-therapeutic abortion." Finally, he finished his pitch by assuring EMG, "we will use our sixteen hundred dollars capital as security. If there are any defaults, the Service will pay." If the service could have secured this agreement, it would have been able to help countless more women get abortions. Using the funds as a guarantor would free up the pathway for pregnant women at the Chicago campus to Planned Parenthood and from there to getting a legal abortion in New York.[47]

It may have been surprising to the coordinators that EMG would not enter into an agreement, given the reporting that same month in *Chicago Today* that the Eastside clinic charged only $130 and depended on volume to profit. However, Zawilenski could not guarantee the number of women who would utilize the services. Offering credit would also disrupt the "cash on the barrel" operation, described in the news story, that characterized provision of abortions generally, with each woman paying the $8 transportation fee before being dropped off at the clinic and then supplying the $130 fee before receiving the scheduled abortion. Moreover, even if the clinic had agreed, Zawilenski had not factored in the fact that the women still had to purchase airfare, and even the cheapest option of a student, standby round-trip ticket from Chicago to New York City was an estimated $85.[48]

Indeed, over time, the high cost of travel led the coordinators of the loan fund to seek out licensed medical providers closer to home. One option for some UI-CC women was to contact the Janes in Chicago. This secretive group of women first served as a much-needed referral service to male providers, helping women secure the clandestine procedure. After several years, a few women in the collective began to perform abortions themselves at reduced rates, cutting out the male providers altogether. The list of numbers to call, from Kathy Mallin's archived ALS materials, includes the number for Jane, 643-3844, but when asked why the service did not just refer women seeking abortions to the local and eventually affordable option, she explained, when "Diane [Ronan] interviewed the women, they were primarily interested in legal abortions." Many women, including most who approached the UI-CC service, chose legality and medical oversight over a less expensive option, if they could.[49]

Ultimately, Mallin began to pursue a third option after Ronan and Zawilenski graduated, EMG refused to accept the insurance payout, and the women coming to her continued to seek legal abortions. In the fall of 1972, she reached out to a clinic in Milwaukee. Her records include a newspaper clipping from *Chicago Today* proclaiming, "Is Wisconsin New Abortion Mecca?" and a copy of her letter to the Wisconsin Women's Medical Group that sought to create a similar insurance payout structure as ALS had attempted in New York City. The public reporting that another referral group was "sending hundreds of women each month to Wisconsin" from ten Midwestern states solidified Milwaukee as a viable, legal abortion option. For Mallin, the advantage of a Milwaukee clinic was clear. Due north of Chicago and only about an hour and half away, it would dramatically decrease transportation costs. Her handwritten notes suggest that the clinic was "already operating" and charging $285 for the abortion and $15 for transportation. Likely reflecting a bus schedule, the women would leave at 9 a.m. and return at 5 p.m. on the same day.[50]

Mallin had also been in contact with the UI-CC insurance office and ascertained that the providers could be directly reimbursed for an "an abortion performed on a female Circle student or the wife of a male Circle student." She assured the Women's Medical Group, "the benefits are sent directly to you" and underlined how much this arrangement would help her "working class" peers. The ALS wanted to solidify its relationship with a closer, legal option, and use the UI-CC student insurance to bring the cost within reach for women. While ultimately unsuccessful, these student efforts to make abortion locally accessible in standard medical environments speak to the consumer preferences of the women seeking abortions.[51]

Across college campuses, women's groups also directly supported those seeking abortions. Female students tried to help fund abortions for women in need. In 1972, for example, students in Carleton College's Women's Caucus independently started an abortion loan fund with a distinctive model born of their woman-centered approach. Like other abortion funds, the loan was available "in cases where one of the parents is enrolled as a Carleton student" and the students placed the funds in the First National Bank. The major difference came in how it solicited money from women to loan to the students in need. Outlined in its "Notice to Students, Faculty and Administration":

> The policy which the Women's Caucus has established is that no more than half the loan should directly come from the account. The rest will come from people who have said they will loan money upon request. The purpose of this is to make the resources available for the maximum number of people possible.... Anyone who has used the fund will understand the continuing needs of others, and should try to repay the loan as soon as possible.[52]

The group solicited donations and "There was also a potluck supper held in the Cave, with all donations going directly to the Abortion Loan Fund. The women intended the bank to not just be a repository, but also hoped to grow the money, when not in use, by earning interest. They were working to ensure a commitment of those who claimed to support abortion rights, by securing 'in-kind donations'" and political buy-in.[53]

The University of Iowa Women's Center also raised money to sponsor abortion loans. A spokeswoman reported that the group raised nearly $900 of their $3,000 goal and distributed fifteen interest-free loans over a three-month span, averaging about $100 per loan. Abortion counselors met once a week to discuss funding requests and only referred women to New York "because abortions there are legal and safe." However, like Carleton, the center never gave "a loan for both transportation and an abortion, so the loans cover only part of the total abortion cost." The center raised money on campus with a table set up in their student union once a week, getting about $25 a week, and solicited donations at the

Women's Center, in both the men's and women's residence halls, and in the dining halls. The group noted that about half of the women who came in for abortion referrals needed financial aid.[54]

Scattered, anecdotal information suggests that informal fundraising from other women was also fairly common. In 1966, Skidmore College students approached the new chaplain to ask for help connecting with an abortion provider; they had raised $700 to help a woman who needed an abortion. Rebecca Sive, a Carleton student in 1968, recalled that dormmates informally raised "money for a friend to obtain an (illegal) abortion." Co-founder of the Black Women's Health Imperative Billye Avery recalled in an interview that a white friend told her "Me and all of my girlfriends had a thousand dollars that we kept. And the thousand dollars were if you needed to go have an abortion. And if you didn't have your thousand saved up within our group, we pooled our money to give to you your thousand so that you could go and do that." Certainly, few women could afford to save toward $1,000, but one anonymous writer describing her quest for an abortion in the *Washington Spark* celebrated three women friends who had "$250 stashed away and offered it to us. (Sisterhood is powerful!)" One abortion provider found it profitable to travel to the University of Maine in Portland "because the girls there had a kitty." She incentivized groups of women to use her services, as she had an "understanding" with them: "it would be $350 for the first one and then $50 for each other." Historian Susan Reverby characterized informal "kittys" as a "Feminist insurance policy."[55]

Students on campuses, from community colleges to large state schools, large and small private colleges and universities, actively tried to support women who needed to borrow money for abortions. College campuses offered women and men the unique opportunity to organize to help people cope with problem pregnancies through abortion loans.[56]

Insurance

The promise that medical insurance, public and private, would help make abortions more accessible to more women, including freeing loan money for the poorest uninsured, pervaded the national discourse. As activists and consumers sought to reform and repeal laws governing abortion in the late 1960s and early 1970s, so too did they turn their attention to health insurance policies and their coverage of abortions. They campaigned for coverage for married women, single women, dependents, and daughters under age eighteen, as well as access to procedures without a doctor's approval. NARAL's first "Statement of Policy and Purpose," issued March 27, 1969, listed as its first policy: "Safe abortions performed by physicians should be readily available to all women on a voluntary basis, regardless of economic status and without legal encumbrance." From the outset, the intention was to ensure abortions were available to all.[57]

However, significant tensions existed over public and private insurance coverage of abortion. One important concern was whether women who traveled out of their community or out of state to have an abortion would be covered. This was especially important to women who had to travel across state lines and across the country to locate a provider. Abortion may not have been legal in the state where the policy holder lived, but proponents argued that the procedure should be covered and accessible where it was legal. Sometimes private insurance companies included abortion coverage, as was the case for students (and their spouses) at UI-CC, as well as for New York state employees when the state legalized abortion in July 1970. One interesting approach came in New York when the Health Insurance Plan of Greater New York (HIP), the first not-for-profit HMO, provided abortions for $100 to patients with HIP insurance at the Flushing Women's Medical Center.[58]

Nationally, two women spearheaded the consumer pressure campaign on insurance companies to cover abortions. Influential financial author and columnist Sylvia Porter, who at the height of her influence reached 40 million readers and advised three US presidents, offered her clear assessment of abortion costs in her syndicated column, "Your Money's Worth." Under the title "Finances Limit Abortion Option," Porter argued in 1972 that even though abortion was "increasingly legalized, lack of money will continue as before to divide the poor from the medically solvent in the market for the service." She encouraged readers to seek out policies that would give them abortion access. "As a consumer of health insurance coverage through group plans," she implored, "you have a right to ask for coverage of legal operations as long as you have the money to back up your demands." She then turned to showcasing the extensive research on insurance and abortion done by economist Charlotte Muller.[59]

Muller's work revealed tremendous inconsistencies in policies and abortion coverage. Moreover, she did not just report on where things stood, but like Porter also encouraged readers to take action to secure abortion coverage, asserting, "There is no conceptual reason why coverage could not extend to all single female employees and to unmarried economically dependent children of an insured father or mother." In her research, she located most abortion coverage in "the maternity provisions of the group health contracts and it is generally severely restricted." She found in her 1971 survey of New York City hospitals, for example, that only 26 percent of abortion patients claimed insurance coverage, which led her to conclude that a lack of financing was impeding the access of legal abortions. She implored, "For those who receive welfare assistance, costs for legal abortion should be reimbursable under Title XIX of the Social Security Act (Medicaid)." Moreover, she concluded of private insurance: "high cost is tantamount to effective denial of access to abortion."[60]

At the "Abortion Techniques and Services" conference in 1971, Muller established that "many out-of-town patients arrive . . . with inadequate funds for medical care and for living, and with no lodging and no friends." The need to provide "total cash payment" before the abortion procedure left economically vulnerable women unable to secure abortions. She surveyed the industry, ascertaining that although abortion was sometimes covered, the ability to access the benefit was severely limited.[61]

For starters, the provision pertaining to abortion was uniformly found in the maternity section of the group health contract. She challenged its placement. The limits on coverage were significant, as many companies reported that "Single women may not be covered" and "Daughters of the insured may not be covered." Even ascertaining if coverage existed at all would have required a phone call to the insurance company or their employer, which exposed the family to the scrutiny of outsiders.[62]

There were other limitations as well. Subscribers learned that even if the girl or woman was ostensibly covered, the woman must have conceived following a mandatory waiting period after acquiring insurance. Having a job with insurance that covered an abortion did not automatically mean it would be covered, as women had to make it through the waiting period. Even then, "benefits may be restricted to a hospital," which meant women could face longer wait times to get an appointment for the procedure, which would then cost more because of the types of procedures performed. There were some merciful exceptions in some companies, with eight of those reviewed creatively waiving the waiting period "if delivery would have occurred after the usual maternity waiting period," and one company applied "regular benefits" if the pregnancy involved rape or threat to life or health. Again, this would have necessitated revealing personal information, but Muller reported on these and other efforts to be more humane as she charged, "There is no reason why coverage could not be written without a waiting period."[63]

However, she was a rare vocal advocate. Critics decried the increased costs borne by policy holders, asserting that abortion claims would dramatically increase premium costs. This line of thinking was advocated by those who could not anticipate needing the benefit and did not want to draw unwanted attention to the sexuality of the women covered by the policy. Those who potentially could have used the coverage held back public support for fear of branding themselves or their family as sexually loose and irresponsible.

Occasionally companies and workers agreed to include abortion coverage openly under the company medical plan. The Columbia Broadcasting System offered such coverage, but employees had to travel to New York to make use of the provision. Muller touted the 300,000 steelworkers who collectively secured "coverage of unmarried dependents' pregnancy claims" and the exceptional coverage achieved by the Federal Employee Health Benefits Program, which covered not only "maternity without waiting periods," but also "any expenses in connection with legal abortions that are medically necessary." She noted, in particular, that the Civilian Health and Medical Program of the Uniformed Services covered abortion: "abortions could be performed 'in military facilities of the United States without regard to local State laws,' and a serviceman's wife could get an abortion at Government expense at a civilian hospital, even if her military doctor opposed the operation, only in states where abortions were legal." Muller offered strong examples of what was possible for those negotiating for insurance coverage, empowering them to request coverage.[64]

Critics of poor abortion coverage contended that women faced undue scrutiny in having to secure a doctor's approval before making use of a health benefit that they paid for, while men seeking a vasectomy were not required to do so. Even those who had relatively straightforward abortion access may have opted not to use their health insurance coverage, for fear of reprisal from their employer or a parent. This may have been true particularly of those for whom the coverage did not meet the full cost of the procedure. In that situation, insurance use may have brought unwanted attention without substantially improving the woman's financial outlook. As Dr. Robert E. Hall cautioned readers in his 1971 *A Doctor's Guide to Having an Abortion*, "Most insurance companies will pay only a fraction of the cost of a private patient's abortion."[65]

For out-of-state women seeking abortions in New York, for-profit referral services and clinics generally did not accept insurance, even if they promoted insurance coverage with their services. For example, one woman, writing about her investigative efforts to discern costs and practices for those seeking an abortion, was surprised when she answered an ad for "professional and safe abortions under $100 with most health plans." Not only did they quote her a price of $200 plus airfare from Chicago, they never mentioned health insurance. When she inquired, she was assured that none of the clinics would allow Blue Cross Blue Shield to cover the cost and that to use her insurance to cover some of the cost would only be possible at a hospital, where the abortion would likely be about $600.[66]

Private insurance, then, was little help even to those who had it, but the situation was worse for women covered by federal programs. Public health coverage, where it existed, proved vital to improving poor women's access. Still, Medicaid coverage of abortion proved to be a political hot potato, with critics charging that the program should not include abortions and supporters contending that without it the poorest women would suffer and not be able to secure safe, legal abortions. Questions about the constitutionality of Medicaid payments for abortion were often fought out in court, with New York courts ultimately declaring payments for elective abortions constitutional. Having clear direction enabled the Kings County Hospital in New York City to have "its own Medicaid inspector, so that anyone who does not have the money for the procedure ($160 for suction or curettage, $270 for saline) can apply. The hospital does not wait for the application to be approved before performing the abortion." Of course, New York City hospitals' residency requirement still proved to be an obstacle for women who were not residents, generally requiring residence in the city itself, but sometimes even dictating which neighborhoods would be served. One feminist abortion referral group, the Women's Health and Abortion Project (WHAP), "loaned out our addresses" to women who needed second-trimester abortions. They offered them "fake addresses so that they could look like they were New York City residents. There was a lot less identification then, and maybe we even gave people our driver's licenses to take with them."[67]

One New Mexico Planned Parenthood director noted that "Costs vary with each hospital and physician," and that "Blue Cross medical insurance covers abortions. Financial help may also be obtained through Medicaide [sic]." When New Mexico passed a reform bill in 1969, it required that women's requests be accompanied by letters from two physicians. In spite of these onerous requirements, the state saw a substantial increase in the number of women seeking therapeutic abortions.[68]

Cash flow and profit also led doctors and hospitals to require cash payment up front, even if women had insurance or Medicare, and then had their office assist *the woman* in getting reimbursed, rather than the provider. WHAP evaluated *The Abortion Game* in a 1972 booklet, including a chart that outlined payment information. They noted, "The clinics that handle insurance require women to pay the fee at the time of the appointment; they fill out insurance forms so that women can be reimbursed *if their policy covers abortion* and/or D&C." Instead of taking the insurance and awaiting payment, these in-demand facilities forced women to pay up front and bear the financial burden of waiting for reimbursement. Some facilities offered staggered payments, and a WHAP chart offered descriptions of the various plans. Eastern Women's Center, for example, offered staggered payments, "but bills are sent if not paid," which could potentially expose a woman's pregnancy when mail arrived from the center. Other facilities outright said no or yes to payment plans, hedged with a "sometimes/hard to get," or in one case specified, "Yes; half in cash at the time of appointment."[69]

Some facilities that accepted insurance or Medicaid depended on reimbursements, which were often delayed for up to a year. Thus, they did not necessarily have the ability to offer services without payment. Others, of course, as described by Susan Reverby, who worked the phones and the desk at one abortion clinic, brought in so much cash, it was hard to believe. She remembered, "They brought in piles of money. They would count it out in piles, hundreds of twenties, like Monopoly money, and then take it to the bank." By the time Ron Hammerle was brought in to secure the clinic license for Women's Services, four months after it opened, clinic staff carried "$20,000 to $30,000 in cash . . . to the bank each week down the streets of New York City." A doctor similarly reflected, "We often got paid in small money—singles, even coins—and counting it was time-consuming." Clinics did the heaviest volume on the weekends when the banks were closed, and as one doctor remembered, "By the end of the weekend, you'd open a door and walk into a sea of money." Watching that kind of cash flow, Reverby happily provided women who arrived and could not afford their abortions at the Women's Medical Group a reduced fee.[70]

By 1972, Title VII of the Civil Rights Act brought legal pressure to bear on insurance companies, who were forced to provide "maternity benefits to single women" and greater access to abortion. The equity only went so far, however. Nationwide insurance, for example, still required a doctor to provide a statement regarding the necessity of the abortion, while it did not make the same demands of a man making a claim for a vasectomy. From big-name companies to the federal government, insurance coverage of abortion risked exposure, generally excluded poor women and women of color, and left the poorest vulnerable to sterilization.[71]

"Package Deal"

Ultimately, Medicaid coverage facilitated public hospitals in profiting from poor and Black women. In one instance, a hospital insisted that a young patient submit to a hysterectomy to address an incomplete abortion rather than giving the "D&C procedure" that would leave her reproductive capacity intact. Thankfully for the Black woman who recounted her 1965 experience, her mother stopped the hospital from sterilizing her. As an employed clerk stenographer at the Federal Aviation Authority earning $91 every two weeks, she had federal insurance, but the hospital staff still sought to profit and maim her, rather than care for her after her abortion. This pattern of tying abortion access to coerced or forced sterilization remained a vulnerability for women when they sought abortion care, particularly for the women of color who had to rely on insurance (private or public) to pay the bill. Maryland may have made it illegal to withhold welfare benefits to compel abortions in 1968, but just five years later researchers found Baltimore hospitals "'pushing' elective sterilization" on women. As Dr. Helen Rodriguez-Trias noted, "Lack of access to abortion services may also push women to get sterilization," with some women coerced or outright forced to "consent" to the procedure.[72]

Profitability drove the hospital practice of sterilizing poor women and women of color seeking abortions. Dr. Richard Hausknecht commented that he and his colleagues would do hysterectomies six weeks postpartum to offer women reproductive control before *Griswold v. Connecticut* (1965). He acknowledged that "It was prehistoric, absolutely prehistoric. From a training point of view we were delighted by this cause we got a chance to operate." He later explained that racial prejudice and training opportunities for new obstetrical fellows helped fuel sterilizations of Black and Puerto Rican women, tubal ligations and especially hysterectomies. The profit differential between the two in 1974 was extraordinary; rates ranged from $250 for a tubal ligation to more than $1,500 for a hysterectomy. As one doctor noted, "It can mean a new mink coat for a doctor's wife."[73]

In addition, the motive of punishing women for getting pregnant and having an abortion should not be forgotten. Two Canadian hospitals publicly shared their sterilization policies; one of the sanctioned reasons a woman could be sterilized was if she had a therapeutic abortion. The rationale was that if the abortion was justified on a health basis, then a woman should not have any more children. An obstetrical nurse interviewed in 1971 wanted abortion to be legal, but with stipulations. She said, "After one abortion, if she gets pregnant again and wants another abortion, she should have to agree to sterilization or be satisfied to have the baby."[74]

Critics in the early 1970s charged doctors with hard-selling sterilization to poor Black and Puerto Rican women. Ralph Nader's Public Citizen, Inc. formed the Health Research Group, headed by physicians who charged that "these operations have been 'sold' to the public in a manner not unlike many other deceptive marketing practices." Their study claimed that "considerable 'pushing' of elective sterilization and 'hard-selling' of these procedures" to women had taken place at hospitals in Los Angeles, Baltimore, Boston, New Orleans, Nashville, Chicago, and Louisville. While historians Johanna Schoen revealed the sterilization abuses done by committee in North Carolina and Alexandra Minna Stern revealed the abuses in state institutions in California, this transactional abuse was taking place by individual doctors in hospitals all across the United States. Rather than providing medical training for abortions and creating an effective way to profit from volume, hospitals' cost-benefit analysis embraced sterilization profits gained in addition to surgical training and long hospital stays.[75]

Hospitals and doctors evaded the laws and wielded power to make women who wanted an abortion submit to their authority. Republican pundit and *National Review* editor William F. Buckley Jr. editorialized in a 1971 national newspaper column that poor couples who had a child out of wedlock should be jailed and the child institutionalized. "For the second bastard, the parents should be sterilized," he condemned. The *New York Times* trumpeted a declining birth rate in 1972, particularly in couples with Black women or white men most likely to be sterilized. However, the vast majority of Black women were not seeking out sterilizations; they were being coerced, manipulated, and forced into having the operation, including when they sought an abortion. By 1973, doctors characterized the demand for sterilization in exchange for an abortion as a "package deal."[76]

"The Price I Had to Pay"

This analysis of the financial costs borne by women and men, families, and communities should be read with an understanding of the additional cost paid. Implicit in the decision to seek an abortion is the vulnerability of all girls and women who revealed an unwanted pregnancy and exposed themselves to hateful and violent words and actions. From the thirteen-year-old girl whose mother called her a "whore" to the doctor's decision not to use anesthesia for a D&C to punish a woman, millions of women desperately scrounged for and paid hundreds of dollars to be treated cruelly. Women seeking an abortion were desperate and abortions were illegal across most of the country, so women could hardly hope to be discerning consumers; few women could storm out if they were extorted for sex or demeaned before, during, or after the procedure. Their very desperation for a "disreputable" procedure opened them to abuse.[77]

As one woman, Valerie, described in her testimony before an abortion tribunal in Cleveland, "I found myself looking through the yellow pages trying to guess which one of the many physicians listed there might be sympathetic." Valerie's definition of a sympathetic person, however, was not predicated on treating her competently and with dignity, but just on a willingness to terminate her pregnancy. Her cost in Cleveland in 1968 was extraordinarily high: "The price I had to pay for this therapeutic abortion, in addition to the several hundred dollars for a hospital procedure and then the humiliating requirement of psychiatric approval, was forced sterilization." Pressured by the doctor, her husband gave his approval, which most hospitals required for a woman's sterilization, and left for the night. Valerie recalled how trapped she felt as she again asked for an abortion without being sterilized:

> the doctor said to me, "I want you to know that nobody will ever help you again. I want you to sign this card." And he handed me the pen. I was terrified that he would refuse to do the abortion

> unless I signed. I realized that it was probably hopeless, right from the minute I stepped into his office, that sterilization in exchange for abortion was his policy and probably that of the hospital. I signed the card and the next morning after the abortion, I was sterilized.[78]

She knew that the demand was wrong and did not want to be sterilized, but like so many women, she was threatened and coerced into "agreeing" to the procure. Years later she testified, "Even now, it seems an unnecessary and drastic step. In a country that has the technology to send a man to the moon, it seems incredible that a good and safe contraceptive with no ill side effects cannot be developed, with free abortions as a backup procedure and no forced sterilizations."

Instead, women across the country experienced demeaning treatment, endured humiliating mental health examinations, and lied about or confessed their mental states before medical professionals sitting in judgment, as well as paid exorbitant sums of money for abortions. Throughout, women endured degrading, even criminal exploitation, sexual abuse, and, for the most vulnerable, sterilization, denying their ability to control their own bodies. The cost was very high, indeed.

3

Buying and Selling Information

IN THE FIRST HALF of Super Bowl V (1971) in Miami's Orange Bowl, nearly eighty thousand fans looked up from the matchup between the Baltimore Colts and the Dallas Cowboys to see a plane skywriting overhead. Naomi Smith watched between sips of her pineapple-orange juice as the pilot spelled out: A-B-O-R-T-I-O-N I-N-F-O, followed by the all-important phone number, 716-285-9133. Using a massive stage to reach those in need of the elusive, critical phone number was the most visible evidence of a new for-profit industry that emerged with legal abortion access. Even with legalization in July 1970, few people outside of New York City could navigate the vagaries of abortion information. The efforts of two stalwart organizations, the Clergy Consultation Service (CCS) and Planned Parenthood, remained shrouded in euphemisms adopted in a time when they needed to protect their reputation and shield themselves from legal action. When businesses could finally say "abortion," the vague names did not work as well in successfully reaching women adrift in the abortion market.[1]

Particularly after legalization and before *Roe*, nonmedical, nonreligious, non-woman-centered businesses flourished. Male entrepreneurs created explicit abortion referral businesses to provide the contact information that unlocked abortion access. Women paid for the referral and the abortion—often in advance—with some companies scheduling the abortion appointment only upon receipt of a money order. Others only collected a referral fee, while expecting the woman to pay the clinic upon arrival there. This pay-to-play system, though, offered a fast, direct opportunity to purchase an abortion. Whether it was sixty cents to buy *Consumer Reports*' analysis, $1.25 for a paperback book that explained the process, or a $10 fee to secure an abortion at a New York clinic, people needed information and were willing to pay for it to help them navigate the abortion market.[2]

With high demand and short supply, clinics and hospitals were free to charge whatever the market could bear. With doctors poised to make $150,000 a year in extra income for just a few hours of work a day, entrepreneurs determined that if they could deliver patients, they could get a cut of what promised to be extraordinary profits. Rarely did the men running referral agencies tout their huge profits, as most observers thought their business was immoral and wrong. To counter their dubious reputations, entrepreneurs sometimes offered anecdotal evidence that they were trustworthy and saved the lives of desperate women.

Those critical of the referral businesses that emerged after legalization in New York urged the state's attorney general Louis Lefkowitz to crack down on illegal activity. Those operating in the state found themselves under investigation for criminal activity, including fee splitting, kickbacks, and deceitful advertising. While the legal system aimed to address the abuses, the window of opportunity remained open through 1970 and into 1971, and those operating in other states were out of New York's reach.

This legal wrangling eventually ensnared Martin Mitchell, but for two years he was the most prolific abortion advertiser in the country. Following the Super Bowl he reflected, "I advertise in Miami simply because when you advertise there, you advertise to the whole country." Other men used newspaper ads to great effect, but Mitchell dominated the roadways, the airwaves, and the skies. He saw himself as the consummate business professional. He maintained, "I do what the big boys, the smart boys do. If you've got a product or a service to sell, advertise it. If a woman doesn't know where to go to get an abortion, she needs to know. Advertising makes sense." It was this business approach, meeting consumer demand for a newly legal product heretofore hidden, that distinguished Mitchell and other referral competitors, almost all of them men.[3]

The entrepreneurs who embraced a for-profit approach to abortion information understood that building abortion facilities and hiring staff would not, in itself, generate business. They knew that the business required publicizing the resources. According to referral operators, they did not have to counsel women because they had already decided. Moreover, they did not have to determine any health questions, beyond capturing a woman's self-reported week of pregnancy. By operating truly as middlemen, the individuals and companies, especially those that proliferated in the two-and-a-half-year era of legalization in New York, met the needs of hundreds of thousands of women to find abortion providers.[4]

Proponents of abortion access reacted to the emergence of the abortion referral agencies with hostility. They bemoaned the injustice of fees charged to women already facing steep financial obstacles. Although the agencies were disparaged as deceptive, exploitative, evil profiteers by many, there were still some who welcomed the effort to meet the enormous need that existed. While many women and men learned of free services offered, many more did not. Planned Parenthood, for example, wary of alienating supporters and betraying their mission, generally did not advertise widely, and when they did, rarely used the word "abortion" in their ads. The national clergy network feared legal prosecution and did not mention abortion in their full name, Clergy Consultation Service for Problem Pregnancies. The group's advertising principally consisted of a listing in the phone book and attracting media coverage. Moreover, while the phone call was free, the organizations still exacted a cost, though not necessarily financial. Women had to wait to hear back from the religious counselor on call, navigate family planning or religious counseling, and then make the appointments and travel arrangements themselves. Just as the Women's Health and Abortion Project (WHAP) discerned that there were not many differences between profit-making and nonprofit clinics at the patient-care level, so too it may be that the differences between for-profit and nonprofit referral agencies were less obvious for the consumer. Knowing the number of a free referral service did not immediately secure the abortion. The cost in lost time of calling an answering machine, fielding a call back, and enduring even sympathetic counseling when the woman had already made up her mind made the fee a small price to pay.[5]

Referral services became a big business in 1970, and this chapter explores abortion referral companies and the multitude of ways that consumers learned about how to access abortions. Information about how to locate an abortion provider appeared in medical columns, magazine articles, books, and pamphlets created by organizations. Abortion consumers, whether local, national, and international, knew what they wanted to buy and looked for guidance on where to go and how to get it. As clinic telephone operator Joan Mellon remembered it, "These women who called knew what they wanted was the fastest way to schedule an abortion that was safe and legal and that's why they were calling." The only guidance they needed and wanted was an appointment for the abortion.[6]

Mitchell Family Planning

Martin Mitchell, the most significant abortion advertiser, operated his business from Michigan. His network extended through the Midwest, Kentucky, Pennsylvania, Texas, Florida, and Canada. From his own accounting, within the first month of setting up his operation he received phone calls from the "'tip of Florida to the top of Canada.'" He eventually placed two hundred abortion information billboards in forty states and adopted a model of targeting small cities of about a hundred thousand people. He set up a clinic in Niagara Falls, New York, an upstate location near the Canadian border, because it was easier for women to go there from the Midwest and Canada than to go all the way to New York City. Hailing from Brooklyn, Mitchell also likely knew it was less intimidating for rural and small-town women to travel to another small city, and they could combine it with sightseeing. Moreover, with a head start in introducing a clinic in the area, he hoped to edge out any competition.[7]

Three vital threads fueled Mitchell's business. First, he zeroed in on a broad market and reported that about half of his business were married

FIGURE 7. In this 16 November 1970 press photo, Martin Mitchell stands before a billboard advertising his vasectomy and abortion referral service. Mitchell was the leader in promoting abortion information nationally, including putting up billboards with his phone number in small cities and on highways. © John Collier—USA TODAY NETWORK.

women, and another 25 percent were single, working women over age twenty-one. He reported that a sizable number of inquiries for abortions came from men. Moreover, he also promoted vasectomies, which broadened his appeal as well as his market and gave him credibility about wanting to reduce the population. He saw both women and men as potential markets for that effort. Unlike other referral businesses and clinics, he did not seek an alliance with Planned Parenthood or focus exclusively on the college market.[8]

He also reached a second important conclusion: He had to advertise widely. He did not try to hide his message to avoid legal scrutiny or shield it with coded language; instead, he spent money to legally defend his right to advertise. Mitchell Family Planning explicitly and boldly sold abortions. He hired an advertising agency to handle his account, reflecting how substantial the business was and the importance of advertising to his business model.[9]

Mitchell believed that public, visible advertising was the answer to the desperate unspoken question faced by millions of people: How do I secure a safe, legal abortion? His approach showed his respect for the consumer who wanted to avail themselves of a legitimate service and needed the information. He also noted that people were willing to pay to get an appointment for an abortion. Critics of Mitchell and other profit-making entrepreneurs claimed that if people just called a different number, they could get the information for "free." But they ignored the national vacuum of abortion information. Mitchell understood the need and sought to sell the information with the help of advertising.[10]

The billboards not only generated consumers, but also elicited controversies. Mitchell contended that any complaints likely emanated from only one or two people, but they were generally enough to bring down the signs. After his billboard had appeared for two months on Eight Mile Road near Interstate 75 in Michigan, for example, a sign company painted over it at the behest of the local city council. Despite setbacks, Mitchell wanted to "erect signs within six months in every Midwest city with a population over 100,000" people. The contretemps generated newspaper coverage, but without the phone number visible, it was hard to sell his service. As he noted to one Iowa reporter, "A sign like that is not like advertising for a soft drink where you see it and then buy it." Instead, "It takes about a month or more to tell what kind of response you're getting from these things." He theorized that it took time to register what he was selling, and it was only when there were enough unwanted pregnancies over time that he would start to get calls. It was information that needed to be visible when the need struck. It was only after appealing to consumers over time that Mitchell believed he could confidently determine the effectiveness of local advertising.[11]

In addition to the billboard companies refusing to put up the signs or succumbing to the pressure to paint over them or take them down, Mitchell faced social and legal challenges to his signs across the country. Perhaps hoping to capture college students at Earlham College, travelers going to and from Ohio on Interstate 70, and residents of the small city,

Mitchell contracted a billboard in Richmond, Indiana. It soon drew the ire of a local woman who pressured politicians to remove the advertisement. At times, people's objections were rooted in a sign's proximity to a church or school, as was the case for a billboard in Painesville, Ohio (just outside of Cleveland). Others felt a billboard's existence in the community was enough to warrant its removal. Beyond the legal challenges, community members took matters into their own hands. Two men in New Miami, Ohio, climbed up and tore down a sign in 1971. Mitchell was not intimidated by these reactions and seemed to relish the local fights over his right to advance his business.[12]

Mitchell also employed other strategies that had significant reach. He quickly determined that Cleveland was an important companion city to Detroit in generating business. He worked with individual owners to paint his abortion information on buildings, hoping to capture the attention of urban residents, suburban shoppers, and workers who frequented the downtown. As with so many of Mitchell's efforts, it was the controversy that generated a historical record. His signs drew the attention of the county prosecutor, who alleged that they violated Ohio's Medical Practices Act, and the chief police prosecutor, who warned that the signs violated the city's building code. While Mitchell continuously challenged these legal maneuvers to shut him down, he had to contend with people who, even if they agreed with his business and his rights, were not willing to risk themselves socially, financially, and legally to persist in running the ads.[13]

In addition to billboards and painted buildings scattered across the country, Mitchell also took to the air waves. He noted that none of the local television or radio stations in Cleveland would accept commercials, nor would the newspapers accept his ads, so he had to find another way to reach women. He did so by endeavoring to appear on a variety of radio and television programs, and also by using small-scale advertising like matchbooks, still sought after by a smoking population. Most famously, he joined another man who took white, middle-class, middle-aged women seriously in this era, Phil Donahue. Donahue fostered thoughtful discussions, starting with his first television show in Dayton. When he began national syndication, he brought on Mitchell to discuss abortion on at

FIGURE 8. A plane pulls a banner between Miami and Fort Lauderdale in January 1971, aiming to reach Midwestern vacationers who took down the number and called when they got home. The banner read: ABORTION INFORMATION 716-285-9133, Martin Mitchell's abortion referral number. Author's collection.

least three different occasions, starting in October 1970. Whether alone or paired with someone in opposition, Mitchell was able to share his referral business and beliefs on the air, circumventing the ban on advertising.[14]

With his billboards across the country, appearances on television and radio, and the Super Bowl stunt, Mitchell understood the importance of national exposure and prioritized reaching consumers in the states from which most women traveled to New York for abortions. Aware of the postwar vacation culture, which put Florida's beaches in easy reach for Midwestern Americans, Mitchell contracted with Wynn's Aerial Service to pull his "Abortion Info" banner behind a plane twice daily along the beaches between Miami Beach and Fort Lauderdale. One article described the experience: "Tourists tanning on south Florida beaches Tuesday looked up and saw a blue sky, fluffy white clouds, and a banner boasting New York abortions. The streamer, pulled by a low-flying airplane, read: 'Abortion Information' and listed a New York telephone number." As with his

Super Bowl advertising, Mitchell reported an excellent response to his aerial advertising; he received two hundred to three hundred calls a week, mostly from women (about 75 percent); husbands and boyfriends called, too. Mitchell noted that people frequently wrote down the number in Florida but waited to call until they got back home.[15]

Not only did consumers see his phone number in real time, but the objections also meant there was news coverage as well. Interviewed about the paid banners, the aerial service pilot that pulled them stated that he had no reservations; he had five children and valued access to abortion. The Miami Beach mayor did not object, as the sign was both legal and not obscene. But within a few weeks opposition to the banner appeared in the skies. An "advertising battle featuring World War I 'Red Baron' type airplanes" emerged. An opponent paid to have another plane pull an anti-choice banner over the same stretch of the coastline. The Broward County sheriff then threatened to arrest the pilot if he flew Mitchell's ad again. Ultimately, Mitchell's ads flew unencumbered from December 1970 until mid-April 1971, and he claimed that even without the opposition he was going to end the campaign, because it was the end of the tourist season.[16]

The final part of Mitchell's vision was to develop a distinctive business model. While he initially described himself as a "middleman," who brought together people in need and doctors who wanted to discreetly provide abortions (and make a profit), in reality Mitchell tried to do everything but the procedure himself. As a licensed pilot, he ferried pregnant women seeking abortions back and forth in a day. He also chartered flights from Cleveland and Detroit to the Niagara Falls clinic, found doctors to perform abortions, and subleased use of the clinic to them. One reporter who accompanied him described Mitchell scouring the airport looking for a missing client. From his own accounting, Mitchell seemed to handle the finances, appointments, public relations, and business writ large as well. At times, though, he hired help, including women to answer the phone (weekdays, 9–5), an ad agency, and a public relations firm. He sought to grow his business with an eye toward more control and profit.[17]

The centerpiece of his vision was to both guarantee access to reduce the population and own the profits from the abortions themselves, knowing that each phone call could be slotted into an appointment book in his clinic. He also chose Niagara Falls because it had an airport where he could fly or be flown to the clinic with the women, leaving Detroit in the morning and returning in the evening. In advance of opening his clinic in October 1970, he "leased a 22-passenger DC-3 and a 44-passenger Convair to make shuttle flights" and planned to charge the women $100 for the round-trip airfare. There was absolutely no competition in Niagara Falls, as four months after abortion was legalized in New York the heavily Catholic area had no hospitals or clinics providing abortions. Whether he struggled to find local doctors or wanted more control and profit, Mitchell also reported flying in the doctors.[18]

Mitchell drew the ire of both local and state leaders, who were outraged at his cavalier fly-by-day operation designed to serve out-of-state women. The acting Niagara County health commissioner said he would "not interfere with Mitchell's clinic as long as it abided by health standards." Mitchell detailed the proposed clinic's location across from the Niagara Falls Medical Center, so that any emergencies would be treated in the emergency room. Still, despite early assurances, the local government continually hindered his opening and operation with legal and zoning burdens. Community and state leaders fought him every step of the way, with one resident wailing that they did not want the city to be converted from the honeymoon capital to the "Abortion Capital of the World." Eventually, Mitchell was able to secure a clinic near the city and ferried the doctors and patients by station wagon from the airport.[19]

The demand for abortion referrals proved strong and consistent. A year after he began, *Time* reported that his venture was booming, with 175 cases a week; a chartered plane flew in women three times a week, while others arrived by car. Mitchell's $300 charge for an abortion was twice that of one in New York City. What explains his success, then? Mitchell himself asserted that "I ask for money only from people who want abortions, and that's the American way . . . I'm cutting the mustard better than the groups who are reluctant to give abortion information. Their way is the naive way." In addition, he chalked up his success to the "personal service" that he offered, arranging both abortions and travel.[20]

While critics contrasted his high cost with New York City clinics, they did not contrast his prices with those charged to women who tried to secure therapeutic abortions in local hospitals. Women who navigated the lengthy process of securing two or three psychiatrists who would certify that the pregnancy would endanger their well-being, gained permission from a board of doctors, and then found someone willing to perform the procedure had to spend precious time and about $500. Most women who ran this gauntlet did *not* secure an abortion. Mitchell was expensive, but shopping for abortions was rarely apples to apples, and women generally had very little information or time to make their decision.

While critics maintained that "hustlers" were "capitalizing," the truth was that in the first eight months of legalization in New York more than forty thousand women from Michigan alone made their way there for abortions. CCS claimed to have helped more than fifteen thousand Michigan women, leaving more than twenty-five thousand women to seek out what an Associated Press reporter called "the most lucrative new business of the year." Mitchell had competitors like Ken Oliver, who had a chartered limousine service ferrying women from Detroit to New York clinics, with Buffalo about a four-hour drive each way. However, the ability to sell the faster air travel and pocket fees of $50 to $100 per woman meant "Abortion Merchants Thriving."[21]

Mitchell claimed to channel the fees into the business and rejected the suggestion that by taking a salary he obviated his business's standing as a nonprofit. In one of his first interviews, he stated, "I'm not in this for the money" but clarified that he was not running a charity. A month into the business, he maintained he was "a long way from paying off my initial investment" and expected to earn a salary "commensurate to what is going on in the business." He later noted, "I'm providing a service. When you tell me that the director of the YMCA, or the United Campaign, or Blue Cross Blue Shield, all so called non-profit organizations does not collect a salary, then I won't either."[22]

Forced to pay to advertise, he critiqued organizations' nonprofit cover that permitted them to have free and plentiful advertising. Moreover, organizations with free referrals then sent women to for-profit clinics. In newspaper and magazine coverage of abortion referral services,

TRAVELING ALONE to a place where abortions are legal can be frightening. Because the Missouri law forbids abortions, except in cases where the mother's life is endangered, many women are forced to go abroad or to New York. Clergy Consultation Service of Missouri helped this girl make arrangements. The service charges no fee. (Post-Dispatch Photo by Renyold Ferguson).

Abortion Information Agencies

FIGURE 9. Entrepreneur Martin Mitchell charged that Planned Parenthood and the Clergy Consultation Service benefited from free advertising of their services. Newspapers and magazines promoted not-for-profit agencies; the caption reiterates, "The service charges no fee." With permission from the *St. Louis Post-Dispatch* (21 March 1971). Photo by Renyold Ferguson.

Planned Parenthood and CCS got to promote their network and provide the phone number to secure abortions. Mitchell was disdainful of the "funny business" the organizations put women through and contrasted his service favorably with theirs, noting, "We don't want a woman's life history, we treat her like an individual, not like a five-year-old who can't make her mind up. She either wants one or she doesn't. We don't have her come in and sit down and talk about it." Mitchell believed women who called him had already reached the decision to have an abortion and did not need to talk, they needed to act. He sold fast access.[23]

As a thirty-year-old, married father of one, Mitchell provided abortion information between 1970 and 1972 and claimed from the outset that his efforts reflected a devotion to the ideology of the Zero Population Growth (ZPG) movement. ZPG, an action-oriented group, wanted to slow the nation's population growth by targeting the white middle class of the United States. Mitchell embraced this ideology in his personal and professional life, calling himself a crusader. This, along with his simultaneous focus on sterilization, provided a measure of cover not afforded other companies' abortion advertising. This was not just about abortion and profit; it was about people having control over their reproduction. This was not just about women, but about men, too, being able to control their bodies. While he did not generally talk in terms of women's rights, he did assert that women were adult decision-makers and concluded in an interview with the *Miami Herald*, "no woman should be forced to be a baby factory."[24]

While many wondered at the time if women advocating for abortion access had themselves had abortions, Mitchell publicly asserted his vasectomy as consistent with his ideology. He noted, "I believe that 90 per cent of our social ills are due to overpopulation in a society that already has it priorities screwed-up." He asserted his own sterilization after one child as a point of pride in "walking the walk" of trying to limit overpopulation, and it helped to diffuse the focus on abortion in interviews.[25]

In a nod to the consumer protection turn of the 1970s, Mitchell also asserted that he was "the Ralph Nader of the abortion business." Nader's popularity as a consumer advocate was running high in this period, following his 1965 book about car safety and efforts to ensure food safety, and it speaks to Mitchell's understanding of himself as a consumer advocate that he saw Nader as his model. He said, "If people call for advice, we tell them to talk to someone they respect, to make up their own minds. Then we can refer them for medical service." He consistently reported his respect for women as consumers—he was selling what they wanted to buy—information and abortions. He did not ever intend his business model to include counseling: "I'm doing what a travel agent does when you want to go to the Bahamas." And according to his advertising agency, it made him a "a very wealthy man."[26]

Pregnant? Need Help?

Although Mitchell had the biggest reach, he was not the first to capitalize on the tremendous need for information about abortion. Some men operated referral services free of charge and reached thousands of women, including Yippies co-founder and radical activist Paul Krassner and population control and abortion advocates Lawrence Lader and Robert McCoy. More common, however, was a business model with multiple partners, like the one developed by Wray Morehouse in California. While no business records remain, the news reports suggest a decentralized model, with multiple individuals providing referrals on a city-by-city basis as the business grew. The earliest coverage of Morehouse offering "Pregnancy Advice" appeared in 1968, with a Lincolnesque photo and "A message for girls in trouble: Wray Morehouse at your service." He claimed to have started offering his assistance five years earlier, and in 1967 claimed he had fielded two thousand calls.[27]

With his medical knowledge limited to "some time in pre-medical school for dentistry" and "two uncles who are doctors," Morehouse explained that he was compelled to discover a reputable abortion provider after his girlfriend got pregnant in 1963. He concluded, "what she went through, I wouldn't wish on anyone . . . Back-alley chiropractors or going south of the border and asking a taxi driver for an abortionist is just a quick way to die." If his early involvement sounds organic and plausible in alerting him to this open market, his financial role is decidedly more suspect.[28]

Morehouse's monetary start was never really explained; instead, all of the coverage reported the same nondescript, shifting (and likely apocryphal) story: "The expenses are mainly paid by a woman in San Francisco whose daughter died of an illegal abortion in Los Angeles." Already twenty-seven years old in 1968 and still a college student (psychology major), not only was he answering the phones, but "with a girlfriend" he was also "constantly" checking the hospital quality and following up with women who had abortions. He fully understood how lucrative referrals could be when he told a reporter that illegal abortions were a "$100-million-a-year business." While it is unclear how he first came to do abortion referrals and then to set up a national network, like Mitchell, he was an adherent to a belief that the world was facing an "overpopulation problem."[29]

Morehouse shifted from ads in the underground college paper, the *Berkeley Barb*, in the spring of 1969 that asked, "Pregnant? Need HELP?

FIGURE 10. Wray Morehouse, one of the earliest people to publicly solicit business for abortion referrals, used the direct appeal "Pregnant? Need help?" in newspaper advertising. His ads, like this Michelangelo-inspired one in the *Berkeley Tribe* (22 August 1969), first appeared in California but soon expanded nationally. Author's collection.

Call 415/848–6036," to ones listing three different men, cities, and phone numbers in the fall. While he initially imagined opening offices in New York and Los Angeles, instead he hired people to staff offices in smaller cities across the country. In addition to his main office in Berkeley, California, ads and articles mentioned Atlanta, Dallas, Denver, Houston, Los Angeles, Milwaukee, Omaha, Phoenix, St. Louis, Springfield (Illinois), and Williamsburg (Virginia), largely complementary to Mitchell's Midwest and Northeast emphasis. However, while he may have been able to open these branches, the grueling hours proved hard to staff. One office head thought that it was unlikely anyone lasted longer than three months, while another revealed that in addition to being "chained to the phone," the pay was terrible, "just enough for a food allowance."[30]

It may be that those at the top of the organization were the only ones raking in money, because by November 1970, Bob Matson, one of the men working with Morehouse, reported that "the counseling service operates three abortion clinics in Mexico City, California, and New York." It appears from the description of each that the Mexico City clinic handled the majority of the clients and likely was the most lucrative, with a fee of about $300. The organization was able to bundle the women in groups of two or three, and this insured their combined travel, lowering transportation costs and guaranteeing business to the doctor(s). The Mexico clinic claimed to have performed more than seven thousand abortions.[31]

Starting in 1970, Matson took control of the company and made some significant changes, including renaming the service. For years the phone number was the most significant through line and was usually accompanied by a line drawing of outstretched hands reminiscent of Michelangelo's Sistine Chapel ceiling fresco, *Creation of Adam*. In 1970 the business began to be called the Problem Pregnancy Counseling Service and then Problem Pregnancy Information Service, Inc. (PPIS).

Matson prided himself on his business acumen, asserting to a reporter that he worked in volume to "arrange cut-cost group rates with doctors, hospitals, motels, and even airlines." He even asserted that PPIS was Southwestern Airline's second biggest customer. He bragged in an August 1971 ad that "We have been here in LA two months and as promised abortion prices have been reduced by 30%. We expect this policy to continue."[32]

The company's advertising shifted with the emergence of legal abortions, and Matson offered more traditional packages to women seeking abortions. While the Atlanta office that sent women to New York could not charge an outright referral fee, those sending women to California did. The ad promised that, for a small fee, "An appointment can be made with 48 hours notice. . . . Transportation is provided to and from the airports and hotel accommodations are reserved in advance . . . no age restrictions and financial aid is available." All of the familiar promises and reminders about acting quickly and a counselor available by phone twenty-four hours a day rounded out the ads. By August 1972, an ad in the *LA Free Press* even included a price for an abortion in Los Angeles ($160), and the "services included" section noted that Medi-Cal insurance cases were accepted. From a one-man operation to a national referral organization, the evolution of the service reflected the maturity of the market, evolving laws, and the downward price pressures evident nationally.[33]

Abortion Referral Service

The Abortion Referral Service (ARS) emerged in Philadelphia in the fall of 1970, allegedly to help Temple University students seek abortions. The creation myth helped explain why someone would call Philadelphia to arrange an abortion in New York City. Unlike Mitchell and Morehouse, there was no single namesake founder to generate publicity or answer questions. Local newspaper accounts credited Mike Noshay and Allan Lieberman as being founders of ARS, but nothing is revealed about them, and different names appeared in advertisements and letters soliciting business. Existing only as a phone number and a Philadelphia address where the women should send their information and money via Western Union, ARS could be whatever the consumer imagined.[34]

The company solicited business with national newspaper ads targeting college towns and students, including a community college in Colorado, cities with Catholic colleges, and a Presbyterian college in Utah. It appears that its reach stretched west across the Mississippi more often than other referral groups for New York abortions, bridging a dividing line that made travel both more involved and more expensive. The alleged premise of the business was that it was seeking to expand while remaining nonprofit "and must operate on donations." In one letter to the *Fort Lewis Independent* (Colorado), the ARS proclaimed success, stating, "In only a few weeks time we have been flooded by requests for help by colleges around the country. We are now associated with the finest clinics in New York City." The company set up an appealing prospect—information readily available—with honorable volunteers staffing the phone line day and night at a not-for-profit business.[35]

The advertising, starting in October 1970, appeared in three forms: traditional small ads, letters that newspaper editors readily published, and billboards. The editors of the Great Bend (Kansas) Community College newspaper published the letter "as a public service," even though the company said ARS would pay the paper's rates. The company's early advertising tended to be male-centric and tone deaf, with patronizing language and letters published to "Dear Sirs" and referencing the "will of the mother." ARS also solicited schools with male student bodies that

FIGURE 11. New York state prosecuted the for-profit Professional Scheduling Service, which charged $75 for a referral. The company advertised in college papers and in public settings with billboards, generating controversy in communities where the ads appeared. Author's collection.

focused on technology, such as MIT and Worcester Tech. One letter imagined a male consumer when they promised, "In any case, we will return her to you smiling, healthy, and much relieved, though slightly tired. . . . You can help by carefully reading her 'Instructions' . . . and by feeding her." The ad content affirmed the service as trustworthy, legitimate, and medically sound, including a proclaimed membership in a fictional organization, the National Organization to Legalize Abortion. Early ads promised that it was a "pregnancy counseling service," but one later ad did not even spell counsel correctly when they encouraged consumers to call "For Information and Council on Legal Abortions."[36]

The willingness of college newspaper editors to publish what was effectively a lengthy, detailed ad for free as a "public service" stemmed from the information vacuum confronting college-age consumers for whom unwanted pregnancy could be catastrophic. When nearly 70 percent of Auburn University students believed their student government association should provide a pregnancy counseling service to students, it is no surprise that the student paper devoted pages to abortion coverage, including a detailed article headlined "Agencies Offer Referral Service for Women Seeking Abortions." The Alabama students were desperate for information and naïve to the fact that all of the listed referral groups would be under criminal investigation by New York state in the coming months.[37]

ARS's reach ranged from Rice University's *Thresher* in Houston, Texas, to the Presbyterian Westminster College's *The Forum* in Utah. Like other referral services, ARS advertised heavily in particular markets and did so with a variety of names, wording, and style. The one constant was the holy grail that they offered consumers: the phone number—(215) 878-5800. Political sympathies for abortion law reform in North Carolina, along with college abortion funds and the public sex-ed campaigns undertaken by Dr. Takey Crist at University of North Carolina-Chapel Hill made the state one of its key targets. The company also placed a surprising number of ads in Indiana. The state did not appear to send a lot of women to New York for abortions, as opposed to neighboring Michigan and Illinois, which sent large numbers of women. ARS placed ads in South Bend's local papers under the classifieds' "Abortion" heading, undoubtedly hoping to reach women from the surrounding area, including Notre Dame and St. Mary's students whose college paper would not carry the ad. Also distinctive was the appearance of the company's ads in the papers of junior and community colleges, like the Harrisburg Area Community College's *Vanguard*.[38]

The rush to provide legal abortions in New York state left it an open playing field for doctors, clinics, businesses, and entrepreneurs. With no residency restrictions, no need to justify the procedure, and no one else in the world set up to provide this volume of abortions, the number of consumers seemed boundless. This new business market attracted people seeking to make a quick profit. Critics of the new industry called for changes to the law in the fall of 1970. By 1971, newspapers nationally were filled with headlines like "Abortion Aid: Service or Profiteering?"

and "Abortion Referral: Big Business," and articles detailing the misdeeds and alternatives to the companies. The investigation into ARS was part of a larger 1971 quest by New York's Bureau of Consumer Fraud (in the state's attorney's office) to reform and ultimately eliminate the abortion referral businesses. The contention throughout this period was that it was not legal to advertise medical procedures; those advertising referrals claimed that they were only selling information and did not need medical authority to do so.[39]

Quite often the articles offered examples from ARS advertising to contrast it with Planned Parenthood, which, they continually reminded consumers, gave its referral services free of charge. College papers, like the *Buffalo Spectrum*, also encouraged students to use the referral services available through the student health service or local feminist groups. In their exposés of companies like ARS, journalists frequently placed the emergence of the "new quick-profit business" in historical context. They cautioned that some firms required women to send a "deposit" or "reservation fee," while others were expected to send the full amount of money for the abortion even before securing her appointment, and contrasted the companies making money from referrals against free services. Newspaper coverage cautioned consumers that companies used package deals to disguise the true charges and pad the bill. As one college reporter noted, just months after legalization, some companies demanded that women wire the total $395 in advance without any accounting of the bill. He warned against using "free" pregnancy tests, as they could be manipulated into securing payment for an abortion, even if the woman was not pregnant.[40]

The investigations and prosecutions of those companies and individuals operating with kickbacks and fee-splitting did not deter the ARS business. In 1971, the business expanded to create an office in Miami, headed by Randy Lazarus and Charles Spector. The men asserted their new location was a help to the twenty-five to thirty-five women they sent weekly from Miami to New York, securing a $35 referral fee per woman. The men considered aerial ads (like Mitchell) but ended up buying ad time on a local rock radio station, again targeting a largely male audience, and had a local obstetrician who did pregnancy tests on the women and billed the referral group.[41]

Men's morality and involvement in abortion referral was rarely seen as suspect, while women brokers seeking the same economic opportunities and access for other women faced public criticism. A consumer medical reporter in Miami covering the "booming" abortion referral business described the men's strategies after disparaging how "Miss Marion plies her trade at the Medical Referral Agency." The few businesswomen in the industry tended to self-identify as a "Mrs." to deflect criticism, such as "Mrs. Saul."[42]

In interviews with the *Philadelphia Inquirer*, Noshay played up the companies' righteous humanitarianism and concern for women. He said, "We charge as little as the girls can afford. A lot of our cases are purely charity. We try not to turn down a girl just because she can't pay." Lazarus challenged the contention that their service was problematic and maintained, "We preserve lives by eliminating the market for illegal, unsafe, and unethical abortions." Charles Spector claimed that they opened the Miami affiliate to save lives. He asserted that Alabama, Florida, and Georgia had the highest rates in the country of deaths from illegal abortions, that women there needed a referral service, and that the company was doing "plenty of charity work for kids with no money who are desperate." The company even claimed to cover transportation costs sometimes.[43]

Critics of ASR (and its affiliates) largely disdained the very existence of abortion referral businesses. Editors explained that they could not in good conscience include referral ads for companies that charged "exorbitant" fees for "a few phony words of reassurance." Feminists in a local chapter of the National Organization for Women in Philadelphia organized an abortion information referral service and offered a phone number in the *Inquirer*. One feminist condemned ARS as unnecessary and a racket, and charged that they were "making a profit off women's needs." While some newspapers defended them, others condemned the ads for exploiting women and reported that they were no longer going to carry ARS ads. The exclusion of ARS was pointedly based on its profit-driven motives, with editors pleased to offer nonprofit abortion referral phone numbers in their reporting.[44]

Ultimately, some people contended that ARS was not the worst of the bunch. The president of the Association for the Study of Abortion (secretly funded by eugenicist Cordelia Scaife May), Dr. Robert E. Hall, saw value in the service they provided. He conceded, "They are making a profit, but it's a small one, and they are keeping the price down at a price college kids can afford." He continued, "You have to distinguish between the (profiteers) and the good guys. I'd put these guys near the top with the good ones."[45]

Abortion Information Agency, Inc.

At the top of everyone's list for the worst offender was John Settle's Abortion Information Agency, Inc. (AIA). Settle started and operated the British Referral Service and Travel Agency after England legalized abortion. He sent women from the United States to England with the British travel agency Cook's Tours, Inc. Along with Ellen Glascock and attorney Roy Lucas, he created an agency to offer women information to secure a legal abortion at Dr. Ronald Shaw's hospital in London. Then, with New York's legalization, Shaw established the Park East and Park West hospitals in New York. Settle shifted his efforts to domestic referrals, and with a high volume of referrals at a low cost ($10), he maintained a staff of up to forty-five women answering the phones, three directors, an executive director, a publicist, a president, and an attorney.[46]

Having worked with Shaw, Settle would have been well aware of the importance of referrals and setting up your own hospital. A November 1969 NBC television program, *First Tuesday*, reported on English abortions. Dr. Ronald Shaw, whom the producer referred to as "an abortion tycoon," stated that in England he cooperated with the Student Advisory Service to give abortion counseling to pregnant girls. Nineteen-year-old Richard Branson started the nonprofit *Student* magazine and reached 55,000 young people with his first issue. Branson quickly set up the Student Advisory Service, and news coverage described it as the "pace-setter" of the emerging nonprofits, nearly doubling its reach in a year. One of the biggest areas of demand from young people was abortion referrals; Shaw reported that Branson and his volunteers referred three thousand girls and women for abortions in six months.[47]

FIGURE 12. Richard Branson, organizer of the Student Advisory Service, in London on 30 July 1969. With volunteers assisting him, in just six months Branson referred three thousand girls and women for abortions in England. PA Images / Alamy Stock Photo.

When the British *Daily Telegraph* interviewed Settle about his first referral business in March 1970, he claimed, "We are not blazing any trails," knowing that Branson had been active for about a year. He also knew that his British agency captured only a minuscule number of wealthy American women who wanted to have an abortion. He continued, "We are making it easy for people who have money to get abortions. The whole thing is a jungle and has always been used by exploiters and profiteers." He charged a fee of $155 for each woman referred to England, the equivalent of more than $1,200 in 2024.[48]

AIA received referral fees and kickbacks from the Park East and Park West hospitals, and the agency also operated the Wickersham Hospital, all of which specialized "primarily—even almost exclusively—in abortions." This setup exploited women not only with the fees charged up front, but also by AIA taking a cut of the abortion cost.

Telephone operators at AIA promised callers that they would be referred to a board-certified hospital. In the only abortion referral ad to run in *The Observer* at Notre Dame and in similar ads across the country, the agency implored, "If you need information or professional assistance, including immediate registration into available hospitals and clinics, telephone." The company frequently appeared to have two names, with ads headed by Abortion Counseling, Information, and Referral Services, with AIA at the bottom, followed by the agency's address on West 86th Street in New York City, the phone number, and the operating hours, 8 a.m. to 10 p.m., seven days a week.[49]

The agency also ran long column ads, with much more detail. Some ads could plausibly be confused with a brief news article and included the phone number embedded in the text as well. With more text, the company made a persuasive pitch for board-certified obstetricians, gynecologists, and anesthesiologists operating in fully licensed and accredited general hospitals. One 1970 ad contrasted the excellence of the service provided with the "unacceptably high rate of complications" in "free-standing out-patient clinics." Underlining consumers' sense that "you get what you pay for," the ad explicitly raised fears of medical complications if women used a competing legal abortion provider. In addition, it offered a range of costs for a variety of procedures, linked to the weeks of pregnancy, and assured prospective consumers that the agency was on their side: "You should not have to pay exorbitant charges for any of these services."[50]

By February 1971, eight months after legalization, and just four months since the company started advertising, the ads also began to tout volume. In the *Michigan Daily*, for example, the company claimed to have helped 22,000 women to get a safe, legal hospital abortion. A month later, the company added a new ad style to their repertoire. Building on the scientific reporting issued by the Population Council and New York City, as well the studies that the Women's Service bragged about, the AIA headlined their ads: "Information Study Reveals 28,000 Women Have Safe Abortions." Beyond the incredible numbers being reported, the ads did two other distinctive things. First, they introduced a lot of women, such as Sharon C. Peters, the executive director of the agency. While articles about AIA noted the male founder of the agency, most ads did not make mention of the men, and when they did include people, they were generally women. The ad encouraged anyone unable to pay the regular charges to reach out to Mrs. Melanie White, listed as the director of the agency's social services division. There was no separate number, but asking for

Mrs. White would have alerted the operator taking the call that the person was in financial need.[51]

Finally, ads made mention of another vital piece of the agency's advertising: the twenty-page booklet *A Need Fulfilled*. Giving consumers, organizations, doctors, and medical professionals something to distribute was gold. By March 1971, ads claimed that the agency had distributed two million copies of the booklet—without charge. Written in a conversational tone, directed to women, it relied heavily on the *you*: "You have the freedom of choice"; "If you want this pregnancy terminated"; and "You no doubt have many questions." Organized around answers to frequently asked questions, the brochure tackled technical questions about abortion, outlined what the agency did and who it served, and detailed the process women would experience if they chose to schedule their abortion with AIA.[52]

In the *A Need Fulfilled* brochure and elsewhere in their advertising, the agency explicitly noted that it charged a $10 registration fee. Payment of the fee and the cost of the abortion had to arrive at the office through a Western Union money order, paid in full, and then the consumer could call and get the appointment. What the consumer did not know, however, was that the agency was in league with the clinics and hospitals in a cost-sharing scheme and served as a sort of front office, funneling patients directly to the hospital.[53]

One phone operator, Joan Mellon, recalled that it was through the efforts of the young women working there that Settle agreed to set up financial assistance for those who needed it. Aware of how much money the agency was making and conscious of the daily desperation on the other end of the phone, the women approached Settle and asked him to do "what was right." The thirty women working there in two shifts liked the work because it paid well, was part-time, and had flexible hours. The women enlisted their friends to work there. As Mellon described it, "The work was pretty routine like taking orders at Starbucks but oh, so much more important, because the women were desperate." Mellon also said, "One of the benefits of the job was the access we had to getting an IUD at one of the doctors' offices associated with the agency." In spite of the advertising claims, Mellon did not recall any of the women doing anything other than coordinating the care for women by phone, while Settle operated the business side of things.[54]

A reporter referred to Settle as a "Columbia College graduate, a dark-haired, mustachioed string-bean of a man." Mellon described his "overall manner" as "business-like but easy-going—and very efficient. The worker bees dressed in a more casual manner of the time. This easy-going and efficient feeling was reflected in the AIA office environment, a non-slick atmosphere that felt at ease and trustworthy." In his public dealings, however, Settle was all business. He adopted Shaw's strategies and sent out "Dear Doctor" letters following legalization, but in one clear way he tried to get a jump on Shaw. He also sent out "Dear Doctor" letters *before* legalization, soliciting New York licensed ob-gyn doctors who "would like to be of assistance in our work, please do not hesitate to call me at 212-873-6650, day or night."[55]

While it operated, Wickersham existed as a hospital on two floors of an office building and was owned by a medical group of twenty doctors. Observers for WHAP who evaluated abortion providers described the general atmosphere as "uncomfortable and confusing" and noted with alarm the attempt to cover up the death of a woman seeking an abortion. The WHAP emphatically stated in its review: "We cannot stress strongly enough to avoid this service. There are plenty of other, medically responsible services in New York, and no woman should accept a referral to Wickersham."[56]

With all of the for-profit nonmedical businesses that set up *medical* shop in New York after legalization, the city moved to investigate. The city's Bureau of Consumer Fraud scrutinized dozens of services that emerged after legalization, and the attorney general began his inquiry within a few months. Martin Mitchell found himself on the witness stand not only for operating a medical establishment in the state, but also for fee splitting and nonprofessional advice. In addition, there were several other "similarly situated" businesses that used kickbacks and fee splitting, including S.P.S. Consultants and Manhattan Pregnancy Advisory Service. They all followed similar models of advertising in college and underground newspapers, and ran ads in more unusual publications, like the *New Republic* and the *Baltimore Afro American*.

They charged all consumers referral fees and profited further through kickbacks.

New York charged Settle and co-defendant physician Irving Saxe in February 1972. It was the AIA's explicit financial involvement in securing business and offering medical services that crossed the line, according to the state's attorney general. Settle revealed that women who used the agency paid $285 cash ahead of time for an early abortion. The hospital only billed Settle's agency $175, which he asserted was a "discount based on volume," leaving the agency $110 in profit. The courts considered it a kickback, in violation of the law. It also meant that operating from 8 a.m. to 10 p.m., every day of the week, Settle was grossing $70,000 a week in 1970. Roy Lucas represented several referral agencies in cases brought by New York State. He explained to a critic who had voted to remove him from the board of NARAL that he had "long favored price regulation" because all of that prohibition had just driven referral businesses out of state. Moreover, he contended that disallowing referral advertising would jeopardize efforts to reach the masses and threaten family planning communications. As a co-owner of the AIA, Lucas continued to represent the company and John A. Settle Jr. when the state brought suit in June 1971. The attorney general called AIA a broker in the sale of medical and hospital abortion services that exploited misery. Lefkowitz condemned these businesses as "abortion bonanzas, with a mass merchandising, assembly line type of operation."[57]

The state's Supreme Court declared Settle's AIA abortion referral business to be illegal, and the city decreed Wickersham an unlicensed clinic. However, a reporter in January 1972 responded to "One of the most impressive brochures" produced by AIA and called the number. A recording in a woman's voice made a "direct pitch for pregnant women to patronize Wickersham Women's Medical Center." Wickersham continued to operate its "Model Abortion Program" and advertised itself as a community abortion service affiliate with a metropolitan hospital. A 1972 Wickersham ad assured consumers, "No referral needed. No referral fee or contribution solicited ever." The student editors at the *Hill News* of St. Lawrence University (New York) had to publish an apology after running the ad in January 1972, when unbeknownst to them "legal action has been taken to close the center, which has been described as one of the largest unlicensed abortion clinics in New York City."[58]

Consumer Reports

Atop the teal cover of the July 1972 issue of *Consumer Reports* came the questions: "Legal abortions: How safe? How available? How costly?," appealing to American consumers who subscribed to the advertising-free, independently researched consumer magazine because they sought "Facts You Need Before You Buy." Along with abortion, the issue carried reports on subcompact station wagons, ranges, and air conditioners.[59]

In April 1972, Massachusetts resident Carolyn Schneider wrote to the magazine and made her case that it should study and report on the topic. She said, "It is my hope that *Consumer Reports* will publish findings regarding the facilities available in New York and elsewhere in the country in order that women may more ably choose that which suits their individual needs." Indeed many of the concerns facing consumers that she raised, including "traveling to New York in order to terminate unplanned pregnancies," formed the basis of the magazine's five-page article on abortion. She also captured the importance of this study in serving both women seeking to make a costly consumer decision and the private physician who, "located at some distance from New York[,] has neither the time nor the resources to research the facilities." Moreover, she noted, "Some women have no access to private physicians or any referral service. Such a report would be of tremendous value to *all* individuals involved—women, men and physicians."[60]

The author of the article offered prospective consumers a detailed consideration of the process of securing and having an abortion, including the medical procedures, their safety, and costs. The focus was not on reviewing individual clinics, but more so on offering a sense of the overall process. The coverage centered on New York, given that it alone served out-of-state women at will, but also included a full consideration of availability in other states. The report discouraged pursuit of abortions in states where mental health provisions were "interpreted narrowly" and those that had residency requirements. For states with a more open interpretation of mental health, like Kansas, Maryland, and New Mexico, readers learned about residency requirements.[61]

With insights from doctors, public health officials, and abortion referral specialists, the reporting contained detailed descriptions of every part of the process. It offered a meta sense of how many women had abortions—according to Dr. Christopher Tietze, quoted as "an authority on population and abortion statistics," the number ranged over one million before 1967. Even with legalization in New York and other states, he estimated that in 1971 there were probably about 600,000 illegal abortions. This kind of analysis was important for consumers in this time period, making sense of their purchase in the context of national trends and needs.[62]

From coast to coast, New York to California, *Consumer Reports* reflected the incredible improvements in maternal mortality and the many fewer injuries associated with abortions. The recordkeeping on legal abortions affirmed that the legal procedure was exceedingly safe and "evidence shows that access to legal abortion cuts health risks substantially." This was reported in the section addressing the fraught legal situation, with state laws constantly being struck down, reinstated, and contested in court.[63]

In addition to offering consumers a context for selecting a location, the author offered rudimentary advice, similar to what the referral organizations and agencies did. An important starting point was to determine if a woman was, in fact, pregnant. All businesses were set up to take someone's money, even if they did not need a procedure. *Consumer Reports* introduced some readers to the existence of pregnancy test kits then just beginning to be sold over the counter in drugstores. It cautioned that the reliability of the tests was still being determined and encouraged women to seek out a test in a health department or hospital. It then emphasized, "No one should try to abort herself."[64]

The author strenuously discouraged any efforts to terminate one's own pregnancy in any way. This consumer caution was especially important for those who had likely heard and read supposed remedies to their problem or had been told that there was a way to terminate a pregnancy on their own. Letting people know that the *only* way to terminate a pregnancy was by a professional saved women's lives. After establishing the importance of medical intervention, the magazine laid out the variety of medical techniques and when they were appropriate.[65]

For those who did want to get an abortion, the authors encouraged consumers to shop locally to save on travel expenses, and especially to be close to their provider for any follow-up care. Callers might also seek out local Planned Parenthood or CCS referrals, with the clergy reportedly handling more than a hundred thousand abortion referrals in 1971. The article encouraged national efforts to facilitate free referrals, including phone numbers and addresses for the Family Planning Information Service and the CCS.[66]

Finally, the article concluded with the costs. As painfully expensive as abortions remained, the author contextualized the $125 likely cost with the hundreds of dollars charged before liberalization and legalization of the laws. Offering consumers a sense of the upper end of what the various procedures should cost, based on length of pregnancy, helped insure that fewer people would be financially gouged. The article concluded with more consumer advice from the Consumers Union: "Note that many abortion clinics and hospitals offer birth control services as part of their overall care. CU urges patients to take advantage of those services." Just as an author might have encouraged consumers of appliances to take the warranty coverage, so too this author argued that buying and using birth control would help stave off the need for another abortion purchase.[67]

Two issues later, the magazine published letters to the editor written in response to "Legal abortions," including some from readers who were "shocked" and "grievously insulted" and some from those who appreciated the article as "a very valuable public service" that would save the lives of "anguished souls" who otherwise might have sought out an illegal abortion. The editors concluded the letter section by calling on democratic principles: "In a pluralistic society such as ours, each must be willing to respect the constitutional rights of others to freedom of belief, conscience, and action—so long as individual actions do not violate the laws governing us." In providing thorough, dense reporting, the editors affirmed the right to choose a safe, legal abortion and asserted that "most would agree that that right does not extend to denying others either their rights that are theirs under existing laws or the information about what those laws provide."[68]

Nor was *Consumer Reports* alone in their efforts to provide information. Just as student editors sought to provide information to their community, so too did organizations, newspapers, magazines, and book publishers seek to produce helpful guides, or direct people to them. These guides were often promoted in advice columns or listings of "Things to Write for." Just as *Consumer Reports* analyzed abortions along with self-cleaning ovens, so too did *Kiplinger's Personal Finance*, another financial magazine. Amid promotions of pamphlets offering cleaning tips and helping parents teach young children how to behave around a dog, they offered a guide to legal abortions.[69]

Opponents of abortion condemned those providing information, while supporters of abortion access critiqued those gatekeeping information. Critics like Susan McConnell charged in the *New York Times*: "Abortions are big business. There's profiteering going on. It should not be done that way." Yet the referrals and those providing the service continued to carry an air of illegality. The difficulty in not knowing if the service provider would be an honest broker left consumers vulnerable. The farther one was from New York City, the harder it was to get information. And most people seeking abortions in New York, particularly in the for-profit clinics, were not from the city. While they waited for the day when you could say "'I'm going to my abortionist today,' the way you say 'I'm going to my dentist,'" consumers had to navigate the unknown. Even if their private doctor made a referral, the pregnancy and abortion itself remained a mystery to most. By putting forth information, from defining terms to explaining that women needed a pregnancy test and telling them how to get it, entrepreneurs met the tremendous need for abortion information.[70]

One of the most significant markets for their advertising were young people on college campuses. The next chapter explores how students found abortion information and their efforts to ensure that everyone had access to it.

4

Seeking Information on Campus

IN THE MID-1960S at Skidmore College, a student hid her pregnancy and gave birth to a baby in her dorm room. The woman survived, but the baby she delivered alone died. Colleges in the 1950s and 1960s, before abortions became legal and accessible, were filled with pregnancy, efforts to hide or terminate pregnancies, and the consequences of having done so. For some, seeing a pregnant woman denied the right to an education and a bright future—forced to take a leave for a "breakdown," or expelled—while the man who impregnated her continued unimpeded, revolutionized their thinking. It inspired a belief that they had a right to reproductive resources; activists sought to ensure that their colleges would help them. In addition to financial assistance, explored in Chapter 2, students wanted information. Without access to good medical care, information about their options, and a phone number to get an abortion, frantic women navigated unwanted pregnancies alone. With the emergence of better birth control and the legalization of abortion, students wanted to make the abortion market accessible to college campuses across the country.[1]

Students applied pressure to their college's administration and student government to offer sexual health services. Some schools responded by funding student groups, providing sex education materials, offering hotlines, and, most critically, providing medical help to those who wanted an abortion. Alongside these institutional efforts was the appearance of advertisements for abortion referral companies in college and underground newspapers.[2]

The arrival of abortion referral advertisements in the fall of 1970, following the legalization of abortion in New York, prompted several reactions. Some embraced the opportunity to discover this coveted information and access this market, while others sought to banish the ads and the editors who placed them. Tens of thousands of young women made phone calls and traveled to New York (as well as to California and the District of Columbia), but the ads also resulted in threats and punitive measures by campus, local, and state authorities designed to discourage their publication.

The colleges, used to regulating women's behavior, had to shift to empowering women to make decisions for themselves. From William & Mary women governed by a handbook that dictated they must wear a London Fog raincoat over their gym shorts to Penn State University women lined up around the block to get the Pill, students increasingly challenged administrations to meet their needs. The American Association of University Women (AAUW) affirmed their actions, calling for access to birth control resources as necessary for women to achieve an equal education. Feminists and free speech advocates on campus worked to fill the information vacuum, even as the law and obstructionist recalcitrants stood in the way. Through both the advertisements and campus services, women found opportunities to learn about and buy abortion services.[3]

"'She's Bleeding to Death!'"

With the increased number of women attending college, institutions of higher education found themselves, starting in the late 1960s, tasked with providing more and better services to their female students. This was especially true as first the birth control pill and then legal abortions became widely available in the fall of 1970. The women, paying the same tuition, room, and board bills as male students, began to assert the same rights as men in throwing off oppressive dress codes and gendered policies regulating their behavior, and also increasingly demanded that the schools provide both medical professionals and reproductive health services.[4]

Those tasked with answering these demands for reproductive services generally started with the simplest response: No. No, the institution will not hire a gynecologist. No, it will not outfit you with a diaphragm or prescribe birth control. No, it will not offer pregnancy tests. No, it will not refer you for an abortion. The arguments against providing these resources generally came down to two arguments: money and morality. Deans, health directors, and presidents all claimed that even if they wanted to, there was not enough money in their budgets to provide even a part-time gynecologist or enough counselors to meet the seemingly insatiable demand for information about contraceptives. Wayne State University had a "sexual counseling clinic," but even at a school "where women outnumber men," the head of the clinic claimed they could not hire a gynecologist because "there is not enough money." Without a doctor, the clinic could not "dispense contraceptives," and referred pregnant women to the Michigan Clergy for Problem Pregnancy. At Bennington College, the health director believed that "birth control was the responsibility of private doctors, adding that she did not feel it was her duty to 'either pierce ears or prescribe premarital contraceptives devices, or medication.'" Of course, some colleges persisted in not having doctors of any kind, such as Wright State University (Ohio), which had only had nurses on staff in 1971 and had to refer students not just for abortions but for all medical care to outside providers. Many did not see the injustice of denying reproductive care, such as the dean of students at Towson State in Maryland, who obtusely stated, "activities which are not directly related to education, like this, would be low in priority here."[5]

For institutions that did offer services and staff, there was student need in every quarter. At one exemplary program at the University of North Carolina's Health Education Clinic, approximately eight hundred women visited the clinic in its first year and a half; doctors prescribed birth control to almost every one of them. The growing numbers of women students and the increasing variety of reproductive care services available combined to create tremendous demand for college health clinics.[6]

GAMECOCK

Vol. LXIII—No. 15 University of South Carolina, Columbia, S. C. 29208 Thursday, October 19, 1972

Sometimes a problem can become too large to handle alone. When this happens expert, confidential help is as close as the telephone

ABORTION REFERRAL HOTLINE 777-4256 (hours: 7:30 p.m. until 9 p.m.)

COUNSELING BUREAU 777-5223

THE BOSOM 252 3601

PSYCHOLOGICAL SERVICES CENTER 777- 4864

COLUMBIA HOTLINE 758-2191

Abortion : "I'm glad I had it done."

BY CHARLES FELLENBAUM

Last weekend, Karen (not her real name) a 19 year old USC sophomore from Columbia walked into the Women's Medical Center of Washington, D.C. for an abortion. This is the story of her experience.

"I'm glad I had it done," she said. "If my mother had found out about it it would have killed her, and my boyfriend's parents too."

"My first guilt feelings occurred when I was on the table. Sometimes I still feel guilty because I realize there will never be another baby like the one I lost.

"The people at the clinic said I took it very well. I don't feel a lot of guilt about what I've done.

"The whole thing takes about three hours. I was in at 9 a.m. and back at the motel at 1 p.m. I really believe a girl could go through it by herself but it's nice to have someone there. My boyfriend went with me. He wouldn't let me go by myself. There were a lot of boyfriends, fathers and mothers there in the waiting room.

"The place was very new and very sanitary. If it would have been bad I would have walked out. I called them last week on Tuesday for a Saturday 9 a.m. appointment, made plane reservations and got in at 2 p.m. We spent the night and went in the next day.

"The first thing you do is fill out release papers, the clinic is not liable. Then they take lab tests to make sure you're not RH negative. Then there is a session with a trained counselor. I was surprised how nice and understanding the people were. The counselors stay in the operating room with you and help you with breathing exercises.

"They give you a shot to cause labor contractions but they (the contractions) are not strong or painful. Although it was pretty painful for me, I'm different inside and other girls there didn't feel near as much pain. They used the vacumn tube method. It causes a lot less bleeding and pain. The whole process takes about 15 minutes. They block your view.

"You're in the recuperating room about an hour and given antibiotics and pills to stop the bleeding. I was with six other girls in the room. There is more counseling and they tell you all about birth control methods. We later all sat around and discussed our personal feelings. There was a 45-year-old lady whose kids were grown. She got pregnant during menopause. She and her husband decided on an abortion.

"All the other girls were from the south except one who went to the University of Maryland. They were from North Carolina, Tennessee and Virginia. I was the only girl from S.C.

"I still can't believe how good the people there were. They advise you after three weeks to go for follow-up care with a doctor and if you don't have one they'll give you a name of a good one in your area. If you live in the area they offer free follow up care.

★ ★ ★

"It wasn't a hassle like most girls would think it would be. I thought I might be very upset if it ever happened, but I was pretty calm. I was nine weeks pregnant when I had the abortion. I went to a local doctor, but she didn't know of any clinics. She told me to go to Planned Parenthood for information. I didn't know about the abortion-hotline on campus.

"The cost for my abortion was $125, plus $64 round trip plane fare to D.C. per person. My boyfriend paid for most of it. We were planning to get married anyway, and now we probably will over the Christmas holidays. The name of the clinic is the Women's Medical Center of Washington., Washington, D.C. 20006, 202-298-9227.

FIGURE 13. College newspapers provided abortion referral information and featured stories about students seeking abortions. A story on the 19 October 1972 front page of the University of South Carolina *Daily Gamecock* helped students considering an abortion learn who to call to arrange it, as well as what to expect about the travel, the costs, and the procedure itself. With permission from the *Daily Gamecock*.

Of course, resistance to providing birth control also helped contribute to the tremendous need for abortion information. Commercial referral services knew they were meeting consumer demand by placing plentiful advertising in college papers, and thousands of students called volunteer-staffed hotlines where students could get free abortion referrals. University of South Carolina (USC) graduate and law student Vickie Eslinger told a *Gamecock* reporter, "Every year I lived on campus from 1966 to 1970 I knew of at least one illegal abortion being performed on a girl in my dorm. One year they found a dead fetus in a garbage can at South Tower." The doctor who operated the university's health clinic refused to provide birth control to women who were not engaged to be married. Eslinger was motivated to act by the reality that illegal abortions were the leading cause of maternal death at the time. She said, "I did know that people shouldn't die," and started a hotline. The university president only acceded to the hotline after insisting that it be "incorporated independently of the university" and checking "with the state attorney general to make sure such a service would be legal." The Abortion Hotline reported that in its first year and a half of operation student volunteers "handled over 2,000 calls." Director Clisby Williams reported in 1972 that, "some 35 callers were going to New York for abortions each month." Many women and men strove to give women control over their lives, including the need to control their own bodies and seek an abortion. Nor were Esligner and the USC hotline unique.[7]

The response from students and health care providers reflects an understanding of these services as essential consumer needs. Without the services, women would be likely to get pregnant and either be forced from the institution (to give birth) or seek out dangerous and potentially deadly illegal services. Most damningly, lack of services would likely disproportionately affect the poorest of the students. While some schools did help, many resisted publicizing and identifying their efforts, even to their student body. The same kind of fear of publicity that plagued abortion funds shaped the ways institutions provided care, counseling, and referrals. Worry that angry alumni, trustees, taxpayers, parents, and politicians would withhold funds and support for the institution, or that the police or attorney general might prosecute them, led to fears of tapped phones and the publication of materials that drew too close an association of the institution with the project.[8]

Concomitant with the urgent demand for help came the vitally important imperative for privacy. Parental rights to be informed about the health of their child had to end to allow for true access to sexual health information at college health centers. Many women at Mount Holyoke, for example, believed the rumor that every urine sample supplied to the campus health center was tested for pregnancy and that parents were informed of any pregnancy. Doctors at college health centers were at pains to assure students that they were legally entitled to confidential care. At Penn State University, Karen Carnabucci reported on the state law that anyone age eighteen or older, "or who has graduated from high school, or who has been married, or who has been pregnant is entitled to confidential medical and dental care—and the consent or advice of no other person is necessary." She further detailed that students could confidentially get prescriptions for birth control pills, IUDs, pregnancy tests, and vasectomies, with the health center reporting sixty to eighty women seeking "information on contraceptives" every day.[9]

In a savvy appeal to the paranoia about parental involvement and the oppression of *in loco parentis*, Planned Parenthood "advised students to take the position that 'by denying the health-service doctor the right to dispense contraceptives, [the administration] is interfering with the doctor-patient relationship; then, you can pressure your health service to get going and set up a clinic or at least an open referral policy to direct girls to a private doctor.'" Those students who did achieve quality health centers also "demanded a greater say" in how they were run and what services were offered. In 1970, the role of the students, according to the American College Health Association, was predicated on their "growing consumer power," and the students were tasked with giving "insight into student health services 'through the eyes of the consumer.'" The organization's president declared that "[i]f students 'are expected to pay the bill for the program . . . they should have a major role in setting priorities and developing the specifics of services which are offered.'"[10]

Reproductive services, including abortion referral, proved popular among men and women across the country. At a large, public, Southern institution, Auburn University in Alabama, by November 1970, 68 percent of "the students believe that the Student Government Association should provide a pregnancy counseling service to students." Students were supported in their quest in 1971 when the AAUW issued its "Guidelines for Academic Equality," which called for "availability of counseling for birth control, pregnancy and knowledge of community resources" as one of their twenty-one demands. The chair of the committee who formulated the guidelines, Dr. Mabelle McCullough, explained that institutions that adhered to them could "avoid confrontation with the Federal Office of Contract Compliance on the matter of sex discrimination." The subtle "knowledge of community resources" language regarding pregnancy was astutely reported as requiring abortion referrals. The AAUW Standards for Women in Higher Education, which addressed both students and faculty, called for universities to provide sex counseling, ensure that both women and men were encouraged to use it, and, if there were no such resources, asked if the students had access to an outside service. Even in 1972, a survey by the National Student Association found that only 47 percent of schools had gynecological services, and less than a quarter prescribed birth control.[11]

So with a push from students and a pull from the federal government (with threats of sex discrimination), many colleges and universities began to incorporate changes into student health services. There was an incredible range of services, from the paltry referral providers to the Yale team's exemplary Sex Counseling Service, which offered medical advice on masturbation, sexual pleasure, and birth control, and help navigating and securing an abortion. A desire for bodily autonomy compelled many women to seek out and use university health services for their reproductive health.[12]

Philip and Lorna Sarrel at Yale University took a revolutionary approach in 1969, heralding the arrival of five hundred undergraduate women to the previously all-male undergraduate campus with the Sex Counseling Service. What the Sarrels—Phillip was an obstetrician/gynecologist and Lorna was a psychiatric social worker—and their colleagues had been able to do with sex education classes expanded to modeling health discourse and providing medical services. They ensured that any pregnant Yale woman could secure a therapeutic abortion in New Haven and Philip would do the procedure. Friendship with the university president gave them carte blanche to implement a top-down program, and although they credited the students for making it happen, the decision to bring the Sarrels was predicated on Phillip's success in educating over five thousand undergraduates in the northeast and (hopefully) guaranteeing that the newly coed university would not be embarrassed by pregnant women, or female students caught getting an illegal abortion. Even at Yale, though, a student described the all-too-common scene experienced by girls and women across the country:

> A woman in their dorm started hemorrhaging one night after going through an illegal abortion. The girl's roommate had pounded on their door. "Call the police! Call the police! She's bleeding to death!" An ambulance arrived, and the student was saved, but she was never able to bear her own children afterward.[13]

Although it did not reach all students, Yale ultimately provided safe, legal therapeutic abortions to about twenty undergraduates in its first three years.

Moreover, the university actively encouraged the use of the birth control pill. Margaret Homans recalled that as an undergraduate, "Yale's student health services . . . pushed the pill on us all so hard, my impression was that Yale students just didn't get pregnant. I am sure I was wrong about that, but that was my belief at the time." Indeed, in spite of access to birth control and abortion, Yale women did indeed find themselves pregnant, and, like so many others, they dropped out. As a Yale sophomore reflected when she learned why one of her classmates had left, "It was like women, whether in high school or college, just faded away once they became pregnant."[14]

Even in a university with truly exceptional support for sex education and resources, students organized to help provide information to those who needed it. Along with her friends, Homans answered phones for the Women's Abortion Referral Service, which was part of the New Haven Women's Center at Yale. The student volunteers understood that only Yale women and women of means could access abortions. The hotline was designed to reach girls and women in the New Haven community. Most of their efforts centered on the referral, calling women back after they left a message on the answering machine and helping facilitate appointments with two Yale-connected doctors. The doctors, a white woman and a Black man, Virginia Stuermer and Marshall Holley, "provided their services for free or reduced rates. I recall $225 or $255 or

$285—something like that—as the usual fee; I remember it was a project to try to get the fee down as far as possible." Grateful to have a shared woman-only experience in the still heavily male environment, Homans recalled that the group approached their service as providing abortion information rather than counseling women about their options. Embracing the group's "anti-war, anti-establishment, social/racial justice point of view," she believed "these are women who know what they need and we are helping them access services they are asking for. I do recall horror stories about women being sterilized against their wishes during abortions, and feeling confident that our doctors would never do this."[15]

Homans and her friends did not intervene with the doctors or the women, or involve themselves with securing payment or services, beyond setting up appointments. The only exception involved helping four Black women who had appointments in New York City, and she drove them in a borrowed car in a snowstorm. For Homans, at the wheel of a borrowed car, sliding around on the slick highway at night, it was a perilous journey, but she was grateful to be able to safely deliver them to an abortion clinic. Student efforts generally focused on pushing their school to provide services and sometimes stepping up to do counseling and referrals themselves.[16]

The situation at William & Mary, a small, public university in Virginia, was markedly different. The heartache, stress, and consequences of an unwanted pregnancy fell squarely on the woman. At William & Mary in the fall of 1970, a pregnant student, unable to secure an abortion in time, had to leave school and carry her pregnancy to term in a Florence Crittenton home. At the home, "A member of the staff told her, 'Don't worry, honey, the doctor will stitch you up so tight no one will ever know.'" She was not allowed to return to school. The experience of watching a woman deprived of a chance for an abortion, forced to give birth, and then having the injury compounded by being unable to continue her schooling led a few women in the college community to band together. The Women's Equality group, aligning itself with the Environment Committee of the Student Association due to their shared concerns about "the importance of birth control in an effort to preserve the environment," got an office in the basement of a dorm. With their desk and telephone, they were able to establish a hotline to help women get reproductive information.[17]

Interviewed by the student paper, Winn Legerton remarked of the hotline's significance, "Considering the ignorance on this campus about birth control methods . . . and also the number of women students who have had abortions this year, we sincerely hope this information service will prove beneficial." Legerton's quoted comments led to condemnation by the university president and complaints of printing "obscenities" by the dean of the law school. Another complainant was a business professor, who wanted the editor "relieved of his post" for the "vulgar and obscene language" and for ruining the reputation of the college. The president charged that "to imply that a significant number of William and Mary coeds, much less one, have been engaged in this tawdry business is, unless substantiated, a most insulting example of gossip." Beyond the college, local businesses also took offense and refused to advertise in the *Flat Hat*, resulting in a "substantial loss" of revenue. Students, offended by this financial pressure, in turn took to boycotting the businesses.[18]

Hoping to ensure women's freedom and to decrease the need for abortions, Ellen Spears, Chris Faia, Dorothy Riddle, Winn Legerton, and others in the group found two local doctors willing to accept referrals for birth control, so when the calls came in, they had information to share. As a feminist activist and the wife of a faculty member, Chris Faia recalled that there were two ministers active in the Clergy Consultation Service and a woman connected with an abortion clinic in Brooklyn that charged only $200. The Women's Equality hotline helped William & Mary women connect to the health care they needed, especially with the increased access afforded by the changes to the laws in the nearby District of Columbia.[19]

Evolving from a separate handbook governing women's behavior and an administration offended by the "indecency" of a student discussing abortion in the student paper, the tradition-bound institution emerged into the 1970s distributing four thousand copies of the *Birth Control Handbook*; bringing Bill Baird to galvanize the students' quest for reproductive rights, as he had done on so many campuses; and offering birth control information and eventually abortion referrals through hotlines staffed by volunteers.[20]

DAILY PRESS, NEWPORT NEWS, VIRGINIA, SUNDAY MORNING, JULY 12, 1970

Four leaders of the student Women's Lib group at William and Mary are, from left, Dr. Dorothy Riddle, Winn Legerton, newly elected president of the student body, Marcia Yancey and Joy Dickinson. They plan to send a letter outlining their purpose and activities to all incoming freshmen as their first action this fall. (Photo by Bill Hoyle)

FIGURE 14. Hoping to decrease the need for abortions at the College of William & Mary, Dr. Dorothy Riddle and Winn Legerton (pictured to the left) helped find two local doctors willing to prescribe birth control. The women and their allies then founded an abortion referral service. Photo by Bill Hoyle. With permission from the *Newport News* (Virginia; 12 July 1970).

For some students, coming face-to-face with unwanted pregnancies and illegal abortions up and down their dorm hallway, in their group of friends, or even in their own family galvanized them. Jane D. Brown's experience at the University of Kentucky was a convergence of all three. She arrived in Lexington in the fall of 1968, after seeing two friends from her Maryland high school graduate pregnant (one got married; the other disappeared to give up the baby for adoption). At the university, the trend continued. Her roommate and seven other women in her dorm that first year got pregnant and approached her for help. Ultimately, they all dropped out of college. Already attuned to the issue and politicized in her anti-war activities, Brown faced a terrible and immediate crisis—her twin sister got pregnant in the summer of 1969.[21]

Like so many hundreds of thousands of others, Brown, her sister Judi, and her sister's boyfriend tried to find an illegal abortionist. The more calls they made, the more scared they got. Brown remembered, "We kept calling and whispering and questioning around. It was getting pretty late." Ultimately, Jane made the decision to call their mother, who was able to secure help from the family physician for a therapeutic abortion. It was hugely expensive, their mom paid for three psychiatrists to affirm that Judi would be mentally injured if forced to continue the pregnancy, a doctor to perform a D&C, and a two-day stay in the hospital. All totaled, the abortion cost $750, and according to Jane, it was a "humiliating awful experience."[22]

Even in New York State, women faced hurdles in getting abortion information. A group of Cornell University students, including Deborah Ross, Laura Peck, and Peg Spear, formed the Ithaca Women's Abortion Project, which offered free abortion referrals, lightening the load of the local Planned Parenthood and the university health center. Students could get a free pregnancy test at the campus health center, and pregnant women were instructed to call and arrange the desired abortion. Between June and October 1970, the group estimated that it received a hundred inquiries and arranged fifty abortions, with calls coming from Cornell students and women from the surrounding area. To promote their service, the group printed up business cards and placed ads promising referrals to fast-safe-inexpensive-legal New York clinics. Sometimes pregnant women traveled to Scarsdale; others went to New York City by train, with women disguising it as a shopping trip.[23]

A small group of committed women in Ithaca also shared health information more broadly. The Ithaca Women's Health Project met in a community co-op, above a grocery store; there, they taught local women about birth control and their bodies. After some Cornell women got involved in the fall of 1970, they developed a curriculum for the Women's Community Education Program, using the in-development, not-yet-published *Our Bodies Our Selves*. The women also connected with national organizations like the Women's National Abortion Action Coalition and wanted to secure legal abortion access. With the leadership of Rosalind

Kenworthy, the university's first sex counselor, brought on in November 1971, the health center also gave referrals to New York City clinics, and made about ten referrals each month.[24]

The efforts of college health services to meet the needs of students who needed abortions expanded nationally. The Student Health Service of the University of Maryland at College Park (UMCP) brought on a full-time gynecologist and started doing abortion referrals, "with an average referral rate for abortions of about ten a week." The service first directed students to New York and then, with legalization, sent them to the District of Columbia. Offering up their experience as a model, Dr. Margaret W. Bridwell, the UMCP staff gynecologist, and Dr. Louis W. Tinnin, the senior psychiatric consultant in the student health service, published their findings in the *Journal of American Medical Women's Association.* The doctors assured, "We try to give the patients kind, supportive, non-judgemental care during this crisis," and their one-sentence conclusion was equally direct: "Abortion counseling, including referral and post-abortion care, can be done within the confines of a student health service with success."[25]

Another school rising up to meet the challenge was Emory University. By March 1971, Emory students had access to four doctors to consult for unwanted pregnancies, including two full-time doctors at the student health services, as well as one through Planned Parenthood and one through the school's ob-gyn group. The doctors made referrals to three or four "reputable" New York clinics, "on the basis of a special trip made by several doctors."[26]

The University of Rhode Island (URI) appeared to address the problem of unwanted pregnancies by creating a new position, Director of Health Services. The new director worked to create a gynecological clinic that could provide contraceptive information and devices; in explaining his motivation, Barry Solomon told a WEAN radio interviewer in November 1970 that 250 unmarried URI students had already had abortions that semester. The university president demanded the doctor provide evidence or retract his statement, and even fired him in December 1970. The president faced tremendous pressure both from students who wanted preventative services and politicians like a Republican gubernatorial candidate who "stated vehemently that he would go to the courts if necessary to prevent the sale of birth control devices at a state-supported institution." Despite the scrutiny and criticism, Solomon not only got reinstated but also persisted in meeting student need; in April 1971 he stated, "It is not an exaggeration to say that we see at least one girl a day who's pregnant." At the health center, women could meet with a part-time gynecologist, a medical professional to receive an abortion referral, or a social worker provided free of charge from Catholic Social Services.[27]

For many students in the western half of the country, necessity and local activism informed reproductive health services. Touted in a *Mademoiselle* article, the University of Colorado–Boulder "student-run birth control information commission" also operated "as an abortion referral service." Founded in the spring of 1969, the group was initially made up of mostly men. Their application for recognition as a student organization revealed the early, close history between population concerns and sex education: "To be a center for discussion about ideas and distribution of literature concerning sex education, birth control and the population explosion. To educate students and community about the urgency of these problems. To provide information about obtaining contraceptives to anyone who desires it." One of the men, David Schoen, went on to be the leader of the renamed Birth Control Information Commission, and proposed a $10,000 budget for the 1971–1972 school year, planning for an ambitious agenda of speakers, travel, literature, and an education program. He touted the group as "one of the most progressive and most active centers of this type in the country."[28]

In addition to distributing the McGill students' *Birth Control Handbook*, in 1970 Schoen put together *The Boulder Birth Control Handbook*. Along with Planned Parenthood and NARAL, he included "Helpful Organizations" like Zero Population Growth (ZPG) and the Population Crisis Committee, as well as books by Paul Ehrlich. Schoen's booklet elicited a complimentary note from Dr. Takey Crist, who praised it as "fine work." The progressive efforts to discuss and provide birth control in some schools were rooted in male concerns about overpopulation and were not necessarily advanced based on women's rights.[29]

The approach of students at the University of Washington in Seattle (UW) captures an outlier in the quest for colleges to provide abortion information and services, composed entirely of women and partnered with an established community group. A local YWCA connected to the UW campus, along with the student group Committee for Abortion Reform that was forced off campus for advocating politically, joined forces to create the Abortion-Birth Control Referral Service. Founded shortly after Washington became the first state in the nation to pass abortion reform by popular referendum, the group took an active role in advocating for abortion access by providing abortion referrals and assembling the entire process into an operating handbook.[30]

The Abortion-Birth Control Referral Service's reputation for openly supporting women drew Katherine Saltzman from Colorado, where she was writing a dissertation on abortion access in northern Colorado and planning to set up her own referral service in Denver. She reflected in an interview, "I traveled to Seattle and stayed with a woman there who had started an abortion service, stayed with her for about a week, met all the women there who were involved in abortion—asking how are you doing it and how can I do it right?" The twenty-page *Handbook for Operating an Abortion-Birth Control Referral Service* wound its way across the country.[31]

So too did the Associated Students of the University of Washington (ASUW) want to announce the passage of the new abortion law in November of 1970, which made abortion at up to sixteen weeks legal for residents who had lived in the state for ninety days, including for those over age eighteen without parental permission. The ASUW Women's Commission published *How to Have Intercourse Without Being Screwed: A Guide to Birth Control, Abortion, and Venereal Disease.* Touting the free health care services and discounted contraceptives available, the guide alerted students to "morning-after treatment" and "abortion referral." In the extensive resources section, the guide also detailed seven other options available for "Abortion Referral or Counseling." Sixty-nine percent of the abortions performed in Washington in 1971 were done in King County, home to the university, and the process for UW students was relatively easy and accessible.[32]

After two years of access to legal abortion in Washington and with several referral services in operation, nearly half of the students voting in an opinion poll supported a proposal that the campus health center provide *free* abortions on demand. A local news article reported on the narrow defeat by just 183 votes, noting, "The vote, held Thursday in conjunction with Associated Students of the University of Washington elections, was 1,910–2,093." The headline pronounced, "Free Help Idea Loses." Even if the students had voted for free abortions on demand, the opinion poll would not necessarily have been enough to compel the administration to provide the free procedures, but the students and the citizens of Washington did make clear at the ballot box their strong support for abortion access. And like so many students across the country, they made clear their belief that their university should help them.[33]

"Applaud and Appalled"

Starting in the fall of 1970, with the legalization of abortion in New York State, businessmen calculated that they could sell abortion referral services in college and underground papers. They invested money, aware that college students often sought out illegal abortions, desperate not to interrupt their young lives and derail their scholarly pursuits. When students returned to campus, many abortion referral companies decided to place ads in college newspapers.

The National Educational Advertising Service (NEAS), the clearinghouse for most abortion ads, experienced tremendous growth in the late 1960s, with ad volume increasing by 70 percent between May 1965 and May 1966. Owned by Reader's Digest Sales and Services, Inc. until December 1970, NEAS had a monopoly on national advertising placed in college student newspapers across the country. From December 1970 until December 1972, the advertising company earned nearly $5 million in commissions. Taken to court to break their monopoly, NEAS revealed that they had secured access to college students through a combination of written and oral agreements. "With 1103 college newspapers, including virtually all 100 schools with the largest enrollments," NEAS had a lock on the market. Their contracts were infinite, could only be terminated

Typical ads from abortion brokers aim for the coed market.

FIGURE 15. This collage, including a line drawing of a clergy member, captured the abortion information most students found in their college newspapers. Appearing in the student paper of Montclair State University in New Jersey, the focus on neighboring New York was readily apparent. With permission from the *Montclarion* (26 February 1971).

with twelve months' notice, and had a strict no-compete clause. NEAS also proved to be recalcitrant in negotiating or compromising on their ad bundles, even when the ads broke a state's laws.[34]

Chasing college students' purchasing power, believed to be $35 billion a year, NEAS made inroads across the country. The company invested in the growing market, with the number of college students expected to balloon from 7.5 million in 1969 to more than 9 million by 1975. Most student newspapers welcomed the much-needed revenue; for example, ad revenue made up 75 percent of the operating budget of the University of Georgia's *Red and Black*. Moreover, as growing tensions emerged over governance and censorship, more papers declared themselves independent from their universities, to free themselves from political and financial pressures. This ultimately led most papers to an even greater reliance on advertising revenue.[35]

According to NEAS, about 20 percent of their clients refused to run the ads they sent. By the end of 1971, the company reported that "493 college newspapers are currently carrying the ads of 10 different abortion agencies, many of them located in New York, Philadelphia and California." With a fairly steady number of college papers running ads, in spite of legal challenges and discomfort over charges of profiteering, the company succeeded in presenting abortion options to consumers across the country.[36]

According to the *Chronicle of Higher Education* in 1971, "The publishing of advertisements in campus newspapers for abortion referral services has caused almost as much controversy as the services themselves." After the University of Notre Dame *Observer* carried an abortion referral ad in their independent student newspaper on October 26, 1970, the editors announced the next day that they had erred in running it. The students at the Catholic university offered a column in response to the letters "that poured in from all circles criticizing the 'ethical' judgment of the *Observer* for allowing the abortion counseling ad. . . ." From a position of principles and objectivity, the men asserted, "It is not the purpose of any newspaper to play the censor in order to protect its readers from internal conflict that may result from the reading of something they didn't know or didn't want to believe existed." The editors asserted their impartiality in running ads, noting that the editors did not "endorse" any of the products or services that advertised in their pages and that the NEAS "have always been of quality and name-associated corporations and interest groups. . . ." They rejected the expectation that the *Observer* would "investigate all of its ads. This would mean reviewing all movies before they were advertised."[37]

At the time, Notre Dame was still men-only, but the student newspaper and the *Scholastic* magazine were joint ventures with St. Mary's, a nearby women's college. Moreover, Notre Dame was moving toward becoming coed, with women from St. Mary's able to take classes there. The St. Mary's women's reputation appeared to provide cover to the editors at the student paper. The day after their intellectual defense of

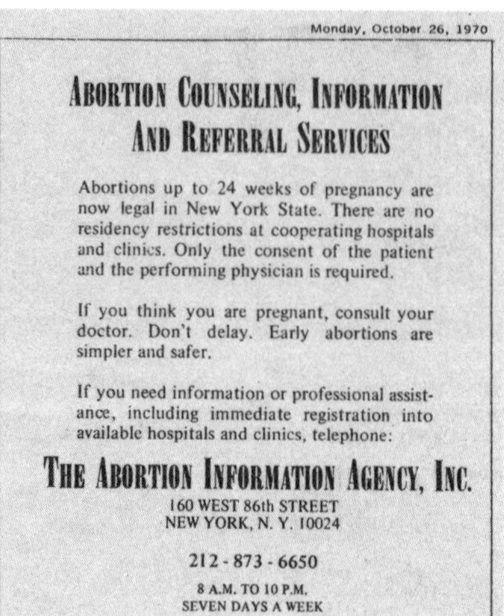
Monday, October 26, 1970

ABORTION COUNSELING, INFORMATION AND REFERRAL SERVICES

Abortions up to 24 weeks of pregnancy are now legal in New York State. There are no residency restrictions at cooperating hospitals and clinics. Only the consent of the patient and the performing physician is required.

If you think you are pregnant, consult your doctor. Don't delay. Early abortions are simpler and safer.

If you need information or professional assistance, including immediate registration into available hospitals and clinics, telephone:

THE ABORTION INFORMATION AGENCY, INC.

160 WEST 86th STREET
NEW YORK, N. Y. 10024

212 - 873 - 6650

8 A.M. TO 10 P.M.
SEVEN DAYS A WEEK

FIGURE 16. This Abortion Information Agency, Inc., ad appeared in Notre Dame and St. Mary's Colleges' *Observer* (26 October 1970), the only abortion referral ad to appear in the paper. New York State prosecuted and dismantled the for-profit agency for price fixing and kickbacks. With permission from the Notre Dame Archives.

running the referral ad, the newspaper ran a blank space in the size and shape of the Abortion Information Agency, Inc. ad and claimed, "This was the space allotted for the abortion referral agency ad. We have omitted the ad because of the ill-will it generated over at St. Mary's." Nor was this isolated coverage; Notre Dame engaged with abortion throughout that fall. As the *Observer* editors noted, the campus hosted a "Representative of Zero Population Growth."[38]

The university's *Scholastic* magazine also ran an abortion referral ad that appeared on the inside of the front cover--squarely facing every reader who opened it. The magazine editors, too, responded to the "outrage" and vowed to talk "about the whole issue with openness and charity." The magazine then ran four essays, two offering critiques and two in support of abortion rights, including one arguing for the repeal of abortion laws (making abortion legally available) and the other a "zero population growth position paper," offering a "relatively new rationale for abortion as an essential means for preservation of the human species. . . ." Notre Dame fully engaged with abortion questions in the fall of 1970.[39]

A year later, the student paper at the all-male Mount St. Mary's College in Maryland ran an abortion referral ad. The *Mountain Echo* editor,

Michael C. Keenan, reflected on his rationale for placing an ad for abortion referrals, remembering that it "fit my counterculture mode at the time, I figured 'the powers' wouldn't like it but my paper was for 'the people,' so I ran it. Frankly, I had no idea it would get noticed and create tumult to the degree that it did." And indeed the innocuous ad that offered help to women seeking abortions appeared in a multitude of underground and campus newspapers that October, promising sincere guidance without judgment or discrimination. The ad resonated with the editor as both legitimate and useful.[40]

Much of the male student body was outraged when the dean of student affairs "confiscated and burned" six thousand copies of their student paper, likely in the big coal furnace that fueled the campus. The dean, Father James Forker, asserted that his actions were justified because the issue was "extremely distasteful" and "a violation of the basic philosophy of this institution." In this instance, there was no pretext about the advertising being illegal, but instead, Keenan explained, "the fact that it was against the core precepts of the Catholic Church was made eminently clear to me by Father Forker." Some students supported the dean's action, including one who maintained, "an ad for abortion has no place on an all-male campus," and some faculty, too, concluded that "suppression in this case is the lesser of two evils."[41]

The newspaper staff and their supporters, however, vehemently disagreed. The next issue commemorated their seized newspaper, "incinerated and reduced to ash," with black mourning bunting. The front page carried two stories covering the advertisement and the mixed reaction by faculty, described as "Applaud and Appalled." The box atop the masthead sarcastically proclaimed: "Here it is again, folks! The notorious journal that was banned in Emmitsburg.—Rated X." The newspaper did not run any further abortion ads, but the editor published an "Abortion Contortion" column in the next issue. Thereafter, returning to the newspaper's offices, Keenan discovered that the administration had padlocked the door. There was no public denouncement, but the students were locked out. Keenan and a friend went to find Sister Basil, who watched the door while the two students rustled up a bolt cutter from the maintenance room. With a snap of the cutters, they broke the lock and regained access to the newspaper office. The administration did not respond to the students reclaiming the paper, and it was never mentioned again.[42]

Abortion ads proved to be especially contentious at some religiously focused schools, with Notre Dame approaching the incidents cerebrally and the editors at Mount St. Mary's locked out with their paper incinerated, but the tensions and reactions occurred to varying degrees on campuses across the country. Some students were dismayed to receive abortion referral ads in their contracted NEAS bundles. The managing editor of the University of Massachusetts-Amherst (UMass) student paper, the *Daily Collegian*, explained to NEAS on November 20, 1970, "Because of the Massachusetts State 'Laws against Chastity,' no newspapers in this state can legally accept and print any advertisements dealing with artificial birth control or with abortion." He asked to cancel two November ads and requested that the company "Please discontinue sending any ads of a similar nature in the future." The paper's accountant followed up on December 7, acknowledging the placement of ads for Playtex tampons and a poster service, but insisting that "our newspaper has repeatedly returned all birth control and abortion ads to your firms, as we cannot run this type of ad. . . ." She reiterated past pleading to discontinue the ads, insisting, "You're wasting your postage as well as ours." A week later she fired off another letter, alerting them she would not engage with NEAS regarding these ads because running them was "against the law." While the student newspaper at UMass rejected the advertisements and appealed to NEAS, most other school papers carried the abortion referral ads in the fall of 1970.[43]

For many newspapers, an imperative to offer information to women in need combined with the "bonanza of revenues" gave providing abortion advertising a doubly positive purpose. While at many colleges, such as Middle Tennessee State, the newspaper's faculty advisor and the students succumbed to "considerable pressure" and did not run ads, at others, such as the University of Nebraska—Omaha, the faculty advisor advocated for mature content, stating, "We are not a family newspaper or a television station that reaches into homes of eight-year-olds." Richard Goldman, the editor of the student paper and one of the five student organizers of the abortion referral service at Towson State University, asserted, "This is not the medieval age. It [pregnancy] is a fact of life, not a social stigma." The editors themselves actively chose to carry—or not carry—the ads. An editor at Rollins College in Florida stated, "I cannot think of a better place to put these advertisements, it is a service that a college newspaper should provide in that it concerns deeply, the well-being of the students." The advertising director for the *Daily Iowan* contrasted ads that could be charged as "obscene" and therefore illegal, such as ads for "a call girl or a homosexual partner" because they "pander prostitution" or promote "homosexual acts," with the abortion referral ads he ran.[44]

A few editors, though, resisted running ads on the grounds that it violated their sense of morality and decency. One rationale took issue with the immorality of referral companies' price gouging of people in need. At Skidmore College, for example, an editorial asserted that "any business that thrives on the desperation of others cannot have a fair price." In the fall of 1970, the paper declared its policy: They would carry no recruitment ads for General Electric or other war contractors, or abortion ads of "questionable integrity." The editors acknowledged that this would come at a price of considerable loss of income, but believed it was the right choice for the paper. In February 1971, the newspaper aligned itself with the attorney general of New York, who was investigating "the moral legitimacy of such a business" and concluded that they would not "support those segments of society who become the parasites living off of these changes." Another issue that inspired students to reject abortion referral ads was a belief that abortion itself was immoral. In the case of the University of Cincinnati, the students' editorial column "Why No Abortion Ads" explained, "we find abortion completely indefensible under any circumstances" and "that agencies which argue they are merely offering students a service are whoremongers."[45]

Feminists also brought pressure to bear, objecting at Northwestern University that "The Daily is more concerned with accepting the money from these ads than with the health and welfare of pregnant women at Northwestern. The Daily has willingly allowed itself to serve a system which puts its primary value on money rather than on people." The women advanced the names and numbers of free alternatives and called for action. While not shifting their policy of accepting abortion referral ads, the editor noted that the subject of the women's ire was an ad "canceled several weeks ago."[46]

(Male) Legal Challenges

Just as abortion laws varied from state to state, so too did laws governing its advertising vary widely. College administrations used the threat and uncertainty of these laws and their enforcement to constrain editors of college papers. With all of the social and political turmoil of the late 1960s and the 1970s, abortion referral ads contributed to tensions between students and administrators over interpreting the laws and the freedom of the press. Students contended that efforts to censor the paper were unconstitutional. Critics who despaired at college newspaper articles about the sexual revolution, women's health, and options for controlling reproduction reacted sharply.[47]

A study of the college press from 1969 to spring 1971 found many newspapers in conflict. The "crackdowns" by administrators, boards, and state legislatures included "censorship, outright firing of editors, withholding of funds, copy blackouts, . . . and in some instances complete reorganization of publications." One observer of the ongoing conflicts characterized the students as in a "battle of 'fascistic repression.'" The crackdowns intensified in the fall of 1970. One of the most widely reported crackdowns took place at Concordia College in Minnesota, after the student paper ran an abortion ad in December 1970. The college president turned his building rage at student behavior against the newspaper and its student editor, Omar Olson.[48]

The president "informed Olson that the paper was in violation of a 1909 Minnesota Penal Code statute making it illegal to advertise any means of terminating pregnancy," unilaterally removed him as editor, and shuttered the paper. Olson did not believe the president's claim and called the Minnesota attorney general's office; he was assured that the 1910 Minnesota statute "did not apply to ads, only to means whereby an abortion was induced presumably meaning medical devices. Otherwise, the sister Lutheran colleges, state schools, and other state media who also carried the ad would have run an illegal ad as well." Moreover, Olson noted that the ads were pervasive across the state; he decided if they were running at the University of Minnesota, with their law school, then there was nothing to worry about legally. The state attorney general came out with his official ruling and stated that it was not clear that abortion ads were illegal, and most significantly, he did not plan to prosecute college newspapers that ran the ads. Olson found tremendous support for his position.[49]

The ads created intense angst for college and underground newspaper staffs across the country. Some student editors acted preemptively to pull the abortion referral ads, worried that running them would break the law, while others learned from their university and legal counsel that running the ads would endanger the standing of the newspaper.[50] While hundreds of newspapers ran the ads, usually two to three an issue, without any concerns, for many the ads proved to be a legal lightning rod. The question of whether the ads constituted advertising or medical advice, and as such were governed by state laws like the 1901 law in Arizona that "made it illegal for any person to provide, supply, or administer any drug, substance, or instrument to a pregnant woman with the intent to produce an abortion," brought many editors and lawyers together. The laws often also explicitly "banned the advertisement of contraception and abortion." Arizona's abortion laws, like those in Michigan, Montana, and many other states, dated to the late nineteenth and early twentieth centuries.[51]

The city of Tempe charged the editors of the *New Times* with running a Problem Pregnancy Information Service ad, and the Maricopa County Superior Court convicted the editors of violating "a state law against advertising abortions." Immediately after the ruling, the University of Arizona's *Daily Wildcat* filed suit for the right to run the same ad. The students wanted the courts to declare unconstitutional the "law banning advertising of abortion and contraceptives" and hoped a declaration judgment against county attorney Rose Silver "would prevent any prosecution for running abortion service advertisements." The Arizona Civil Liberties Union was aware of and supportive of the cases. The question of how to interpret laws created to govern selling drugs or tools to induce abortion in states where abortion was still illegal—but where the advertised medical service was in a state where it was legal—persisted in each state until each attorney general made a ruling. Not until *Roe v. Wade* were state laws and their interpretation made moot.[52]

At times there was also a concerted effort by religious organizations and politicians to test laws on universities to advance an antiabortion stance. A Michigan state representative "dug out a 1911 law" and proceeded to send "letters to all college and university presidents and strongly worded warnings to the president of Eastern Michigan University and University of Michigan," condemning the ads run in their students papers as "illegal" and noting that the offense carried a $600 fine, a one-year jail term, or both for "distributing advertising of any 'immoral services' and lists of abortion referrals." The University of Michigan students continued to run the ads, and defended their right to do so while the matter was investigated, "because it believes removal of these advertisements would constitute censorship."[53]

In February 1971, the working-class-focused *Virginia Weekly* newspaper, published by a collective of University of Virginia students, decided to publish an abortion ad. With limited information about abortion availability in central Virginia, Jeff Bigelow remembered that the group made a decision to run the ad to offer the needed information: the name and phone number of a referral service in New York, where abortion was legal. The decision to publish the ad also immediately followed a letter from the state's attorney general "to the presidents of all state institutions" cautioning them "about accepting advertisements from legal abortion referral or information services." Unbeknownst to the students, a member of a local antiabortion group brought charges against the paper, under a Virginia statute that "had never before been used since it was passed in 1878."[54]

A few months later, at 11:30 at night, Charlottesville police arrived with an arrest warrant and took Jeffrey C. Bigelow, a University of Virginia student and the managing editor of the paper, into custody. With the timing designed to ensure that he had to spend the night in jail, Bigelow was ultimately arrested four separate times and tried and convicted "of encouraging or promoting the procuring of abortion by publication, advertisement, sale, or circulation of the *Virginia Weekly*, a newspaper published in Charlottesville, in violation of Code § 18.1–63." Attorney John Lowe, supported by the American Civil Liberties Union, represented Bigelow and the *Virginia Weekly* and successfully appealed the ruling "on grounds that the Virginia law banning abortion advertising is unconstitutional." The judge did not address its constitutionality and did not agree with the appeal argument that "the advertisement did not encourage or persuade women to obtain abortions, but instead merely informed those who had already rejected their pregnancies that services were available for legal abortions." The judge concluded that "the commercial nature of both the advertiser and the advertisement is patently revealed." The court asserted that the value and right to distribute information about abortion trumped the fact that it was an advertisement.[55]

Not content with that outcome, Virginia then appealed the case to the US Supreme Court. Although the case was initially remanded back to the state, after the passage of *Roe v. Wade*, the state court claimed that *Roe* did not mention "the subject of abortion advertising" and sent it back to the high court. According to legal scholar David L. Hudson Jr., "In Bigelow v. Virginia, 421 U.S. 809 (1975), the Supreme Court established that at least some commercial advertising, in this case an abortion ad, should receive First Amendment protection, thereby laying the groundwork for its ruling the next year in Virginia State Board of Pharmacy v. Virginia Citizens Consumer Council, Inc. (1976), which established the modern commercial speech doctrine." Justice Harry A. Blackmun, writing for the 7–2 majority, "determined that the abortion advertisement at issue was not pure commercial speech." As Hudson noted, "Had it been so, it would not have been entitled, by the precedents of the day, to any legal protection." Blackmun explained, "The advertisement in appellant's newspaper did more than simply propose a commercial transaction. It contained factual material of clear public import." Of particular importance to abortion advertising, Blackmun pointed out that the Virginia law "sought to limit what 'Virginians may hear or read about New York services'—an interest, he wrote that was entitled to 'little, if any, weight.' The First Amendment, according to Blackmun, prohibited the state from shielding its citizens from truthful information." Ultimately "public interest," including most especially the interest of those who would not otherwise have access to the information, was affirmed by the court.[56]

Other Virginia students also fought back against the censorship and financial pressures wielded by their schools. Although Bigelow was unique in being arrested, fifteen students at George Mason College of the University of Virginia brought a suit against their institution because "they were being threatened by school officials with a fund cutoff if they continued publishing abortion information." The female staff of the Mary Washington College student paper aligned with their peers at George Mason when "college officials threatened to interfere with the publication of the newspaper," if they published advertisements and information regarding the availability of abortions. Two students writing in to the Mary Washington *Bullet* also affirmed the Mason editors, proclaiming, "We are 100 per cent behind you. Forbidding advertisements or publications concerning abortions is as ridiculous as forbidding advertising concerning contraceptive foam and family planning."[57]

A Florida editor explicitly sought a conflict to challenge Florida's antiquated abortion laws. Like most newspaper editors in colleges across the country in 1971, the University of Florida editor was a man and a senior. The semester had just gotten underway when student editor Ron Sachs courted trouble for *The Alligator.* He stated, "We wanted to publish the information and get court standing so we could challenge the law which we believed to be unconstitutional." It was this direct, intentional strategy that provoked the university president's condemnation, drew publicity, and led to a warrant for his arrest.[58]

Sachs was not the first to try to challenge the Florida laws governing abortion information. Several other Florida colleges had run abortion referral ads and did not face consequences. The editor of the Florida Atlantic University's *Atlantic Sun* in October 1971 had "printed abortion referral ads in 'nearly every issue' of the weekly paper since he took over as editor in March." He decried the inconsistent application of the state law, noting he had been informed by the assistant state attorney that "this office would not prosecute anyone who advertised in the State of Florida abortions to be legally performed," and yet Sachs was prosecuted. A reporter for the *Sarasota Herald-Tribune* trumpeted in a headline, "New

College Abortion Info Preceded UF Controversy," and emphatically noted that students had published referral information seven months earlier. The editors of the New College paper reprinted the article and an ad in support of "freedom of the press," Sachs, and the women of New College.[59]

Sachs, new to the position of editor in the fall of 1971, took a different tack in drawing attention to his publication. Instead of running an abortion ad, he made printing abortion information the legal test. When the newspaper's printer refused to print abortion referral information, Sachs, with the help of colleagues, was able to mimeograph the information and insert ten thousand flyers into the student paper overnight. The flyer drew on accessible sources like *Redbook*, *Playboy*, and *Cosmopolitan*, and he argued that newspapers had the right to reprint publicly available information of interest to the community. Sachs was arrested, charged, tried, and "convicted by a Florida lower court of publishing an abortion advertisement."[60]

Sachs garnered a great deal of attention. Newspapers across the country carried the story of a college editor facing a year in jail and a $1,000 fine, sparking fundraising and close coverage. Closer to home, both his local journalism society and the *Miami Herald* (his hometown paper, where he had been an intern) created defense funds for Sachs, and the student senate passed a resolution on October 12, 1971: "whereas, The editor of the Florida Alligator was placed under arrest exercising his duty as a journalist and editor . . . therefore, be it resolved that we the Student Senate applaud the Alligator for its valiant efforts and pledge our support to it."[61] Eight months later, when the university president tried to seize control by making the newspaper a university publication, the student senate again offered its support. Their resolution proclaimed the paper as "the only legitimate means for constructive dissent on this campus" and warned that converting it "to a University publication will destroy the freedom of the press and free speech and end the independence of the Florida Alligator after 65 years of existence." Ultimately, on appeal, Sachs's conviction was overturned by the Florida Supreme Court, which decreed "the law unconstitutional for vagueness and said that it also violated Sachs' First Amendment rights (State of Florida v. Sachs)."[62]

Bigelow, Sachs, and their First Amendment college compatriots were not the only ones to take to the courts to press for the right to publish meaningful consumer information under the umbrella of free speech protection. For Atlanta's underground newspaper, *The Great Speckled Bird*, the legal battle unfolded in April 1972, when the United States Postal Service (USPS) refused to mail material "giving direct or indirect notice of how, from whom, or by what means an abortion could be obtained." Harkening back to the Comstock Act (1873), which outlawed the mailing of "obscene" materials, the postmaster of Thomasville, Georgia, refused to mail the newspaper with an offending ad. Of course, by the time of this refusal, the *Bird* "had carried advertisements, for, and a directory of, abortion referral services for the past two years." The publishers of the *Bird* brought suit against the USPS on behalf of its readers "who desire to receive it free of government censorship," and challenged the constitutionality of the law on the grounds that it violated "rights to freedom of speech and freedom of the press." The *Atlanta Constitution* reported in September 1972 that "Abortion Material Ruled Mailable," with the three-judge federal court ruling the federal laws unconstitutional and affirming that "abortion referral information 'falls within the protective ambit of the First Amendment. The fact that it is transmitted in a commercial setting or for profit does not remove that speech from the protection of the First Amendment.'" Abortion advertising proved to be a point of contention from localized communities to national distribution, but time and again, newspapers triumphed in their right to carry abortion ads and information, even if abortion was not legal in their state.[63]

"You Don't Have to Be Crazy"

In addition to the weekly presence of abortion ads distributed by agencies and the NEAS, college and underground editors also promoted abortion referral information in another important format: articles and columns. One popular way they did so, which also pervaded most major dailies, was to write articles that showcased a company or organization and served as de facto ads. The reporters detailed services and costs, and provided a phone number. The headline for one article at Westminster

College in Salt Lake City proclaimed: "Hang On To These Numbers—You May Need Them Someday." A great deal of college coverage focused on the "unscrupulous practices" of the for-profit services and concluded that to avoid the "Abortion Rip-Offs" women should use one of the listed services that did not charge for the needed information. Not-for-profit organizations also occasionally used traditional advertising and secured placement with donated space. Both newspapers and the Advertising Council stepped forward to support sharing these public service announcements.[64]

The Clergy Consultation Service for Problem Pregnancy (CCS) and Planned Parenthood depended on newspaper coverage of their services, which were positioned as the honorable, free alternative to the for-profit companies trying to gouge women. Articles allowed for persuasive writing and contrasted prices and services against "big business." One article at the University of Buffalo declared, "Planned Parenthood offers its referral services free of charge. Planned Parenthood is one of the most reliable places to go if a woman thinks she is pregnant." In addition to their main marketing strategy of obtaining listings in the phone book, garnering newspaper coverage, and running ads in the classifieds, Planned Parenthood also occasionally hoped to reach abortion consumers with direct advertising of their services.[65]

In 1971, Planned Parenthood pursued a broader strategy, trying to reach diverse groups of people with multiple advertising messages centered on their theme: "Children by Choice. Not Chance." Its campaign appeared in newspapers, on radio, and on television, walking a fine line of trying to appeal to young people while not offending with poor taste or racial insensitivity to Black people, to say nothing of the omnipresent risk of offending Catholics. There was a lot at stake, because $10 million to $15 million of donated space by the Advertising Council meant Planned Parenthood would have tremendous reach across the country. The organization emphasized the concept of every child being a wanted child (estimating that half of all pregnancies were unplanned) and left unspoken whether prevention was achieved through birth control or abortion.[66]

Another adopter of promoting abortion information in college and underground papers was ZPG. Like Planned Parenthood and CCS,

ZPG frequently emerged in local efforts, promoting population control through meetings, forums, and articles, listing phone numbers for their referral service, and advertising a national network of abortion providers in college papers. A largely male effort, the group offered public talks; tried to reach people through newspaper, radio, and television; and began to offer an abortion referral service all with the aim of encouraging people to voluntarily limit their reproduction to two or fewer children. Judy Kunofsky was a ZPG member at the University of California, Los Angeles, where she and a medical student ran the campus "Overpopulation Information Center," distributing birth control information at a weekly table.[67]

The initial efforts to start a ZPG "Abortion Referral Service" in the fall of 1971 were limited to announcements in student papers. Promising free information and low prices, and requiring women to write away and wait in hope of a written response, the group initially only offered a mailing address, which undoubtedly added at least a week to the woman's timeline. ZPG advertising slowly improved to include phone numbers in the spring and fall of 1972. Even though the group's referral action was limited, ZPG still generated great concern from Planned Parenthood, which initiated its Student Community Action program to answer the intense interest in the "population explosion," and tried to compete with ZPG.[68]

ZPG-New York's irreverent ads, with bold questions like "When was the last time you had your period?" and phone numbers at the ready with the reminder, "Keep this near your contraceptive. If it doesn't work, this will," appeared in college newspapers. The ads tried to compliment a reader who was smart but not knowledgeable about securing an abortion, acknowledging "You can be a straight 'A' biology major and still not know how to get an abortion." They promised practical know-how for getting "a legal, safe, inexpensive abortion. By an M.D. in a clinic or hospital." The University of Delaware's *Review* delineated that it donated the ad space, offering the information but not complicit in profiting from the referral, as ZPG assured that "there's no charge for our service."[69]

In a direct appeal to those offended by the laws and policies governing therapeutic abortions, ZPG-New York ran another ad that appeared in college papers. The headline stated, matter-of-factly, "You don't have to be crazy or raped to get a legal abortion." Challenging the requirements that most women faced to receive a therapeutic abortion in a hospital, after scrutiny and approval by psychiatrists and doctors, ZPG assured the reader, "In several states, the only requirement for an abortion is that you're pregnant. And we can help." The final assurance, after detailing the cost, reiterated that "you don't have to be crazy or raped. Or rich."[70]

Directly appealing to men was another of ZPG's unusual advertising tactics, imploring, "Every guy should save this ad." They positioned the ad as valuable information "If the girl you're going with should ever want an abortion," and suggested that the man put the number in his wallet or hang it on the wall to keep it available. This appeal to men was consistent with health educators seeking to involve men in sexual health, as well as with the experience of clinics and hospitals that knew men frequently made the first phone call and accompanied their partner to an abortion.[71]

Whether appealing to women, men, or couples, abortion referral ads pervaded the print media available to young people in college towns. Sometimes their reach was greater than they imagined. The *Kentucky Kernel* offered a large number of articles about abortion and its availability. In one article, "Nancy" described her desperation to find a legal abortion she could afford, recalling how she was "walking through the Student Center, and saw the Women's Lib advertisement. So I called Suzie and she gave me the number of the place I finally went to." First names, local phone numbers: The ease and personalization made it possible for students to access the information. Jane Brown recalled her most poignant experience doing referrals:

> Once we set up this phone system, advertising a phone number to call (my phone number), then we would get women who needed to talk about it. There was not much counseling: how much does it cost?, where do I go?, how do I do it? Have you confirmed that you're pregnant, do you have transportation, do you have money, how much can you get, costs $200 in NY, plus plane fare.
>
> We were mostly doing University of Kentucky students but it began to spread. Got a phone call from a young woman in Eastern Kentucky, never been out of her *county* before, forget getting on

> an airplane to NYC. A most impossible thing. If she continued the pregnancy believed that her father would kill her. That part of Kentucky was alien to us, it seemed like another world. We believed her, that her father would kill her. She told us, "I can't get to the airport. I have no money. I am desperate, my father will kill me."
>
> We raised the plane fare and arranged for the abortion. One morning while it was still dark, I borrowed my roommate's car, met her at the end of a dirt road, drove her to the airport, she went and did it—young and unmarried—what were we thinking, all sorts of things could've gone wrong. She had instructions, had to take subway to New Rochelle to the abortion clinic. I learned later that stewardesses recognized that women were making this journey and took care of them. . . . There was no way to check on her, we didn't know what happened. Late that day I went back and met the return flight. She got off the plane and she said: you have saved my life.[72]

The advertisements had tremendous reach and offered tens of thousands of women and men elusive information for how to procure an abortion. Even if they did not need it on the day they saw it, they knew that their school or community newspaper was a valuable resource. While many chose to pay for the referral information, student editors and local leaders tried to put free information in front of them as well.

Colleges played a central role in shaping abortion discourse and access in the late 1960s and early 1970s. For many students, the tensions between free speech and censorship played out on the question of abortion service advertising. Administrators, boards of trustees, and political figures all played critical roles in determining how to respond to the consumer demand for information. With ardent activism, sometimes separate from and occasionally in alliance with their college, students demonstrated real need for health services and abortion referrals. For most women, tearing out referrals from their school paper or getting a phone number from their health clinic after a positive pregnancy test enabled them to make an appointment, find out the cost, and head to New York to have a legal, safe abortion before *Roe*.

5

Traveling to Islands, Cities, and Small Towns

IN THE 1960S, a single woman in a small city in Indiana discovered she was pregnant. With a new career working as a nurse in a hospital, she needed an abortion. Her medical colleagues provided the phone number of someone who traveled from Kentucky to Indianapolis each weekend to provide abortions. Her boyfriend sold his car to pay for the abortion and accompanied her to the appointment. For both the doctors and the women seeking abortions, traveling away from home offered a buffer of distance, dramatically reducing the likelihood that women would see someone they knew and providing a space where they could leave their actions behind.

Historians Christabelle Sethna and Leslie Reagan have both written extensively on women who traveled for abortions, and this chapter builds on their understanding of not only what motivated women but also where and when they traveled. Businesses occasionally tried to sell women in need the façade of tourism, to shield them from scrutiny and the law, but it was the abortion they were seeking, never the destination per se. Women did not have the luxury of comparison shopping for providers, as all illegal providers risked prosecution, resulting in changing patterns of availability. The women generally shopped for an abortion in one location and then traveled somewhere else to secure it.[1]

A New York doctor reflected in 1963, "One of the curious things about abortions is that women generally go somewhere else to have them performed. Our women here seem to like Puerto Rico. In California, they make their way to butcher shops in Tijuana." While it does appear that women may have preferred to travel to have an abortion, travel was usually recommended to access a provider. Sometimes it necessitated leaving the woman's city or state, even the country.[2]

The Clergy Consultation Service (CCS), founded in 1966, tried to legally protect women and the clergy who referred them by sending women out of state. The secrecy and subterfuge, necessitated by the punishing laws and risk of prosecution, were familiar to women used to speaking in code about their reproductive lives. One woman, describing a friend, recounted that she had gone in for some "dusting and cleaning" (a D&C, a common abortion procedure). Moreover, working the phone and writing letters were familiar techniques for women long denied more traditional avenues to achieve social and political aims, and both helped to secure abortion information. While some wanted to travel to achieve anonymity, for others it was an absolute requirement to access an abortion. Even states that intended to liberalize abortion laws permitted only a tiny number of women to get legal abortions. Without local access to legal abortion, travel was a forced choice.[3]

Most women seeking abortions had to travel long distances, which inevitably increased costs. For some, the hospital or the airport itself was the destination. One woman took a bus, spoke no English, had only $5, and stayed overnight in the hospital bathroom after her abortion. One doctor set up his operation in a hotel, moving from room to room to treat the women. In Pennsylvania, Dr. Robert Douglas Spencer provided housing so Black women could stay the night and avoid the discrimination they would face in his small town. For women seeking abortions, the procedure was the point; there was no tourism.[4]

One oral history of abortion in Montana before *Roe* revealed that every major town had at least one abortionist, and so women stayed in the state but traveled to different towns for privacy. A great many of the unknown abortion providers never drew national attention. Instead of medical doctors who courted arrest and brought legal cases, lay women quietly served their communities doing abortions, often for decades. The 1961 arrest of a sixty-three-year-old grandmother in Dayton, Ohio, revealed that Myrtle Berlin provided about two thousand abortions over eleven years, and police recovered over $4,000 dollars squirreled away all over her house. The reporting described her as a "bespectacled, white-haired widow." A seventy-nine-year-old widow in Rapid City, South Dakota, Lavagne Michael, charged from "$25 to whatever the market could bear" for the eight or nine abortions she performed each week. Even though her small, white calling card attracted women across the country from 1932 to 1962, she only faced jail after a woman from neighboring Minnesota pressed charges. The local sheriff had given up hope of building a case against Michael, even though he reported that "virtually the entire town knew what went on in her attractive bungalow just a few blocks from the county courthouse." As evidence of the town's admiration for her, just three weeks before her arrest she was awarded "Gold Star Mother of the Year."[5]

The city of Portland, Oregon, also tolerated an abortion provider for decades. By the time of her arrest in 1966, Ruth Barnett, a seventy-five-year-old grandmother, had completed forty thousand abortions since her start in 1918. One reporter discovered that she was "the best in the business" in a Medical Board file, and from his investigation surmised that she was the "chief abortionist on the West Coast." She claimed that during the Second World War, she performed abortions for "an estimated 50 women per day" at her Portland clinic. All told she was estimated to have earned $10 million.[6]

States like Rhode Island and West Virginia could reject legalizing abortion (for any reason other than the life of the pregnant woman) because its citizens could easily travel for abortions to New York and Washington, D.C. In contrast, the remoteness of Hawai'i and Alaska informed their decisions to be among the first, in 1970, to legalize abortion for their citizens. They also implemented a thirty-day residency requirement, to emphasize their intent to provide care for their citizens and to discourage out-of-state travelers.[7]

The complexity of laws, language, time zones, and the expense of phone calls all contributed to the rise of entrepreneurs who sold "package

FIGURE 17. A 1968 photograph of Ruth Barnett in front of her Portland, Oregon, clinic. She completed about forty thousand abortions from her start in 1918 and was estimated to have earned $10 million. She operated openly and served as one of the largest providers on the West Coast. Photo is the property of Oregonian Publishing Co.

deals" like travel agents. While critics denounced $1,000 abortions plus travel costs as the "Great Rip-Off," national referral agencies were able to operate across the country, charging a "package price and then 'selling' the patient to the lowest bidder in the appropriate state." While these companies profited, they also provided a valuable service and care at a time when perhaps no one else was willing or able to help. One person at a nonprofit group that did referrals reflected, "It was very frightening. Some of these women had never left the south side of Tucson, let alone get on a plane and go to California . . . it was overwhelming to a lot of them." It was not just Arizona women who were scared, but women nationally who headed off to the unknown and wanted assurance.[8]

Abortion access and acceptance in the United States emerged from women's continued desperation, entrepreneurs and doctors driven by profit, and fears that the population was out of control. Unlike the "Green Books" helping Black Americans to find safe travel accommodations or the "Damron Address Books" helping white gay men find each other, which remained secreted in those communities, abortion information emerged publicly, in small-town newspapers, the *Ladies' Home Journal*, and *Playboy*. Starting in 1970, women and men found widely disseminated information that facilitated national and international abortion travel.[9]

This chapter will consider some of key places that provided abortions before *Roe*, with the following chapter focused entirely on New York. It is no surprise that islands across the globe, both literal and metaphorical islands, first embraced legal abortions or tolerated illegal abortions. Where physical barriers of great distance precluded other options, isolated communities were forced to make choices about the need for safe abortion care. Just as with Dr. Henrie in Oklahoma, illegal abortion providers in the United States found support from the communities they served. Islands providing abortions first included Cuba, Puerto Rico, Japan, and England. The chapter then considers Mexico before turning to cities across the United States.[10]

While this analysis cannot be exhaustive of all places that provided abortions, abortions were available across the country, and newspapers frequently covered their availability. Some organizations and companies offered information and checklists, especially for those traveling to Mexico and Japan, while others provided only a phone number or address. While we cannot know how many traveled where and when, we do know from public print media coverage that women and men could see where and when abortion was available and learn how to get one.

C'mon, Jet Happy: Islands

Cuba and Puerto Rico

In the 1940s and 1950s, Cuba was an abortion destination for wealthy Americans, part of the island's identity as a hedonistic vacation spot, replete with gambling and prostitution. There was a ferry service from Key West, and as airfare costs dropped, it became an accessible destination for even more Americans. For those on the East Coast, especially, it was a relatively close option for women seeking an abortion provider, and travelers did not need a passport. Journalist Susan Brownmiller remembered her experience, bleeding all the way back to New York, and abortion activist Lawrence Lader described the prospect of going to Cuba as terrifying for a woman he remembered seeing off at the airport. In a 1959 letter to a desperate woman, Dr. Robert Douglas Spencer of Pennsylvania offered explicit instructions for finding the correct medical doctor and advised her on what to eat, where to go, and how to avoid the rackets being run by anyone who suspected she was there for an abortion. After the 1959 Cuban revolution and subsequent embargo, abortion-seeking Americans turned to Puerto Rico and the half dozen clinics operating illegally and in plain sight there. Some of them were staffed with Cuban doctors, forced to flee, so there was no learning curve of either process or procedure as the demand shifted to Puerto Rico.[11]

From 1960 to New York's legalization of abortion in the summer of 1970, Puerto Rico attracted an estimated ten thousand women seeking abortions a year. What had previously been known as a "Havana Weekend" was rechristened the "San Juan Weekend." One woman who sought an abortion there in 1963 described the clinics as running "the gamut from tarantulas crawling on the walls . . . to hospital clinics and well-appointed doctors' offices." The women seeking abortions, too, ranged from working women earning $100 a month to the well-off staying in "plush hotels." A New York *Daily News* reporter's four-part series and local reporting in *El Mundo* and the *San Juan Star* revealed the tensions playing out in the island's abortion scene, with the procedure illegal but easy to arrange. Attorney Roy Lucas had a life-altering experience when he accompanied his girlfriend to Puerto Rico in 1967 and was inspired to write the first scholarly legal article on abortion.[12]

Critics, including especially the Puerto Rican Medical Association, tried in vain to quash the island's identity as an abortion destination. The association offered a $10,000 reward to anyone who could get a conviction of a doctor doing abortions, but there was little appetite to stop the trade. Moreover, a woman who had an abortion would implicate herself in the criminal action and face years of jail time if she testified against her doctor. Not surprisingly, few doctors were ever charged, and none convicted. Another proposed strategy was to go after the money, charging the doctors with tax evasion on their unreported income, but that also did not happen. One doctor speculated that the abortion doctors' power came in "skeletons in the closet," recounting a story of an arrested doctor who threatened that if he faced charges, he would expose the names of the wives of the politicians on whom he had performed abortions. Exposing the abortions of mistresses would have been an implicit threat as well.[13]

Instead, doctors like "King" performed an estimated five thousand abortions a year and raked in millions of dollars, tax free. Providers did so in a complex web of word-of-mouth advertising and payoffs to other doctors (30 percent of the fee) and cab drivers ($25 per patient delivered and for delivering payoffs to the doctors). And they did so with the assistance of airlines who touted inexpensive getaways to Puerto Rico, particularly with the promise that women could leave on a Friday and return on a Sunday. While critics hoped for a public relations campaign "to frighten away women seeking abortions and those who wish to establish abortion factories here," the business message Puerto Rico sent to mainland Americans in 1963 was in fact welcoming.[14]

Eastern, Pan Am, and Trans Caribbean airlines all serviced Puerto Rico, bringing women from cities like Chicago, Cleveland, New Orleans, and Philadelphia, with the vast majority coming from the New York/New Jersey area. In 1965, Trans Caribbean ran an ad in the *Daily News* featuring a smartly dressed young woman, one leg kicked back, ticket in hand, purse in the other, that appealed, "C'mon, Jet Happy." The ad anticipated the carefree, single-woman imagery of *The Mary Tyler Moore Show* and built on the popular song "Get Happy," whose lyrics encouraged listeners to "shout hallelujah c'mon get happy, We're goin' to the promised land." The airline promised for $104 to whisk women to "Sunny Puerto Rico." Some of the ads were even more direct, speaking to those who sought to go away for the weekend, including one from Eastern Airlines that included a "Bargainer's Weekend" to San Juan for $145. The cost covered airfare and four days and three nights at the Condado Ritz Hotel, as well as free cocktails, chaise longues, and both pool and beach access.[15]

Some encouraged women to pursue their abortion quest in a haphazard fashion, with the argument that making appointments necessitated phone calls or letters, both of which could be intercepted and used as

FIGURE 18. With imagery of a carefree, single woman, the airline promised to whisk women to Puerto Rico for only $104. Appearing in the New York *Daily News* (14 May 1965), the ad referenced the lyrics of a popular song, "C'mon Get Happy," which promised, "We're goin' to the promised land." Airlines solicited abortion consumers for weekend trips, leaving Friday evening and returning on Sunday.

evidence against them. Women therefore found their way to Puerto Rico but arrived uncertain where to go. Generally, all but the wealthiest and well-connected women were just told to go to the island. The women then secured the name and address of an abortion clinic in Puerto Rico only after scouring the phone book or generously tipping cab drivers, bellhops, and waiters. Abortion referral groups also sent women to the island, striving as they always did to ensure quality care and (relatively) low prices.[16]

In 1963, one woman struggled to find a reputable provider in the mainland United States and was grateful to get a lead in Puerto Rico. Moreover, she was

> Given all the specifics down to what to pack in my overnight case—a toothbrush, a change of underwear. I was told to wear low-heeled shoes and to take along some Modess because I could not use Tampax afterward. I was told not to eat anything before I went to see the doctor and various specifics like that.
>
> I was also instructed as to the convenient flight to take to San Juan. The specific flight that was recommended to me was a weekend flight, which would mean I would not lose any time from work. I could leave Friday evening and be back to work on Monday morning.[17]

All totaled, she estimated that she wasted about $200 on her fruitless mainland quests and then spent another $500 going to Puerto Rico on airfare, abortion, hotel, and taxi. When she found herself pregnant four years later, she went back to the same doctor in Puerto Rico and haggled again. She found four years of experience and improved technology made it a better experience.[18]

Some women got referrals from the CCS. The group relied heavily on referrals to Puerto Rico when they formed, before they could build a mainland stable of doctors to whom they could send women. The CCS based referrals on both quality of care and low prices. Circumstances on the island, with a booming demand for abortion, meant that doctors did not have to lower their prices—some even boosted their prices. Nearly every woman's account included a demand upon arrival that she pay exorbitantly more than the promised price. Nor did the doctors have to rein in their worst behavior to please the CCS. A large drawing accompanied a New York *Daily News* article about the doctors; the article and image depicted the sexual degradation and assault that awaited women. Both journalists and women seeking abortions reported on the rampant abuse women received, including sexual assaults and demands for sex in exchange for lower fees. The CCS turned, when they could, to better-supervised providers in the United States.[19]

Most referring doctors across the United States wanted to be able to refer patients to a specific doctor, and harangued their counterparts, desperate for information. Other wealthy and connected people seeking information about Puerto Rican providers in New York reportedly just had to ask: "the right bell hop in any of the major cities in the States can furnish that." Even more common, though, was that wealthy women had private physicians who maintained connections in order to serve their patients. A New York obstetrician told a reporter in 1963 that dozens of his patients went to Puerto Rico. He also had a colleague who claimed that at his country club it was "considered almost a status symbol to have had an abortion in Puerto Rico. He says he knows of at least a dozen women there who have gone to San Juan for illegal operations." For the wealthy, "knowing a guy" through a private doctor meant access to the illicit operation, while those without money and private medical care struggled.[20]

The legalization of abortion in New York destroyed the power held by providers in Puerto Rico. A September 1970 newspaper article in Allentown, Pennsylvania, described an obstetrician who received cards and letters from abortion providers in both New York and Puerto Rico. He noted of the Puerto Rican doctors, "I know they were getting a lot of business. They have a lot of private hospitals. They must be hurting for business with this new law." After ten years, Puerto Rico's status as an important destination for women seeking abortions had ended. For some vulnerable, desperate women, it had solved the problem of an unwanted pregnancy, but at a cost.[21]

England

England looms large in the understanding of where American women traveled for abortions. It created an oversized impression by offering legality, a shared language, and relative proximity to the East Coast and New York's all-important media market. The number of abortions done for American women by British providers in the first ten months following legalization in 1968, however, was only 185. The following year, the number climbed to 1,594. With New York's legalization of abortion without restrictions in 1970, all incentive for someone on the East Coast to spend $400 on a procedure and $300 on a plane ticket evaporated.[22]

Entrepreneurs tried to capitalize during the two-year window. Ellen Glascock wrote in her college's alumni magazine in 1972, "Deeply concerned with the population explosion . . . a friend and I decided to tackle the crisis by helping to ease the abortion situation." The company they set up, the British Referral Service and Travel Agency, was inspired by the legalization of abortions in England. Women, as nonresidents, could pay to have an abortion in private clinics. Another company, operating out of Springfield, Massachusetts, set up a similar service, charging $1,250 for a "London Trip & Abortion."[23]

Headlines in the United States expressed alarm: "American Girls Hooked on Abortion Deal" (Fort Myers, Florida) and "'Pirates' Hijack Women" (Tampa Bay, Florida). The language was explosive, claiming that the abortion business was booming, and travel agencies were deluged with phone calls, with one headline touting an investigation of "Mass Abortions in London." Newspapers chronicled the profits secured by the travel agents in the United States and the commissions scored by the touts at the London airport with a weary sense that the duped women had overpaid. One captioned photograph of a woman in London for abortion read, "the country has been flooded with unwed mothers on 'vacation.'" The coverage ignored women's desperation and purpose.[24]

It was primarily those with means who could travel abroad: either wealthy women, a man who could pay, or those working who could borrow and repay the steep costs. A 1969 reporter criticized women who went off to "some other country for the grand rest cure" but returned home silently, not fighting for abortion law repeals so that all women could be "cured." In part this is not surprising, as few women returned home from having an abortion fired up to make social or political changes. While they shared the experience of desperate abortion travel with millions of other American women, unlike with most tourism that was documented and savored, these women wanted to immediately put the experience away and forget it. It was more than a decade later, as a leading women's rights activist, that Gloria Steinem publicly acknowledged her 1957 illegal abortion in London.[25]

And yet, for all the hype with NBC reporters on the ground in London, it was not truly a big event. Relatively few American women went to England for abortions. It may be that travel to England was not foreign enough, or that it was too expensive, or that it took too long to fly there, be hospitalized for the procedure, and fly back. One travel package stated that the trip "usually lasts five days." When the largest London clinic (Langham Street) complained that its clients were being "hijacked" by competitors in 1970, they reported losing only three or four women a week.[26]

Japan

In contrast to England, Japan was relatively unseen as an abortion destination. Women who got abortions on the island nation secured distance, legality, and exceptional expertise. In 1955, Japan recorded 1.2 million abortions, which dropped to a still-staggering 740,000 in 1967. Most of the abortions were done by the twelfth week, but the country's 1952 Eugenic Protection Law allowed for abortions up to the twenty-eighth week, so the doctors had experience, particularly distinctive for late-term abortions.[27]

Japan, therefore, stood out as the one place where American women could safely go for abortions after twelve weeks. Given the country's proximity to the West Coast, the Association to Repeal Abortion Laws, supported by Cordelia Scaife May, included Japan as an option, with detailed instructions. Newspapers published this information as well, with headlines like "Abortions: $20 in Japan, $550 in Mexico." The CCS appears to have held Japan as an option for women in need of more specialized care, as with one woman who needed an abortion at twenty weeks. She traveled to England but the British doctor would not take the case, and so her desperate ob-gyn in the Shenandoah Valley reached out to a minister with the CCS who supplied the name of a doctor in Japan. The minister reflected that the woman in crisis got help, and it was a very positive experience for him to be able to send her to someone experienced and legally able to help. For the woman's part, it was extraordinarily expensive to pay travel expenses to two countries and nerve wracking to face the deadly consequences of continuing the pregnancy.[28]

Nor was the CCS alone in referring women to Japan. A San Francisco doctor recounted that he sent his upper-class patients to Japan; the relatively inexpensive procedure ($75 in 1967) helped offset the $700 airfare. It appears that Japan was a very good option if women could afford the flight. The airfare costs certainly escalated for those traveling from New York, with Sheila Raskin detailing that she paid $2,600, which included bringing a friend, "you know, because I felt I couldn't quite handle all of the details myself." She traveled to Japan after a failed attempt in New York, and emphasized the contrast, noting that while it was "very, very expensive," Japan "was a very pleasant, warm kind of an experience. The doctors were humane. . . . I didn't feel like a criminal . . . people treated me like a human being."[29]

The most hyped attention to Japan's legal abortions came with the publicity surrounding Sherri (Finkbine) Chessen's 1962 quest to terminate her pregnancy after it was revealed that the thalidomide she had taken could harm her fetus. Determined to discourage Americans' interest in Japan as an abortion destination, after Chessen was denied a therapeutic abortion in Arizona, Japan did not offer her a visa, forcing her to turn to Sweden. So, on the media-saturated international stage, the country said no, but newspaper reporting and the efforts of abortion referral groups tell a different story. The Japanese Medical Society had a "policy against performing abortions on foreigners," and during the 1964 Tokyo Olympics, the newsletter of the designated abortion providers' group Nichibo underlined the importance "of not giving foreign visitors the impression that it was easy to get an abortion in Japan." The Japanese press was aware that its policies were attractive to foreigners who could not secure abortions in their own country. In the United States it appears that Japanese doctors and officials made subtle efforts to encourage abortion business, as well as general tourism, as long as it was not a featured story in the news.[30]

Japanese newspapers generally reacted negatively to the country's identity as an "abortion paradise," including the 1967 coverage of a Tokyo ob-gyn's letter—in English—sent to doctors and hospitals in the United States. Just as American providers and hospitals solicited for referrals and promised kickbacks, this doctor promised to give doctors what they needed—a referral, the assurance that he spoke English and could communicate with patients, and a record of success. He noted that "Some of our patients flew back to America on the next day of their arrival here, with relief and satisfaction." "You might be asked for your advice on these matters," he wrote. "Simply let her fly to Tokyo and leave the rest to us. Your introduction will be appreciated and 10 percent of the patient's payment for operation fee will be paid to you as your introduction fee." Another American doctor recalled English-language solicitations saying "Fly your patient to Japan. She'll be met by an English-speaking driver and taken straight to the clinic."[31]

Japan Air Lines had a monopoly on the routes from New York, Honolulu, San Francisco, and Los Angeles to Tokyo through at least 1968, when they faced increased competition from US carriers. The government of Japan owned more than half of the company and did not appear to discourage the effort to market to women seeking abortions to increase ridership. Moreover, as we saw in Chapter 2, the airline worked with the Bank of Tokyo to offer credit as well. A California doctor reported that an airline was offering package tours that included round-trip airfare, two nights at a good hotel, abortion, and hospitalization. Travel agencies in Seattle and Honolulu sold Japanese "abortion package tours," including one for four days, with a day of sightseeing built in to it. That may have been to appease a Japanese consulate-general who asserted that the country only issued visas to those wishing to travel to Japan and "to promote tourism and trade relations." The Association to Repeal Abortion Laws cautioned in the list of guidance provided to women seeking abortions: "It is not legal to go to Japan for an abortion. If anyone knows of your purpose to Japan, your visa can be denied." An abortion inquiry into a travel agent in Salem, Oregon, found complete support and forthcoming information. The agent said, "It's all done in the Central Clinic in Tokyo by Dr. Eto. It's sparkling clean. It's really very simple. There's not a thing to worry about." Especially along the West Coast and in Hawai'i, Japan subtly allowed abortion providers to play up their availability to women in need.[32]

Mexico

Of all the known destinations for illegal abortions, Mexico is probably the best studied historically. Scholars have studied the significance of white American women's abortion travel and the Mexican people working in the industry in the border towns, as well as exploring its social, medical, and political effects for both countries. Historians Lina-Maria Murillo, Alicia Gutierrez-Romine, and Leslie Reagan have offered excellent analyses of the abortion experience along the shared border. Both real-time coverage and historical studies of Mexico have described the efforts of activist Patricia Maginnis and her organizations, the Society for Humane Abortion and the Association to Repeal Abortion Laws. Along with Lana Phelan and Rowena Gurner, the California organizations offered information about safe abortions in other parts of the world, which included Puerto Rico and Japan, and most especially neighboring Mexico.[33]

This consideration of Mexico as a destination for abortions, therefore, builds on this nuanced understanding, but shifts the focus from the experiences of Anglo women seeking abortions along the border to consider how organizations and businesses across the United States funneled patients to the capital, Mexico City. It was an almost entirely male enterprise, with the CCS, Planned Parenthood, and Bob McCoy's Minneapolis referral service joined by entrepreneurial men who created a national business largely centered on delivering women to Mexico City. Of course, women were active in sending women, too, but most organizations appeared to be nonprofit. One organizer, Catherine Cameron, remembered making phone calls and appointments for women at University of California, Santa Barbara, in 1967. She was part of a network of women, including a sorority at UCLA, that helped women fly to Mexico. Even with frequent crackdowns, continual payoffs, and referral kickbacks, it was an incredibly lucrative business for providers in Mexico.[34]

A document created for women who sought referrals from the CCS offered detailed instructions about how to proceed. Empowering women to know what to bring, what to say, and even where to turn left into the "Banco Nacional de Mexico," the typewritten guide also offered women guidance on how to catch the right cab, what they would have to pay for it, and assurances about the hotel suite they would share with three other women. Unique among the travel guidance, the clergy suggested that women avoid raw fruit, vegetables, and tap water, encouraging them to "drink Cokes" instead. The advice was both very specific and vaguely generic, referencing only "other fees involving your visit" that would need to be paid in US dollars and not traveler's checks, with no specific details concerning the abortion.[35]

In a July 1970 typewritten "confidential" document, someone in the Chicago CCS detailed the costs for an abortion in Mexico City, ranging from $200 to $400 (through sixteen weeks). The Mexican provider encouraged women to wear a white ribbon so they could recognize each other, but to remove it before entering the country. The description of the facility to which the women were taken was tantalizing: "The clinic is housed in a beautiful Spanish mansion, and is spotless. The whole staff is extraordinarily hospitable, and all speak English." The doctor arranged for the accommodations as well, reserving "four suites of two rooms each in the following first class hotel on Mexico's finest boulevard." Women were instructed to tell the desk clerk that "Mr. Tony sent them." With assurances from the clergy and instructions on which flights to book, Chicago-area women working with the CCS to obtain abortions in Mexico City were well prepared.[36]

In 1970, the Iowa Planned Parenthood organization sent some of the seventy-five Iowa women they saw each week to Mexico City. Bob McCoy's private referral service encouraged Minnesota women less than fifteen weeks pregnant to fly to a clinic in Mexico City, operated by Dr. Armando Ponce. For a fee of $550, plus travel costs, the Mexican clinic made hotel reservations for the women at the San Jorge Hotel, which McCoy described as "posh and rather fabulous." He contrasted it with some of the domestic options available to women in the United States, which he described as dirty and dangerous, and assured women that the Mexican doctor he worked with was safe and reliable. McCoy reported sending the majority of the 650 women he referred to Ponce in Mexico over ten years. Even when they secured proximity to legal abortions in Kansas, some abortion referral groups in Missouri and Nebraska preferred to set up trips to Mexico City, which promised lower costs and less red tape.[37]

The Problem Pregnancy Counseling Service (later renamed the Problem Pregnancy Information Service), from 1970–1972, relied heavily on Mexico to provide abortions for five thousand women. With advertisements and a dozen offices across the country, the men offered local phone numbers and a supportive service that advised on the hotel and flights and arranged abortions for a set price. A sixteen-year-old girl who flew from Florida to Atlanta to Mexico City remarked that "It's almost like a travel agency. The counseling service works out every detail in advance and answered all my questions." In October 1970, the service offered women a choice of Mexico City or New York; at that time Mexico was the cheapest and the most popular choice. Counselors encouraged women to take more than just a small case, so that they would appear to be tourists, and then offered clear instructions about which hotel to call, how to change their money, and a description of the car that would pick them up.[38]

Of course, many American women went to abortion providers in Mexican border towns like Ciudad Juarez, Nogales, and Tijuana, as well, as they also came recommended and were within driving distance of the US border. Mexican doctors generally charged less than American providers, with one in 1970 telling an Austin patient that he provided six abortions a day, six days a week, and charged $350. However, one appeal of Mexico City, far in the interior of the country, was that by necessitating air travel, it avoided the scrutiny of crossing the border. It was easier for women to disguise the true intention of the trip, bringing more luggage and buying conspicuous tchotchkes. Newspaper coverage in June 1970 described one clinic in a quiet suburb of Mexico City, dubbed "casa de las gringas," as "one of the world's busiest abortion mills." The doctor charged $1,300 per abortion and reportedly spent some of it for protection locally and "kickbacks for referrals from the U.S."[39]

While many of the Mexican clinics relied on referrals from Maginnis's list, some also employed traditional marketing strategies like flyers and letters. The *Medical World News* magazine estimated that one provider in Ciudad Juarez, Mexico, mailed a hundred thousand solicitation letters to US doctors "from California to Connecticut" seeking referrals. With disdainful language, the reporters investigated the "shady operation," in a border city "already famous for quickie divorces," to capture the "sordid account of misrepresentation, bribery, and greed." The reproduced letter described the equipment, and the reporters noted a special reference to "the most modern Japanese surgical suction equipment." Using that country's decades-long experience and technological knowhow, along with the guise of medical authority, to promote abortions in

Mexico in 1968, the clinic scaled up their service. At the height of the Ciudad Juarez abortion juggernaut, competing with "dozens of clinics," the clinic reportedly did twenty to twenty-five abortions a week.[40]

Serving a Region

Kansas

In the middle of the country, Kansas citizens lived on what was effectively an island, separated by the greatest distance from more visible abortion providers on the coasts, and with no legalized abortion in any surrounding states. Along with fears of overpopulation, concerns about fairness, changing attitudes on the part of the medical profession, and the growing women's movement, geographic context is important to understanding why Kansas chose to reform its abortion laws. Adopting a therapeutic model that allowed for abortions with permission from three doctors was seen as a humane way to address the estimated five thousand to seven thousand illegal abortions performed in the state. Kansas doctors then approved 98 percent of those seeking abortions as having met the emotional or physical danger to the woman's health provision, if they had been approved by three doctors, at least one of whom had to be licensed by the state. As the key advocate, Kermit Krantz, framed it, the proposed 1971 law aimed to "bring the problem of abortion out of the dark ages and make it into the instrument of human charity that it is." The local newspaper the *Lawrence Daily-Journal World* carried a syndicated article that explored why over 80 percent of students emphasized the inherent fairness in legalizing abortion, with the arcane laws penalizing the poor disproportionately.[41]

It is perhaps reflective of the overall acceptance of the state's decision to enact abortion reforms that many of the articles covering the law and supportive editorials appeared deep in the newspaper, rather than snagging above-the-fold, front-page coverage. This was true of the more plentiful coverage focused on New York's new law as well as Kansas's. The *Wichita Eagle*, for example, placed its abortion reform coverage on the first page of its "Of Interest to Women" section. Of course, it could be that the newspapers hoped to mute the coverage and quietly enable adoption of the law without much notice. The male legislature relied heavily on the medical authority of Krantz and his male colleagues to advance the reformed law.[42]

Kansas's border with Missouri, and especially the conjoined twin Kansas Cities, likely helped determine that there would be no residency requirement. Unlike other states that passed reform bills, the intention to provide equity of care for all women in need gave doctors the authority to approve women's abortion requests. This provision empowering doctors' authority (along with the requirement that the procedures be done in approved hospitals) appears to have fueled medical support for offering legal abortions.[43]

With the required bureaucracy, the cost of abortion stayed high ($400–$600), but some hospitals aimed to meet the needs of those who could not afford to pay. As a leading ob-gyn at the Kansas University Medical Center (KMC) in Kansas City, Kansas, and longtime advocate for the reform of the state's abortion laws, Kermit Krantz argued, "We can no longer have first and second class levels of care." Although he began his efforts in 1962 concerned with the threat of overpopulation, he soon turned to publicly championing women's rights and the needs of the poor. He called for "the assurance of 'equal justice under the law'" and the principle that a "human being is a human being regardless of economy," and strived to ensure that the cost of abortions at KMC was "based on the patient's ability to pay."[44]

Kansas women also had abortion access in many locations, including fifty accredited hospitals in the largest cities (Topeka, Wichita, and Kansas City) as well as in fifteen smaller communities. This unusual and extensive geographical access existed in spite of the fact that the law did not require doctors or hospitals to provide abortions. The state also decided not to release information about these hospitals individually, so as to discourage scrutiny and harassment; only year-end statistics about abortions performed were provided. When state officials completed their report on the 8,500 women who had abortions in the first year of legalization, they discovered that more than a quarter of the abortions were done at the small, fifty-bed Douglass Hospital. This was surprising because the facility, founded by the African Methodist Episcopal Church as a nursing school and hospital for Black patients, was not accredited and could not legally do abortions under the law. The number exceeded that of the KMC (about 2,200) and the Wesley Medical Center (about 2,000).[45]

The Douglass administrator, responding to a *Kansas City Star* reporter, detailed how the hospital got into the abortion business two months after the law went into effect, recognizing that it could pick up unmet demand from other hospitals, including women who faced delays of five to six weeks or had been outright rejected. The Douglass Hospital also solicited business from referral organizations like the Women's Liberation Abortion Collective (WLAC). The WLAC concluded that "the accreditation requirement is unnecessary and would force Douglass to substantially raise its fees." Patients welcomed the lower price, $250 or $350, rather than the accredited hospital charge of $550. Moreover, a Douglass Hospital administrator affirmed, "We're a charity institution and we try not to turn away anyone in need."[46]

Legalization in Kansas had a national impact. From its central location, Kansas drew 61 percent of its patients from thirty-one other states in the first year alone, including Illinois, Iowa, Nebraska, and Oklahoma. Douglass Hospital reported that 95 percent of its abortion patients came from outside of Kansas, and that "practically all of them look like college girls."[47]

The most significant state to benefit from the new availability of abortions, however, was Missouri, whose residents accounted for two thousand abortion patients in the first year. The president of the Missouri Blue Cross insurance company confirmed that any policy holders in Missouri, as well as their dependents, would be covered for an abortion obtained in Kansas. Missouri media reported on this phenomenon, with headlines like "Abortions in Kansas Affects Birth Rate," taking note of the 2,400 women who obtained abortions in Kansas in 1971, and the 2,000 others who traveled to New York State to do the same. Broader national concerns with population growth and the reported decrease in local birth rates, particularly in Kansas City, Missouri (a decline of 12.8 percent), and St. Louis (8.3 percent), fueled newspaper stories.[48]

An historical marketing analysis of the distribution of abortion services found that Kansas's 12,200 abortions in 1972 delivered on meeting its citizens' needs. In just over two years of providing legal abortion care, the state not only met demand, but found that nearly two-thirds of the abortions served out-of-state women. Although the number of women from Illinois traveling to Kansas declined, residents of neighboring Oklahoma, which like Illinois and Missouri also reported zero legal abortions, increased their totals in Kansas to 1,020.[49]

A state with only one-tenth California's population succeeded in delivering nearly one-third as many abortions to out-of-state women. While current accounts and historical memory tend to locate abortion access in New York or California, Kansas provided the fourth most abortions between legalization in 1970 and *Roe v. Wade*. To offer a contrast, Colorado passed the first liberalized abortion law in 1967, spurred by zero population growth advocate Richard Lamm, and is often mentioned in histories detailing early reform efforts. However, Colorado doctors remained reluctant to care for out-of-state women, who comprised only a few hundred of the dramatically smaller number of the state's 5,300 abortions in 1972.[50]

The rarely mentioned New Mexico had a similar experience to Kansas. In 1971 the *Albuquerque Journal* reported on the strategies imported from New York City and adapted to the state. Two that proved efficient and thus lucrative were to transform the ward within a hospital into an outpatient clinic for abortions, and to rely on volunteers from Planned Parenthood to give instructions and counseling for birth control. Planned Parenthood placed classified ads in Corpus Christi, Texas newspapers encouraging people to call them directly, proclaiming, "Abortion. Legal in New Mexico." The Presbyterian Hospital Center in Albuquerque calculated in 1971 that about forty percent of the abortions were for out-of-state women, with the majority hailing from Texas. In 1972, statewide, New Mexico doctors and hospitals provided six thousand abortions, with nearly 70 percent of them going to out-of-state women.[51]

District of Columbia

New Orleans is famous for being both of the South and distinct from it. So too is Washington, D.C., unique and also intricately connected to the Southern experience with regard to abortion. Although hundreds of thousands of women flew to New York City for abortions, it is clear that many Midwestern and Southern women preferred D.C. While the proximity was especially compelling for women in neighboring Delaware, Maryland, Virginia, and West Virginia, the reach extended to the Deep South. Nor was it accidental. In addition to increased visibility in 1971, reporters discovered that "Thousands of leaflets publicizing the ready availability of abortions in Washington have recently been mailed to doctors in North Carolina, South Carolina, Virginia, and Maryland. Thousands more are being sent to Georgia, Kentucky, and Florida." In August 1971, one D.C. clinic reported women coming from Georgia, Florida, and Missouri. Women doing abortion referrals in Louisville, Kentucky, shifted their clients from New York City to the closer, easier D.C. location starting in December 1971.[52]

The District's identity as a place where anyone could get an abortion, like New York's, was long-standing. In 1950, nearly two decades before complete legalization, the *Evening Star* concluded "Abortion Is a Flourishing Racket Here." As in so many cities, hospitals, especially those serving the poor, faced a deluge of those injured, maimed, or killed by illegal abortion attempts. A representative of D.C.'s Medical Committee for Human Rights conservatively estimated that at least ten thousand illegal abortions were done in the city in 1967. While the poor had limited options for providers and emergency care, the wealthy had many more opportunities. A 1969 Women's Liberation newsletter included not only phone numbers and information about referral options, but also a scathing critique of the city's role in the quest for an abortion. Likely overstating the extent to which a "middle-class woman resident" could get an abortion if she had money, they astutely condemned the horrors that awaited poor women. In 1967, the newsletter alleged, the D.C. General Hospital completed only seven legal abortions, all while caring for eight hundred women endangered by illegal abortions. Meanwhile, in June 1970, a one-woman enterprise operated out of D.C., taking care of passports, vaccinations, and appointments, before shuttling women to London for legal abortions. The wealthiest women could rely on discreet doctors, locally or by traveling.[53]

In March 1970, a federal court decision overturned the District's abortion laws, finding them unconstitutional. The court ruled, "We hold that the right to refuse to carry an embryo during the early stages of pregnancy may not be invaded by the state." As D.C. awaited the appeal to the Supreme Court, the city lacked policies governing emerging businesses, so profiteering quickly took hold. Businesses like the Abortion Information Service sent out hundreds of letters to doctors across the southern United States. After D.C. banned charging for referrals, companies settled in Pennsylvania and Maryland. One underground paper in Baltimore turned the tables, requiring cash-in-advance payments for ads and only accepting those referring women to D.C.[54]

In addition, D.C. was home to many activists, accustomed to skirmishes over not only the city's laws but also the nation's. The Women's National Abortion Action Coalition and the Population Council both opened offices in the nation's capital, and the dual concerns of abortion rights and population control converged with the opening of the Preterm clinic. Two alumni of the Population Council, Harry Levin and Nan McEvoy, moved into the D.C. market and opened Preterm—short for "pregnancy termination." The clinic grew out of both Levin and McEvoy's commitment to controlling population growth. In D.C., Preterm's founders claimed to have gotten $125,000 in gifts and loans that had to be repaid, and therefore put their prices at $200, $50 more than the going rate in New York City. The clinic, according to McEvoy, was created to demonstrate that "abortions could be given outside of a hospital, quickly and cheaply, and at no danger to a woman's life." The support came from Boston, New York, and Washington "benefactors and foundations interested in population control."[55]

Some of the doctors appear to have been solely focused on women's right to an abortion, like Dr. Barbara Roberts, co-founder of the Women's National Abortion Action Coalition, and Dr. Jane Hodgson, the first doctor in the United States to be convicted of performing an illegal abortion in a hospital. In contrast, a male doctor appeared to share Levin and McEvoy's commitment to population control. Preterm began in 1970 as a research organization studying "the problem presented by the increasing population of the world, and the relation of contraception, abortion and sterilization to that population growth."[56]

FIGURE 19. This photo of phone counselors at Preterm clinic shortly after it opened captures the volume of calls as consumers, especially Southern women, sought out legal abortions in Washington, D.C. (*Evening Star* [Washington, D.C.], 12 December 1971). Photo: Rosemary Martufi, courtesy D.C. Public Library Washington Star Collection © Washington Post.

Local Black women who did not have access to a private medical doctor for a referral were among the first to appear at Preterm, but over time the race of the women who sought abortions in D.C. abortion clinics ended up being about 60 percent white. In 1972, newspapers in thirty-one states carried an Associated Press story about abortion in D.C., which one Mississippi paper headlined, "Washington Moving Into the Abortion Ranks." A 1972 reporter captured the geographic diversity of patients at one D.C. clinic. He noted, "Eighty percent of the Maternal Counseling's patients don't live in the District. They come from as far away as Massachusetts and Nebraska. The great majority of them are white girls from small communities in the South, the more remarkable because the clinic's two doctors and most of the nursing and counseling staff are black." Abortions remained, in general, more expensive in D.C. than in New York, with the cheapest abortion, for a pregnancy in the first ten weeks, costing $200. Moreover, referral groups found it more difficult to get free abortions for needy cases in D.C.[57]

San Francisco and Los Angeles

Despite its early abortion reform, introduced by State Representative Anthony Beilenson and signed by Governor Ronald Reagan in 1967, California's optimism and anxiety about its potential identity as an "abortion Mecca" quickly stalled. In the first year after moderate reform was passed, prices and access remained prohibitive, and the state received less than a dozen out-of-state applicants. Even for its own citizens, there were only 518 legal abortions; physician fees and hospital charges made the average cost about $650. One woman said in 1968, "You have to be rich, crazy, or a victim of rape to get an abortion legally in this state. I got mine on a back street for $200 and I'll do it again if I have to." Prices across the state remained high and the number of legal, therapeutic abortions stayed strikingly low, at less than 21,000 through 1969. Of those, only a tiny percentage were done for non-California residents.[58]

Many advocates encouraged a loosened interpretation of the new law and were heartened by the California Supreme Court's 1969 ruling in favor of Dr. Leon Belous, who had been arrested and convicted for a referral two years earlier. Those who wanted to provide abortions and referrals found reason for encouragement. Justice Raymond Peters's majority opinion held "there no longer is a justification for 'the great and direct interference with a woman's constitutional rights' to have an abortion if she so chose." With this new legal landscape, an independent legislative analyst in February 1970 suggested that, to reduce state spending on welfare benefits, there should be a further liberation of abortion laws "so that needy expectant mothers could choose to undergo a therapeutic abortion." The argument he made was that the reduced number of payments for births ($1,500), even offset by abortion costs ($750), would save Medi-Cal $8.8 million, estimating that about one-third of pregnant women on welfare would choose an abortion. This kind of financial argument, hoping either to reduce spending or to increase tax revenues, fueled legislative debates in some states, but did not seem to publicly motivate voters or legislators to provide more accessible or affordable abortions. Still, in a significant change, some California hospitals began to more liberally interpret those under the age of twenty-one as legally emancipated minors, which enabled many more college students to secure abortions.[59]

Others believed that allowing those with little or no financial resources to secure abortions was an equity issue and bemoaned the limited geographic access, with the vast majority of abortions available only in San Diego, San Francisco, and Los Angeles, and still costing upward of $500. The state's Bureau of Maternal and Child Health warned that "concentration of abortions in a few hospitals moves away from the concepts of family practice and a continuing patient-doctor relationship" and wondered how women could "secure their rights if hospitals or physicians do not provide therapeutic abortions in their communities." Planned Parenthood reflected on its role in supporting those with marginal income—new and underpaid workers, college students—and supported affiliates who provided access to low-income patients. All the while, enterprising individuals set up services "selling" (by phone) the "information that may mean the difference between life or death."[60]

Dr. Edmund Overstreet, a professor of obstetrics and gynecology at the University of California School of Medicine, advocated for abortion access where he could, at conferences, to reporters, and in medical journals. He bemoaned the limited number of hospitals willing to do abortions, calling for "some sort of regional distribution centers" and recognition of the perilous economic position of the "lower middle-class woman, just above welfare." His father was a member of the American Eugenics Society and he advocated for a "program of population limitation in his article 'Role of Female Sterilization in Population Control.'" Overstreet argued that America needed "to substitute pregnancy-prevention for pregnancy-obliteration," before population growth took away the choice. Overstreet quoted eugenicist sociologist Kingsley Davis, who coined the terms "population explosion" and "zero population growth," and "pointed out, no nation has yet demonstrated that population growth can be slowed by voluntary family planning methods—unless elective abortion is also used." Using his medical authority and research to demonstrate the need and ability to perform abortions without hospitalization, Overstreet hoped to lower costs and improve access to abortion.[61]

Eugenicist Prynce Hopkins and Joseph Sunnen, philanthropists devoted to population control, funded Planned Parenthood's San Francisco Center for Legal Abortion, subsidizing a drop in the cost of an abortion in California by about half, to $300. Across the bay, Dr. H. B. Van Maren in Oakland had already performed four thousand abortions after legalization in 1967. By the start of 1972, his Special Care Center offered two distinct options that most clinics did not. The first was that he accepted Master Charge and BankAmericacard, early credit cards; most places required cash, which often meant securing a loan. The other significant feature of his practice was that he did saline abortions for pregnancies between thirteen and twenty weeks. He did more salines than any doctor in California, about 15 percent of his total abortions, and did all salines "from Houston, Dallas and Fort Worth." Van Maren took on the more time-consuming procedure, advised for pregnancies beyond fifteen weeks, and facilitated payment with correspondingly higher prices. Desperate women flocked to him from Colorado, Idaho, Nevada, and Oregon. One more feature of his clinic is worth noting: He invested $3,000 in a suction pump that operated from a central point in the office, so the patient did not hear the sounds of her abortion. In San Francisco, the Pregnancy Control Center at Cathedral Hill Medical Center drew women from Texas, Arizona, and Minnesota, and performed five hundred abortions a month. The center's executive director estimated that as many as 20 percent of their patients came from the Midwest. And the smaller Birth Control Institute, doing seventeen abortions in a day, set aside Saturday appointments for girls and women from the area, drawing from Sunnyvale and Los Gatos.[62]

A *San Francisco Examiner* story, "The Business of Abortion," explored area enterprises, reporting on the practices of doctors and hospital business administrators who were remitting a portion of each fee to referring agencies, either in cash or by offering indigent women a free abortion. An Associated Press article that appeared in other states characterized a $250 abortion at Cathedral Hill as "a Cut-Rate Clinic," suggesting that lower prices would be reflective of poor care. Business managers and doctors understood that sticking together to keep costs high was good business. The referrals came in from Planned Parenthood, the Department of Public Health, private doctors, and the Zero Population Growth's San Francisco office—which referred three thousand women in nine months.[63]

Los Angeles, too, had financially savvy practitioners and clinics as early as 1967. Ob-gyn Dr. John Gwynne and psychologist Harvey Karman estimated that together they helped five thousand women get abortions. In 1970, their new location, the Community Service Center and Abortion Clinic, provided ten to fifteen abortions a day—asking only for donations. They depended instead on feminist organizations like the Women's Liberation Front and the National Organization for Women for funding. Gwynne and Karman were two of about fifty other doctors heavily involved with abortions in the Los Angeles area.[64]

Researching this period of widening abortion access in California, sociologist Michael S. Goldstein studied twelve doctors whom he categorized as physician entrepreneurs, men who dominated the emerging market of abortions and aimed to mass-produce abortions by gaining control over small, financially strapped hospitals. As evidence of this dominance, he found that in Los Angeles County, less than 5 percent of the hospitals performed over 90 percent of all abortions between 1967 and 1972. In Goldstein's interviews, the entrepreneurial doctors, who owned and operated their own clinics, reported that financial gain was their primary motivation.[65]

In 1972, state and national media attention focused on two intertwined aspects of abortion emerging in California: the increased arrival of out-of-state women and the bonanza to for-profit referral agencies in kickbacks from hospitals. For the first time, profit-focused Los Angeles reported the most abortions in the state, with San Francisco trailing behind. Geographic proximity and marketing in states like Nevada, Arizona, and Texas helped referral agencies drum up business. With a steady stream of customers, the organizations could then develop a "group fare flight that leaves Dallas every Saturday for Los Angeles. It's always full and never popular. To qualify you have to need an abortion."[66]

FIGURE 20. This drawing told the story of thousands of women flying from Southwestern states to California to secure abortions. Nationally, the number of women traveling, usually alone, often with just a small suitcase, made them identifiable to flight attendants, some of whom trained to care for them. Problem Pregnancy Information Service claimed to be Southwest Airlines' second-largest ticket buyer. Drawing by Dean Waite. With permission from the *Argus-Leader* (Sioux Falls, South Dakota, 16 April 1972).

The Problem Pregnancy Information Service (PPIS) agency put together the package deal, charging $346 for plane, transportation, doctor, motel, hospital, and counseling for women in Dallas and Houston. The agency's welcome team in Los Angeles greeted about seventy girls and women a week, transported them to the motel, and then picked them up at 5 a.m. to make the trip to the twenty-two-bed hospital. One woman decried the assembly-line practice of the doctor, who operated on each woman in just a few minutes before moving on to the next, making "a fortune off of our misfortune." In her back-of-the-napkin calculation, she realized that, for not even a full day's work, at $50 a person, the doctor was easily pulling down $100,000 a year. The chief of California's family planning service toured an L.A. hospital that performed "1,000 abortions a month, many of them for out-of-state women through a package arrangement with an airline and motel and decided, 'it's not ideal, but it's better than knitting needles and crochet hooks.'"[67]

The takeover of small, "Mickey Mouse" hospitals in financial trouble was key to the success of the California physician entrepreneurs and the referral agencies. As Goldstein concluded: "the entrepreneurs tried to monopolize the market for legal abortions by changing them from a commodity typically delivered in a traditional individualized doctor-patient relationship to a standardized, mass-produced commodity in facilities specially created or modified for this purpose." One doctor recalled that by November 1969 he was making $22,000 a month, and three years later he was clearing over $2 million a year. Another doctor invited Goldstein to tour his facility, where TV monitors ensured all employees kept working efficiently. The doctor had left a traditional hospital and started his own to ensure that he was able to "do big numbers." The traditional institution "wouldn't touch advertising or making the referral connections you needed to keep the numbers up." Also alleviating the time and space pressures on the doctor and hospital, the groups did birth control counseling at their home airports the night before, with thirty to fifty women on each flight. At one twenty-two-bed "Mickey Mouse hospital" the owner had given the doctor a percentage of the profits to turn the hospital's finances around, and he brought in 1,700 abortion patients a month.[68]

Giving the hospitals financial life gave the doctors control, because a doctor could "threaten to remove his business unless the hospital reduced its charges" or otherwise complied with his demands. This meant enterprising doctors dominated the hospital's finances and work rules, to ensure more profits for themselves. The hospitals certainly stood to profit, too. In 1972, one observer calculated that the hospital's charges, at $75 per abortion for five minutes in the operating room, could mean over $3,500 a day, yielding over $1 million in one hospital, in one year.[69]

The marriage between supply and demand that enabled hospitals to profit and retain doctors was brokered by the referral organizations—nonprofit and for-profit alike. Tulare County's Family Planning Program adhered to the state guidelines that no money go toward abortions to such an extent that they called collect when they wanted to make a referral to a hospital. The director of PPIS, Bob Matson, generated so much business that he rented a fleet of station wagons and vans "that moves constantly between the airport and a hotel where girls coming in stay overnight." Workers in a two-bedroom apartment in El Segundo fielded a hundred calls a day, and the volume of women seeking abortions enabled Matson to "arrange cut-cost group rates with doctors, hospitals, motels and even airlines." According to Matson, PPIS was the second biggest customer of Southwest Airlines in 1972. Big profits meant lots of consumers, which meant looking out of state. The organization averaged six hundred referrals a month to Bel Air Hospital and others.[70]

By keeping costs high, abortion providers generated staggering profits. With California reporting 138,600 abortions in 1972, analysts determined that only 16.1 percent were for out-of-state women. Those 22,176 women—equivalent to the number of women who got abortions in Washington, D.C., that year—received care almost entirely from fifty-six Los Angeles physicians. One of the leading actors in finding those women was Henry "Hank" Dubin, who made $100,000 in 1972 working as a "business agent for at least five Los Angeles–area hospitals." He was encouraged to hustle patients for them, starting out making 10 percent of the fee on each woman. Dubin told a reporter for a short-lived weekly newspaper that after three months in the business "they're calling me 'Mr. Abortion,'" and she heralded him as the reigning abortion king. Three months later *Newsweek* reported that he had moved to St. Michael's Hospital, where he expected to net $1.5 million from facilitating abortions.[71]

The Feminist Women's Health Center got $50 for each of the 150 to 200 referrals they sent to Dubin each month. The Women's Clinic had a smaller volume (sending only 40 to 50), but it is likely that they were able to get a finder's fee, too. Carol Downer, head of the Feminist Women's Health Center, told *Newsweek* that Dubin "wants good care for women," and that he had lowered prices, but did not acknowledge that the Center also got a referral fee. George Collins, a doctor who gratefully relied on his abortion referrals, thanked the day he met Dubin and estimated

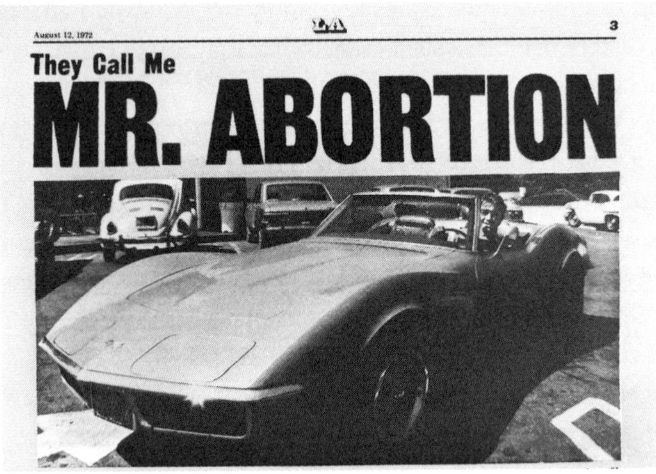

FIGURE 21. California had a booming private abortion industry, fueled by entrepreneurs who worked with small, struggling hospitals. They picked up women who flew to Los Angeles, arranged overnight accommodations, and transported them to the procedure. One of the most successful, Henry "Hank" Dubin, made $100,000 in 1972, working as a "business agent for at least five Los Angeles–area hospitals" (They Call Me Mr. Abortion," *LA*, 12 August 1972). Author's collection.

that his income had increased tenfold to $240,000. Whether they merely tolerated the entrepreneurs or embraced them fully, feminists, referral groups, doctors, and hospitals all stood to gain in California.[72]

Conclusion

Traveling for an abortion was often not a woman's first effort to terminate her pregnancy. Faced with a pregnancy, many girls and women tried desperately to terminate themselves. Although the coat hanger is a symbol of these efforts, it was not the only instrument of an improvised self-abortion. In a 1969 abortion speak-out, Gloria Steinem said that when she was faced with an unwanted pregnancy in the late 1950s, "I had been doing all of the foolish things that we then did [to terminate a pregnancy], like riding horseback, throwing ourselves down stairs." At age nineteen, a college student was hysterical about her pregnancy; she later recalled in a deposition that she had tried drinking a lot of gin, ingested a lot of nutmeg, and taken mustard baths, but nothing happened. A doctor told her to take a large quantity of pills intended for headaches, to trigger an abortion. Instead, "I became deaf for 12 hours. I thought I was going to die." At that point, she "[h]adn't been to school in a month or six weeks, and not out of bed . . . nothing.'" In the 1972 movie *To Find a Man*, a pregnant teenage girl away at boarding school tries jumping from heights, drinking castor oil, and douching with soda, but other girls and women tried even more dangerous and deadly efforts. Then, as now, nothing short of medical intervention would safely terminate a pregnancy, and it demanded searching for someone to do it.[73]

Sociologist Nancy Howell wrote *The Search for an Abortionist* in 1969, based on the research she did for her Harvard dissertation. The most important takeaway from studying pregnant women who searched for someone to do an abortion was that their mission was desperate. They were not comparison shopping or looking for deals; they needed someone to help them, and time was of the essence. In studying the process, Howell found that many women considered and tried several methods of abortion before seeking an operation—legal or otherwise. Twenty-five of the 114 women, for example, attempted to do "Unusual exercise or exertion." Thirty-two took "Hot or cold baths." Even when the woman (and sometimes her partner) began looking, it was not a linear path. The 114 women studied went to a total of 324 people directly for help, with some people getting lucky and finding an abortionist in just a few tries, but with some having to start over repeatedly and consulting nine or more people.[74]

A 1972 study of three referral agencies in Phoenix found that most women got their referral to the agency through the newspaper, friends, a doctor, or other advertising, with each group finding success in different avenues. Reflecting the overwhelming racial composition of those seeking abortion referrals, 86 percent of the clients were white, and two-thirds were either students or working women. In comparing the women who contacted each organization, the study speculated that the PPIS may have been "less threatening and therefore more appealing to students" with their over-the-phone counseling.[75]

Travel was not always an option for girls and women, due to cost, school and work obligations, health, or childcare demands. We will likely never know very much about the millions of abortions that took place on kitchen tables, in closed offices in the dark, and at any number of untoward locations. Small-scale operators could not generally command the same kind of fees as medical doctors and often only promised to start the bleeding, with the expectation that women would need to go to the hospital to have the abortion completed.[76]

The women and girls who could fund the trip had a life-altering experience. Whether they traveled to a place where abortions were legal or one where illicit providers paid off those who otherwise might have cracked down, the outcome was the same: money paid, procedure procured. The ritual ensured that she could return home not pregnant and resume her life. Traveling provided the physical and mental distance to allow the abortion to be compartmentalized and locked away.[77]

The financial desire for lucrative business was offset by fears of becoming what was consistently referred to as the "abortion capital"—whether of the country or the world, it was a title no one seemed to want. Residents of cities like Grove, Oklahoma, Peoria, Illinois, and Portland, Oregon, and states that wanted to broaden access decried their identity as an abortion destination. The biggest destination for US women, however, was New York, the subject of the next chapter. New York purposefully chose to legalize abortions for all up to twenty-four weeks. The vast majority of abortions helped women at twelve weeks or less, and the public attention to the safe, new, and increasingly affordable access led more women to New York, with the rate of those arriving later in pregnancy declining between 1970 and 1972. Home to many doctors, hospitals, entrepreneurs, feminists, and national media outlets, New York City, and the entirety of the state, transformed abortion access in the United States.[78]

6

Making New York City the Abortion Capital

WHEN NEW YORK STATE legalized abortion in 1970, it unleashed a torrent of ambitious business plans to provide abortions. Feminists, abortion providers, entrepreneurs, and administrators laid the groundwork for a July 1 opening date. Intending abortions to be available to all, the lawmakers enabled abortions "on demand"—meaning a woman did not have to justify or explain her rationale to anyone, did not have to be from New York, and as long as she was eighteen she did not need permission from a parent. New York's abortion market held out an abortion to any woman who wanted one.[1]

Analysts anticipated a staggering demand for abortions. With only a couple of months to get everything ready, the situation favored those with business experience and abortion know-how. The emerging clinics and private hospitals operated with budgets, shift work, regulations, and advertising strategies. Whether fueled by compassion for women who needed abortions or a get-rich scheme, New York brought people together in pursuit of the best, safest way to provide abortions.[2]

Leading figures in the abortion law repeal movement debated how to prepare for the expected deluge of women. Only nine hundred women had secured legal, therapeutic abortions in the city in 1968, and working estimates anticipated 20,000 to 100,000 city residents seeking abortions.

With no residency requirement, however, there was also tremendous uncertainty about how many women would be arriving from the rest of the country, or the world, and estimates reached as high as a half million additional women descending on the city starting on July 1, 1970.[3]

Grave concerns emerged about the lack of medical knowledge and experience. One worried observer noted, "The operation was not done in large enough numbers for doctors to develop a widely shared body of knowledge." The average New York City gynecologist, for example, did "about one abortion a year." To support his colleagues' new role, Dr. Bernard Nathanson "organized a day-long training session on the techniques of out-of-hospital abortions." The hope for some was that by allowing doctors to perform abortions in their offices, abortion could be a shared responsibility for all doctors and achieve the normalcy of other standard procedures, like a "tonsillectomy, with no more red tape, committees, humiliation or exploitation."[4]

Policymakers and researchers wanted data to substantiate that legalization transformed the procedure from one that killed women to a safe one with few complications and no deaths. Building on a history of monitoring pregnancies and births dating back to the nineteenth century, the city required "certificates of termination of pregnancy for every abortion performed." For the municipal hospitals, the city demanded a daily phone call tabulating numbers of abortions, and for all facilities, a weekly report. Medical scholars like Jean Pakter and Frieda Nelson created questionnaires to measure everything they could about abortion consumers and the people and places providing abortions. Nine months later, when the first terminated pregnancies would have otherwise been born, they proudly reported on what New York had delivered: an excellent record, besting those held by countries with much more experience. As the *New York Times* reported, "well over 100,000 legal abortions have been performed in New York City. The rate is now about 15,000 a month and it shows signs of increasing steadily rather than abating. New York City has, in fact, become the abortion capital of the country. And, remarkably, its medical resources have been quite successful in meeting this vast new demand." The city rose to meet the challenge.[5]

One policy that evolved within the first few months responded to the fact that initially any doctor could perform early abortions anywhere, including in their office suites. Before the city outlawed them, "An undetermined number of abortions—mostly on out-of-town women—were performed in physicians' offices." Thereafter, and with a new emphasis on licensing, the city tightened its grip on abortion providers. The need to capture the number of abortions, to ensure safe conditions, and to monitor the process, led the NYC Board of Health to take the action of eliminating this option. With the new Health Code (Article 42), the city required that a non-hospital abortion service "have a formal connection with and be within 10 minutes travel time of a hospital in case of complications or emergencies." If the provider did not have a backup, they had to purchase a daunting number of emergency elements that cost about $250,000. Clinics had to have an "operating room capable of performing abdominal surgery, and have x-ray, laboratory and blood bank facilities, adequately staffed in all these areas." Some doctors found workarounds, shuttling patients by limousine across city lines, where they would do the procedure before sending them back, or buying offices just over the city line or near the airport to circumvent the health code, but most were forced to reckon with increased scrutiny and oversight. Activist Susan Reverby argued in 1970 that prioritizing hospitals, despite scientific evidence that the clinics were as safe—if not safer—was a travesty. She contended that the new law put power in the hands of men operating the hospitals. After they eliminated the doctor's offices, the city introduced draconian demands on the new clinics that successfully met the tremendous out-of-state demand.[6]

As one Atlanta reporter reflected after a full year of legal abortion, the "law of supply and demand created, almost overnight, clinics and 'groups' to meet the needs of women flooding New York City. . . ." Hospitals, clinics, and referral groups worked to provide 181,821 abortions.

Fortunately, by the time legalization took hold, many practitioners brought experience with the procedure and benefited from steady improvements in tools and techniques. One transformative aspect of legalization was the ability to safely use localized pain medication. The localized anesthetic also made the experience faster and much more tolerable for women.[7]

The Miami Herald
For and about WOMEN
Sunday, September 27, 1970 Section H

Florida Mother Goes to New York

'I Had a Legal Abortion'

'I want to tell how I went about it so other women won't be afraid. I was afraid but it was the best decision I ever made. My husband thinks so, too, but my doctor blew his stack.'

FIGURE 22. Newspapers across the country reported on women who traveled to New York for an abortion, offering assurance that it was safe, easy, and affordable. Drawings like this one helped women picture the experience as sisterly and relaxed, and a trip they could take. It included an excerpt from the article, concluding "I was afraid but it was the best decision I ever made. My husband thinks so, too." Drawing by Cathy Eignus. With permission from the *Miami Herald* (27 September 1970).

Not only did the city deliver on nearly 200,000 reported abortions in that first year, it also achieved, according to a report at the 1971 annual American Public Health Association meeting, "the lowest maternal mortality rate in New York City history, a marked drop-off in deaths associated with abortion, and a significant decrease in out-of-wedlock births." The majority of the women were in their twenties; teens accounted for another quarter of those who had abortions in New York City. With legalization, the city became tied to abortion to such an extent that popular comedian Milton Berle could joke that the only reason he left California to come to New York was for the abortions. The city also earned the deep appreciation of patients and doctors across the country. A Michigan doctor spoke up at a medical meeting to "'thank New York for its remarkable job' and said that he and his colleagues were 'extremely grateful there is some place we can send our patients and know they will receive safe, excellent care.'" Clinics and hospitals in New York City, which housed just 2 percent of the US population, served about 10 percent of "the national 'demand' for termination of unwanted pregnancy." With pioneering political and medical leadership, the state of New York, and particularly New York City, met the challenges with new legislation and policies to provide safe, legal abortions.[8]

Suburban and Upstate New York

Following the legalization of abortion in New York, clinics opened not just within New York City but also in three major population centers north, northwest, and east of the city. Just over the Hudson River, Rockland County had about 200,000 residents. Westchester County north of the city was home to 900,000 people, with a population larger than San Francisco and Washington, D.C. Nassau County, Long Island, had a population of one and half million, with Hempstead, its largest city, home to about half of them. Operating a clinic in the suburbs offered lower overhead, better parking, and commuter rail, with easy access to doctors for hire.[9]

One of the towns that was an abortion destination was Monsey, in Rockland County, New York. Doctors opened the Monsey Medical Center in 1971 and appealed directly to college students, including those at the University of Cincinnati, University of Missouri, and Wake Forest University. Offering both addresses and phone numbers, the ads tried to present the clinics as honorable and affordable, to contrast with the more profiteering referral services. With an eye toward women's consumer demand for abortions in Massachusetts, where abortion was illegal, *Boston* magazine, produced by the city's Chamber of Commerce, carried an article that explored one Massachusetts woman's experience getting a legal abortion in Rockland County.[10]

The Pelham clinic opened in Westchester, north of the city, and completed over 25,000 abortions in its first year and a half of operation. When the clinic confronted legal pressures from the village, it responded with "one of the slickest public relations campaigns in the country." Sometimes clinics like Pelham offered discounts for slower days and times. A June 1972 Abortion Rights Association pamphlet listed Pelham's $150 price, but a footnote promised that a woman could save $49 if she specified the "evening program" when making her appointment. Another encouraged women to schedule an abortion on Wednesdays between 3 p.m. and 8 p.m., when it only cost $101. The first director of the clinic recalled that there was "no community reaction against it."[11]

New York magazine's "Special 8-Page Handbook" for abortion services described another Westchester clinic. The Dobbs-Ferry Medical Pavilion, Inc., was in "a quiet, residential area" with "plenty of couches, and picture windows." An article in the *New Republic* described how a Kent State (Ohio) student learned that for a flat fee, the Clergy Consultation Service (CCS) would take care of everything—transportation to and from the airport, plane tickets, a car to the clinic in Dobbs Ferry, as well as her trip home. A driver came and picked her up at her dormitory to take her to the airport, and she noticed another girl sitting inside the car. When she arrived in New York, a man was waiting at LaGuardia Airport to shepherd her and several other women into three vans.[12]

The clergy sent thousands of women to Westchester. For example, Reverend William Kirby, a leader in the Missouri chapter of the CCS and a chaplain at Stephens College, a small, private women's school in Columbia, Missouri, described getting students from the campus to Dobbs Ferry: "They were shuttled to the St. Louis airport, where they would catch an American Airlines flight to LaGuardia, using a specific American Airlines flight because a nurse that worked with them had trained the flight attendants so that they knew what to do if a woman began to hemorrhage on her journey home." From his chapter alone, he estimated that he sent three thousand Missouri women to Dobbs Ferry.[13]

With the Long Island Rail Road and easy access to the airports, the Abortion Rights Association's Clinic Directory recommended two clinics on Long Island: Dr. Saul Bilik, who did about 350 abortions a month in June 1972, and the largest clinic on the island, Eastgate Medical Center in Garden City, which did about a thousand abortions a month. The vast majority of the nearly nine thousand abortions in its first two years

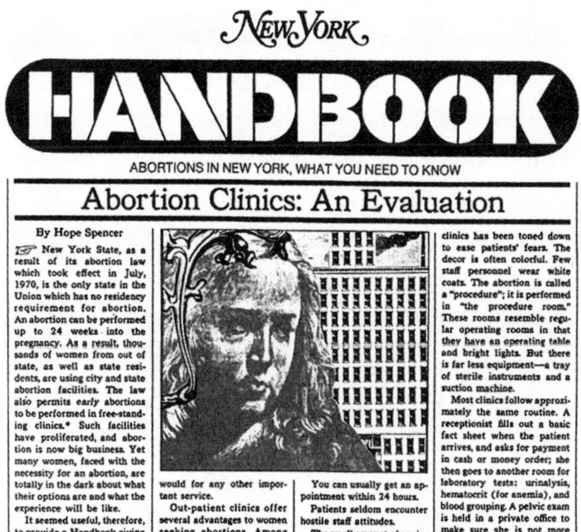

New York

HANDBOOK

ABORTIONS IN NEW YORK, WHAT YOU NEED TO KNOW

Abortion Clinics: An Evaluation

By Hope Spencer

New York State, as a result of its abortion law which took effect in July, 1970, is the only state in the Union which has no residency requirement for abortion. An abortion can be performed up to 24 weeks into the pregnancy. As a result, thousands of women from out of state, as well as state residents, are using city and state abortion facilities. The law also permits *early* abortions to be performed in free-standing clinics.* Such facilities have proliferated, and abortion is now big business. Yet many women, faced with the necessity for an abortion, are totally in the dark about what their options are and what the experience will be like.

It seemed useful, therefore, to provide a Handbook giving

would for any other important service.

Out-patient clinics offer several advantages to women seeking abortions. Among

You can usually get an appointment within 24 hours.

Patients seldom encounter hostile staff attitudes.

The small amount of equip-

clinics has been toned down to ease patients' fears. The decor is often colorful. Few staff personnel wear white coats. The abortion is called a "procedure"; it is performed in "the procedure room." These rooms resemble regular operating rooms in that they have an operating table and bright lights. But there is far less equipment—a tray of sterile instruments and a suction machine.

Most clinics follow approximately the same routine. A receptionist fills out a basic fact sheet when the patient arrives, and asks for payment in cash or money order; she then goes to another room for laboratory tests: urinalysis, hematocrit (for anemia), and blood grouping. A pelvic exam is held in a private office to make sure she is not more

FIGURE 23. New York had just a few months to prepare for legalization. Abortion consumers needed help connecting with abortion providers, so *New York* magazine published a special eight-page pull-out guide to New York abortion facilities, which offered evaluations of providers and clear guidance on locations, costs, and the process (24 July 1972).

were for out-of-state women. Two of the founders of a referral group in Louisville, Kentucky, Nancy Gall-Clayton and Johanna Camenisch, reflected, "Because we made so many referrals to Eastgate, we were able to negotiate for one in ten abortions at no cost." By February 1972 the Kentucky women had made more than a thousand referrals. This type of arrangement was common, with a discount ensuring loyalty and care for poor women.[14]

For some women, traveling to or within upstate New York was easier and cheaper. Upstate abortion clinics, though, struggled to find doctors willing to work. For most local ob-gyn doctors willing to do abortions, the procedure was not their sole or even primary focus, and filling their schedule with these patients risked agitating or losing their regular ones. Many upstate doctors and anesthesiologists refused to work on weekends, the most popular days for women seeking abortions. The clinic administrator for Erie Medical Center in Buffalo, which did twenty-six abortions a day, six days a week, claimed that "Finding doctors is one of the biggest problems of the clinic. Doctors generally have their own practices and precious little time." The upstate clinic had to import doctors for the work. As a satellite of the Pelham Medical Group in New York City, the Erie center had the advantage of experience in operating a clinic and a stable of doctors they could fly in to staff its clinics. Upstate patients relied heavily on New York City doctors and others who flew in like Gilbert Higuera and his assistant, who commuted from Michigan every weekend to offer abortions from a small office.[15]

Upstate providers did not struggle to find patients, however. One hospital in Rochester was fully booked with late-term abortions for the first three weeks after legalization, reflecting pent-up demand. With a price of $750 per procedure, the income for hospitals and clinics was tantalizing. Still, even with the potential profits, the Planned Parenthood in Syracuse knew that there were no clinics or hospitals willing to perform abortions in the "conservative, Catholic community." Its director, Ellen Fairchild, later claimed that she and the medical director, Dr. Jeff Penfield, had previously intended to open a clinic to challenge the law, so they were ready and did four abortions on the first day of legalization. In the first year, the center went on to terminate an average of twelve pregnancies a week, at an average payment of $150, with 20 percent of the patients on welfare.[16]

Nearby Cortland had two medical doctors doing abortions in an office suite. In the small city, 95 percent of the abortion patients were college students. With 2,500 female students at the State University of New York in Cortland, the office did three hundred pregnancy tests a year and provided about fifty abortions a year to students. The office also afforded women a degree of bureaucratic anonymity, allowing students to bring in urine to be tested under a pseudonym and affirming that pregnancies were not reported to the college or to the women's families.[17]

Canadian women drove a great deal of the tremendous demand for abortions in upstate New York. Of those women seeking abortions in New York (city and state), Canadian women appeared in the top ten states/regions. While about nine hundred Canadians made their way

FIGURE 24. Abortion clinics in upstate New York struggled to find doctors. To meet the demand, the Syracuse Planned Parenthood started providing abortions. Here the counselors and nurses meet with Dr. Ellen Fairchild in September 1970. Author's collection.

to England between legalization there in 1968 and 1972, plentiful marketing to Canadians through newspaper coverage, word of mouth, and advertisements lured most Canadians abortion travelers across the border into the United States. Between legalization in July 1970 and the end of 1972, nearly eight thousand women traveled from "Canada & other countries" to New York to have the procedure. Although some Canadians found their way to border cities like Seattle and Detroit, for the vast majority, New York proved to be the favored destination.[18]

The Canadian magazine *Chatelaine*, with more than 1.2 million French and English readers, engaged women on the abortion question and supported legalization and access. Reader surveys solicited in October 1970 discovered that the vast majority of English-speaking respondents thought that abortion should be "The decision of the woman and her doctor." Only a few months after legalization in New York, 262 Canadian readers reported that they had had a legal abortion in the States.[19]

Contemporaneous researchers like Christopher Tietze and historical analysts tried with some difficulty to capture the number of Canadians who obtained abortions in the United States. One scholar noted that their estimate of 6,573 Canadian abortions done legally in the United States was "Based on the incomplete reports from some of the states." The most famous and complete Canadian study, the 1977 Badgley Report, acknowledged that before national legalization with *Roe*, the vast majority of Canadian women seeking American abortions found their way to New York. Initially, most ended up at one of the forty or so clinics and proprietary hospitals in New York City, but business-minded men endeavored to bring the services closer to the border. What initially demanded a full-day trip with air travel was achieved by a much shorter jaunt. Bus travel, markedly less expensive, also brought down costs.[20]

In addition to cost, an important sell for Canadian women was timeliness. One referral agency promised students "Low cost, safe, legal abortion in New York scheduled immediately." The struggle to secure one of the limited numbers of therapeutic abortions in their own country, generally reserved for wealthy Canadian women who could afford to pay for the psychiatrists and doctor's appointments, led thousands of women to head to New York. On the first day of legalization, a reported 250 Canadian women were on a waiting list seeking an abortion in upstate New York. A few months later, a reported wave of "Dozens of women who can't get past hospital abortion committees in Ontario and Quebec are hiking to New York State, where abortion is available upon request." According to a New York doctor working close to the border in 1971, "Eighty per cent of our patients who come to get an abortion in Champlain Valley Medical Center in Plattsburgh are Quebec girls."[21]

Urban Woodstock

New York City, the largest city in the United States, had many factors that helped make it the abortion capital of the country and of the world. With car, bus, train, and plane access, women found their way to the city. The trip to get an abortion was an intimidating one. Traveling for an extended distance, perhaps leaving their state (or country) and traveling by plane for the first time, and then navigating unfamiliar highways, subways, and streets made it a truly stressful experience. If they could afford it, women brought someone with them—a parent, a friend, a partner. Most, however, traveled alone with just a handbag or a small case, making them easily identifiable at the station or the airport.

The familiar London scene reported years earlier, with taxicab drivers trying to get kickbacks from clinics, played out in New York City, too. One reporter characterized it as a "macabre mini-industry." Taxi drivers overcharged three and four times the one-way $7 fare from the airport to the city. Compounding these financial fears were "bodysnatchers" who would "whisk her away to a competing abortion clinic," where they would get a commission.[22]

Some referral services and clinics took the precaution of hiring drivers to shepherd women from the airport, to keep the wolves from picking off their clients. The most ostentatious promised women a "chauffeured limousine." Local travel for the pregnant woman was often included in the cost, but sometimes there was a small fee for the transportation. Eastside Medical Clinic did not have a formal relationship with United Airlines but instructed arriving patients to "sit near the window" in the United waiting room and wait for someone to pick them up. According to one account in *Chicago Today*, the airline's "waiting lounge has become the rendezvous for the abortion traffic." Two men rounded up the women and drove them to the clinic: "'It's not hard to spot the girls,' said Ben, who averages 10 round trips a day. 'They have a kind of bewildered look. They're scared. That's why we wear these badges, so they won't be startled when a strange man comes up to them.'" Their station wagon "limousine" held eight passengers. "It is usually full." The $3 round-trip charge recouped some of the costs and was a smart investment by the clinic, cutting down immensely on the upscale neighborhood's "complaints about the taxis that would line up and wait for the girls to return to the airport."[23]

Faced with the extraordinary expense of an abortion, some families traveled together. Ellen Glascock, who worked at Park East Hospital, was bemused by people who tried to set up their RV camper on the streets of New York City; they "had no idea they should probably stay in a hotel."

She found "most people frightened by the size of it, the subway, I told them it's not a wise idea to drive. They thought it was comparable to Chicago or Detroit. NYC is incomparable, so people were frightened by the size, complexity." She helped them find a place to stay—"most of them had never been off of the farm"—and "could point them to a Broadway show—safe things they could do." The care was not just of the girls and women, but also of the families and boyfriends that accompanied them.[24]

One of the doctors at Women's Services, Don Sloan, described the scene in Manhattan that first summer, with the heat and humidity as the backdrop: "The day started a little after dawn, and we worked into the wee hours of the night. . . . Sure, there were supposed to be appointments, but friends brought friends and some just showed up . . . Many came from far away, often spending their last few dollars getting the plane or bus fare or their vans filled with gas and camping out until we saw them. Imagine camping out in a van in midtown Manhattan in the silk-stocking district!" Sloan was amazed not only by the women who mobbed the clinic, but also by their visibility in the streets. He captured the scene on his way to work: "People had spread sleeping bags or blankets in doorways or in their vans and cars and were sacked out everywhere. It felt like walking through some gigantic sleep-in, a city Woodstock." And as he left, at 10 p.m., 11 p.m., or later, "the crowds were building up. Many were the friends and consorts of the patients, waiting for their people to be discharged. They sat on the curbs, playing guitars and eating sandwiches and pizza, drinking beer and soda."[25]

While Sloan recalled the scene idyllically, Frances Kissling suggested that arriving to open her Westchester clinic in the mornings was more akin to *The Night of the Living Dead*, with patients arriving "after driving from Kentucky, sleeping all night, scared, not knowing what's going to happen." People were more frightened than relaxed, more "shell-shocked" than calm. Regardless of their mental state, women flooded into the city in these years, drawn by the promise of the care and services so desperately needed.[26]

Some of the services and amenities advertised were fairly standard, and included counseling, qualified professionals, and set rates. For women who faced the prospect of endless "add ons" for testing and medications, the assurance that the fees were all-inclusive was important. The Eastern Women's Center promised free pregnancy tests without an appointment, a low-cost way to bring in prospective customers. Promises of special extras in the ads included orange juice, Coke, Oreos, music, televisions, private rooms, and Broadway tickets.[27]

The Women's Referral Service picked up the women at the airport and delivered them to the company's office, where the women completed forms and answered questions, and the company "chauffeured" them to the contracted hospital or clinic. The offices had a waiting room for companions and the women waiting for a return flight, and promised refreshments, TV, and music while they waited. The service also reconfirmed plane reservations and made hotel reservations, if needed. "Nothing is too much to ask of us. We are at the complete disposal of each woman using our services." It was not so much what they did, but the sense that this was a concierge-type service, that justified the $300 fee.[28]

Offering assurances of all kinds not only helped justify the extraordinary expense but was also especially important because the long-standing illegality of abortion and its related unseemliness continued to permeate the minds of people across the country. In all likelihood, women going to the clinics were traveling from a place where it was illegal. A clinic director later reflected, "as far as they were concerned it was illegal. The mentality was still clandestine even though it was legal." Sabra Moore, a counselor, concurred, "Most patients at our clinic are from out of town. For these women, coming to New York City for an abortion often involves secrecy and deception. It is an illegal abortion to them." For patients, seeking an abortion was scary and shameful. Having a welcoming, supportive office helped legitimize the experience and reduce their anxieties. Stories in student newspapers emphasized the relief and ease of getting an abortion in New York.[29]

Proprietary Hospital (for Profit)

Attorney Roy Lucas was one of the earliest to profit from creating a referral service. He worked with Ellen Glascock and John Settle to set up the British Referral Service in 1968; the service specialized in sending women seeking abortions on exorbitant package tours to Dr. Ron Shaw's clinic in London. This experience proved invaluable when New York legalized abortion. Dr. Shaw took his London experience and purchased the for-profit Park East and Park West hospitals in "an area of the city where addresses are spelled out . . . in elegant script and where, it's said, even the garbage dares not to smell." Glascock moved from sending patients to London to working directly for Shaw in New York City. She remembered, he "brought with him nurses, anesthesiologists, etc.; we already had some contacts. . . . It was up and running minutes after the law was passed." He imported his proprietary model, a "high-yield, pay-in-advance abortion business." An analysis of expenditures revealed that out-of-town women likely paid the most, frequenting proprietary hospitals and clinics without a resident's access to New York's Medicaid or the municipal hospitals, nor the "time or the knowledge to 'shop around.'" The statistics breaking down payments to proprietary hospitals reveal the bait-and-switch, with nearly 80 percent of women paying from their own funds, 16.9 percent paying with insurance, and a minuscule number of abortions done for Medicaid payment or no payment at all. Private, for-profit proprietary hospitals also charged much higher abortion fees, on average.[30]

Seeking to turn a quick profit in New York, Shaw undertook a unique advertising strategy. To announce the hospital's arrival on the scene, he sent out a "Dear Doctor" solicitation letter with services and prices to forty thousand medical offices around the country. The American Medical Association (AMA) loudly denounced the letter, but in doing so, it helped spread information about Park East. An editorial criticized abortion referral solicitation letters, characterized the advertising as "in violent disregard of medical ethics, tradition and ordinary good taste," and concluded, "That these mailings constitute objectionable solicitation of referrals is beyond question." The *Journal of the American Medical Association* (*JAMA*) urged its readers to apply pressure to curtail "trafficking in abortions." Attorneys general in other states also challenged the mailings as "violating federal law against mailing matter concerning abortions."[31]

The scandal, though, was most welcome by the hospital. Shaw protested, "we're not advertising . . . People don't know where to go and they're arriving in New York when it is late and the abortion is dangerous." The letters encouraged tremendous publicity that always carefully detailed that it was Park East Hospital in New York City that sent the letter. Moreover, some newspaper coverage detailed the letter's contents. The *Orlando Sentinel*, for example, quoted several paragraphs from the letter, including an overview: "Our facilities consist of 200 private and semi-private rooms, eight operating rooms, and ancillary recovery rooms, and full complement of nursing staff." They also detailed the costs,

> We propose to charge the patient a Hospital fee of $325.00 which will include the Anesthetist's fee for a General Anesthetic. We have ascertained that the fee of a qualified surgeon in Ob-Gyn on our staff or those who have privileges at our Hospital will be approximately $250.00, making a total of $575.00 If for any reason it is found necessary for the patient to stay longer than 24 hours or to receive further medical care, no extra charges will be made.[32]

With the letters, Park East advertised its professional service and facilities to doctors who would, they hoped, see it as a trusted hospital to refer patients who sought to terminate their pregnancies; the abortion would be legal, completed by physicians, and have a set price. The *Sentinel*'s coverage even included a "'Package' Cost" breakout box that answered the question: "How much would it cost a Central Florida woman to have a legal abortion in New York?" The reporter estimated for readers a round-trip airfare of $146, coupled with the fees, and concluded that the total cost would be $721. A *Medical Economist* editor credited the hospital's "flying start with advertisements in medical journals" and the letter for its early success leading "all the rest in number of abortions performed."[33]

The condemnation from doctors, "the AMA Judicial Council, and the Medical Society of the State of New York" all provided opportunities for Park East. Shaw immediately wrote a follow-up letter to all forty thousand doctors, apologizing. This clever tactic enabled the recipients to remember that they had already been solicited by Park East and let the hospital look humbled, while simultaneously serving as a second ad. Instead of going in the circular file, many of these letters got saved. Doctors and clinics then drew on Park East when women came in seeking an abortion referral.[34]

To the woman who could afford it, Park East offered the advantages of qualified doctors and nurses, a counselor, and privacy. Unlike the stories of New York City public hospitals overwhelmed by demand, the reporting promised women, "There are no long queues in front of a clerk who fires rapid personal questions at an embarrassed woman." The media coverage revealed both doctors and consumers hungry for abortion referral information. Just a month after the hospital opened, it reportedly provided abortions to thirty-eight Florida women. By August 20, nearly two months after legalization, the hospital reported that for Florida alone the letter has led to "up to 100 responses," "mostly from the Miami and Fort Lauderdale areas."[35]

Shaw encouraged the idea that women needed the help and support of Park East, claiming that "since some women arrive in an 'emotional state having traveled 1,000 miles to New York for the first time, we have to help them organize.'" He explained to the reader, "that includes checking return tickets, hotel reservations if they're staying in New York and family planning brochures and assistance from doctors on that subject if they want it." As the final "service" offered, "Patients even get a 'hospital-pack' which includes [a] gown and cold cream." One thousand miles anticipated women traveling from cities like Minneapolis, Des Moines, and Tampa, and women across the country sought out the business.[36]

Not content to wait on responses to their letter-writing campaign, Shaw also sent Ellen Glascock across the country to make appeals to local clergy and Planned Parenthood organizations. She built an itinerary around friends she could stay with. Glascock said of her work for Park East, "The first thing I did was a fair bit of travel—to Missouri, to Oklahoma, all over the place. Started with places I knew people. It wasn't normal for a young woman to be traveling over the country, soliciting for abortions." She reflected, "I guess that was whatever advertising we did at that point. We'd contact someone through Planned Parenthood or CCS, get a local counseling person . . . so I would go out and interview them, and talk to them about what we could do." Glascock promised more than just a referral. According to medical economist Howard Eisenberg, women who obtained their referral through Planned Parenthood received a dramatically reduced price. Instead of the customary $575, women who used Planned Parenthood's Family Planning Information Service could secure an abortion at Park East for $300. Eisenberg also credited the early jump on clients to the hospital's collaboration with Planned Parenthood.[37]

Glascock tapped into her alumni network at the Connecticut College for Women as well. She knew that the women and their families would be a lucrative word-of-mouth network. In the guise of a professional announcement in the alumni notes, she noted that, "The hospital handles 250 legal abortions per week and Ellen's staff tries to provide personal contact for each patient." Later she contributed a three-page article detailing her work, again using its eighteen-month safety record providing twenty thousand abortions to solicit more patients.[38]

Shaw's strategy of buying the hospitals to specialize "primarily—even exclusively—in abortions" was predicated on ease and volume. He would have liked to jettison all other in-patient procedures to focus on abortion only, as demand increased, but was never able to do so. For doctors who thought all abortions should be performed in a hospital, Park East offered the assurance of quality care and services that they feared could not be matched by an affiliated clinic. Like the clinics, proprietary hospitals only wanted to take on the fastest, cheapest, and safest abortions, those pregnancies at twelve weeks or less.[39]

Dr. Howard Weitzner, part owner and chief of gynecology at Madison Avenue Hospital, took a different tack to drum up business at his for-profit hospital. Under questioning by a New York legislative committee, he testified that not only did he "set up an agency to steer patients to his hospital," but also a "referral service—Women's Pavilion, Inc. The service also paid him $24,000 a year as its medical consultant." A for-profit hospital—Madison Avenue Hospital—created a for-profit referral service to solicit women, dressed up in the guise of supporting them. Women's Pavilion, Inc., assured women that they could help. The lyrics "need someone to talk to" appeared in Carole King's popular new album, *Tapestry*, and the sense that the referral agency and the hospital

FIGURE 25. The abortion referral service Women's Pavilion was a prolific advertiser in college papers. While their ads claimed that they sent women to accredited hospitals and clinics, they funneled consumers to Madison Avenue Hospital in New York City. Although they were expensive and profit-driven, for-profit hospitals like Women's Pavilion helped meet the tremendous need from out-of-state women that emerged following legalization (*The Maine Campus*, University of Maine, 18 March 1971). With permission from *The Maine Campus*.

would be there for women at all hours of the day and night suggested a supportive, empathetic agency. While they were expensive and profit-driven, for-profit hospitals that specialized in providing abortion care for out-of-state women met the tremendous need that emerged following legalization.[40]

Municipal and Voluntary Hospitals (Nonprofits)

Most of the public criticisms about abortion access centered on the exorbitant costs charged by proprietary (for-profit) hospitals and clinics compared to the charitable, nonprofit efforts of voluntary hospitals and clinics. Seemingly outside of the conversation rested the "elephant expected to carry the heaviest load," the city's municipal hospitals. On the day before the New York law legalized abortion, an assessment of the "14 aging and already hard-pressed city hospitals" was bleak. Bellevue was one of the most important, serving "all of lower Manhattan from 42nd Street below" (along with the only voluntary hospital, Beth Israel). As at all municipal hospitals, bed space was at a premium. Bellevue had been allotting only "four beds a day. That is 20 women a week" for abortion care. One assessment characterized the lack of beds "for *all* kinds of patients" as a "major obstacle," and noted that it was not uncommon "to have to wait two-and-a-half to three months for elective surgery."[41]

Even with the new law in effect, the response by the municipal hospitals was anemic. The number of days and hours that the hospitals served abortion patients was exceedingly inadequate to the need. Bellevue offered their abortion clinic only three days a week: Monday, Wednesday, and Friday, from 8:30 a.m. to 4:30 p.m. Fordham, Greenpoint, and Harlem hospitals delineated days and times women could register, and then different days and times they would have to come back for the abortion clinic. At Bellevue and other hospitals, even though a "patient is not to be refused because she is unable to pay," there were attempts "to recover partial payment and follow-up billing is done." Not only did that place a financial burden on poor girls and women, who could have an abortion aged seventeen years and older without parental consent, but the follow-up billing also had the potential effect of exposing them to their families.[42]

So, too, did hospitals cut costs and expose women to scrutiny by sending patients home to complete abortions. The Bronx Municipal Hospital Center (Jacobi) did its salting out procedure "on a non-inpatient basis, the patient is encouraged to return to the clinic for fetus expulsion the next day." Most girls and women likely shared their living space, which made enduring this process a particularly difficult burden. For those women expected to labor and expel the fetus at home, Jacobi provided women with "a specially designed bag, with the picture of a fetus on its side" to return the material to the hospital. Many argued that later-term abortions should be done in the hospital, but for the poorest in need, municipal hospitals sent women home rather than provide them with a hospital stay. At Kings County Hospital, considered "one of the best hospital abortion facilities," the saline patients were sent home and then would return "to the hospital when labor begins and stay in a special six-bed room attended by a medical student." The law enabled abortion availability in theory, but did not truly address the inequities in access, care, and comfort.[43]

Still, even though they did not start with a fresh new purpose, these already-burdened hospitals met tremendous demand, performing about fourteen thousand abortions in the first six months after legalization. Moreover, the municipal hospitals completed the most abortions for pregnancies between thirteen and twenty-four weeks, the category of abortion with the highest risks. Kings County Hospital, "fourth largest hospital complex in the United States," eventually performed about 150 abortions a week, more than any other hospital, and was the only one that accepted cases up to week twenty-four. Kings tried to support its patients by having its own Medicaid inspector to aid in the application for abortions ($160 for suction or D&C and $270 for saline), and did not hold up the procedure awaiting a response to the application. In reports reflecting on the hospital's performance after the first year, doctors concluded, "our voluntary abortion service has adequately and safely discharged its responsibilities." Municipal and voluntary hospitals provided an important service to the communities they served, and with financial support from the city's contingency fund, by the end of 1972, had provided "about half the abortions for City residents." Medicaid paid for nearly half of abortions in municipal hospitals, and for "two-thirds of the ward patients in the voluntaries."[44]

Although proponents argued that it was safer to perform abortions in a hospital, ironically, they tended to be performed by less experienced medical professionals. Abortions were performed "primarily by junior house staff under attending supervision." In one report, 90 percent of abortions at Bellevue were done by residents. In another, the vast majority of 925 curettages (D&C) "were performed by junior gynecology residents and junior general surgery residents who were rotating for the first time through a gynecology service and had no prior experience with interruption of pregnancy." From this experience, doctors concluded that "with proper supervision and training physicians with no prior experience in terminations of pregnancy can quickly become safe and proficient practitioners. . . ." Of course, these findings, coupled with the exceptional rate of success for clinics with much cheaper, safer, less invasive methods, like vacuum aspiration, also suggested that people with some medical training and supervision could in fact complete abortions for patients at twelve weeks or less in a clinic.[45]

Despite their nonprofit status, municipal hospitals embraced profit-making abortion policies, primarily through extending the length of time for the procedures. For example, Bellevue insisted that a patient nine to twelve weeks pregnant have a D&C and "spend two full days in the hospital—even though the patients do nothing the first day but lie in bed and receive a shave and an enema," at a time when clinics were completing abortions on an outpatient basis, with recovery completed in just a few hours. The hospital policies not only burdened poor women with a painful two-day procedure instead of a two-hour one, but also tied up the staff and the bed, leaving the hospital to care for fewer women. By holding on to an old model, even as the vacuum method proved its merits, the hospitals maintained the ability to bill for a two-day stay and did not create a clinic within the hospital to meet the demand. The need for medical control and good billing is measurable in both the inertia and the resistance. Municipal hospitals, which existed to serve their communities, still operated as businesses. Moreover, delays in payment to cover the costs incurred for indigent, welfare, and insurance payments meant that hospitals had to find ways to stay afloat. Lacking the ability to advertise to draw in more paying patients, "One Brooklyn hospital is said to have made an arrangement with a referral agency because it was awaiting a million dollars in Blue Cross payments and was short of cash."[46]

While legalization removed the onerous costs and social capital that defined the city's therapeutic abortions and ostensibly extended abortions to all women, it also kept abortion access the privilege of those with economic means. Moreover, it exacerbated tensions within the hospitals and the communities they served, as doctors and nurses who opposed abortion legalization felt free to disparage and abuse the girls and women they treated. Some nurses refused "to aid in abortions beyond the twelfth week." In some instances, the animosity was expressed behind closed doors, like one doctor who angrily asked, "You mean that under the new law we'll *have* to give the little whore another abortion?" Some women called the Clergy and Lay Advocates for Hospital Abortion Performance, a consumer group formed to monitor hospital abortion services in New York City, to report cruel behavior.[47]

Black and Puerto Rican women, in particular, faced limited abortion access in their communities, compounded by the preference of doctors and clinics who did not need to accept Medicaid. High prices for abortions put them out of reach. A clinic "In one of the lowest income areas in the most depressed areas in the south Bronx," did not accept Medicaid and charged a flat fee of $400, according to Alfred Moran of Planned Parenthood. Moran said the practice "leads me to believe that what they're really saying is that those patients can borrow $400 from a loan shark" and that the clinic believed the "Medicaid rate of payment for an abortion on an outpatient basis much too low to be really attractive and profitable to them." Even the city's fifteen municipal hospitals could count only a "few black abortion patients" among the 120 abortions they completed a day, while "some doctors who had hoped to set up free or inexpensive abortion clinics for the poor" claimed to be "reluctant to do so in the ghetto," because of a fear of Black male militancy against abortions for Black women. More likely, the doctors lacked altruistic funders or financial support.[48]

The death of thirty-one-year-old Carmen Rodriguez at Lincoln Hospital—the first abortion-related death, less than three weeks into legalization—drove home the importance of the long-standing efforts to make the municipal teaching hospital more responsive to the needs of the poor, Puerto Rican community it was supposed to serve. Rodriguez had a health condition that should have precluded her from having an abortion, but either the doctors neglected to read her chart and/or they did not want her to have a third child out of wedlock. Her death and the poor care Puerto Ricans received at Lincoln Hospital mobilized the Young Lords, along with the Health Revolutionary Unity Movement and Think-Lincoln groups, who had already been working for meaningful change at the hospital, having meetings, setting forth demands, and organizing strategic actions. With participation and allegiance from the community and some Lincoln staff and doctors, the protesting groups charged that the only hospital that served their community was a "butcher," with shoddy care, filthy conditions, and disengaged doctors.[49]

Access proponents also charged that "some hospitals make it as difficult as they can for a woman to get an abortion." *Time* magazine characterized it as a "reluctance on the part of many hospitals to cooperate fully in the program" and observed, "relatively few hospitals are performing relatively few abortions." On top of the limited hours and days and small number of beds and appointments allotted, the accusation rested on the "inconsistent but largely restrictive hospital policies" that governed abortion access. The long list of requirements to get an abortion varied from institution to institution; they included residency requirements; parental permission for patients under age twenty-one (or under eighteen, or under seventeen); consent from husbands; reviews by committees; overnight stays; and complete workups, including chest X-rays. All the restrictions and policies seemed designed to discourage care. Dr. Robert E. Hall objected, "A girl who's old enough to get pregnant is old enough to have an abortion."[50]

Critics directed their sharpest critiques at hospitals that were supposed to serve the poor but refused to do abortions at all. The Women's Abortion Project denounced hospitals: "St. Vincent's, which is receiving $1 million in ghetto medicine for increased outpatient facilities, has absolutely refused to handle abortions." Surveys of doctors and hospitals across the city and state revealed the same disregard for the need. A municipal hospital like Fordham, staffed by primarily Catholic doctors, put a negligible amount of money toward their abortion program. Sheila Doran and her colleagues argued that if the law maintained that this medical procedure was legal and there was need among the poor, which was one the principal reasons it was passed, then the municipal hospitals should meet that need. She cited a study of 55,000 women over the last ten years who had given birth in a municipal hospital. Asked whether the women wanted their last pregnancy, 75 percent said no. Poor women did not have a choice in deciding to carry through with their pregnancies. Susan Reverby, writing for the Health Policy Advisory Center in December 1970, decried the delays and quotas imposed on the number of women getting abortions when the municipal hospitals had been "given a $3.5 million grant out of the city's emergency fund to pay for abortion services." With such financial help, why would a woman seeking an abortion at Kings County Hospital be "handed a slip of paper explaining the charges, demanding payment prior to the procedure if she is not on Medicaid." At Cumberland Hospital, an executive medical secretary summed up women's choices: "Either they have cash, medical insurance or take a loan, or they're turned away."[51]

Reverby further maintained that the city's guidelines "have compounded the delays and increased the costs." Despite the city's generous funding, "Women are told 'Sorry we are full today,' or 'We're not registering any more women now, etc.' without any other referral within the hospital system." She noted that by delivering "the abortion package into the hands of the hospitals and their doctors," the city "enabled quality control to be synonymous with hospital control." Beyond the limited capacities and care, in October 1970, public hearings also revealed "inhumane treatment, unsanitary conditions, and inflexible regulations" in the municipal hospitals. Without any "consumer" pressure, the high prices and long wait times, and the consequent health ramifications of unwanted births, dangerous illegal abortions, and financial devastation, continued to plague New York City's municipal hospitals and harm the poorest women.[52]

In much of the discourse of the time, municipal hospitals were held up as a straw figure against the evils of for-profit entities. However, the explosion of clinics did not have any bearing on women who sought abortions at municipal hospitals. The clinics generally did not serve the poorest women, and neither did most of the hospitals. Time-consuming and discouraging barriers forced some women to turn to other alternatives, while for others hospital policies pushed pregnancies too far for women to be eligible for abortions at all.[53]

Abortorea (Free-Standing Clinics)

In May 1970, an article in *New York* magazine introduced the word "arbortorea" to define a new medical service and space. The author, a professor of obstetrics and gynecology at Mt. Sinai, Dr. Richard Hausknecht, defined the new process as "ambulatory abortion," "a brief minor surgical procedure, performed under local anesthesia, in settings of varied descriptions." He believed that the clinics "represent a medical compromise brought about by a large number of patients and overcrowded, over-utilized medical facilities." He credited two men not only with establishing ambulatory abortions in New York City, but also with providing a counselor-oriented model. First, he heralded Hale Harvey, who brought his extensive experience performing (illegal) abortions in New Orleans, as well as his insight that using counselors—young women, especially those who had had an abortion—to explain the procedure and process reduced stress and improved medical outcomes. Along with Harvey, Hausknecht noted the importance of Reverend Howard Moody. Moody and other ministers, rabbis, and supporters through the CCS helped women across the country find good, safe abortions, and with legalization in New York, used the power of numbers to help drive down the costs.[54]

Hausknecht should also have included Barbara Pyle, whose foresight and planning enabled these two men to come together in the Center for Reproductive and Sexual Health, often called Women's Services (and later Women's Group). The *New York Times* characterized the clinic in April 1971 as the city's "best-known clinic." Early scholarly work on philosophy and abortion brought Harvey and Pyle together, and at his bequest, she "researched the legalized abortion system in England." She wrote to him after the New York legislature legalized abortion and asked, "'Why don't we start a clinic?' I knew all about it from the research I'd done in England. He sent me $30,000 and that's what it took—two months' supplies and everything, drugs, medications, pumps and everything. I figured we would make Hale's money back in six weeks and we did." In their collaboration with the CCS, the twenty-two-year-old Pyle and Harvey shared a commitment to the lowest cost they could achieve and the highest quality of care, with an emphasis on counseling and making the procedure as painless as possible. The Judson Church and CCS provided $250,000 to make the clinic operational. Freed from financial strain and assured of patients, with CCS's steady supply of "700 patients per week," Women's Services was able to put its priority on care.[55]

Another proponent of free-standing clinics was Dr. Alan Guttmacher, who, along with his staff at Planned Parenthood-World Population, took on evaluating the city clinics' facilities, techniques, and conditions. What he found was excellent care and facilities. While some doctors expressed dismay at the degree to which both women (advocates) and lawmakers controlled both facilities and procedures, Hausknecht thought the counselors, serving as patient-advocates, functioned so well it might benefit "other areas of medicine." It also points to the unusual role legislators and the Board of Health took in dictating what would typically be determined by medical professionals.[56]

More than two dozen New York City clinics opened following legalization, and by November 1971, the *Daily News* counted about seventy clinics, operating as either physician-oriented or counselor-oriented. With few reported complications and no deaths in any clinics, Hausknecht explained that the major difference in care between physician-oriented and counseling-oriented clinics came down to counseling. Aligned with Planned Parenthood, he argued against those who believed all abortions should be performed in hospitals and asserted that it appeared from the evidence that "ambulatory abortions are safer." Harvey and Pyle concluded in their analysis of four thousand completed abortions that "early abortions (12 weeks or less) are safe and free from serious medical complications . . . provided no general anesthetic is used." They drew an analogy between an early abortion and having a tooth pulled: "Each usually involves use of a local anesthetic, very little blood loss, can be done quickly on an ambulatory basis and has similar 'non-fatal' complications and dangers occurring in the range of one per thousand cases." Collecting the data allowed supporters of the free-standing clinics to prove their safety vis-à-vis hospitals.[57]

Proponents of physician-oriented clinics claimed to offer counseling, including follow-up services. However, clinics premised on a counseling-oriented approach distinguished themselves from the high costs and perfunctory counseling of these physician-oriented practices with a truly hand-holding, supportive approach to counseling. Critics of "more efficient" physician-oriented clinics, who performed abortions "at a far faster rate," concluded that they did so by shortchanging the female patients of emotional care in pursuit of generating "a profit to their owners." Hausknecht offered a description of these contrasting experiences, emphasizing the missing counseling when doctors' profits were the aim: "In clinics which are counselor-oriented, the patient then joins a session of either group or individual counseling which may last from 10 to 15 minutes up to an hour. In physician-oriented clinics the patient is brought into a treatment room, undressed, examined by a physician, and given vacuum aspiration under either general or local anesthesia." To critics, it was not just a philosophical difference. Prioritizing profits demanded a system that enabled as many abortions as quickly as possible. This meant organizing facilities for expediency and profit, not for counseling or providing other forms of care. Critics also took issue with the emphasis on profit; charging exorbitant fees was not providing good care that benefited the patient; it profited the clinic and the doctor.[58]

Indeed, many men imagined abortion clinics would serve to recoup investments in underused medical facilities (like the struggling hospitals in California) or as a get-rich-quick scheme. Alfred Moran, the executive vice president of Planned Parenthood, was a beacon for those hoping for referrals and up-front cash. He generally dismissed offers like that of a Manhattan dentist who "spent a lot of money renovating this office" and was "looking to defray the costs" by making his office available after hours or by subdividing. No better, for Moran, were those doctors who wanted to work with Planned Parenthood by doing abortions as an outpatient procedure in their suite of offices, which he characterized as an opportunity to "capitalize on an investment." He spelled it out for New York City radio listeners on the day legalization took effect: "Really, if you do the arithmetic in terms of serving 100 patients a day at an average cost of $600 to $800 a patient, you can do the arithmetic and see what this comes to in the way of money."[59]

Fairly quickly, particularly through the efforts of Women's Services, in collaboration with the CCS, Planned Parenthood, and other counselor-oriented clinics, the cost of abortions in free-standing clinics plummeted. Heavy consumer demand and the relative ease and low cost of performing vacuum abortions were transformative, and incremental decreases followed. Competition and increased medical efficiency helped to lower costs.

To achieve the lowered rates, nonprofit referral services had to promise volume, such that doctors would still profit. The cost negotiations, therefore, largely centered on what the clinic had to pay the doctors. Harvey's clinic, for example, started with a maximum cost to patients of $200, of which the doctors took a percentage. However, all of the staff doctors had to agree to "perform up to 25% of their cases at no charge for welfare or indigent patients." Even the poorest women, though, were expected "to pay a token fee of $25." Reporting on their clinic, Harvey and Pyle claimed, "We believe this clinic has been a major force in breaking the high costs of abortion service—high costs which had seemed likely to continue in New York."[60]

Writing on the history of the CCS referrals, one analyst characterized its consumer advocacy as a "kind of pre-Internet Yelp," using consumer responses to clinics to continually ensure a high quality of care and fair pricing. If a doctor "charged more than the agreed upon price or added fees, the CCS would stop referring him, cutting off a lucrative source of patients until he agreed to their terms." Patients, then, played an important role in keeping prices low, by reporting back efforts of doctors to charge more than the agreed-upon price.[61]

Women's Services started as a counselor-oriented clinic. Hale Harvey shaped the identity of the space by putting posters on the walls and potholders on the stirrups, hiring feminist counselors, and expecting doctors to provide excellent medical care and be respectful of the patients. There were two major goals of counseling: reducing pain from the procedure and preventing what some professionals referred to as "recidivism." The counseling was intended not only to support the abortion, but to offer guidance and immediate help with birth control to prevent more unwanted pregnancies. However, it would be a mistake to leave Women's Services in the counselor-oriented category. Four months after it began, the clinic adopted a physician-oriented approach. To assert its identity as a medical clinic, Nathanson removed the "posters from the walls and potholders from the stirrups," and succeeded in creating a "more traditional professional medical atmosphere." With the help of Ron Hammerle in establishing a stable financial system (payroll, taxes, insurance) and the formation of a board, Women's Services passed its state inspection and avoided closure. To achieve this momentous step toward medical and state accrediting, however, the clinic stripped itself of the very qualities that defined it as counselor-oriented.[62]

Further supporting the clinic's physician orientation were the arrangements for those unable to pay. While the clinic was initially structured to provide one in four patients a reduced-fee abortion, Howard Moody and Arlene Carmen of the CCS argued that it was only through those paying full price that the clinic could enable the price break. Moreover, Moody rejected making abortions free. Unlike Dr. Robert E. Hall, who thought poor women should receive free abortions, Moody argued that "no woman should receive a free abortion." He believed that such "charity would damage a woman's dignity and self-respect." In their accounting, Moody and Carmen remembered that they imposed this requirement on a "very reluctant Harvey." When the doctors agreed, under pressure from the CCS, to lower their price for first-trimester abortions to $125 in November 1971, the clinic also reduced the proportion of those receiving the $25 rate from 25 percent down to 20 percent of patients. With 80 percent of women paying the full fee of $125, by 1973 the clinic was a "million-dollar enterprise." It continued to help only a small number of poor women and insisted that they pay 20 percent of the abortion fee.[63]

The CCS had long known that "their counseling, though free, was useless to poor women because the services they referred to were so expensive." With legalization, the group continued to funnel almost exclusively those with means to the clinic. The clinic counselors objected to this bait and switch, believing the clinic betrayed the promise of caring for those in need by only serving white women who could afford to both pay for travel and the full cost of the procedure. Ninety percent of women seeking abortions in New York that first year were white. The policy also meant clinics were abandoning those most in need. Feminist counselors requested that the CCS "approach community groups in black and brown neighborhoods to see if they would be interested in referring women to the clinic" and "hire more black and brown counselors," but these ideas were "quietly forgotten."[64]

The CCS served women coming to Women's Services from out of state, so the travel costs plus the cost of the procedure (even at a reduced $25) put the trip out of reach for those of limited economic means. Although Women's Services was one of the first clinics to accept Medicaid, the number of poor women served in 1971 actually declined, "as women came from regions further from New York City." Referrals from the South sent only 9 percent, and only 11 percent came from the Midwest, as people struggled to find funds to get girls and women to New York City. This left the clinic free to tout its generosity and values, while its counselors criticized its inaccessibility for those in need. Moody and Carmen actively fought efforts to serve the poorest women and complained that other referral groups and clinics "dumped the poor" on Women's Services. The clinic reported that it cared for six thousand women who paid $25 or less across thirty months. While the CCS leaders did not provide a figure for the total number of abortions completed, even a conservative estimate would leave the poorest making up less than 8 percent of the total number of women served by the clinic.[65]

When Harvey proposed using the profits generated from the clinic in the summer of 1970 to open a new clinic to serve local poor women, Moody strongly objected. Moody did not see poor women as his focus. The head of the New Jersey CCS reported, "We couldn't figure out a way to help the women who really needed the help . . . who never could have been helped out by our so-called 'counseling service' anyhow." The model and principle of Moody's clinic was cash on the barrel, designed to serve women of means.[66]

Arlene Carmen criticized the efforts of clinics that solicited business, and she charged that "a lot of clinics had traveling salespeople going around to visit the clergy, inviting them to come to New York and see their clinics." However, the clergy and Planned Parenthood independently contributed to the uneven distribution of referrals.[67]

Moody and Carmen ensured that the national CCS held the power in driving pricing and ensuring that clinics met their demands by playing the clinics against each other. They did so by ensuring dispersal of clients to multiple providers. As with smaller referral operations like Pat Maginnis's in California, any "major complication, mistreatment, or repeated overcharging resulted in a doctor being dropped from the referral list." When there was a dearth of providers, the clergy prioritized competence and safety and compromised by accepting shaming or insensitive behavior. Not permissible, though, were financial dealings between the clergy and the clinics. When Detroit tried to arrange kickbacks for the referrals they sent to New York, Moody intervened, objecting that becoming beholden to the provider would compromise the groups' discretion to limit or drop them. He also suggested that any effort to provide care at a reduced rate, even as was purported to be the case at Women's Services, might have the appearance of impropriety, akin to "the sale of indulgences."[68]

All the clinics in New York City performed thousands of abortions in short order. Hausknecht's Eastern Women's clinic completed three thousand in four months. One doctor, writing in to the *JAMA*, reflected on his experience operating a fertility clinic sandwiched in between two floors of an abortion clinic that performed forty thousand abortions in one year, by his calculations, noting that one floor worked six days a week, while the other "took no rest or respite even on Sundays" and operated from 8 a.m. to 10 p.m. Of New York's abortions, about "25% were performed at this single location. My office building was unquestionably the largest abortion center in the United States." While many had worried that the out-of-state demand "would swamp the City's resources and deprive residents of services," "the health system expanded to meet the demand," with most women traveling to New York City to profit-making hospitals and clinics. Clinics also expanded their staff and hired doctors from places like St. Louis and Nashville to fly in to do abortions on the weekends.[69]

At Women's Services, initially the emphasis on care was evident in the "60 women counselors, many of whom have had abortions themselves, who spend an hour and a half with each patient, developing a supportive relationship with her and seeing her through the entire procedure." The CCS recruited Sabra Moore and other artists from a local group, Women Artists in Revolution, and hoped they would be empathetic and passionate, having experienced "hasty, desperate, seedy abortions" themselves. Moore and the other women working as "doctor's assistants-counselors" believed fully in their supportive, trained role. She reflected, "The job is indescribable because although abortion is a medical procedure, an unwanted pregnancy is not a medical problem." The counselor meets the needs of a woman by explaining the procedure and assisting the doctor: "This method takes into account the woman's total being." Moore contrasted the experience with that of one patient who described an abortion at an Astoria clinic, where "No one spoke to me. It was like a factory." In describing abortions as something transformative that "affected the whole woman," Moore concluded of the abortion process that "her emotions were as important as her uterus, and that doctors, assistants and patients could together evolve a special and real benefit from a crisis situation."[70]

The emergence of this new category of worker, cloaked in an expectation of women's experience, sisterhood, and counseling, had a rocky start. More than once, the leadership (doctors and administrators) clashed with the underpaid and underappreciated female staff, hired purportedly because counseling was vital to the process, but then paid only $50 for an emotionally weighty eight-hour day. The new industry created new kinds of workers, which did not fit the pattern of a female nurse supporting a male doctor in his work. The counselors saw their work as not just supportive but integral to a successful procedure. Moore said in her memoir,

> I doubt that the [CCS] has foreseen the dynamics of hiring feminists who had endured illegal abortions to staff the new clinic alongside male doctors, none of whom had participated in consciousness-raising let alone criticism/self criticism. Suddenly, the doctors were being required to speak gently to a woman in crisis and be assisted by a group of newly trained paraprofessionals, each with a passionate identification with the patient on the table before them.[71]

The experience of Moore and her counterparts harkened back to a long history of male doctors usurping the role of female midwives in delivering babies. Historically, female friends and relatives supported a birthing mother, and even as doctors began to assert their professional place as birthing authorities, women still called on other women for support. However, male doctors began to limit the number of women in the delivery room to just one or two so that he could have control of the delivery as a medical procedure, reflecting a significant change from a female-centered to a male-centered and controlled experience. The ideological, financial, and organizational differences between the feminist paraprofessional counselors and the doctors and clinic administrators proved to be profound. The supportive, woman-centered approach at Women's Services was short-lived.[72]

On a day-to-day basis, Women's Services' policies generated tensions. One policy was that counselors wore ordinary street clothes—except during the procedure, when they donned lab coats—to encourage a "woman-to-woman" relationship. The counselor stayed with each patient throughout her time at the clinic, before, during, and after the procedure. This dynamic of a nonmedical person participating in a medical procedure had not existed previously, and the tensions of age and gender—with older male doctors and younger female counselors—played out in abortion clinics across New York City. The counselors soon faced new demands "to speed up the process and spend less time with each patient." The administration started to break down the counseling with Taylorism, pressuring counselors to limit the counseling. Instead of counselors having the latitude to spend forty-five minutes with a patient whose birth control had failed or "two hours with a fourteen year old," the counseling timing had to match the procedure timing, creating "a competitive situation between the counselors." Those who finished counseling quickly and could take on more patients got paid more. The financial value placed on speed over quality and care also applied to the doctors. Even at Hale Harvey's vaunted clinic, "Most of the doctors were rushing. They had a financial incentive—they were paid by the number of abortions performed during each shift."[73]

Eventually, the women counselors decided to unionize. Moore noted, "We were all political activists, so we knew how to organize and fight." The women prioritized not being rushed, caring for each woman, and having a voice in shaping the clinic and its ideals, as well as more familiar concerns like hours and wages. The female counselors were tired of supplying the labor, while the men made the decisions. Beyond grievances like not being able to take a lunch hour or a break, they hoped that

"A union would clarify what our real position was as workers in the traditional capitalist structure we now had at the clinic." They also sought "basic, safe physical conditions for both the staff and patient." To try to break support for the union, the clinic "stopped hiring women identified with women's liberation" as counselors. According to Moore, the clinic also "hired nurse-practitioners, whom we trained, and who were not in the union." She remembered that the CCS "called us mercenaries" for seeking to provide the best care. The very qualities that made them excellent counselors (passionate, experienced) were the same ones that made their role easy to dismiss as "women's work." Their effort to receive fair pay and good work conditions was dismissed as unethical and motivated by greed. Tellingly, the CCS did not criticize the male doctors negotiating their pay, only the female counselors.[74]

Doctors and Nurses

Regardless of the laws and statutes governing abortion, money was the one constant that women needed to find providers. Money ensured medical professionals would perform abortions. From its time as an illegal operation to the ruling on *Roe*, profit was a driving force in luring people into the work.

In contemporaneous analyses, however, abortion access proponents bemoaned the few doctors willing to perform the procedure. Dr. Robert E. Hall reflected on two points of resistance from doctors, centered on financial concerns. First, colleagues who did take up the work found themselves regarded as not much better than "the back-street abortionist," performing the procedures out of greed. However, he criticized the junior residents for claiming that "doing several abortions a day for a few months interferes with their over-all training experience" and was "boring and messy." He claimed that junior residents' resistance was rooted in greed, because they were willing to do more abortions "if remunerated for their work" and were "almost universally eager to moonlight in abortion clinics at $12.50 an hour," the equivalent of about $100 an hour in 2024.[75]

Medical residents in this era watched attending doctors take on profitable positions in the new abortion clinics. For example, the clinics first wanted and then had to have a hospital affiliation in case of an emergency case, and proudly advertised affiliated doctors, like Dr. Hausknecht, an attending ob-gyn at City Hospital Center in Elmhurst. The hospital charged only $34 for an abortion, but Hausknecht was the medical director for a clinic that charged $150. Unlike hospitals, clinics had long hours and operated seven days a week. Junior residents could see the profits accruing to those doctors who could charge for their services and affiliations.[76]

Moreover, the perennial poverty of medical residents meant that they moonlighted frequently to get more experience and make ends meet. Dr. Don Sloan recalled his experience as a resident in Philadelphia treating self-abortions in the emergency room, and his delight at finding a way to make money and make a difference in saving women's lives when he moved back to New York and moonlighted there. For those in training in New York, being asked to do a few abortions a day not only served the financial and moral needs of the hospital, but also ensured that all doctors would leave medical school with the experience necessary to safely perform abortions.[77]

The second point of resistance from male ob-gyns centered on the belief that patients generally and pregnant women especially should only be told what procedures or treatments they should receive. They did not see patients as consumers. Women's expectations of birth control and abortions on demand undermined doctors' sense of themselves as authorities in the care of women. Armed with abortion information and legal access, women began to approach the doctor as a practitioner who offered a service for a set price. Hall believed that the demands for abortion threatened the male doctor's sense of potency and masculinity. He agreed with another doctor who said, "This flaunting of traditional subservience may be one of the more powerful and less conscious determinants of our irrational opposition to granting women the right to decide matters in this crucial area of their lives." Sabra Moore, at Women's Services, argued that the tension extended beyond abortion on demand. She noted that many doctors "had been used to performing surgery under anesthesia and weren't accustomed to a situation where the patient talked back. They weren't used to having their authority questioned" in the procedure room. Historian Johanna Schoen also found that doctors at "feminist clinics struggled with their lack of influence over clinic policy and with the nontraditional atmosphere of the clinic." One doctor believed the women "were running him," while another complained, "I was reduced to being a technician." As Dr. Michael Levi characterized it, the clinics introduced "a new concept of medical practice." The result was removing a doctor from "his pedestal." As Levi saw it, "It's all between the skilled man who can do it and the woman who says 'I want it.' It's a 50–50 and not 100 per cent the doctor's way any more." As an outgrowth of feminist efforts both in the clinics and in the larger women's health movement, women told doctors what procedure they wanted.[78]

There were also degrading verbal and sexual interactions, and hostility inflicted by male doctors onto female patients, reflecting abortion's long history as a shameful procedure and evidence of sex. While there may have been an expectation that these cruelties disappeared with legalization or continued only in poorly run places, incidents did not abate. One male doctor at Bellevue Hospital, for example, showed a callous disregard for his patients' feelings by conducting research on saline patients with the fetal monitor "placed right next to the woman's bed." He said, "Well, I don't like doing abortions, so I might as well get something out of it." Merle Hoffman described confronting doctors at her clinic who spoke despicably to patients by saying things like, "Come on, you knew how to spread your legs before you got here, you can spread them for the exam." She tried to discipline their misogyny, which placed the center in jeopardy, but had to balance her role as a young, nonmedical woman telling medical men who deeply resented her what to do.[79]

Doctors also resented counselors who criticized them for sexual and racist attitudes, comments about a patient's weight or build, and even their abortion technique. Moore recounted one doctor at Women's Services "'who raised his hand in greeting and said, How,' when introduced to a Native American woman" and another "who insisted that the speculum was 'no bigger' than the penis that had impregnated the woman." Initially, under the direction of Hale Harvey, the clinic aspired to be a caring place for women. Hale empowered the counselors to speak directly to the doctors to improve the experience for patients. However,

"Structurally," according to Sabra Moore, the counselors "remained in a position of subservience to both the doctors and the administration." Quickly, Hale's attention shifted toward expanding the clinic, and his influence faded entirely with his exposure four months later as an unlicensed doctor. With his removal, the counselors lost their advocate, and the male doctors' power increased.[80]

It was not just Catholic hospitals or male doctors who objected to doing abortions or treated the women seeking them as immoral criminals. Many nurses in hospitals that provided abortions not only refused to work in providing abortions or aiding recovery, but also acted with cruelty toward the patients. Most providers had no provision for a "conscience clause" for those who objected to abortion based on a moral or religious belief, and nurses found themselves assigned to work with patients getting and recovering from abortions. Dr. Levi found that nurses took out their "hang-ups" "on the lady who is there for an abortion. Some nurses have refused a woman her food." Another doctor recalled, "Nurses were absolutely cruel. I can remember one woman who was forty, had hypertension—. . . . Had twin fetuses . . . When the nurse saw her chart, they took her down to the nursery and showed her twins that had just been born. And this was in a hospital where the nurses were wonderful nurses, caring nurses,—my friends!"

This animosity emerged from a population that was "less supportive of abortion rights than physicians, social workers, or Americans generally." Within the nursing profession, there was also a distinctive hierarchy of abortion support, with those most likely tasked with abortion care most opposed to it. In one 1968 study of all registered and licensed practical nurses at the University of Washington Hospital, only "7 of 102 nurses in obstetrics-gynecology and pediatrics (none of the 28 nurses in the post-partum units) were in favor" of abortion. Broadly speaking, on all of the abortion questions studied, the "Eleven nurses working in the premature care center were more in favor of abortion for all reasons than were the nurses in the delivery rooms, postpartum units, nursery, and pediatric services." One woman reported to the CCS that during pre-abortion counseling in a New York City municipal hospital she was told by a nurse, "We stick a long needle into your belly and kill the baby."[81]

Nor did things improve over time. A year and half after New York's legalization, a *New York Times* headline proclaimed, "Even Now, Helping With Abortions Is Traumatic Shock For Some Nurses." The reporter found that "Some nurses left hospitals, some transferred to different departments and a number went through group therapy and counseling sessions." Some nurses asserted that they were "degraded and abused" in having to care for women having abortions and were upset by the job requirement. As historian Karissa Haugeberg demonstrates, nurses caring for abortion patients did so in the context of long-standing labor shortages, overwork, and paltry pay. With little or no training, no institutional anticipation of what the experience of caring for the most difficult procedures would entail, and no oversight or consequences for their callous behavior, nurses resented abortion care.[82]

For other nurses, their concerns closely echoed those of the clinic counselors. Rather than objecting to the work or the pay, they disliked that the care "was being done like an assembly line and that women became objects." The nurses wished they could develop a "personal relationship" and help the women, but "The women were in and out of the hospital so quickly, most of them the same day." These nurses resented the "impersonal manner" of the procedure, at a time when most surgeries and childbirth required several days in the hospital. The speed of the abortion, including preparation and recovery, left some nurses feeling unable to do their job in a supportive manner. Some nurses expressed the desire to spend more time aiding the patient's recovery, including one who asked to move from the termination room to the recovery room, where she "could give the patient the emotional support she needs at the time." She was opposed to abortion for herself but wanted to work with the women who sought abortions, "based on her beliefs that 'a woman has rights over her own body.'"[83]

Indeed, supportive nurses could be incredibly kind and caring. One called every social agency she could to find a place for an aborting woman to await labor from the saline procedure because she was separating from her husband. When she could not find a place, she kept the patient on the abortion unit overnight. Another patient's whole family slept overnight when their caregiver died just before the procedure and there was no one to watch them. No small feat for a nurse in a busy unit that cycled through four shifts of patients every day. In another hospital, the head nurse of a prenatal clinic proclaimed herself "staunchly in favor of population control." She acknowledged, "Women have been having abortions all along. This was just a safe way of doing it."[84]

While the belief was that hostile attitudes and behavior were harder to screen for in hospitals and much "easier for a clinic to weed out," first-hand accounts from both hospital and clinic experiences reveal the cruel attitudes and behavior of staff, nurses, and doctors. Although clinics sold themselves as caring places, contrasted against the stereotypically impersonal hospital experience, doctors and staff continued to operate with impunity. Given the scarcity of those willing to do the work, those who would, however grudgingly, wielded power.[85]

Drawing girls and women across their reproductive lives from across the nation and many countries abroad, New York met the tremendous need for legal abortions. In the two and a half years between legalization and the passage of *Roe v. Wade*, New York doctors performed more than 332,237 abortions. New England residents alone made up nearly 56,000 of the patients, while more than 83,000 women from the mid-Atlantic states made their way north. The Midwestern states of Illinois, Michigan, Indiana, and Ohio cumulatively sent over 105,000 women, while Wisconsin and the upper Midwestern states west of the Mississippi were home to an additional 22,000 patients. More than 55,000 girls and women in Southern states east of the Mississippi also made their way north to New York.[86]

Despite the tensions that emerged in these two and a half years, the overall impression for most who traveled to New York was one of safe, relatively affordable access. As the city and state contested the profiteering that emerged simultaneously with the new law, they massaged bureaucratic tensions between hospitals and clinics, particularly the efforts to curtail abortions in doctor's offices, and contended with the emerging distrust between male doctors and female staffers. New York maintained a calm, welcoming outward façade. Women could read anonymous accounts of women flying into New York to get an abortion "all in the same day" and be assured that clinics would "help any girl, regardless of race, religious belief, age or financial status. Prices can be adjusted according to the ability to pay." Women had a clear destination in mind if they sought a safe, legal abortion, and over time their consumer power would help drive down prices. Men saw the opportunity to profit from the strong, immediate demand. Legalizing abortion helped to generate strong economic growth for New York, and the abortion market attracted hundreds of thousands of consumers.[87]

Conclusion

A REPORTER CLAIMED IN 1969, "The abortion mills are among the most ghoulish and lucrative rackets in this country. They favor the rich who can pay the high fees." Even with legalization, reporters persisted in advancing a social taboo of abortion providers as necessarily suspect. Disparaging abortion providers as lucrative rackets, abortion rings, and abortion mills revealed the intense discomfort that Americans, even those supportive of legal abortion access, felt toward the procedure.

Without a belief in abortion as a part of good and legitimate health care, the only abortion providers that achieved respect—in retrospect—were elderly small-town doctors at the end of their careers. Their dedication to the broader health of the members of their communities secured loyalty and legal cover. Having to stay put, they could only charge about one-tenth of the going rate for an abortion, and less for those who could not afford it. Observers therefore heralded only these doctors as honorable. Journalist Susan Brownmiller wrote of Dr. Robert Douglas Spencer in 1969: "And then there was Spencer with his clinic on the main street of a small American town, who charged $50, who believed in abortions, and who was kind." Doctors who had to stay put provided other medical care, enmeshed in people's lives on "main street," that offered full social and economic benefits to offset the moral cost. Before his death in 1969, Dr. Spencer estimated he did about thirty thousand abortions in Ashland, Pennsylvania. "I've been here since 1919. I daresay I've helped out half the town. Even on the abortion end, there is probably one of my patients related to a family in half of the town. I think most of the town would stand up for me." An official who commented on Spencer during a 1959 trial in which he was acquitted of manslaughter concurred, "There aren't too many people in this county he hasn't helped."[1]

So too did coverage like Brownmiller's enshrine Spencer as the "angel of Ashland," or a saint who seemed to not want to charge. Rhetorically it worked to emphasize that Spencer was not motivated by profit but was instead a principled doctor who cared for his community. Preventing his identity from tipping from doctor to "abortionist" depended on his community. In his case, his atheism may have been an even more offensive identity, but neither did that turn his neighbors against him. Every indicator suggests that he did not turn away any patients, and for those truly impoverished, he sent them baskets of food or gave them bus fare to get home. His kindness inspired women who sought abortions from him to later bring their daughters, reflecting the consistency of his good reputation across forty-three years of practice.[2]

From relative isolation on liminal islands, doctors who performed abortions enjoyed an unexpected tolerance that enabled them to market themselves with their constancy. One pregnant woman returned home to Montana in the summer of 1963, following a failed effort to secure an abortion in New York City. She sought out Dr. Sadie Lindeberg, arriving in Miles City to find a "big white house and the lovely little old lady." Heralded in the newspaper the following year on her eightieth birthday, she was acclaimed for delivering eight thousand babies, but on this day Dr. Sadie first prescribed her "spirits of turpentine" and then a series of pills, none of which worked. The doctor finally had to put her patient under to complete the abortion.

All the doctors continued to practice medicine, including performing abortions, as long as they were able. These rural doctors offered a challenge to the social taboo surrounding abortion and provided an opportunity to think about the work of an abortion provider in a rational abortion market. Providers had a product for sale that consumers wanted to buy.[3]

Moralizing about capitalism and a denigrated medical procedure converged to vilify abortion providers. This tendency was compounded with New York's legalization of abortion. In the spirited debates that ensued, the question of how to best provide safe medical care got wrapped up in efforts to ensure transparency for fair and accurate pricing, as well as profit. The medical profession, including office managers, hospital administrators, medical doctors, and medical schools, each played a role in limiting where and when abortions could be performed, to such an extent that affordable abortions could only be done in clinics. Landing on a model that moved this safe, simple procedure from a doctor's office to an abortorium designated it as something distinctive and separate. Instead of all doctors training in a procedure that could be provided to patients, abortion stopped being taught at all. Analysts in 1970 studied and supported having abortions done by paraprofessionals trained in the procedure. With legalization, though, abortions persisted in being required to be performed in offices and hospitals by doctors (especially doctors-in-training), where the procedure remained marginalized and costly. Whatever profits an entrepreneur would imagine in setting up a stand-alone facility would be offset by the long-standing difficulty in providing doctors and the emerging need in the last quarter of the century to defend employees, patients, and the clinics against harassment and domestic terrorists.[4]

Language and attitudes struggled to evolve from "butcher" to "abortionist" to "doctor." As abortion was delegitimized by the medical profession, removed from (or never added to) medical training, and degraded as a subspecialty of someone who had no other options, the language remained fixated on *the abortionist*. As Susan Brownmiller observed more than fifty years ago, "the image of an abortionist, through books, plays, movies, articles, or whatever, was of an evil, leering, drunken, perverted butcher, at worst, and a cold mysterious money-hungry Park Avenue price-gouger at best." No other doctor was thus demeaned and reduced to a denigrated procedure. Sociologist Nanette Davis concluded in 1973, "Abortion promises to continue to be a costly and problematic health commodity for producers and consumers alike." The social, legal, and political climate thwarted efforts to make first-trimester abortions available by paramedical professionals or doctors-in-training at outpatient clinics, all of which served to make access to abortion expensive and theoretical for most women across the country.[5]

In 2024, nearly two-thirds of Americans support access to abortions, recognizing that abortions are a life-saving medical procedure and understanding that there are a multitude of valid reasons that people seek them out. Opponents have been able to impose their minority opinion by legally destroying the protection afforded by *Roe v. Wade* for fifty years. Not content to limit or restrict abortion, ideologues in states across the country have denied legal, therapeutic abortions to people dying from their pregnancy and are strategizing about how to revive the Comstock Act, a nineteenth-century law, to prohibit sending abortion pills through the mail. As historians have demonstrated, about one in four American women have had an abortion. Making abortions illegal will not stop people from having them. It will only stop people from having safe abortions. Abortion access should be available to all who need it, ensuring that people can get safe, affordable health care where they live.[6]

NOTES

Preface

1. Matthew Connelly, "Population Control Is History: New Perspectives on the International Campaign to Limit Population Growth," *Comparative Studies in Society and History* 45(1) (Jan 2003): 145–46. Lawrence Lader noted that the French company that developed RU-486 gave the US patent for the drug to the Population Council, the most significant population control organization (Elizabeth Mehren, "Champion of Choice," *Los Angeles Times*, 30 November 1995).

Introduction

1. With thanks to William Jennings Bryan Henrie Jr., Jennifer Hansen, and Sheila Stogsdill.

"Preliminary Set March 27 On Abortion Count," *Grove Sun*, 16 March 1961; Bob Shaw, "Friends Honor Prison-Bound Doctor," *Miami News-Record* (Oklahoma), 16 July 1962; Mike McCarville, "Mark Left on Grove by 5,000 Abortions," *Daily Oklahoman*, 17 November 1963; Mike McCarville, "Abortionist Keeps Technique Secret," *Daily Oklahoman*, 18 November 1963; "Parole Docket, October 1963" and "Summary: Dr. J. Bryan Henrie, OSP #67109," from the October 1963 Pardon and Parole Board meeting minutes file, Oklahoma State Archives; Lawrence Lader, *Abortion* (The Bobbs-Merrill Company, Inc., 1966), 53; Letter from Henrie to Roy Lucas, 4 December 1970, Box 21, Roy Lucas Papers, Special Collections and Archive, Wesleyan University; Ann DeFrango, "Decision Rests Heavy on Physicians' Shoulders," *Daily Oklahoman*, 30 June 1971; Sheila K. Stogsdill, "Grover Abortion Doctor Is Subject of Film," *Oklahoman*, 20 August 2006; Sheila K. Stogsdill, "Group Prays at Site of Old Abortion Clinic," *Oklahoman*, 8 April 2012.

2. Birth notice of daughter of Mr. and Mrs. Robert Byron at Bryan Henrie Clinic, *Miami Daily News-Record*, 23 July 1959; "Doc Henrie's Farewell," *Newsweek*, 30 June 1962; "Goodbye, Dr. Henrie" photo and caption, *Miami News-Record*, 16 July 1962; Bob Shaw, "Friends Honor Prison-Bound Doctor," *Miami News-Record* (Oklahoma), 16 July 1962; "Osteopath Is Planning Book on His 5000 Abortions," *Springfield News-Leader*, 18 August 1964; Delaware County Historical Society, *Heritage of the Hills: Delaware County History* (Delaware County Historical Society, 1979), 59.

3. Bob Shaw, "Friends Honor Prison-Bound Doctor," *Miami News-Record* (Oklahoma), 16 July 1962; William Jennings Bryan Henrie, *Rendezvous with Destiny* draft, circa 1964, in author's possession; "Osteopath Is Planning Book on His 5000 Abortions," *Springfield News-Leader*, 18 August 1964; Sheila K. Stogsdill, "Grove Abortion Doctor Is Subject of Film," *Oklahoman*, 20 August 2006; Mike McCarville, "Mark Left on Grove by 5,000 Abortions," *Daily Oklahoman*, 17 November 1963; William Jennings Bryan Henrie, *Rendezvous with Destiny* draft, circa 1964, in author's possession; "Did Murder Victim Visit Henrie's Office?," *Miami Daily News Record* (Oklahoma), 23 March 1964; Society for Humane Abortion conference in San Francisco, KTUV television news coverage, 9 January 1966; "First National Conference on Abortions Laws, NARAL, Schlesinger, MC313, Box 1.1; "Tracing the Legacy of an Enigma: The W. J. Bryan Henrie Legacy Project," *In Touch with Information Technology* (Gettysburg College): Winter 2007.

4. Bob Shaw, "Friends Honor Prison-Bound Doctor," *Miami News-Record* (Oklahoma), 16 July 1962; William Jennings Bryan Henrie, *Rendezvous with Destiny* draft, circa 1964, in author's possession; "Osteopath Is Planning Book on His 5000 Abortions," *Springfield News-Leader*, 18 August 1964; Sheila K. Stogsdill, "Grove Abortion Doctor Is Subject of Film," *Oklahoman*, 20 August 2006; William Jennings Bryan Henrie Jr., phone interview by author, 28 August 2022.

5. Garrett Hardin claimed that Dr. Alan Guttmacher found most abortions were done by doctors, not quacks. Guttmacher estimated 80 percent of all abortions were done by medical doctors, while Dr. Calderone went even further with her estimate of 90 percent (*Abortion and Human Dignity*, Public Lecture, University of California, Berkeley, 29 April 1964, Society for Humane Abortion, Inc., 1964–1973, undated; Abortion collection, Sophia Smith Collection, SSC-MS-00428, Smith College Special Collections, Northampton, Massachusetts.

6. Mike McCarville, "Mark Left on Grove by 5,000 Abortions," *Daily Oklahoman*, 17 November 1963; Mike McCarville, "Grove Abortionist Story Incredible," *Daily Oklahoman*, 19 November 1963; Mike McCarville, "Select Few Asked for Release of Abortionist," *Daily Oklahoman*, 20 November 1963; Paul Krassner interview with Spencer, *'60s Icon Paul Krassner Reveals His Early History with Abortion*, AlterNet.com, 6 February 2013; Richard Metzger, "Paul Krassner: How A Satirical Editor Became a One Man Underground Railroad of Abortion Referrals," dangerousminds.net, 7 February 2013, https://dangerousminds.net/comments/paul_krassner_how_a_satirical_editor_became_a_one_man; William Jennings Bryan Henrie Jr. phone interview with author, 28 August 2022.

7. Dr. Alfred Kennan is in a similar mold, performing about 10,000 abortions between January 1971 and January 1972 at the Midwest Medical Center in Madison, Wisconsin. An article about the abortion patients at Kennan's clinic included six photos of women who publicly stated in 1972 that they had abortions, including historian Barbara Tuchman, singer Judy Collins, tennis player Billie Jean King, and actor Lee Grant ("Abortion Clinic Stirs Up Madison," *New York Times*, 2 May 1971; Lloyd Shearer, "Who Gets an Abortion," *Fort Worth Star-Telegram*, 11 February 1973).

8. David J. Garrow, *Liberty and Sexuality: The Right to Privacy and the Making of Roe v. Wade* (University of California Press, 1988).

9. $100 1962 to 2024, https://www.usinflationcalculator.com/ (accessed 5 June 2024); Cari Romm, "Before There Were Home Pregnancy Tests," *Atlantic*, 17 June 2015.

10. Molly Sinclair, "Abortions Are Hard for Poor to Obtain," *Miami Herald*, 25 January 1971; Alan Charles and Susan Alexander, "Abortions for Poor and Nonwhite Women: A Denial of Equal Protection," *Hastings Law Journal* 23 (November 1971): 147–70; Emily Langer, "Norma McCorvey, Jane Roe of Roe v. Wade decision legalizing abortion nationwide, dies at 69," *Washington Post*, 18 February 2017.

11. *Abortion Rap*; Mary Ziegler, "Roe's Race: The Supreme Court, Population Control, and Reproductive Justice," *Yale Journal of Law and Feminism* 25(1) 2013, 30–34; David J. Garrow, *Liberty and Sexuality: The Right to Privacy and the Making of Roe v. Wade* (University of California Press, 1988).

12. Harriet Pilpel, "The Right of Abortion, *The Atlantic*, June 1969; Oral history interview with Byllye Avery, 2003, Physicians For Reproductive Health And Choice Oral History Project, Columbia University; Leslie Reagan, *When Abortion Was a Crime: Women, Medicine, and Law in the United States, 1867–1973* (Berkeley: University of California Press, 1997), 193; David T. Beito and Linda Royster Beito, *Black Maverick: T.R.M. Howard's Fight for Civil Rights and Economic Power* (University of Illinois Press, 2009); Lisa Lindquist-Dorr, Email regarding Black providers, 16 May 2024.

13. Harriet F. Pilpel, "The Public and Private Aspects of the Problem," *New York Times*, 14 June 1970.

14. Harriet F. Pilpel, "The Public and Private Aspects of the Problem," *New York Times*, 14 June 1970; Mary Ziegler, "Roe's Race: The Supreme Court, Population Control, and Reproductive Justice," *Yale Journal of Law and Feminism* 25(1) (2013): 18, 27; Ziegler, "Reinventing Eugenics: Reproductive Choice and Law Reform After World War II," *Cardozo J.L. & Gender* 319 (2008): 323–24, 337–39, 344; *Population Growth: Family Planning Programs*, Proceedings of the Annual Population Symposium, ed. Alexander Doberenz (College of Human Biology, University of Wisconsin—Green Bay, 1971).

Abortion advocates and public health proponents argued that high death rates, purportedly caused by illegal abortions, were a reason why abortion laws should change. Dramatic photos and the disproportionate loss of women of color helped propel the discourse, but as in all battles, and not surprisingly for one lived in the shadows, the numbers were hard to nail down and easy to inflate. For numerical accountings, see Dave Behrens, "Personal Views, Moral Issues Complicate Abortion Question," *News Day*, 27 March 1969; Glenn Kessler, "Planned Parenthood's False Stat," *Washington Post*, 29 May 2019.

15. "Two Men Seized in Warren County Abortion Racket," *Journal Herald* (Dayton), 4 September 1959; "Abortion, Birth Control Needed, Says BH Medic: Described as Only Means to Halt Overpopulation," *Herald-Palladium* (Benton Harbor, Michigan), 3 February 1970; Mary Ziegler, *After Roe: The Lost History of the Abortion Debate* (Harvard University Press, 2015), 99 and 289fn11 and fn12; Mary Ziegler, "Reinventing Eugenics," 335; Nicholas Kulish and Mike McIntire, "Why an Heiress Spent Her Fortune Trying to Keep Immigrants Out," *New York Times*, 14 August 2019.

16. Martin Ebon, ed., *Everywoman's Guide to Abortion* (Universe Books, 1971), 52–53.

17. Edwin F. Dailey, "Repeat Abortions in New York City," *Family Planning Perspectives* 5, no. 2 (Spring 1973): 89–93.

Chapter 1

1. "The Real Cause of War; Is It Over-Population," *Gazette* (Cedar Rapids, Iowa), 12 February 1916; Connelly, "Population Control," 140.

The debates about the causes of and solutions to eradicating poverty are longstanding. The approach advanced by Reverend Thomas Malthus and satirized in the character of Ebenezer Scrooge dates to the early nineteenth century in England. The ghost of Christmas present shames Scrooge when he hopes Timmy will be spared by quoting Scrooge back to him, "If he be like to die, he had better do it, and decrease the surplus population" (John Broich, "The Real Reason Charles Dickens Wrote A Christmas Carol," *Time*, 29 April 2021).

2. "The Real Cause of War; Is It Over-Population," *Gazette* (Cedar Rapids, Iowa), 12 February 1916; "Predicts Overpopulation," *Idaho Statesman*, 1 Mar 1922; "Campaign to Check the Population Explosion" ads in *New York Times*: 7, 16, and 21 January 1968; Matthew Connelly, *Fatal Misconceptions*, 118, 129–134, 160–62; "Margaret Sanger Is Dead at 82," *New York Times*, 7 September 1986.

3. Linda Gordon, "The Politics of Population: Birth Control and the Eugenics Movement," *Radical America* 8(4) (1974). 81-82; Connelly, "Population Control," 133–34; "From Geneva to Cairo: Margaret Sanger and the First World Population Conference," Spring 1994, The Margaret Sanger Papers, https://www.sanger.hosting.nyu.edu/articles/from_geneva_to_cairo/ (accessed 11 May 2024).

For insights into Sanger and eugenics, Planned Parenthood submitted its internal 2016 analysis to the Supreme Court: https://www.supremecourt.gov/opinions/URLs_Cited/OT2018/18-483/18-483-2.pdf (accessed 11 May 2024).

4. Human Betterment Association of America, "The Place of Sterilization in Heredity Counseling," dinner conference, 1 November 1957, New York City, Human Betterment Association of America—Correspondence, 1957, American Philosophical Society, Philadelphia, Pennsylvania; "People Don't Talk About Birth Control," *Lima News*, 12 December 1965; Harriet Pilpel, "The Right of Abortion," *Atlantic*, June 1969; George Langmyhr, "The Role of Planned Parenthood—World Population in Abortion," *Clinical Obstetrics & Gynecology*, 14 (1970): 1190–1196; "Population Council Gives Findings on Abortion," *Times-News* (Twin Cities, Idaho), 16 December 1971; International Planned Parenthood Federation, *Medical Handbook* (Paul & Mathew Ltd, 1962, 1967, 1971); Miles A. Powell, "'Pestered with Inhabitants': Aldo Leopold, William Vogt, and More Trouble with Wilderness," *Pacific Historical Review*, 84(2) (May 2015): 217–20; Betsy Hartmann, *The America Syndrome: Apocalypse, War, and Our Call to Greatness* (Seven Stories Press, 2017); Mary Ziegler, "Roe's Race: The Supreme Court, Population Control, and Reproductive Justice," *Yale Journal of Law and Feminism* 25(1) (2013): 13; "Population Growth: Family Planning Programs."

Matthew Connelly also notes the close association between population control and eugenics and that "fear of population growth" was "still cast in terms of race and class conflicts" (*Fatal Misconception*, 8, 59–60, 98–99, 103–106, 117–20, and "Population, the U.S. Problem, the World Crisis," 127).

Planned Parenthood would not have another woman as president again until Faye Wattleton in 1978, five years after *Roe* (Faye Wattleton, "Unfinished Agenda: Reproductive Rights," *Sisterhood Is Forever: The Women's Anthology for a New Millennium,* ed. Robin Morgan (Simon & Schuster, 2007), 26.

5. "Population Boom Termed Perilous," *New York Times*, 12 May 1961; "World Population Emergency Campaign—History," The Margaret Sanger Papers Project, https://sanger.hosting.nyu.edu/aboutms/organization_wpec/; "From Geneva to Cairo: Margaret Sanger and the First World Population Conference," Spring 1994, The Margaret Sanger Papers, https://www.sanger.hosting.nyu.edu/articles/from_geneva_to_cairo/ (accessed 11 May 2024).

6. "The Population Explosion," *New York Times*, 15 May 1961; Paul and Ann Ehrlich, *The Population Bomb* (1968), 73; Richard Bowers, "Initiative Signature Project Needs Help," *SHA Newsletter*, Spring 1970; Derek S. Hoff, *The State and the Stork: The Population Debate and Policy Making in US History* (University of Chicago Press, 2012), 178–81, 322n105 and 106; Linda Greenhouse and Reva B. Siegel, *Before Roe v. Wade: Voices That Shaped the Abortion Debate Before the Supreme Court's Ruling* (Creative Commons, 2012); Mary Ziegler, "Reinventing Eugenics: Reproductive Choice and Law Reform After World War II," fn 288; and Mary Ziegler, "Roe's Race: The Supreme Court, Population Control, and Reproductive Justice," *Yale Journal of Law and Feminism* 25(1) (2013): 20; Sierra Club, "History of Accomplishments," https://www.sierraclub.org/sites/www.sierraclub.org/files/sce/north-star-chapter/SierraClub_Timeline_webversion.pdf (accessed 6 June 2024).

For membership estimates, see: Judy Klemesrud, "To Them, Two Children Are Fine, but Three Crowd the World," *New York Times*, 12 January 1971; Suzanne Staggenborg, *The Pro-Choice Movement: Organization and Activism in the Abortion Conflict* (Oxford University Press, 1991), 166–67; John Caldwell and Pat Caldwell, *Limiting Population Growth and the Ford Foundation Contribution* (Frances Pinter Ltd., 1986). The Pathfinder Foundation reflected on its eugenic past and evolving "population control" language: https://www.pathfinder.org/impact-stories/entering-a-new-era/ (accessed 6 June 2024).

7. Hugh Moore and William Draper Jr., created the Population Crisis Committee, believing that the Ford Foundation and the Population Council were too conservative (Connelly, *Fatal Misconceptions*, 206, 231, 259). Between 1952 and 1982, "the Ford Foundation spent $270 million in the population field" (Connelly, "Population Control," 125); Joan Roelofs suggests that the Rockefeller and Ford Foundations, among others, supported population control because they believed it was necessary to achieve social and political stability (*Foundations and Public Policy: The Mask of Pluralism* [State University of New York Press, 2003], 31).

8. Emily Bazelon, "Talking to Ruth Bader Ginsburg," *Slate*, 19 October 2012, https://slate.com/news-and-politics/2012/10/ruth-bader-ginsburg-clears-up-her-views-on-abortion-population-control-and-roe-v-wade.html (accessed 6 June 2024).

9. "The Population Explosion," *New York Times*, 15 May 1961; Mary Ziegler, "The Framing of a Right to Choose: Roe v. Wade and the Changing Debate on Abortion Law," *Law and History Review* 27(2) (Summer 2009): 283.

Dating back to 1965, the Office of Economic Opportunity funded programs at home that helped Planned Parenthood provide birth control services in poor neighborhoods. Planned Parenthood was aware of the perception and openly discussed it in board meetings. Government agencies and private foundations funded hospitals and organizations that provided abortions and sterilization (Connelly, *Fatal Misconceptions*, 247–55, 271).

The shrinking size of the American Eugenics Society meant that by 1960 scientists and doctors comprised a majority. See American Eugenics Society, Special Collections, University of Missouri, https://library.missouri.edu/specialcollections/exhibits/show/controlling-heredity/america/aes (accessed 14 May 2024).

10. Derek S. Hoff, *The State and the Stork: The Population Debate and Policy Making in US History* (University of Chicago Press, 2012), 322 fn106; Christabelle Sethna, "The Evolution of the *Birth Control Handbook*: From Student Peer-Education Manual to Feminist Self-Empowerment Text, 1968–1975," *Canadian Bulletin of Medical History* 23(1) (2006): 98–101; Mary Ziegler, "The Framing of a Right to Choose: *Roe v. Wade* and the Changing Debate on Abortion Law, *Law and History Review* 27(2) (Summer 2009): 292; and *After Roe: The Lost History of the Abortion Debate*, 111–12; Caitlin Fendley, "Eugenics Is Trending," *Washington Post*, 17 February 2020.

11. Betty Friedan, *The Feminine Mystique* (W. W. Norton & Co., 1963), 31–32; Lana Clark Phelan, "Abortion Laws: The Cruel Fraud," speech delivered at first California Conference on Abortion, 10 February 1968; Betty Parker Ashton, "Feminist Asks Help of College Students," *Richmond Times-Dispatch*, 22 April 1970; Society for Humane Abortion, *Newsletter*, Spring 1970 (Smith College archive); Katherine Seligman, "The Revolution Begins," *San Francisco Examiner*, 9 April 1989; Miroslava Chavez-Garcia, "From 'Tough Love' to 'Street Fight': Garrett Hardin and Cordelia S. May's Battle for Population Control and Eugenics at the Turn of the Millennium," *Revista Brasileira de historia*, 43 (94) (Sep-Dec 2023). Chavez-Garcia found that May and Gardin worked with the "Society for Humane Abortion and the Association to Repeal Abortion Laws (ARAL), to legalize abortion and help those who wanted them to go to Mexico and Japan for the procedure."

ZPG was advised by eugenicists, including Garrett Hardin and Kingsley Davis. Richard Bowers, "Executive Director's Report," 6 September 1969, Box 12, Folder 160, Zero Population Growth, Inc. 1969–1970, University of Illinois at Chicago Archive; "Annual Board of Directors Meeting," *SHA Newsletter*, Spring 1970); Matthew Connelly, *Fatal Misconceptions: The Struggle to Control World Population* (Belknap Press of Harvard University Press, 2008), 239–40, 248–49; Mary Ziegler, "The Framing of a Right to Choose: *Roe v. Wade* and the Changing Debate on Abortion Law," *Law and History Review* 27(2) (Summer 2009): 285, 294; Caitlin Fendley, *Countdown to Zero: A History of Grassroots Population Activism in the United States, 1968–1991* (Ph.D. diss., Purdue, 2023), 210.

Journalist Jane E. Brody characterized those who believed voluntarism could work in the war on overpopulation as doves, while those who thought the government needed to use more aggressive tactics were the hawks ("Overpopulation War Escalated," *New York Times*, 6 January 1969).

The mention in *The Feminine Mystique* was not a fluke for Betty Friedan. Friends with fellow New Yorker and population control soldier Lader, she would go on to invoke the necessity of population control in 1973, stating, "I'm not sure what part women will play in population control. Liberalized abortion laws will of course play a part. But more advanced birth control technology will have to control future growth of the population" (Rebecca Hilton, "They All Had One More Question," *Johnson City Press* [Tennessee], 2 March 1973). In 1974, with Germaine Greer and Margaret Mead, Friedan attended the UN-sponsored World Population Conference in Budapest, and complained that the conference's population plan "made only cursory mention of women" (Barry Waters, "Bias Charged in Population Plan," *Traverse City Record-Eagle* [Michigan], 23 August 1974).

12. John Tierney, "Betting on the Planet," *New York Times Magazine*, 2 December 1990; Ian Dowbiggin, *The Sterilization Movement and Global Fertility* (Oxford University Press, 2008), 141; Derek S. Hoff, *The State and the Stork: The Population Debate and Policy Making in US History* (University of Chicago Press, 2012), 187–88; Mary Ziegler, "Bad Effects: The Misuses of History in *Box v. Planned Parenthood*," *Cornell Law Review Online* 105: 165 (2020): 198–200.

13. Harriet Pilpel, "The Right of Abortion," *Atlantic*, June 1969; Marian Faux, *Roe v. Wade: The Untold Story of the Landmark Supreme Court Decision That Made Abortion Legal* (New York: Cooper Square Press, 2001), 171; Joan Marie Johnson, *Funding Feminism: Monied Women, Philanthropy, and the Women's Movement, 1870–1967* (University of North Carolina Press, 2017), 196.

14. Linda Gordon, "The Politics of Population: Birth Control and the Eugenics Movement," *Radical America* 8(4) (1974); Linda Gordon, *The Moral Property of Women: A History of Birth Control Politics in America* (University of Illinois Press, 1976, 2002), 282; Adele E. Clarke, *Disciplining Reproduction: Modernity, American Life Sciences, and the Problems of Sex* (University of California Press, 1998), 226; Molly Ladd-Taylor, "Eugenics, Sterilisation and Modern Marriage in the USA: The Strange Career of Paul Popenoe," *Gender & History*, 13(2) (August 2001), 301–2; Leslie Reagan, *When Abortion Was a Crime*, 220; Joan Roelofs, *Foundations and Public Policy: The Mask of Pluralism* (State University of New York Press, 2003), 8; Mary Ziegler, "The Framing of a Right to Choose: *Roe v. Wade* and the Changing Debate on Abortion Law," *Law and History Review* 27(2): 283–84.

Roelofs found that the American Council of Learned Societies and Social Science Research Council were created to distribute "slightly laundered" Rockefeller and Carnegie money, so it did not have the same stains. She noted the "buffer" organizations hid their provenance from activists, academics, and the public (*Foundations and Public Policy*, 9, 34). According to historian Joan Marie Johnson, Katherine Dexter McCormick, "like Sanger, was alarmed by population growth. However, this later embrace of population control never overshadowed her feminist beliefs" (*Funding Feminism: Monied Women, Philanthropy, and the Women's Movement, 1870–1967* [University of North Carolina Press, 2017], 201.

Ziegler further claimed in 2013, "It is wrong to treat the abortion-rights, population control, and eugenics movements as indistinguishable from or even similar to one another." Her point is well taken, that it is false to use historical actors and actions to make assertions about modern-day Planned Parenthood and Reproductive Freedom for All. Ziegler's contention that these movements were distinct and different from each other stemmed in part from some historians' mistaken assumption that eugenicists like Margaret Sanger historically opposed abortion. Legal scholar Paul Lombardo, for example, stated, "I've been studying this stuff for 40 years, and I've never been able to find a leader of the eugenics movement that came out and said they supported abortion." However, that is only evidence of how abortion rights leaders avoided identifying themselves as eugenicists, as they let the cloak of overpopulation and even abortion define them.

Historian Wendy Kline observed that eugenics ideology continued unabated after World War II and argued, in fact, that "the most overlooked trajectory of eugenics lies in its connection to the liberalization of abortion law." Individuals and organizations that held eugenic ideals or were sympathetic to them transformed their language and behavior to build toward their ideal world. As renowned women's historian Linda Gordon demonstrated fifty years ago, individuals and organizations aligned with eugenics ideology joined forces with population control and abortion supporters. Ziegler insightfully discovered that eugenics work got rebranded to "reflect the changing norms of the post-war era" and had the appearance and label of "reproductive choice," even as the work became "more openly racist than earlier eugenic legal reform projects had been." Eugenicists and population control advocates worked together as allies to fund abortion discourse, the massive legal fight, access to the procedure, and long-term projects and individuals committed to abortion (Linda Gordon, *The Moral Property of Women: A History of Birth Control Politics in America* [University of Illinois Press, 1976, 2002], 280–82; Mary Ziegler, "Reinventing Eugenics: Reproductive Choice and Law Reform After World War II," *Cardozo J.L. & Gender* 319 (2008); Mary Ziegler, "The Framing of a Right to Choose: Roe v. Wade and the Changing Debate on Abortion Law," *Law and History Review* 27(2) (Summer 2009): 285, 290; Mary Ziegler, "Roe's Race: The Supreme Court, Population Control, and Reproductive Justice," *Yale Journal of Law and Feminism* 25(1) (2013): 1; Lombardo in Eli Rosenberg, "Clarence Thomas Tried to Link Abortion to Eugenics. Seven Historians Told *The Post* He's Wrong," *Washington Post*, 30 May 2019; Alexandra Minna Stern, "Clarence Thomas' Linking Abortion to Eugenics Is as Inaccurate as It Is Dangerous," *Newsweek*, 31 May 2019; Wendy Kline, "Abortion in the United States," in *The Oxford Handbook of the History of Eugenics*, ed. Alison Bashford and Philippa Levine (Oxford University Press, 2010), 518, 546; *Eugenics: A Journal of Race Betterment*, Volume 4, 1931.

Scholars rightly contend that Clarence Thomas "Using eugenics as a rhetorical sledgehammer" is wrong and that making "guilt-by-association" arguments is ahistorical and inaccurate. They also reject his claim that those pursuing birth control and abortion rights were motivated by racism, noting that "the abusive or coercive imposition of sterilization has, historically, been deployed against marginalized communities," and that this was not true of abortion (Alexandra Minna Stern, "Clarence Thomas' Linking Abortion to Eugenics Is as Inaccurate as It Is Dangerous," *Newsweek*, 31 May 2019; Melissa Murray, "Abortion, Sterilization, and the Universe of Reproductive Rights," *William & Mary Law Review* 63(5) (April 2022): 1605–1607, 1635).

15. *Eugenics: A Journal of Race Betterment Through 1931*; Jack Rosenthal, "Birth Rates Found in a Sharp Decline Among Poor Women," *New York Times*, 3 March 1972; Linda Gordon, "The Politics of Population: Birth Control and the Eugenics Movement," *Radical America* 8(4) (1974): 61–98; Linda Gordon, *The Moral Property of Women: A History of Birth Control Politics in America* (University of Illinois Press, 1976, 2002), 280–82; Frank Dikötter, "Race Culture: Recent Perspectives on the History of Eugenics," *American Historical Review* 103(2) (1998): 467–68; Molly Ladd-Taylor, "Eugenics, Sterilisation and Modern Marriage in the USA: The Strange Career of Paul Popenoe," *Gender & History* 13(2) (August 2001): 298–89; Wendy Kline, "Abortion in the United States," in *The Oxford Handbook of the History of Eugenics*, ed. Alison Bashford and Philippa Levine (Oxford University Press, 2010), 518, 546; Eli Rosenberg, "Clarence Thomas Tried to Link Abortion to Eugenics. Seven Historians Told *The Post* He's Wrong," *Washington Post*, 30 May 2019; Alexandra Minna Stern, "Clarence Thomas' Linking Abortion to Eugenics Is as Inaccurate as It Is Dangerous," *Newsweek*, 31 May 2019; Mary Ziegler, "Bad Effects: The Misuses of History in *Box v. Planned Parenthood*," *Cornell Law Review Online* 105: 165 (2020): 199; Connelly, "Population," 138–40.

16. Mary Ziegler, "The Framing of a Right to Choose: *Roe v. Wade* and the Changing Debate on Abortion Law," *Law and History Review* 27(2) (Summer 2009): 285; Wendy Kline, *Building a Better Race: Gender, Sexuality, and Eugenics from the Turn of the Century to the Baby Boom* (University of California Press, 2001), 143–45; Molly Ladd-Taylor, "Eugenics, Sterilisation and Modern Marriage in the USA: The Strange Career of Paul Popenoe," *Gender & History* 13(2) (August 2001): 298–301; Frank Dikötter, "Race Culture: Recent Perspectives on the History of Eugenics," *American Historical Review* 103(2) (1998): 467–68; Anne Overbeck, *At the Heart of It All*, 104; Frederick Osborn, *The Future of Human Heredity: An Introduction to Eugenics in Modern Society* (1968).

17. Osborn, *Future of Human Heredity*; Kline, *Building a Better Race*, 143–45; Ladd-Taylor, "Eugenics, Sterilisation and Modern Marriage in the USA," 298–301; Dikötter, "Race Culture," 467–68; Overbeck, *At the Heart of It All*, 104; Ziegler, "The Framing of a Right to Choose," 285–90. As Melissa Murray notes, the "eugenics movement's interest in racial betterment was primarily directed at improving and purifying the white race." To the extent that they sought to police others, their preferred vehicle for limiting reproduction among the "unfit" was not contraception or abortion, but rather sterilization. "Abortion, Sterilization, and the Universe of Reproductive Rights," *William & Mary Law Review* 63(5) (April 2022): 1605–7.

18. Mary Ziegler, "The Framing of a Right to Choose: *Roe v. Wade* and the Changing Debate on Abortion Law," *Law and History Review* 27(2) (Summer 2009): 285–90, 295–96; Alexandra Minna Stern, "How the *Los Angeles Times* Shilled for the Racist Eugenics Movement," *LA Times*, 28 February 2021.

For a sense of the shifting attitude of Americans, the *New York Times* reported that voluntary vasectomies increased from forty thousand men in 1960 to one million in 1972 ("Vasectomies Increase," 8 November 1972).

19. Osborne list of American Eugenics Members, American Philosophical Society (Philadelphia, PA), 1974; Mary Ziegler, "The Framing of a Right to Choose: *Roe v. Wade*

and the Changing Debate on Abortion Law," *Law and History Review* 27(2) (Summer 2009): 286–87, 290–92; Kevin Begos, "Questions, Answers About History of Eugenics in US," *Washington Examiner*, 20 June 2012.

20. Mary Ziegler, "Reinventing Eugenics: Reproductive Choice and Law Reform After World War II," *Cardozo J.L. & Gender* 319 (2008): 333.

Molly Ladd-Taylor noted that "eugenicists relied on print propaganda and the mass media to change individual attitudes and personal behavior . . . it required convincing normal people." "Eugenics, Sterilisation and Modern Marriage in the USA: The Strange Career of Paul Popenoe," *Gender & History* 13(2) (August 2001), 301, 304.

21. Lawrence Lamb, "Abortion Is Part of Medical History, *Selma Times-Journal*, 26 September 1971, and "Abortion Doesn't Kill Women," *Hope Star*, 18 March 1972; Don E. Weaver, "Freer Abortion Laws Spreading," *Birmingham Post-Herald*, 6 October 1970; David Hendin, "New Abortion Mecca Not Without Its Initial Problems," *Selma Times-Journal*, 18 July 1971; Clyde V. Kiser, Dorothy G. Wiehl, Paul C. Glick, and Wilson H. Grabill, "The Work of the Milbank Memorial Fund in Population since 1928," *Milbank Memorial Fund Quarterly* (49)4, Part 2 (Oct. 1971): 15–66; Kenneth Lammott, "The Anatomy of the Philanthropoid" (review of *The Money Givers*, by Joseph Goulden), *Chicago Tribune*, 28 March 1971; Linda Gordon, *The Moral Property of Women: A History of Birth Control Politics in America* (University of Illinois Press, 1976, 2002), 281; Gene Roberts and Hank Klibanoff, *The Race Beat: The Press, the Civil Rights Struggle, and the Awakening of a Nation* (Sequitur Books, 2008); Susan E. Swanberg, "'Well-Bred and Well-Fed,' the Science Service Covers Eugenics: 1924 to 1966," *American Journalism* 38(2) (April 2021): 202–23; Alexandra Minna Stern, "How the *Los Angeles Times* shilled for the racist eugenics movement," *LA Times*, 28 February 2021; Emily Merchant, *Building the Population Bomb* (Oxford University Press, 2021).

22. "Hawaii Doctors to Convene; Abortion Is Major Topic," *Honolulu Star-Bulletin*, 14 May 1967; Victor Cohn, "Battle for Healthy Babies," *News-Journal* (Mansfield, Ohio), 14 August 1968; Leslie Aldridge Westoff and Charles Westoff, *From Now to Zero: Fertility, Contraception and Abortion in America* (Little, Brown and Company, 1969, 1971): 117–62; John Ensor Harr and Peter Johnson, *The Rockefeller Century* (New York: Charles Scribner's Sons, 1988), 457; Conwell Carson, "Lifting Veil from Genetic Secret," *Kansas City Times*, 19 December 1965; Jerome P. Curry, "'Will Our Baby be Normal?,'' *St. Louis Post-Dispatch*, 28 August 1970; "See Few Valid Reasons for Abortion," *Red Bluff Daily News* (California), 24 February 1971; Kingsley Davis and Judith Blake, "Social Structure and Fertility: An Analytic Framework," *Economic Development and Cultural Change* 4(3) (April 1956): 211–35; Judith Blake, "Abortion and Public Opinion: The 1960–1970 Decade," *Science* 71 (1971): 540–49; Linda Bourque and Valerie Oppenheimer, "In Memoriam: Judith Blake," 2011 Calisphere, University of California.

23. Helena Huntington Smith, "Enter Planned Parenthood," *Parents*, September 1942; Robert and Annabelle Cook, "110,000,000 Babies: Born This Year Will Grow Up in a Teeming World . . . With Population Doubling in Forty Years," *Parents* (May 1960): 36–37, 134–137; Winfield Best and Frederick Jaffe, "Should Abortion Laws Be Liberalized?," *Parents*, June 1965; "Parents Magazine's Awards for Outstanding Service to Children," *Parents*,

January 1969; Jill Lepore, *The Mansion of Happiness: A History of Life and Death* (Alfred A. Knopf, 2012), 132; James Allen Smith, "Legitimizing the Social Sciences," Rockefeller Archive Center, 13 January 2022, rockarch,org.

Dan Gerber, CEO of the namesake baby food company, also favored zero population growth. Derek S. Hoff, *The State and the Stork: The Population Debate and Policy Making in US History* (University of Chicago Press, 2012), 184.

24. "That Population Explosion" cover, *Time*, 11 January 1960; Roul Tunley, "The Environment Crusade," *Seventeen*, February 1970; "A Thoughtful New Student Cause: A Crusade Against Too Many People," *Life*, 17 April 1970; Jean Libman Block, "The Population Bomb and How to Defuse It," *Good Housekeeping*, May 1971; Deirdre Carmody, "Identity Crisis for 'Seven Sisters,'" *New York Times*, 6 August 1990; John R. Wilmoth and Patrick Ball, "The Population Debate in American Popular Magazines, 1946–90," *Population and Development Review* (Dec. 1992); 631–68.

25. "Playboy Interview: Dr. Paul Ehrlich, *Playboy*, August 1970; Mary Ziegler, "Reinventing Eugenics," 342 ("I thought we favored the sterilization of imbeciles and the link in public institutions"); Derek S. Hoff, *The State and the Stork: The Population Debate and Policy Making in US History* (University of Chicago Press, 2012), 178–79; Charles C. Mann, "The Book That Incited a Worldwide Fear of Overpopulation," *Smithsonian*, January 2018; Richard Grossman, "Respect for 'Population Bomb,'" *Durango Herald*, 25 May 2019; Alex Trembath and Vijaya Ramachandran, "The Malthusians Are Back," *Atlantic*, 22 March 2023.

26. "Population, the U.S. Problem, the World Crisis," *New York Times*, April 1972, 5–7.

Matthew Connelly reported on a Ford Foundation representative meeting with USAID officials in 1968, who said, "our primary purpose is to reduce the rate of population growth. Connelly also notes that between 1968–1972, the US government provided four-fifths of all international assistance for population programs." Supplement contributor and US Representative (Hawaii) Patsy Mink viewed abortion as "more of a women's rights cause than of population control . . . the right of termination must exist as a human choice." She noted with concern that "so much of the drive for population control is directed at ethnic minorities," and quoted a Senate report on population growth that stated: "The poor contribute only a small proportion of this overall increase, with most growth resulting from the fertility of middle-class families." The supplement was like the "1619 project" in securing the imprimatur of the *New York Times*, a stand-alone item that suggested something of real importance to be pulled out, shared, and reckoned with. "Population, the U.S. Problem, the World Crisis," 8; *Fatal Misconceptions*, 207, 238–40; "Population, 127."

27. Mary Ziegler, "Reinventing Eugenics, 342–43; Letter from Lawrence Kegan to David Lelewer, 17 November 1971; Letter from David Lelewer to Lawrence Kagan, 24 November 1971, RAC, RA2, 447–449 MKP; PR Form Letter for Lader, PR 1969, 2, MC313_NARAL_24–389, Schlesinger; Rebecca M. Kluchin, *Fit to Be Tied: Sterilization and Reproductive Rights in America, 1950-1980* (Rutgers University Press, 2011), 5, 11, 21, 28-30.

28. Kingsley Davis, "Population Policy: Will Current Programs Succeed?," *Science*, 10 November 1967, 730–39 (abridged) in *Population Crisis: Hearings, Ninetieth Congress,*

First Session, 2 November 1967, 251–66; Derek S. Hoff, *The State and the Stork: The Population Debate and Policy Making in US History* (University of Chicago Press, 2012), 177–79; Lee Rainwater, *And the Poor Get Children: Sex, Contraception, and Family Planning in the Working Class* (Quadrangle, 1960) and *Family Design: Marital Sexuality, Family Size, and Contraception* (Routledge, 1965), 18; Robert G. Weisbord, "Birth Control and the Black American: A Matter of Genocide?," *Demography* 10(4) (1973): 571–90. See, for example, Margaret Mead, "Why Americans Must Limit Their Families," *Redbook*, August 1963; Garrett Hardin, "A Scientist's Case for Abortion," *Redbook*, May 1967; Margaret Mead, "The Crisis of Our Overcrowded World," *Redbook*, October 1969. *Redbook* was a Hearst Media publication.

29. Geoffrey McNicoll, *A Biographical Memoir: Kingsley Davis* (National Academy of Sciences, 2019); Mary Ziegler, "Reinventing Eugenics: Reproductive Choice and Law Reform After World War II," *Cordoza Journal of Law & Gender* 319 (2008): 332 fn102; Mary Ziegler, "The Framing of a Right to Choose: *Roe v. Wade* and the Changing Debate on Abortion Law," *Law and History Review* 27(2) (Summer 2009): 308 fn163, 314; Dorothy Roberts, *Killing the Black Body: Race, Reproduction, and the Meaning of Liberty* (New York: Pantheon Books, 1997), 102–3; Robert G. Weisbord, "Birth Control and the Black American: A Matter of Genocide?," *Demography* 10(4) (1973): 571–90; *Social Biology* Mailing List, American Eugenics Society Papers, American Philosophical Society.

Weisbord maintained that charges of genocide could only be confirmed if the goal of total annihilation was possible, and since it was not possible, according to his calculations, for thousands of years, he asserted that critics were being paranoid (Thomas Krueger, review of *Genocide? Birth Control and the Black American* by Robert G. Weisbord [*Journal of American History*, July 1976, 782–83]).

30. Lawrence Lader, "Chaos in the Suburbs," *Better Homes and Gardens*, October 1958; Lawrence Lader, "Turbulent Years: Harvard 1937–1941," *Sewanee Review* 112(1) (Winter 2004): 106–18; Lawrence Lader, "Laws to Limit Family Size," *Parents*, October 1970.

31. Betty Friedan, *The Feminine Mystique*; Lawrence Lader to Hugh Moore, 30 March 1966, letter regarding support of Sanger and abortion books, and Hugh Moore to Lawrence Lader, 29 August 1966, letter regarding population control, Hugh Moore Fund 153, 2.7, Princeton; Hugh Moore to Lawrence Lader, 29 August 1966, Hugh Moore Fund 153, 2.7, Princeton; Friedan in *Fatal Misconceptions: The Struggle to Control World Population* (Belknap Press of Harvard University Press, 2008), 265; Derek S. Hoff, *The State and the Stork: The Population Debate and Policy Making in US History* (University of Chicago Press, 2012), 180; Lawrence Lader listed as Executive Director of the Hugh Moore Fund, NARAL, MC 313, Box 1, Folder 7; Schlesinger; Lawrence Lader, 18 October 2000: Veteran Feminists of America Pioneer Histories: Lawrence Lader, "18 October 2000 remarks," New York City, https://www.youtube.com/watch?v=nJik_tXwzgc (accessed 6 June 2023).

Globally, questions about what elements of society helped it achieve population stability were constantly being studied. The cruelest responses from some eugenicists were to not feed starving people, including children, who would then die and not reproduce. For those looking for active ways to help a society voluntarily move toward population stability, there were two emerging ideas in the 1970s. The first, described here, was that policies and funding help empower women. If they had food and shelter and opportunities, they would desire to control their own fertility. The other competing idea, which ultimately proves to be most successful, was that the society broadly had to invest in development. The importance of access and opportunity to control reproduction was part of the equation, but choice and motive had to be driven by individuals.

32. "Between the Lines" and Lawrence Lader, "A Guide to Abortion Laws in the United States," *Redbook*, June 1971; Elizabeth Mehren, "Champion of Choice," *LA Times*, 30 November 1995; Lawrence Lader, *Breeding Ourselves to Death* (Ballantine Books, 1971).

33. Helen Hennessy, "Many Believe Abortion Problems Best Handled By Clergy, Doctors," *Iowa City Press-Citizen*, 10 May 1968; Lader, "Between the Lines," *Redbook*, June 1971.

34. Lawrence Lader, "A Platform on Population," April 1970, NARAL, MC 313, Box 24, Folder 378, Schlesinger Library; Lawrence Lader, *Breeding Ourselves to Death* (Ballantine Books, 1971); William Draper Jr. Eulogy of Hugh Moore, Hugh Moore Fund correspondence, PPFAII, Princeton Library.

Unitarians published Lader's paperback *Abortion* (1966) and *Abortion II* (1973) with Beacon Press. The church started supporting birth control to control the population starting in 1962 and affirmed support for legal abortion in 1963 (Unitarian General Resolution on Population, 1962, https://www.uua.org/action/statements/population and Reform of Abortion Statues, 1963, https://www.uua.org/action/statements/reform-abortion-statutes).

Religious support for abortion and population control was not unusual, as Derek Hoff and I have demonstrated, but the public efforts of the UUA are notable, particularly given the church's historic embrace of eugenics ("Former Omaha Pastor Causes Stir," *Bee* (Omaha), 19 December 1921; Mark Harris, *Elite: Uncovering Classism in Unitarian Universalist History* (Skinner House Books, 2010). Hoff also points to the population control position statements by the Presbyterian Church (USA) in *The State and the Stork: The Population Debate and Policy Making in US History* (University of Chicago Press, 2012), 184. I noted the Methodist's Population Institute cash prize awarded to the two-part *Maude* abortion episode, which sought to bring conversations about population control to the public (Katherine Parkin, "The Women's National Abortion Action Coalition & The Abortion Tribunals, 1971–1972," *Journal of Family History*, 2022, 17).

35. Bob Bickel, "Crusader for Abortion Fights His Battles Alone," *Democrat and Chronicle* (Rochester), 1 May 1975; "Baird 'Sick and Tired' of Abuse," *Daily Evening Item* (Lynn, Massachusetts), 19 October 1976; Mildred Hamilton, "The Fiery 'Father of the Abortion Movement,'" *San Francisco Examiner*, 25 June 1980; Elizabeth Mehren, "Champion of Choice," *LA Times*, 30 November 1995; David J. Garrow, *Liberty and Sexuality: The Right to Privacy and the Making of Roe v. Wade* (Macmillan Publishing Company, 1994), 408.

36. Ann-Mary Currier, "Women Fighting Law on Abortion," *Boston Globe*, 15 February 1970; Joan Roelofs, *Foundations and Public Policy: The Mask of Pluralism* (State

University of New York Press, 2003), 8–9, 34; Kelsey Rhodes, Physicians for Reproductive Health, to Katherine Parkin, 26 September 2023, email correspondence; "Physicians for Reproductive Health and Choice Oral History Project, 2000–2003," Finding Aid, Columbia University, Columbia Center for Oral History; "Family Planning Oral History Project Interviews, 1973–1977," Finding Aid, Schlesinger Library, Radcliffe Institute, Harvard University; "Population and Reproductive Health Oral History Project oral histories," Finding Aid, Sophia Smith Collection of Women's History, Smith College; Lawrence Lader Lectureship, https://bioethics.hms.harvard.edu/events/lectures/lader-lecture (accessed 6 June 2024) and correspondence with Louise Perkins King, May and June 2023; Lawrence Lader, *Breeding Ourselves to Death* (Ballantine Books, 1971).

37. Lader used Dr. Lonny Myer's Chicago-based Illinois Citizens for the Medical Control of Abortion conference to launch his own ambitions for a national organization. With Myers and her Chicago colleagues providing most of the funding and doing all the local work to pull off the conference, Lader took the credit and the reins of the new organization. *First National Conference on Abortion Laws*, MC313, Schlesinger; David J. Garrow, *Liberty and Sexuality: The Right to Privacy and the Making of* Roe v. Wade (Macmillan Publishing Company, 1994), 167, 360-361; Mary Ziegler, "The Framing of a Right to Choose: *Roe v. Wade* and the Changing Debate on Abortion Law, *Law and History Review* 27(2) (Summer 2009): 302; Joan Roelofs, *Foundations and Public Policy: The Mask of Pluralism* (State University of New York Press, 2003), 115; "D.C. Abortions Decline Despite Legalization," *Journal News* (White Plains, New York), 11 February 1970; Lonny Myers interview, September 1976, Family Planning Oral History Project, Schlesinger Library; Lawrence Lader interview, Papers of Lawrence Lader, Box 20, Schlesinger Library.

38. Estelle Griswold, Connecticut Hall of Fame, https://www.cwhf.org/inductees/estelle-griswold (accessed 4 June 2023); Lee Buxton in Osborne list of American Eugenics Society members 1974, American Philosophical Society; "Reminiscences of Estelle Griswold: Oral History, 1976," Women's History and Population Issues Project, Columbia Center for Oral History, Columbia University.

The American Eugenics Society explicitly stated that its name change to the Society for the Study of Social Biology in 1972 "did not align with a change in interest or policy" (American Eugenics Society, Embryo Project Encyclopedia, Arizona State University).

39. Betty Friedan to NOW membership, letter, 15 January 1968, https://feminist.org/resources/feminist-chronicles/part-iii-the-early-documents/national-organization-for-women-letter-from-pres-betty-friedan-jan-15-1968/ (accessed 6 June 2023); Betty Friedan, "Abortion: A Woman's Civil Right," 1969 NARAL conference in *Before Roe v. Wade,* ed. Linda Greenhouse and Reva B. Siegel (Yale Law School, 2025); *First National Conference on Abortion Laws*, MC313, Schlesinger; Population Crisis Committee members; Bernard Nathanson with Richard Ostling, *Aborting America*, 1979, 49–50; Mary Ziegler, "The Framing of a Right to Choose: *Roe v. Wade* and the Changing Debate on Abortion Law, *Law and History Review* 27(2) (Summer 2009): 313; Conni Bille, phone interview by author, 21 February 2023; Felicia Kornbluh, *A Woman's Life Is a Human Life* (Grove Press, 2023): 55, 113.

40. Lonny Myers interview, September 1976, Family Planning Oral History Project, Schlesinger Library; California Committee on Therapeutic Abortion, Collection 1195,

Box 1, UCLA; *Conni Bille interview by author, 21 February 2023*; Lawrence Lader remarks, 18 October 2000, New York City: https://www.youtube.com/watch?v=nJik_tXwzgc (accessed 6 June 2023).

41. David McKelvy, "Abortion Support Growing Fast," *Vidette* (Illinois State University), 8 December 1970; NARAL ads, *New York Times*, 22 April 1971 and 28 April 1972; "D.C. Abortions Decline Despite Legalization," *Journal News* (White Plains, New York), 11 February 1970; Roy Lucas, "Statement on Medical Referral Agencies, 27 September 1971 and Roy Lucas to NARAL Board, 1 October 1971 in Lucas papers, Box 25, Wesleyan; *Conni Bille interview by author, 21 February 2023*; Florence Crittenton endorsement, California Committee on Therapeutic Abortion, Collection 1195, Box 1, UCLA; UAW supports NARAL, Papers of Lawrence Lader, Folder 20, Schlesinger Library.

Wealthy eugenicists Beatrice McClintock and Jesse Hartman's donations to the Human Betterment Association generated named sterilization funds that indigent people could apply to use for the operation. Hartman's targeted effort in Berea, Kentucky, was reported on widely (Ziegler, "Reinventing," 337; "Sterilization Plan Backer Considers One for Florida," *Miami Herald*, 8 January 1965).

42. Alan F. Guttmacher, "Medical Application of Genetic Theory," *Eugenic Quarterly* 3(2) (June 1956): 67–68; Alan F. Guttmacher, "The Genesis of Liberalized Abortion in New York: A Personal Insight," *Case Western Reserve Law Review* 23(4) (1972): 761–62; Harriet F. Pilpel, "Abortion: U.S.A. Is Style," *Journal of Sex Research* 11(2) (May 1975): 113–18; Rockefeller funding for American Law Institute noted, https://www.ali.org/about-ali/story-line/.

43. Lawrence Lader, "The Scandal of Abortion Laws," *New York Times*, 25 April 1965; "D.C. Abortions Decline Despite Legalization," *Journal News* (White Plains, New York), 11 February 1970; Alan F. Guttmacher, "The Genesis of Liberalized Abortion in New York: A Personal Insight," *Case Western Reserve Law Review* 23(4) (1972): 761–62; Arthur Freund to Joseph Sunnen, 15 February 1972, Lucas papers, Wesleyan; Mary Ziegler, "The Framing of a Right to Choose: *Roe v. Wade* and the Changing Debate on Abortion Law," *Law and History Review* 27(2) (Summer 2009): 303 fn132.

44. James C. Millstone, "Legalized Abortion Drive Gains," *St. Louis Post-Dispatch*, 20 February 1970; David Garrow, *Liberty and Sexuality: The Right to Privacy and the Making of* Roe v. Wade (Macmillan Publishing Company, 1994), 505, 522; Lucas to Landfather, 16 December 1970; Joan Roelofs, *Foundations and Public Policy: The Mask of Pluralism* (State University of New York Press, 2003), 115.

45. Lucas to Allan Barnes, Rockefeller Foundation letter, 7 September 1970, Roy Lucas papers, Box 25, Correspondence 1972; Wesleyan; Lader letter to Sunnen, 20 April 1970, California Committee on Therapeutic Abortion, Collection 1195, Box 1, UCLA; Lucas letter to Samuel Landfather, Sunnen Foundation, 16 December 1970, Wesleyan. Roy Lucas was the legal officer of NARAL (David Garrow, *Liberty and Sexuality: The Right to Privacy and the Making of Roe v. Wade* (Macmillan Publishing Company, 1994), 354).

46. James Madison Constitutional Law Institute, Prospectus (21); Unsolicited Comments, and Prospectus for Population Law Center; Letter from Lucas to Stewart Mott, 29 December 1970, Box 25, Misc. Correspondence and Money, Lucas papers, Wesleyan;

Harriet Pilpel, "The Right of Abortion," *Atlantic*, June 1969; Marian Faux, *Roe v. Wade: The Untold Story of the Landmark Supreme Court Decision That Made Abortion Legal* (Cooper Square Press, 2001), 170; David Garrow, *Liberty and Sexuality: The Right to Privacy and the Making of Roe v. Wade* (Macmillan Publishing Company, 1994), 502.

Donald Harting, VP East of NARAL, reported that Lucas was Chairman of American Bar Association's Committee on Overpopulation (Harting and Helen Hunter, "Abortion Techniques and Services," *American Journal of Public Health*, October 1971, 2089–90). Morris Dees, co-founder of the James Madison Constitutional Law Institute, provided a $1 million endowment and subsequent financial support from the M&M Charitable Foundation (letter David Greenspan to Morris Dees, 1 December 1970, Roy Lucas papers, Box 25, Money; Roy Lucas, "Federal Constitutional Limitations on the Enforcement and Administration of State Abortion Statutes," *North Carolina Law Review* 46(4) (1968).

47. Marian Faux, *Roe v. Wade: The Untold Story of the Landmark Supreme Court Decision That Made Abortion Legal* (Cooper Square Press, 2001), 170; David J Garrow, *Liberty and Sexuality: The Right to Privacy and the Making of* Roe v. Wade (Macmillan Publishing Company, 1994), 408–9, 502, 505; Joan Roelofs, *Foundations and Public Policy: The Mask of Pluralism* (State University of New York Press, 2003), 5, 115; Lucas to Robert Hall, 6 December 1970, Lucas to Samuel Landfather, 16 December 1970, Memo from Roy Lucas, 19 December 1970, and Lucas to Nat Lerhman (Playboy), Lucas papers, Box 25, Wesleyan; Lucas to David Llelwer, 14 December 1970; Derek S. Hoff, *The State and the Stork: The Population Debate and Policy Making in US History* (University of Chicago Press, 2012), 182; Sarah Weddington, *A Question of Choice* (G. P. Putnam's Sons, 1992), 86. Lucas solicited other individuals, too, like philanthropist Stewart Mott (letter 29 December 1970) in Lucas papers; "The Cost of Abortion Reform" and letter from JDRIII to Cordelia May, 30 December 1970, RAC—JMCLI; Myra MacPherson, "MDs File Abortion Lawsuit," *Washington Post*, 30 September 1969; "State Abortion Curb Challenged in Suit as a Violation of Rights," *New York Times*, 1 October 1969; Fred Graham, "Court Fight for Legal Abortions Spurred by Washington Ruling," *New York Times*, 12 November 1969; Fred Graham, "Abortions: Moves to Abolish All Legal Restraints," *New York Times*, 16 November 1969; "Constitutional Rights," *Time*, 19 September 1969.

48. Lucas letter to Stewart Mott, 29 December 1970, Lucas Papers, Box 25, Money; "Population Council funders of $1000 or more, 1952–1977," in *The Population Council: A Chronicle of the First Twenty-Five Years, 1952–1977* (Population Council, 1978), 163; Bernard Nathanson with Richard Ostling, *Aborting America*, 1979, 54; Lucas to Samuel Landfather, Sunnen Foundation, 16 December 1970, Lucas papers Box 25, Money; Sarah Weddington, *A Question of Choice* (Penguin Books, 1993), 91–93 and *A Question of Choice 40th edition* (Feminist Press, 2013), 308; Robert Mcg. Thomas Jr., "Thomas Cabot, 98, Capitalist And Philanthropist, Is Dead," *New York Times*, 10 June 1995.

49. Lucas to Carol Crawford, Office of Robert Packwood, 8 October 1970, Lucas papers, Box 25, Sept.-Dec. 1970 Money, Wesleyan; Joan Roelofs, *Foundations and Public Policy: The Mask of Pluralism* (State University of New York Press, 2003), 115; David J. Garrow, *Liberty and Sexuality: The Right to Privacy and the Making of Roe v. Wade* (Macmillan Publishing Company, 1994), 540.

50. Linda Greenhouse, "Constitutional Question: Is There a Right to Abortion?," *New York Times*, 25 January 1970; Cyril Means, "'The Phoenix of Abortional Freedom,' Is a Penumbral or Ninth Amendment Right About to Arise from the Nineteenth Century Legislative Ashes of a Fourteenth-Century Common Law Liberty?" *New York Forum* 17 (Fall 1971): 335–410; Elaine Woo, "Lawrence Lader, 86; Activist for Abortion Rights Whose Book Was Cited in Roe Case," *LA Times*, 14 May 2006; *Roe v. Wade* (1973), https://supreme.justia.com/cases/federal/us/410/113/; Lader's *Abortion* (1966) is cited in Calif. Therapeutic law, see "The California Therapeutic Abortion Act: An Analysis" by Brian Pendleton, *Hastings Law Journal* 19(1) (January 1967); G. Alan Tarr, *Judicial Process and Judicial Policymaking*, 294; Felicia Kornbluh, *A Woman's Life Is a Human Life* (Grove Press, 2023): 39–40.

Regarding ASA and Cordelia Scaife May, see: 11 December 1974 memo from Jimmye Kimmeny to ASA Board of Directors and *ASA Newsletter*, 3(3–4) (1973): 8, NARAL, MC 313, Box 18, Folder 274, Schlesinger Library; Jimmye Kimmey, "Abortion Law Reform in the United States," ed. by Linda Greenhouse and Reva Siegel, *Before Roe v. Wade: Voices That Shaped the Abortion Debate Before the Supreme Court's Ruling* (Creative Commons, 2012): 31–33; Miroslava Chavez-Garcia, "From 'Tough Love' to 'Street Fight': Garrett Hardin and Cordelia S. May's Battle for Population Control and Eugenics at the Turn of the Millennium," *Revista Brasileira de História* 43(94) (2023): 175–98; Nicholas Kulish and Mike McIntire, "Why an Heiress Spent Her Fortune Trying to Keep Immigrants Out," *New York Times*, 14 August 2019; Martin Wooster, "Newly Unearthed Documents Reveal Heiress Cordelia Scaife May's Philanthropic Legacy," *Philanthropy Daily*, 30 October 2019.

51. "Free Birth Curb Devices Offered," *Beckley Post-Herald* (West Virginia), 11 August 1965; Gary Ronberg, "He Wants to Be Population Traffic Cop," *St. Louis Post-Dispatch*, 19 November 1972.

52. "Ways to Lower Costs of Legal Abortions Sought," *Daily Independent* (San Rafael, California), 14 May 1971; Health and Welfare Agency press release, "Abortion Rate in California Drops," 25 May 1973, Abortion (I12), The National Women's History Project.

Of the statewide abortion seekers, the vast majority (70 percent) were under the age of twenty-five, and of those twenty and younger, 40 percent relied on Medi-Cal, the state's Medicare program, which provided health services to the medically indigent (Walter Ballard, "California Abortion Statistics for 1971," *California Medicine* 116(4) (Apr. 1972): 55; "The Medi-Cal program—1966–1971," *California Medicine* 114(2) (Feb. 1971): 63.

53. Bernard Nathanson with Richard Ostling, *Aborting America* (1979), 87; Marian Faux, *Roe v. Wade: The Untold Story of the Landmark Supreme Court Decision That Made Abortion Legal* (Cooper Square Press, 2001), 221; Sarah Weddington, *A Question of Choice* (Penguin Books, 1993), 85–86; Roy Lucas, "Statement on Medical Referral Agencies, 27 September 1971 and Roy Lucas to NARAL Board, 1 October 1971 in Lucas papers, Box 25, Wesleyan.

McClintock used her money and standing to support abortion in the late 1960s and early 1970s. She was a participant in the First National Conference on Abortion Laws that created NARAL (where she served as Assistant Treasurer), a sponsor of the Abortion Rights Association of New York; and recruited into the Association for the Study of Abortion by Smith. She was also a member of the eugenically rooted Human Betterment Association and the Population Crisis Committee. (The late journalist Kevin Begos traced the Human Betterment Association's evolution from the earlier pro-choice organization Birthright in "The American Eugenics Movement After World War II," *IndyWeek.com*, 25 May 2011, https://indyweek.com/news/american-eugenics-movement-world-war-ii-part-2-3/)

54. Ralph Montgomery, "Family Agency Aids New Lake Group," *News-Herald* (Willoughby, Ohio), 24 September 1971.

The award total was not recorded. For foundation's eugenic and population control mission and funding of Planned Parenthood and NARAL, see entry in Case Western Reserve's *Encyclopedia of Cleveland History*, https://case.edu/ech/articles/b/brush-foundation (accessed 5 May 2023).

The father-in-law Charles put Dorothy at the head of his agency when his son (her husband) died (Joan Marie Johnson, *Funding Feminism: Monied Women, Philanthropy, and the Women's Movement, 1870–1967* (University of North Carolina Press, 2017), 196; Brush Foundation website: https://www.brushfoundation.org/presidentsmessage).

55. "Albuquerque Doctor Joins Med School," *Albuquerque Journal*, 8 November 1971; Bruce Ferguson, Proposed Fellowship application (January 1971), Western Reserve Historical Society, Mss.4736, 2(29).

56. Bruce Ferguson, 1 May 1971 Fellowship application, Western Reserve Historical Society, Mss.4736, 2(29); Garrett Hardin, "Tragedy of the Common."

57. Ferguson to Weir, 7 September 1971. See, for example, Charles Brenner et al., "Navajo Infant Mortality, 1970," *Public Health Reports* (89) (July-August 1974), 353–59.

58. Charles Francis Brush to David R. Weir, letter 15 July 1971; Carrie Seidman, "The Battle for the Abortion Dollar," *Albuquerque Journal*, 2 April 1995; Bruce Ferguson obituary, *Albuquerque Journal*, 5 January 2014, http://obits.abqjournal.com/obits/show/239793; Brianna Theobald, *Reproduction on the Reservation: Pregnancy, Childbirth, and Colonialism in the Long Twentieth Century* (University of North Carolina Press), 152–53. According to Theobald, on the Navajo Nation, sterilizations "doubled between 1972 and 1978" (*Reproduction on the Reservation*), 153.

59. Christopher Tietze, Samuel R Poliakoff, and John Rock, "The Clinical Effectiveness of the Rhythm Method of Contraception," *Journal of Fertility and Sterility* 2(5) (1951); Christopher Tietze, *Bibliography of Fertility Control: 1950–1965.* Publication No. 23 (New York: National Committee on Maternal Health, 1965); M. L. Meldrum, "'Simple Methods' and 'Determined Contraceptors': The Statistical Evaluation of Fertility Control, 1957–1968," *Bulletin of the History of Medicine* 70(2) (1996): 266–95; Harriet Pilpel, "The Right of Abortion," *Atlantic*, June 1969; Jane Brody, "Abortion Law Linked in Study to 19,000-Birth Drop in City," *New York Times*, 23 February 1973; *The Population Council: A Chronicle of the First Twenty-Five Years, 1952–1977* (Population Council, 1978), 86–97. For a history of the Human Betterment Association and its many other names, see the history page of the organization, https://www.engenderhealth.org/about/history (accessed 21 November 2024).

The Rockefeller Archive Center's Philosophy Roundtable concluded: "From its beginning, the Population Council was associated with eugenics. Its first president, Frederick Osborn, was a founding member of the American Eugenics Society. Eugenics and alarm about population growth were entwined for decades. . . ." https://www.philanthropyroundtable.org/almanac/rockefeller-iii-births-the-population-council/ (accessed 6 June 2023). Mary Ziegler analyzed the Population Council and the Human Betterment Foundation as "pro-eugenic groups redefined themselves and their programs in order to ensure their political survival." In particular, she noted that "Recognizing the connection between eugenic goals and issues of population control was politically significant for the Council" (Mary Ziegler, "Reinventing Eugenics: Reproductive Choice and Law Reform After World War II," *Cardozo J.L. & Gender* 319 (2008): 331–32.

60. Osborne list of American Eugenics Members, American Philosophical Society (Philadelphia, PA), 1974; "Birth Control Meeting," *Eugenical News* (March 1941), https://compass.fivecolleges.edu/object/smith:1349779#page/2/mode/2up (accessed 26 June 2023); Mary Ziegler, "The Framing of a Right to Choose: *Roe v. Wade* and the Changing Debate on Abortion Law," *Law and History Review* 27(2) (Summer 2009): 306–7; Finding Aid, Alan Guttmacher Institute Records, Smith College, https://findingaids.smith.edu/agents/corporate_entities/1081.

61. Wendy Kline, *Building a Better Race: Gender, Sexuality, and Eugenics from the Turn of the Century to the Baby Boom* (University of California Press, 2001), 161–64; Katherine Parkin, "'A Dead Husband Is a Better Ticket to Congress Than a Log Cabin,'" *Suffrage at 100: Women in American Politics Since 1920*, ed. Stacie Taranto and Leandra Zarnow (Johns Hopkins University Press, 2020); Molly Ladd-Taylor, "Eugenics, Sterilisation and Modern Marriage in the USA: The Strange Career of Paul Popenoe," *Gender & History* 13(2) (August 2001): 323–29.

Chapter 2

1. "British Taking a Look at Abortion Profits," *Kansas City Times*, 16 April 1969; Ena Nauton, "AMA Shifts Abortion Stand; 'Profit-Seeking' Is Attacked," *Miami Herald*, 26 June 1970; Annabelle Kerins, "1st Suffolk Abortion Site Planned, *Newsday* (Nassau), 11 November 1970; "Abortion Profits Soaring," *Lubbock Avalanche-Journal*, 4 June 1971; Pennie Sue Thurman, "Midwest's Fastest Growing Industry—Abortion Referral," *Commonwealth Reporter* (Fond du Lac, Wisconsin), 9 December 1971; "ICCS Recommends NY Exclusively For Abortions," *Cedar Rapids Gazette*, 3 February 1972; Betty Yarmon, "Abortion Costs Lower Since Liberalization of Laws," *Muncie Star*, 10 June 1973; Nanette Davis, *The Abortion Market: Transactions in a Risk Commodity* (Ph.D. diss., Michigan State University, 1972), 50.

Hawai'i was the first state to legalize abortions, in March 1970, and a study of abortions there from 1970–1972 found prices ranged from $0 to $350, with traveling to Honolulu an additional cost for women on other islands (Douglas Mardfin, "Economics of Abortion Demand by Pregnant Married Women: The Ultimate Fertility Choice.," Ph.D. diss., University of Hawai'i, 1979).

2. Martin Ebon, ed., *Everywoman's Guide to Abortion* (Universe Books, 1971), 52–53; National Center for Education Statistics, Table 320. Average undergraduate tuition and fees and room and board rates charged for full-time students in degree-granting

institutions, by type and control of institution: 1964–65 through 2006–07, https://nces.ed.gov/programs/digest/d07/tables/dt07_320.asp; "Volkswagen Raises 1971 Beetle Prices for a Second Time," *New York Times*, 16 December 1970; Byllye Avery and Susan Reverby, "Ask a Feminist: Byllye Avery Discusses the Past and Future of Reproductive Justice," *Signs* 46(3) (2021), 760–61, http://signsjournal.org/avery/; Barbara Corday, *The Choices We Made: 25 Women and Men Speak Out About Abortion*, ed. Angela Bonavoglia (Four Walls Eight Windows, 2001), 77.

3. Nancy Howell Lee, *The Search for an Abortionist* (University of Chicago Press, 1969), 91.

4. J. B. Kahn, Judith Bourne, and C. W. Tyler Jr., "The Impact of Recent Changes in Therapeutic Abortion Laws," *Clinical Obstetrics and Gynecology* 14(4) (December 1971): 1130–48; Richard A. Schwartz, "Abortion on Request," *Case Western Reserve Law Review* 23(4) (1972): 843.

5. Judith Arcana, phone interview by author, 18 August 2022; Michelle Mehrtens, "The Underground Abortion Network That Inspired 'Call Jane,'" *Smithsonian Magazine*, 28 October 2022; as told to Patricia Anstett, "I Was Salvaging My Own Life," *Chicago Today*, 1 February 1971; "A Pink Dress and $500 Will Get You an Abortion," *Perquimans Weekly* (Hertford, North Carolina), 27 May 1971; Deborah Ross, Laura Peck, and Peg Spear, phone interview by author, 30 October 2020; Leslie Reagan, "Abortion Travels," *Journal of Modern European History* 17(3) (2019): 337–38 and *When Abortion Was a Crime: Women, Medicine, and Law in the United States, 1867–1973* (University of California Press, 1997), 224–225; Richard Metzger, "Paul Krassner," dangerousminds.net, 7 February 2013, https://dangerousminds.net/comments/paul_krassner_how_a_satirical_editor_became_a_one_man (accessed 11 July 2023).

6. Mrs. X, "One Woman's Abortion," *Atlantic*, August 1965; Nancy Howell Lee, *The Search for an Abortionist* (University of Chicago Press, 1969), 94; David P. Cline, *Creating Choice: A Community Responds to the Need for Abortion and Birth Control, 1961–1973* (Palgrave Macmillan, 2006), 166; David Lowe, *Abortion & The Law* (Pocket Books, 1966), ix.

For example, Jill Fine, who had already gotten a pregnancy test, was forced to pay $500 for another one in New York City, on top of the $1,000 the man was charging for the abortion. She testified that she would have had to pay $25 to three psychiatrists to make her appeal for a therapeutic abortion but opted instead to spend $1,000 for an illegal abortion. An anonymous woman testified that she was quoted $2,000 for a second-trimester abortion (Jill Fine Parks, phone interview by author, 21 February 2021; anonymous speaker and Jill Fine at Houston Abortion Tribunal, 21 October 1972, Wisconsin Historical Society Archives, Women's National Abortion Action Coalition Records, 1969–1973, File 786A/11—"Tapes of Abortion Tribunal Held in Houston, Texas, Including Testimony, 21 October 1972"; "Doreen," 1972, WONAAC Case Western).

One common refrain was needing to borrow a car or get a ride, with most women generally not owning a car or even having a driver's license, especially poor, urban, and rural women (Margaret Homans, email interview by author, 6 June 2020; Katherine Parkin, *Women at the Wheel* (University of Pennsylvania Press, 2017), xvii–xviii, 2–3, 9).

7. Nancy Howell Lee, *The Search for an Abortionist* (University of Chicago Press, 1969), 92; "Comments on Women's Pavilion," South Carolina Clergy Referrals, Correspondence, 1970–1972, Winthrop University, Louise Pettus Archives & Special Collections, Rock Hill, South Carolina; Martin Ebon, ed., *Everywoman's Guide to Abortion* (Universe Books, 1971), 42; "Doreen," Case Western Tribunal, 1972, WONAAC, Wisconsin Historical Society; David P. Cline, *Creating Choice: A Community Responds to the Need for Abortion and Birth Control, 1961–1973* (Palgrave Macmillan, 2006), 35.

Linda Proctor recalled needing to return the $30 her friend lent her for an abortion, and she sent it certified mail because it was so much money (phone interview by author, 1 April 2021)..

8. "Student Presses for Abortion Fund," *The Good Five Cent Cigar* (URI), 14 April 1971; Charlotte Muller, "Health Insurance for Abortion Costs: A Survey," in *Family Planning Perspectives* 2(4) (October 1970): 12; "Cost of Abortion, Various Cities, 1972" table in "Abortion: The Continuing Controversy," by C. E. Behrens in *Population Bulletin* 28(4) (1972): 28; Sam Kindrick, "Offbeat: Abortions Numerous and Expensive in S.A.," *San Antonio Express*, 6 November 1972. Lawrence Lader stated in 1968 that an abortion in Puerto Rico ran "$500 plus air fare and hotel" and that London, all totaled, was "almost a $1,000" (*Abortion in a Changing World, Vol II*, ed. Robert E. Hall (Columbia University Press, 1970), 26.

9. John Bartlow Martin, "Abortion," *Saturday Evening Post*, 20 May 1969, 21; David P. Cline, *Creating Choice: A Community Responds to the Need for Abortion and Birth Control, 1961–1973* (Palgrave Macmillan, 2006), 57; Rickie Solinger, "Extreme Danger: Women Abortionists and Their Clients Before Roe v. Wade," *Not June Cleaver: Women and Gender in Postwar America, 1945–1960* (Temple University Press, 1994), 354; Kelly O'Donnell, "Reproducing Jane: Abortion Stories and Women's Political Histories," *Signs: Journal of Women in Culture & Society* 43(1) (Autumn 2017): 77–96; Nancy Howell Lee, *The Search for an Abortionist* (University of Chicago Press), 91. Lee's 1969 study revealed 36 of 114 couples who appealed to friends or relatives, with 30 of them telling "the real purpose of the loan."

10. "Student Presses for Abortion Fund," *The Good Five Cent Cigar* (URI), 14 April 1971; Sarah Weddington, *A Question of Choice* (Penguin, 1993), 35; an Interview with Carol Giardina, "I Helped My Classmates Get Illegal Abortions Before Roe. We Can't Go Back," *Jacobin.com*, 21 May 2022.

11. Elaine Morrissey, "Fear Stalks Florida Girl Convicted of Abortion," *Dayton Daily News*, 10 October 1971; Katherine Parkin, "The Women's National Abortion Action Coalition & the Abortion Tribunals, 1971–1972," *Journal of Family History* 47(4) (October 2022): 367–400.

The account is post-*Roe* but reflects that some people historically prioritized paying for a desperately needed abortion before food and rent. Written on Christmas Day, the reporter described finding the money for a desperately needed abortion: "In Phoenix, a 13-year-old girl paid with her family's $250 monthly welfare check" (Steven V. Roberts, "Abortion Cutoff Causing Hardship for Poor Women Around Country," *New York Times*, 25 December 1977).

12. Kathy D. (Out-of-state women), Testimony from hearings held by borough president Percy Sutton on October 16, 1970, reported by Susan Edmiston, "A Report on the Abortion Capital of the Country," *New York Times*, 11 April 1971.

13. David Lowe, *Abortion & the Law* (Pocket Books, 1966), 13–14; Nancy Howell Lee, *The Search for an Abortionist* (University of Chicago Press, 1969), 91–92; "Abortion: I'm a Single Working Girl," *Appleton Post Crescent*, 14 June 1970; Barbara Corday, *The Choices We Made: 25 Women and Men Speak Out About Abortion*, ed. Angela Bonavoglia (Four Walls Eight Windows, 2001), 74–75; *Back Rooms: Voices from the Illegal Abortion Era*; David P. Cline, *Creating Choice: A Community Responds to the Need for Abortion and Birth Control, 1961–1973* (Palgrave Macmillan, 2006), 106–7; Anonymous, "When Abortion Was Legalized: One Woman's DC Experience," *Washington Area Spark*, 29 February 1972; Linda Proctor, phone interview by author, 1 April 2021.

14. Nancy Howell Lee, *The Search for an Abortionist* (University of Chicago Press, 1969), 92; Nadine Cohodas, "Abortions on L.I.—A Progress Report," *New York Times*, 27 February 1972.

15. This reflects a woman getting a vacation loan earlier than March 1969. Susan Brownmiller, "Everywoman's Abortions: 'The Oppressor Is a Man,'" *Village Voice*, 27 March 1969.

16. Carole Joffe, *Doctors of Conscience* (Beacon Press, 1995), 113; David P. Cline, *Creating Choice: A Community Responds to the Need for Abortion and Birth Control, 1961–1973* (Palgrave Macmillan, 2006), 42; Nancy Howell Lee, *The Search for an Abortionist* (University of Chicago Press, 1969), 91; *Abortion Rap*, 56. It is not documented if the couples had individual women securing the loans, or if their husbands cosigned the loan.

17. Janet Bowers, "Bank Loans Help Iowans Get Abortions," *Des Moines Register*, 16 September 1972; David Lowe, *Abortion & The Law* (Pocket Books, 1966), 13.

18. Janet Bowers, "Bank Loans Help Iowans Get Abortions," *Des Moines Register*, 16 September 1972.

19. "Abortion: I'm a Single Working Girl," *Appleton Post Crescent* (Wisconsin), 14 June 1970.

20. Janet Bowers, "Bank Loans Help Iowans Get Abortions," *Des Moines Register*, 16 September 1972, 1.

These figures align with what Sylvia Porter outlined in "Your Money's Worth: Learn True Costs Before You Borrow," *Fresno Bee* (California), 30 April 1969.

21. "Court Decisions Nullifying Laws Prohibiting Abortion" and Jackson Credit Co. ad, *Clarion-Ledger* (Jackson, Mississippi), 21 January 1970; "More Liberalized Abortion Views Gradually Being Accepted in US" and Rushville National Bank (Personal Loans), *Rushville Republican* (Indiana), 24 March 1970; "PMA Backs Drive to Liberalize Abortion Laws" and Lebanon County Trust Company ad, *Lebanon Daily News* (Pennsylvania), 30 March 1970.

22. "Church Abortion Views Soften" and Marine Midland Personal Loan ad, *Sunday Press* (Binghamton, New York), 17 January 1971 and "Eugenic Abortion Called Ethical" and Peoples Bank and Trust Company ad, *Gazette* (Cedar Rapids, Iowa), 30 March 1971; "N.J. Medical Society Favors Abortions," and Mid State Bank "Will lend you cash for

just about anything . . ." ad, *Central New Jersey Home News*, 9 May 1972; "Family Financial Protection" column and Carbon Emery Bank, "When you need money, see us for a Personal Loan" ad, *Helper Journal* (Helper, Utah), 27 May 1971; "Abortion Rights Group Explains Plan of Action," and Merchants Bank, "The Big Lenders," ad, *Morning Call* (Allentown, Pennsylvania), 3 June 1971; First National Bank and Abortion Counseling, Information and Referral Services ads, *Wright State Guardian* (Dayton, Ohio), 10 February 1971; National Abortion Council and Family Savings & Loan ads, *Los Angeles Sentinel*, 30 September 1971; Tom Foley, "City Ponders Move Against Dr. Kennan," "Abortion Barrier" and "Bank of Madison" ad, *Capital Times* (Madison, Wisconsin), 13 May 1971, 1, 4; "Wisconsin Abortion Still Legal, Special Considerations Apply" and Appleton State Bank ad, *Lawrentian* (Lawrence University, Appleton, Wisconsin), 28 May 1971; Gail Collins, "Westport Girl Stars in Film About Abortion" and Thomas C. Jackson, "Clergy, Planned Parenthood Offer Abortion Guidance" and Westport National Bank ad, *Westport Fairpress*, 16 March 1972, 60.

23. Linda Greenhouse, "New Abortion Agency Here Arranges Travel, Housing and Care in Clinics in London," *New York Times*, 22 March 1970; Martin Ebon, ed., *Everywoman's Guide to Abortion* (Universe Books, 1971), 50; Thomas W. Bush, "Bank of Tokyo Shows It's Not Bound by Tradition," *LA Times*, 6 June 1969; "'Rush' Procedure for Going to Japan," Society for Humane Abortion Collection, MC289, Box 4, Folder 73, Schlesinger Library and in *Before Roe v. Wade: Voices That Shaped the Abortion Debate Before the Supreme Court's Ruling* by Linda Greenhouse and Reva B. Siegel (Yale Law School, 2012), 8–11; "Bank of Tokyo of California" (San Francisco), Society for Human Abortion Collection, MC289, Box 2 Folder 27, Schlesinger Library.

See Chapter 5 for travel to Japan.

24. Marion Meade, "Credit Crazed Dolls," *Cosmopolitan*, May 1969; Joan Cook, "Help for Credit-Card Losers," *New York Times*, 13 October 1970; Margaret Dana, "If You Lose a Credit Card," *Woman's Day*, November 1970; Elizabeth M. Fowler, "Personal Finance," *New York Times*, 15 May 1972; "Abortion? Bring Credit Card" *Bergen Record* (NJ), 13 September 1970; Rose Eveleth, "Forty Years Ago, Women Had a Hard Time Getting Credit Cards," *Smithsonian*, 8 January 2014.

An ad for a personal loan, appearing alongside a positive abortion article, included the MasterCard symbol, suggesting that women could apply for a credit card and use it to pay for an abortion (Merchants Bank, "The Big Lenders," ad, *Morning Call* (Allentown, Pennsylvania), 3 June 1971).

25. Stuart Hills, "Combating Organized Crime in America," *Federal Probation* 33 (March 1969): 24–25; Mark Haller, "Illegal Enterprise: A Theoretical And Historical Interpretation," *Criminology* 28(2) (1990): 207; Peter Reuter, "The Decline of the American Mafia," *Public Interests* (Summer 1995), 97; Robert M. Lombardo, "The Social Organization of Organized Crime in Chicago," *Journal of Contemporary Criminal Justice* 10(4) (December 1994): 290–312; "Profile of Organized Crime," *Great Lakes Region: Hearings Before the Permanent Subcommittee on Investigations of the Committee on Governmental Affairs, United States Senate, Ninety-Eighth Congress, Second Session, January 25, 26, 31, and February 1, 1984*, 81; Matthew G. Yeager, "From Organized Crime to Illicit

Enterprise" *Contemporary Sociology* 5(3) (May 1976), 272–77; David Lowe, *Abortion & the Law* (Pocket Books, 1966), 6.

26. John Seidl, *"Upon the Hip"—- A Study of the Criminal Loan-Shark Industry*, Dissertation, Harvard University, 1969, 100–1, 106, 126; Lawrence J. Kaplan and Salvatore Matteis, "The Economics of Loansharking," *American Journal of Economics and Sociology* 27(3) (July 1968): 239–52; John Seidl summarized in Matthew G. Yeager, "From Organized Crime to Illicit Enterprise," *Contemporary Sociology* 5(3) (May 1976), 272–77; US Census Bureau, Statistical Abstract of the United States (US Government, 1976), Recent Trends, XX.

Debt was familiar to American households. Economist Annelise Graebner Anderson pegged consumer debt in 1970 at nearly $127 billion, with 80 percent of it being paid on installment, and a per-person average debt of about $634 (*The Business of Organized Crime: A Cosa Nostra Family* [Hoover Institution Press, 1979], 64–69).

27. Tom Mainor, phone interview by author, 8 March 2022; "Restudy Wanted of Abortion Law," *Daily Advertiser* (Lafayette, Louisiana), 20 May 1971; "Presbyterian Board Move, Church to Help Black Banks," *Atlanta Constitution*, 30 April 1971; Ellen Molloy, "Loans, Grants to Women: Presbyterians Get Fund to Assist on Abortions," *Times* (Shreveport, Louisiana), 20 May 1971; Dala McKinsey, "Fund for Abortions: Presbyterian Church Administers 'Fly Now Pay Later' Program," *Camden News* (Arkansas), 9 November 1971; Seth Dowland, *Family Values and the Rise of the Christian Right* (University of Pennsylvania Press, 2015), 115, 118–19; "Presbyterians and Abortion," *Christian Century* 108(6) (20 February 1991): 192.

28. "Presbyterian Board Move, Church to Help Black Banks," *Atlanta Constitution*, 30 April 1971; "With First Honorary Degrees: College Honors Hall, Sanford," *St. Andrews Newsletter* (St. Andrews Presbyterian College), April-June 1971, 1, 3; Terry Sanford letters to Mrs. Riegle (Nov. 4 1971); Mr. Houser (Nov. 4 1971); Mrs. Cox (Nov. 4 1971), Terry Sanford Papers, Abortion Loan, Box 1, Duke University.

29. Ronald F. Banks to Winthrop Libby, 11 September 1973, University of Maine Archive; Jim Mann, "Baird Discusses Abortion and Birth Control Laws," *Maine Campus*, 10 April 1969, 1; Jim Mann, "Baird Discusses Abortion and Birth Control Laws," *Maine Campus*, 10 April 1969, 1; Peter Bergeron to Susan Vogel letter re Baird visit, 18 September 1969, University of Maine Student Senate, University of Maine, General Student Records, UA RG 0009.008, Box 9, 48, Raymond H. Fogler Library Special Collections Department, University of Maine, Orono, Maine; "Senate Committee To Discuss Abortion Loans," *Maine Campus*, 29 October 1970, 3; Ken Johnson, "Baird Takes Abortion Laws to Task," *Maine Campus*, 29 October 1970, 12.

30. "New York Awaits Rush; Abortion Law Now in Effect," *Bangor Daily News*, 1 July 1970.

31. "Senate Committee To Discuss Abortion Loans," *Maine Campus*, 29 October 1970, 3; UPI, "Loans for Abortions Made Available for Co-Eds," *Victoria Daily Times* (British Columbia, Canada), 14 January 1971.

32. Winthrop Libby to Anthony Ezzy, Knights of Columbus, 25 March 1970, UMO Archive. A few years later, Libby published an essay, "The Public Be Damned," in which he

reiterated his assertion that the fund was motivated by humanism, directed by Catholics, did not encourage sex or advertise, and concluded of their efforts to find a way forward, "Students are sensible" (*Crises in Campus Management: Case Studies in the Administration of Colleges and Universities*, ed. George J. Mauer [Praeger Publishers, 1976], 226–30.

33. Ronald F. Banks to Winthrop Libby, 11 September 1973, UMO Archive.

34. "All Students Must Pay for Abortion Fund," *Maine Campus*, 18 February 1971, 3; Ronald F. Banks to Winthrop Libby, 11 September 1973, UMO Archive; Nelson Benton, "Senate Explains Increases in Abortion Loan Fund," *Maine Campus*, 7 January 1971; Dennis Mills, "Orono Campus Students Spur Coed Abortion Loan Fund," *Bangor Daily News*, 11 January 1971; "Maine Students Have Abortion Loan Fund," *Lincoln Journal Star*, 12 January 1971; "Student Loans to Help Coeds with Abortions" *Arizona Daily Star*, 14 January 1971; "Abortion Fund Continues Loans Despite Protests, Investigations," *Daily Princetonian*, 19 March 1971 (article accompanied by an abortion ad on same page).

Bringing Baird to campus not only opened up the public discussions of birth control and abortion, it also gave women like Dr. Susan Tracy access to abortion referrals. As she said, "I knew how to get in touch with him" (David P. Cline, *Creating Choice: A Community Responds to the Need for Abortion and Birth Control, 1961–1973* (Palgrave Macmillan, 2006), 57.

35. Cathy Flynn, "Abortions in New York: Two Girls Tell Their Stories," *Maine Campus*, 6 May 1971; "55 Abortion Loans Have Been Granted," *Maine Campus*, 7 December 1972.

Indeed, most women seeking the necessary abortion information (name, telephone number, address) had already made up their minds to have an abortion. One reverend estimated in 1969 that 95 percent had already decided when they came to his office (Doris Andrea Dirks and Patricia A. Relf, *To Offer Compassion: A History of the Clergy Consultation Service on Abortion* [University of Wisconsin Press, 2017], 68).

36. Students also investigated setting up abortion loan funds at Louisiana State University, University of Nebraska—Lincoln, University of Texas—Austin, Sarasota New College, Coe College, College of the Sequoias, University of North Carolina—Chapel Hill, UCLA, and Florida State University (Leslie Taylor, "UT Budget Facing Big Fund Cut," *Austin American-Statesman*, 3 June 1971; "Regents Change UT Austin Tax," *Prospector* (El Paso), 17 June 1971; Jim Bleyere, "Special Fund Used for Abortions at New College?," *Tampa Tribune-Times*, 14 November 1971; "Coe to Have Abortion Loan Fund," *Iowa City Press-Citizen*, 16 October 197; "Coe College Has Abortion Loan Fund," *Argus-Leader* (Sioux Falls, South Dakota), 17 October 1971; "To Keep Coeds in School: College Weighs Abort Fund," *Independent* (Long Beach, California), 11 November 1971; Lana Starnes, "College Loans for Abortion?," *Daily Tar Heel*, 7 April 1971; Ed Rowland, "Abortion Loan Funds Established on At Least Two Campuses in N.C.," *Danville Register* (Virginia), 3 February 1972; letters of inquiry from UCLA student and LA ZPG President Judy Kunofsky to Larry Zawilenski, 7 March 1972 and Helen Gates to Larry Zawilenski, 17 April 1972 courtesy of Kathy Mallin records; *Florida Flambeau*, 1 May 1972.

37. "Student Presses for Abortion Fund," *The Good Five Cent Cigar* (URI), 14 April 1971.

38. Handwritten minutes from Associated Students of Duke University (ASDU), 11 May 1971, 4, Duke University Archives; Handwritten minutes from ASDU, 18 May 1971, 5–6, Duke University Archives; Bill Kennedy, phone interview by author, 15 April 2022; Hayley Farless, "Before 'Roe,' This University Had an Abortion Fund for Students," rewirenewsgroup.com, 13 February 2017; Duke University's 1971 undergraduate enrollment, Duke University Archives. "Office of the University Registrar records, 1853–2000: Statistics 1925–1999."

39. "Abortion Loan," *Chronicle*, 10 March 1971, 2; Tom Markham, "Abortion Loan Program Readied," *Chronicle*, 25 October 1971, 3; "Abortion Loan" *Chronicle*, 10 November 1971; Hayley Farless, "Before 'Roe,' This University Had an Abortion Fund for Students," rewirenewsgroup.com, 13 February 2017; unpublished, Hayley Farless, "Right to Access: A History of the Duke University Abortion Loan Fund" powerpoint, presented at Duke University, 27 October 2016, in author's possession.

40. Unpublished, Hayley Farless, "Right to Access: A History of the Duke University Abortion Loan Fund" powerpoint, presented at Duke University, 27 October 2016, in author's possession; "No-Interest Abortion Loans Set," *Corpus Christi Caller-Times* (Texas), 27 October 1971; "Loans for Abortions," *Bee* (Danville, Virginia), 28 October 1971; N.d., "Bill Kennedy reported on abortion loan program," handwritten notes, Associated Students of Duke University, Duke University archive.

41. College of William & Mary: Chris Jaaffe, "Birth Control Service to Give Telephone Info," *Flat Hat*, 12 February 1971; "Flat Hat 'Obscenities' Spark Continuing Controversy," *Flat Hat*, 26 February 1971; Will Molineux, "Student Unit Forms Corporation," *Daily Press* (Newport News, Virginia), 23 May 1971; Kelly Morrow, *Sex and the Student Body: Knowledge, Equality, And The Sexual Revolution, 1960 to 1973* (Dissertation, University of North Carolina at Chapel Hill, 2012), 73–76.

42. Leslie Taylor, "UT Budget Facing Big Fund Cut," *Austin American-Statesman*, 3 June 1971; "Regents Change UT Austin Tax," *Prospector* (El Paso), 17 June 1971; Alexis Cheung, "At 16, My Mom Flew to Japan Alone to Have an Abortion," www.thecut.com, February 2017.

It may be that emergency loan funds or short term-loans dispensed through colleges and universities were taken by students for abortions without explicitly identifying their purpose. The Dartmouth student, like students at Indiana University Bloomington, might have listed the reasons for the loan vaguely as "Medical." At Indiana University, a high percentage of the loans granted for medical reasons went to students who received financial aid, suggesting they did not have the financial resources to cope with additional costs (William Ehrich, *A Study of the Short Term Loan Program at Indiana University for the 1970–1971 Academic Year and Summer 68*, Doctor of Education dissertation, Indiana University, 1972, 68).

43. Kathy Mallin, phone interview by author, 16 July 2020; Mary Sue Zivalic, "Student-Run Abortion Service Here," *Chicago Illini*, 7 February 1972; Larry Zawilenski to Dan Gouker letter of response, 24 March 1972, in Kathy Mallin files, held by author.

44. Marie L. Johnson, Dean UIC, letter to student in loan default, n.d.; "Abortion Loan Service—Financial Statement," 26 September 1972; Abortion Loan Program, Revised

Procedure, n.d.; "Dear Faculty Member" letter from Kathy Mallin, 8 May 1972; "Dear Faculty Member" letter from Kathy Mallin, 16 June 1972: all in Kathy Mallin records. Sponsors of the Abortion Loan Service: "Student Government, Zero Population Growth, Women's Liberation, and the Circle Women's Abortion Coalition." In other records, Alternate University is listed as well.

45. Karen Hasman, "New Abortion Loans Helping Circle Co-eds," *Chicago Daily News*, 31 January 1972; Mary Sue Zivalic, "Student-Run Abortion Service Here," *Chicago Illini*, 7 February 1972; "If You're in a Family Way," *Chicago Illini*, 7 February 1972; "Chapter News: Abortion Loan Service," *ZPG National Reporter*, February 1972, 12; "Abortion Loans Made at U. of I. by Campus Group," *Chicago Tribune*, 17 February 1972; Nancy Nist to Larry Zawilenski letter of inquiry re Carleton College, 29 February 1972; Larry Zawilenski to Nancy Nist letter of response, 3 March 1972; Dan Gouker to Larry Zawilenski letter of inquiry, 15 March 1972; Larry Zawilenski to Dan Gouker letter of response, 24 March 1972; Virginia A. Hanson to Larry Zawilenski letter of inquiry, 6 April 1972; UIC Committee on Student Affairs allocation to Women's Liberation re publicity for Abortion Loan and Referral Service, 9 June 1972; "Abortion Loan Service" ad, *Chicago Illini*, 17 July 1972; "Abortion Loan Service" ad, *Chicago Illini*, 30 October 1972: all in Kathy Mallin records.

46. Larry Zawilenski to Nancy Nist letter of response, 3 March 1972; Larry Zawilenski to Dan Gouker letter of response, 24 March 1972; "Insurance Information," n.d, Burton Joseph, Playboy Foundation Executive Director to Larry Zawilenski, Abortion Loan Service letter, 10 April 1972, all in Kathy Mallin records; Olivia Sayre, "Insurance Covers Abortions," *Chicago Illini*, 16 October 1972.

47. Larry Zawilenski to Allan Weiselberg, Eastside Medical Group, 14 March 1972, Kathy Mallin records.

48. Lucianne Goldberg, "Journey to a New York Abortion," *Chicago Today*, 28 March 1972.

49. Kathy Mallin, phone interview by author, 16 July 2020; "Diane 663–2662," Kathy Mallin materials.

50. Patricia Anstett, "Is Wisconsin New Abortion Mecca?," *Chicago Today*; Kathy Mallin to Ms. Moore, Wisconsin Women's Medical Group letter, 5 September 1972; "They are already operating" handwritten page: all from Kathy Mallin records.

51. Kathy Mallin to Ms. Moore, Wisconsin Women's Medical Group letter, 5 September 1972 from Kathy Mallin.

Doris Andrea Dirks and Patricia A. Relf noted that CARES and the Chicago Clergy Service did not send women to Wisconsin, because even with the UIC insurance and lower transportation costs, New York was still cheaper (*To Offer Compassion: A History of the Clergy Consultation Service on Abortion* [University of Wisconsin Press, 2017], 148–49.

52. "The Abortion Loan Fund of the Carleton Women's Caucus," 10 February 1972, Carleton College from Kathy Mallin Archive.

53. "The Abortion Loan Fund of the Carleton Women's Caucus," 10 February 1972, Carleton College from Kathy Mallin Archive; "Women's Concerns," *Carletonian*, 4 May 1972; Sue Swanson, "Abortion and Birth Control Counseling," *Carletonian*, 11 January 1973.

Like many colleges, Carleton reported on Bill Baird's stump speech in their student newspaper in 1969. Carleton students could also see and read about local abortion advocates as well, including alum Dr. Jane Hodgson '34 and Robert McCoy ("Boston Abortion Advocate Discusses Women's Rights," *Carletonian*, 9 October 1969; Jane Dillinger, "Hodgson Speaks About Abortion," *Carletonian*, 11 March 1971).

54. "Women's Center Conducts Abortion Loan Fund Drive," *Iowa City Press-Citizen*, 6 March 1972; "Abortion Loan Fund Slated by U. Group," *Gazette* (Cedar Rapids, Iowa), 7 March 1972; Sue Young, "Loan Fund for Abortions Now Being Fully Utilized," *Daily Iowan*, 5 May 1972; Janet Bowers, "Bank Loans Help Iowans Get Abortions," *Des Moines Register*, 16 September 1972, 1; Sandra Morgen, *Into Our Own Hands: The Women's Health Movement in the United States, 1969–1990*, 90.

55. David Lowe, *Abortion & the Law* (Pocket Books, 1966), 13; Anonymous, "When Abortion Was Legalized: One Woman's DC Experience," *Washington Area Spark*, 29 February 1972; Rebecca Sive, "Feminist Carls," *Carleton Voice*, Winter 2010; Byllye Avery and Susan Reverby, "Ask a Feminist: Byllye Avery Discusses the Past and Future of Reproductive Justice," *Signs* 46(3) (2021), 760–61; David P. Cline, *Creating Choice: A Community Responds to the Need for Abortion and Birth Control, 1961–1973* (Palgrave Macmillan, 2006), 106; Polly Bergen, *The Choices We Made: 25 Women and Men Speak Out About Abortion*, ed. Angela Bonavoglia (Four Walls Eight Windows, 2001), 28; interview with Tom Davis by Eileen McAdam, Skidmore College Retiree Oral History Project, Saratoga Springs, New York, May 13, 2015, https://ssmp.skidmore.edu/exhibits/show/oral_histories/item/252 (accessed 8 September 2023).

Leslie Reagan's discovery of the early insurance policies held by eight hundred "girl clerks" in Newark in 1936 reveals the evident decision to invest in affordable access to abortion. The women paid an abortion provider $2 a month for membership in a "Birth Control Club," which gave them monthly exams and abortions as needed for the low, set fee of $75. As Reagan notes, just as working people made small regular payments for life insurance and funeral coverage, these working women bought a form of health insurance through dues paid to this "club" (*When Abortion was a Crime*), 133–34.

56. David P. Cline, *Creating Choice: A Community Responds to the Need for Abortion and Birth Control, 1961–1973* (Palgrave Macmillan, 2006), 169, 225.

57. Craig Palmer, "Abortions: Insurance Claims on the Rise," *Cincinnati Post*, 25 January 1971.

58. "Cheap, Easy Abortions in New York State Unlikely," *Star-Gazette* (Elmira, New York), 2 June 1970; "Abortion Insurance: Blue Cross of New York to Cover Single Women," *York Dispatch* (New York), 27 June 1970; "Legal Abortion: Who, Why and Where," *Time*, 27 September 1971, 6; "N.Y. Insurance Covers Abortion," *Public Opinion* (Chambersburg, Pennsylvania), 29 June 1970; Merle Hoffman, *Intimate Wars: The Life and Times of the Woman Who Brought Abortion from the Back Alley to the Boardroom* (Feminist Press, 2012), 53–54.

59. Tracy Lucht, *Sylvia Porter: America's Original Personal Finance Columnist* (Syracuse University Press, 2013); Sylvia Porter, "Your Money's Worth: Finances Limit Abortion Option," *Miami Herald*, 27 April 1972.

60. Charlotte F. Muller, "Health Insurance for Abortion Costs: A Survey," *Family Planning Perspectives*

2(4) (Oct. 1970): 12–20; Jean Pakter and Frieda Nelson, "Abortion in New York City: The First Nine Months," *Family Planning Perspectives* 3(3) (July 1971): 6–7; Sylvia Porter, "Your Money's Worth: Finances Limit Abortion Option," *Miami Herald*, 27 April 1972; Charlotte Muller, "Insurance for Abortion" in *Abortion Techniques and Services*, ed. by Sarah Lewit (Exerpta Medica, 1972) (same as *FPP* as above); David Hendin, *Everything You Need to Know About Abortion* (Pinnacle Books, 1971), 148; Guttmacher Institute, "An Early Look at Insurance Coverage of Abortion," https://www.guttmacher.org/perspectives50/early-look-insurance-coverage-abortion (accessed 10 March 2022).

61. Charlotte Muller, "Insurance for Abortion" in *Abortion Techniques and Services: Proceedings of the Conference*, ed. by Sarah Lewit (Exerpta Medica, 1972), 129.

62. Charlotte Muller, "Insurance for Abortion" in *Abortion Techniques and Services: Proceedings of the Conference*, ed. by Sarah Lewit (Exerpta Medica, 1972), 130.

63. Charlotte Muller, "Insurance for Abortion" in *Abortion Techniques and Services: Proceedings of the Conference*, ed. by Sarah Lewit (Exerpta Medica, 1972), 130–33.

64. Robin Adams Sloan, "Abortion," *Indianapolis News*, 29 June 1971; Charlotte Muller, "Insurance for Abortion" in *Abortion Techniques and Services: Proceedings of the Conference*, ed. by Sarah Lewit (Exerpta Medica, 1972), 132–33; "Abortion Insurance Rates?," *Ithaca Journal* (New York), 2 June 1972.

65. Janet Bowers, "Bank Loans Help Iowans Get Abortions," *Des Moines Register*, 16 September 1972, 1; Robert E. Hall, *A Doctor's Guide to Having an Abortion* (Signet, 1971), 36.

66. Nancy Banks, "The Truth About Abortion Referral," *Chicago Reader*, 10 December 1971.

67. Susan Edmiston, "A Report on the Abortion Capital of the Country," *New York Times*, 11 April 1971; Jean Pakter and Frieda Nelson, "Abortion in New York City: The First Nine Months," *Family Planning Perspectives* 3(3) (July 1971): 6–7; Byllye Avery and Susan Reverby, "Ask a Feminist: Byllye Avery Discusses the Past and Future of Reproductive Justice," *Signs* 46(3) (2021).

68. Grace Marie Arnett, "Figures Rise Following Adoption of Liberalized Law," *Albuquerque Journal*, 16 August 1970; Grace Marie Arnett, "Patient Load Necessitates New Quarters," *Albuquerque Journal*, 25 October 1970; Bebe Harris, "Few Insurance Firms Cover Abortion," *Charlotte Observer* (North Carolina), 29 April 1972.

69. Women's Health and Abortion Project, *The Abortion Game* (University of Wisconsin Library, 1972), 18–31.

70. Women's Health and Abortion Project, *The Abortion Game* (University of Wisconsin Library, 1972), 18–31; Susan Reverby, phone interview by author, 2 December 2021; Don Sloan, with Paula Hartz, *A Doctor's Perspective/A Woman's Dilemma* (Donald Fine, Inc., 1992), 58; Doris Andrea Dirks and Patricia A. Relf, *To Offer Compassion: A History of the Clergy Consultation Service on Abortion* (University of Wisconsin Press, 2017), 138; Jane E. Brody, "Medicine/Science: It's Still Difficult to Get an Abortion in New York," *New York Times*, 25 October 1970.

71. Joan Brown, "New Policy . . . Rider Provides Maternity Benefits to Single Women," *News-Journal* (Mansfield, Ohio), 25 September 1972; "Insurance Policies Cover Abortions," *Battle Creek Enquirer* (Michigan), 4 September 1971.

72. Joyce Wilcox, "The Face of Women's Health: Helen Rodriguez-Trias," *American Journal of Public Health* 92(4) (April 2002): 566–69; Patricia Tyson, *The Choices We Made: 25 Women and Men Speak Out About Abortion*, ed. Angela Bonavoglia (Four Walls Eight Windows, 2001), 112–13; Richard D. Lyons, "Doctors Scored on Sterilization," *New York Times*, 31 October 1973; Julius Paul, "The Return of Punitive Sterilization Proposals: Current Attacks on Illegitimacy and the AFDC Program," *Law & Society Review* 3(1) (Aug. 1968), 87–88 fn15.

Extremist views informed the discourse, like the Illinois State Representative and member of the Public Aid Commission who proposed in 1963 that all "prostitutes" be sterilized. William Rutherford (a Sierra Club member) defined prostitutes as any woman who had more than one illegitimate child, and he further contended for the purposes of his proposed bill that "illegal abortion should be treated the same as [sic] giving an illegitimate birth" (Julius Paul, "The Return of Punitive Sterilization Proposals: Current Attacks on n Illegitimacy and the AFDC Program," *Law & Society Review* 3(1) (August 1968), 81–82, fn 6.

73. Les Payne, "Sterilization: Are NonWhite Women Subjected to Discrimination" and "Well, It's Done—That's the End of That," *Newsday*, 3 January 1974; Felicia Kornbluh, *A Woman's Life is a Human Life* (Grove Press, 2023): 1–3.

74. Dona Harvey, "Sterilization 'As a Right' Offends Doctors' Ethics," *Edmonton Journal* (Canada), 12 February 1969; Naomi Rock, "Voluntary Sterilization: One Solution for Family and Population Problems," *Times and Democrat* (Orangeburg, NC), 27 Monday 1970; Nancy Romero, "Tissue or Living Being," *Lima News*, 2 May 1971; Richard D. Lyons, "Doctors Scored on Sterilization," *New York Times*, 31 October 1973; Edward J. Spriggs, "Involuntary Sterilization: An Unconstitutional Menace to Minorities and the Poor," *N.Y.U. Review of Law & Social Change* 4(2) (Spring 1974): 131–32, fn44; Dr. Richard Hausknecht in *American Experience: The Pill* (PBS, 2003).

75. Richard D. Lyons, "Doctors Scored on Sterilization," *New York Times*, 31 October 1973; Edward J. Spriggs, "Involuntary Sterilization: An Unconstitutional Menace to Minorities and the Poor," *N.Y.U. Review of Law & Social Change* 4(2) (Spring 1974): 131–32, fn44; Jack Hitt, "Who Will Do Abortions Here?," *New York Times*, 18 January 1998; Alexandra Minna Stern, "Sterilized in the Name of Public Health: Race, Immigration, and Reproductive Control in Modern California," *American Journal of Public Health* 95(7) (July 1, 2005): 1128–38.

The list includes many more southern than northern cities, and the abusive treatment and continued control of Black women's reproductive lives persists in the South (Alana Semuels, "'I Don't Have Faith in Doctors Anymore.' Women Say They Were Pressured into Long-Term Birth Control," *Time*, 13 May 2024.

76. "Infant Mortality at 'Disaster Level,'" *Miami News*, 14 April 1969; William F. Buckley, Jr., "Punitive Sterilization: Right-Winger Offers Bold Idea," *Omaha World-Herald*, 31 March 1971; "Government to Fund Sterilization Project in Appalachia," *Montgomery*

Advertiser, 2 July 1971; Jane Brody, "Birth Decline Linked to 3 Methods of Contraception," *New York Times*, 3 August 1972; Julius Paul, "The Return of Punitive Sterilization Proposals: Current Attacks on Illegitimacy and the AFDC Program," *Law & Society Review*, 3(1) (Aug. 1968), 79; sociologist Hyman Rodman, "The Ethics of Sterilization," *LA Times*, 19 August 1973; Richard D. Lyons, "Doctors Scored on Sterilization," *New York Times*, 31 October 1973.

77. "Testimony from a 14 Year Old Woman from Cleveland," Case Western Tribunal, 1972, WONAAC, Wisconsin Historical Society.

Rickie Solinger, for example, found evidence of a man who demanded nude photos of the women before he would agree to do the abortion procedure ("Extreme Danger: Women Abortionists and Their Clients Before Roe v. Wade," *Not June Cleaver: Women and Gender in Postwar America, 1945–1960* (Temple University Press, 1994), fn9 p355.

78. "Valerie," Case Western Tribunal, 1972, WONAAC, Wisconsin Historical Society. A woman at the Redstockings Abortion Speakout, March 21, 1969, New York City, also testified that she sought an abortion at eleven different New York City hospitals. She was rejected from ten, and the condition of the abortion at the eleventh was that she agreed to be sterilized. She "was 20 years old" (Susan Brownmiller, "Redstocking Rap: Everywoman's Abortions: 'The Oppressor Is Man,'" *Village Voice*, 27 March 1969).

Chapter 3

1. Terry Johnson King, "Gimmick at Super Bowl: Sky-Writing Lures Women to New York Abortions," *Miami News*, 21 January 1971; Molly Sinclair, "Abortions Are Hard for Poor to Obtain," *Miami Herald*, 25 January 1971.

2. Lana Clark Phelan and Patricia Therese Maginnis, *The Abortion Handbook* (Contact Books, 1969); Martin Ebon, ed., *Everywoman's Guide to Abortion* (Universe Books, 1971); "Legal abortions: How safe? How available? How costly?," *Consumer Reports*, July 1972, 470.

3. William Tucker, "'Abortion Broker' Believes in His Work," *Miami News*, 22 January 1971; Bob Dennis, "He's a Breezy Believer in Abortions and Advertising," *Charlotte Observer* (North Carolina), 1 February 1971.

4. Stan Wittner, "Florida Report," *Tampa Bay Times*, 1 February 1971; Kathy Campbell, "Abortion Referral Poster Stirs Controversy in Area," *Journal News* (Hamilton, Ohio), 5 August 1971.

5. Women's Health and Abortion Project, *The Abortion Game*, 1972.

6. Susan H. Metzger, "Sun Spotlight: A Guide to Abortion," *Cornell Daily Sun*, 10 March 1971; John Sibley, "97,881 Abortions Reported in City," *New York Times*, 6 April 1971; Joan Mellon, phone interview by author, 7 February 2023.

7. Gene Raffensperger, "Cover Up His Abortion Sign," *Des Moines Register*, 12 March 1972; Kideckel, "Abortion Now a Fact of Life . . . If You're Rich," *Varsity*, 2 Oct 1970; Elaine Morrissey, "Detroiter Sets Up New York Abortion Clinic," *Dayton Daily News*, 26 October 1970; Georgia Tasker, "He Operates Referral Service for Abortions," *Miami Herald*, 21 February 1971.

8. Gene Raffensperger, "Cover Up His Abortion Sign," *Des Moines Register*, 12 March 1972.

9. Gene Raffensperger, "Cover Up His Abortion Sign," *Des Moines Register*, 12 March 1972.

10. Q&A column re abortion referrals did not differentiate between Planned Parenthood and for-profit referrals, *Kingsport Times* (Tennessee), 10 July 1972.

11. Mitchell Family Planning v. City of Royal Oak, 5 January 1972, Lucas papers, Box 12, Wesleyan; Gene Raffensperger, "Cover Up His Abortion Sign," *Des Moines Register*, 12 March 1972.

12. "Abortion Promotion Draws Protest; Woman Asks If It Is Against Law," *Palladium-Item* (Richmond, Indiana), 27 May 1971; Kathy Campbell, "Abortion Referral Poster Stirs Controversy in Area," *Journal News* (Hamilton, Ohio), 5 August 1971; "Abortion Billboard to Be Taken Down," *Times-Reporter* (Dover-New Philadelphia, Ohio), 20 January 1972.

13. *Plain Dealer*: "Abortion Sign Dispute Goes to Court," 5 June 1972; David G. Molyneaux, "Drive Against Abortion Signs Allowed," 6 June 1972; "Hearing Ordered On Harassment," 9 June 1972; Thomas S. Andrezejewski, "N.Y. Referrals: Abortion Agent Defends Business," 12 June 1972.

14. Tom Kaib, "Flight to Abortion," *Plain Dealer Sunday Magazine*, 11 July 1971; Phil Donahue show with Martin Mitchell: *Cincinnati Enquirer*, 26 November 1971; *Journal Herald* (Dayton), 26 October 1970; *Daily Kennebec Journal*, 17 December 1971; *Detroit Free Press*, 26 November 1971; "Abortion-Service Head Defends Role in TV Talk," *Buffalo News*, 10 December 1971; "Morning Exchange," *Plain Dealer*, 8 November 1972.

Donahue's first guest was Madelyn O'Hair, famed atheist, and his first gay male guest appeared in 1967, so it was consistent with his desire to reach his audience, build ratings, and get picked up in national production and syndication ("On Being with Krista Tippett: Phil Donahue: Transformation, On-Screen and Off," transcript, 12 December 2013, https://onbeing.org/programs/phil-donahue-transformation-on-screen-and-off/).

15. "Airborne Ads Boost Abortions," *San Antonio Express*, 13 January 1971; Georgia Tasker, "He Operates Referral Service for Abortions," *Miami Herald*, 21 February 1971; Susan H. Metzger, "Sun Spotlight: A Guide to Abortion," *Cornell Daily Sun*, 10 March 1971.

16. *Fort Lauderdale News*: James Kerr, "Fly-By-Day Sign Plugs Licit Abortion," 11 January 1971; "Sheriff Ready to Act on Abortion Ad," 13 April 1971; James Kerr, "Aborted Abortion Ads May Have Rebirth Soon," *Fort Lauderdale News*, 27 July 1971; "Abortion Foes Win Battle of Sky," *News-Journal* (Mansfield, Ohio), 16 April 1971.

17. "Delay Shuttle for Abortions," *South Bend Tribune*, 13 October 1970; Mary Ann Weston, "Oak Parker Secretive on Abortion Service," *Detroit Free Press*, 16 November 1970.

18. "NY Flight Service: Abortions Offered to Michigan Women," *News-Palladium* (Benton Harbor, Michigan), 7 October 1970; "Brydges Assails Proposed Abortion Shuttle Service," *Journal-Register* (Medina, New York), 13 October 1970; "Niagara Falls Opposes Abortion Clinic There," *Advance News* (Ogendenberg, New York), 18 October 1970.

19. "NY Flight Service: Abortions Offered to Michigan Women," *News-Palladium* (Benton Harbor, Michigan), 7 October 1970; "Brydges Assails Proposed Abortion Shuttle

Service," *Journal-Register* (Medina, New York), 13 October 1970; "Niagara Falls Opposes Abortion Clinic There," *Advance News* (Ogendenberg, New York), 18 October 1970.

20. John Hanchette, "N.Y. Abortion: Easy, Fast And Strictly Business," *Exponent* (Baldwin-Wallace College), 5 March 1971; *Time*, 27 September 1971, 68; Thomas S. Andrezejewski, "N.Y. Referrals: Abortion Agent Defends Business," *Plain Dealer*, 12 June 1972.

21. "Abortion Merchants Thriving," *News-Palladium* (Benton Harbor, Michigan), 30 March 1971.

22. "NY Flight Service: Abortions Offered to Michigan Women," *News-Palladium* (Benton Harbor, Michigan), 7 October 1970; Mary Ann Weston, "Oak Parker Secretive on Abortion Service," *Detroit Free Press*, 16 November 1970; Gene Raffensperger, "Cover Up His Abortion Sign," *Des Moines Register*, 12 March 1972.

23. "Adequate Service Here," *Plain Dealer*, 1 August 1971; Kathy Campbell, "Abortion Referral Poster Stirs Controversy in Area," *Journal News* (Hamilton, Ohio), 5 August 1971; "Project Coordinates Services: Pregnancy Problems," *Plain Dealer*, 9 September 1971.

24. Elaine Morrissey, "Detroiter Sets Up New York Abortion Clinic," *Dayton Daily News*, 26 October 1970; Georgia Tasker, "He Operates Referral Service for Abortions," *Miami Herald*, 21 February 1971. This echoed Garrett Hardin who referred to "compulsory pregnancy." "Abortion. Or Compulsory Pregnancy?," *Journal of Marriage and Family* 30(2) (May 1968): 246–51.

25. John Hahn, "Billboards: Abortion Replacing Old Signs," *Corpus Christi Times* (Texas), 17 March 1972; Mary Ziegler, "The Framing of a Right to Choose: *Roe v. Wade* and the Changing Debate on Abortion Law," *Law and History Review* 27(2) (Summer 2009): 283.

26. Mary Ann Weston, "Oak Parker Secretive on Abortion Service," *Detroit Free Press*, 16 November 1970; Kathy Campbell, "Abortion Referral Poster Stirs Controversy in Area," *Journal News* (Hamilton, Ohio), 5 August 1971; John Hahn, "Billboards: Abortion Replacing Old Signs," *Corpus Christi Times* (Texas), 17 March 1972.

27. Paul Krassner, "I Was an Abortionist for the FBI," *Realist*, April 1966; "Paul Krassner," dangersousminds.net, posted by Richard Metzger, 7 February 2013, https://dangerousminds.net/comments/paul_krassner_how_a_satirical_editor_became_a_one_man; Art Beeghly, "A Message for Girls in Trouble," *Phoenix* (San Francisco State College), 31 October 1968; Harry Themal, "Man Fights for Abortion; Why?," *Evening Journal* (Wilmington, Delaware), 29 March 1971; Ruth Winter, "Opposition Rising to Resist Abortion Law Liberalization," *Tucson Daily Citizen*, 28 June 1971; Sam Newlund, "Suburban Man Arranges Abortions," *Star Tribune* (Minneapolis), 17 January 1971; "ND Women Can Get Referral Service," *Bismarck Tribune*, 3 February 1971; "Paul Krassner, Radical Activist, Dies at 87," politico.com, 21 July 2019, https://www.politico.com/story/2019/07/21/paul-krassner-radical-activist-dies-at-87–1424334 (all accessed 22 May 2024).

28. Art Beeghly, "A Message for Girls in Trouble," *Phoenix* (San Francisco State College), 31 October 1968.

29. Ari Beaghly, "A Message for Girls in Trouble," *Phoenix* (San Francisco State College), 31 October 1968; Beverly Koch, "Abortion Not So Hush-Hush Now," *Akron Beacon*

Journal, 10 April 1970; William O. Tome, "Flights to Abortion," *Billings Daily Gazette*, 9 September 1970; Jan Jarboe, "Diverse Groups Advocate Change," *Daily Texas* (Austin), 10 November 1970; Sally Smith, "Charlotte Needs a Counseling Service," *Charlotte News*, 19 June 1970.

30. Ad: *Berkeley Barb*, 28 March 1969; *LA Free Press*, 26 September 1969; *Great Speckled Bird*, 26 October 1970; Beverly Koch, "Abortion Not So Hush-Hush Now, *Akron Beacon Journal*, 10 April 1970; Kay Holmquist, "Abortion Quest Narrows," *Fort Worth Star-Telegram*, 26 July 1970; PPIS ad, *LA Free Press*, 18 August 1972.

31. Jan Jarboe, "Diverse Groups Advocate Change," *Daily Texas* (Austin), 10 November 1970.

32. PPIS ads: *LA Free Press*, November 1971 and *Great Speckled Bird*, 15 February 1971; Jonathan Beaty, "Abortion May Be Only an Airfare Away," *Alabama Journal* (Montgomery), 25 September 1972.

33. PPIS ads: *Kaleidoscope* (Milwaukee), 1 October 1969 and *LA Free Press*, 18 August 1972; John Pennington, "Abortion," *Atlanta Journal and Constitution Magazine*, 30 January 1972, 15–16.

34. Mr. Lewis ARS ad, *Heights* (Boston College), 28 October 1970; Patricia McBroom, "Abortion Aid: Service or Profiteering?," *Philadelphia Inquirer*, 9 February 1971; Robert Fensterer, "Abortion-Aid Billboards Pressured Off the Expressway," *Philadelphia Inquirer*, 22 July 1971; D. M. Levine, "Liberal Laws Aiding Abortion Business," *Montclarion*, 26 February 1971.

35. ARS ads: *Heights* (Boston College), 28 October 1970; *Fort Lewis Independent* (Colorado), 30 October 1970; *URI Beacon*, 4 November 1970; *Forum* (Utah), 25 February 1971.

36. *Fort Lewis Independent* (Colorado), 30 October 1970; *Rice Thresher* (Texas), 19 November 1970; *Concordian* (Minnesota), 4 December 1970; Gary Rice, "Juco Paper Abortion Ad Run as 'Public Service,'" *Wichita Eagle*, 9 December 1970; "Abortion Referral Service Begun," *Tech News* (Worcester), 2 December 1970; *Guardian* (Wright State), 7 January 1971; *Lance* (North Carolina); *Forum* (Utah), 25 February 1971.

37. "Book Prices, Curfews Hit in SGA Poll" and "Agencies Offer Referral Service for Women Seeking Abortions," *Auburn Plainsman*, 13 November 1970.

38. *Rice Thresher* (Texas), 19 November 1970; *Concordian* (Minnesota), 4 December 1970; *Lance* (North Carolina) and *Forum* (Utah), 25 February 1971; *Vanguard* (Harrisburg, Pennsylvania), 12 March 1971; *South Bend Tribune*, 1 October 1972.

39. "Abortion Aid: Service or Profiteering?," *Philadelphia Inquirer*, 9 February 1971; "Profit Major Force for Abortion Service" and "Abortion Referral: Big Business," *Spectrum* (Buffalo), 26 April 1971.

See Chapter 4 for legal cases about advertising abortions in newspapers.

40. Dick Saylor, "Abortion Facts to Know," *Guardian* (Wright State), 21 October 1970; "Profit Major Force for Abortion Service" and "Abortion Referral: Big Business," *Spectrum* (Buffalo), 26 April 1971.

41. Robert Fensterer, "Abortion-Aid Billboards Pressured Off the Expressway," *Philadelphia Inquirer*, 22 July 1971; Gillian Frank, "Discophobia: Antigay Prejudice and the 1979 Backlash Against Disco," *Journal of the History of Sexuality* 16(2) (May 2007): 281–82.

42. Ena Nauton, "Abortion Referral Business Is Booming," *Miami Herald*, 8 March 1971; Mrs. Saul ad, *Daily Princetonian*, 8 April 1971.

43. William Tucker, "'Abortion Broker' Believes in His Work," *Miami News*, 22 January 1971; Bob Dennis, N.Y. Abortion Referral: A Booming Business," *Charlotte Observer*, 31 January 1971; Robert Fensterer, "Abortion-Aid Billboards Pressured Off the Expressway," *Philadelphia Inquirer*, 22 July 1971.

44. "Abortion Referral," *Bowling Green News*, 19 January 1971; Mary G. Larkin, "NOW Works to Keep Women Away from Inept Abortionists," *Philadelphia Inquirer*, 21 January 1971; Patricia McBroom, "Abortion Aid: Service or Profiteering?," *Philadelphia Inquirer*, 9 February 1971, "Abortion Ad Discontinued; Davenport Outlines Service," *Lance* (St. Andrews), 25 February 1971; "Dear Sirs," *Blue Banner* (UNC Asheville), 2 March 1971.

45. Patricia McBroom, "Abortion Aid: Service or Profiteering?," *Philadelphia Inquirer*, 9 February 1971; anonymous, "How to Get a New York Abortion," *State News* (Michigan State University), 23 February 1971; "How to Avoid Abortion Rip-Offs," *Journal* (UNCC), 22 April 1971; Larry Zawilenski to Dan Gouker letter of response, 24 March 1972, Kathy Mallin archive; Miroslava Chavez-Garcia, "From 'Tough Love' to 'Street Fight': Garrett Hardin and Cordelia S. May's Battle for Population Control and Eugenics at the Turn of the Millennium," *Revista Brasileira de historia* 43 (94) (Sep-Dec 2023).

46. Carol R Richards, "Abortion Enterprise Pays Off," *Rockland County Journal-News*, 11 February 1971.

47. Leslie Tuft, "A 'Fire Brigade' for Young Newcomers to London," *Birmingham Post*, 8 October 1969; Richard K. Shull, "English Abortions Subject of NBC's 'First Tuesday,'" *Paducah Sun* (Kentucky), 18 November 1969; Diana Pulson, "Journey to the Unknown," *Liverpool Daily Post*, 17 September 1970.

48. Henry Miller, "£488 Four-Day Abortion Trips to London," *Daily Telegraph* (London), 23 March 1970; $155 conversion on 8 December 2024, https://www.dollartimes.com/inflation/inflation.php?amount=155&year=1970.

49. AIA ads: *Observer* (Notre Dame), 26 October 1970; *Daily Tar Heel* (UNC), 1 November 1970; *Michigan Daily*, 13 February 1971; Susan Edmiston, "A Report on the Abortion Capital of the Country," *New York Times*, 11 April 1971.

50. AIA ad, *Oakland Tribune*, 21 March 1971.

51. AIA ads: *Oakland Tribune*, 21 March 1971; *Daily American* (Somerset, PA), 24 March 1971; *Salt Lake Times*, 23 April 1971; Elaine Morrissey, "Women Libs Lend Support to Abortion," *Dayton Daily News*, 13 October 1970.

52. "A Need Fulfilled," *Daily American* (Somerset, PA), 24 March 1971; Abortion Information Agency, *A Need Fulfilled* (October 1970), NARAL—Printed Materials, "New York-Clinics," PR-3, Box 4, Schlesinger Library; Abortion Rights Association, *Listing of Selected New York State Abortion Clinics* (October 1971).

53. Abortion Information Agency, *A Need Fulfilled* (October 1970), Schlesinger.

54. Joan Mellon, phone interview by author, 7 February 2023.

55. John Alden Settle, Jr to Dear Doctor, 15 June 1970 and 15 September 1970, author's possession; Joan Mellon, phone interview by author, 7 February 2023.

56. Women's Health and Abortion Project, *The Abortion Game*, 1972.

57. Henry Miller, "£488 Four-Day Abortion Trips to London," *Daily Telegraph* (London), 23 March 1970; Lucas to Pilpel, 3 January 1972, Lucas papers, Box 19, SPS; The People of the State of New York, Plaintiff v. Wickersham Women's Medical Center, Irving Saxe and John Settle Jr, Defendants, Supreme Court, Special Term, New York County, February 8, 1972; John Pennington, "Abortion," *Atlanta Journal and Constitution Magazine*, 30 January 1972.

58. Abortion ads, *New Republic*, 28 November 1970, 33; *Baltimore Afro American*, 12 January 1971; Ellen Frankfort, "Making Abortions Pay," *Village Voice*, 10 December 1970; Abbe David Lowell, "Abortion Referral Agencies Thrive," *Columbia Daily Spectator*, 7 December 1970; Wickersham ad, *Hill News*, 18 January 1972; John Pennington, "Abortion," *Atlanta Journal and Constitution Magazine*, 30 January 1972, 13; "Status of Abortion Center Clarified," *Hill News*, 17 February 1972.

59. *Consumer Reports*, July 1972, cover. With thanks to Jacqueline Reid Wachholz at Duke's Hartman Center.

60. Carolyn Schneider to *Consumer Reports*, 10 April 1972, Hartman Center, Duke; "Legal abortions: How safe? How available? How costly?," *Consumer Reports*, July 1972, 466. The article was likely written by or with Dr. Alan Guttmacher, who collaborated on the 1962 *Consumers Union Report on Family Planning*.

61. "Legal abortions: How safe? How available? How costly?," *Consumer Reports*, July 1972, 466.

62. "Legal abortions: How safe? How available? How costly?," *Consumer Reports*, July 1972, 466–67.

63. "Legal abortions: How safe? How available? How costly?," *Consumer Reports*, July 1972, 466.

64. "Legal abortions: How safe? How available? How costly?," *Consumer Reports*, July 1972, 467.

65. Christopher Tietze and Sarah Lewit, "Joint Program for the Study of Abortion (JPSA): Early Medical Complications of Legal Abortion," *Studies in Family Planning* 3(6) (June 1972): 97–123 (published by Population Council).

66. "Legal abortions: How safe? How available? How costly?," *Consumer Reports*, July 1972, 469–70.

67. "Legal abortions: How safe? How available? How costly?," *Consumer Reports*, July 1972, 470.

68. "Legal abortions," *Consumer Reports*, September 1972, 554, 617.

69. "Abortion," *Kiplinger's Personal Finance*, December 1970.

70. Stuart Auerbach, "Quickie Abortions Bringing Thousands to New York," *Morning News* (Wilmington, Delaware), 15 January 1971.

Chapter 4

1. Wendy Anthony email to author, relaying story shared by Skidmore historian Mary Lynn, 1 December 2021; "Interview with Tom Davis," *Skidmore Saratoga Memory Project* (accessed 23 June 2024); Anne Gardiner Perkins, *Yale Needs Women: How the*

First Group of Girls Rewrote the Rules of an Ivy League Giant (Sourcebooks, 2019), 204; Patricia A. Lyons, "URI Personnel Voice Their Opinions on Abortions," *A Good 5c Cigar*, 14 April 1971; Heather Munro Prescott, *Student Bodies: The Influence of Student Health Services in American Society & Medicine* (University of Michigan Press, 2007), 148; Kelly Morrow, *Sex and the Student Body: Knowledge, Equality, and the Sexual Revolution, 1960 To 1973* (Dissertation, University of North Carolina at Chapel Hill, 2012); an Interview with Carol Giardina, "I Helped My Classmates Get Illegal Abortions Before Roe. We Can't Go Back," *Jacobin.com*, 21 May 2022.

One 1966 Smith alum applauded Gloria Steinem's protest against illegal abortions at their 1981 reunion, reflecting, "Someone in our class died from a coat-hanger abortion. It was all hushed-up—but we knew" (Gloria Steinem, *We Are All Each Other's Allies: 50 Years of Speaking Out* [Smith College, 1981]), 28. Gabriela D. Noa Betacourt analyzed an illegal abortion in 1963 that resulted in the death of a Tulane undergraduate ("If the Newcomb Walls Could Talk: The Story of June Wall," *Women Leading Change* 1(2) (15 July 2014): 5–15).

2. "Underground/Alternative Newspapers History and Geography," University of Washington's Mapping American Social Movements Project, https://depts.washington.edu/moves/altnews_intro.shtml (accessed 8 July 2022).

3. Ellen Griffith Spears, phone interview by author, 8 June 2022; Angela Z., email interview by author, 23 February 2022.

"Standards for Women in Higher Education," in Standards in Higher Education Committee, 1967–1972, Box 1, Folder 12, Mabelle G. McCullough papers, University of Minnesota Archives; "AAUW Gives Guidelines for Academic Equality," *Times Herald* (Port Huron, Michigan), 26 September 1971.

4. Emily Hoffman, Tufts University, "'Lax on Jaxon Slacks': The Abolition of Dress Codes at Jackson College," undergraduate paper, 15 December 2017, http://hdl.handle.net/10427/014607 (accessed 18 June 2022); Renée Lansley, *College Women or College Girls? Gender, Sexuality, and In Loco Parentis on Campus* (Dissertation, Ohio State University, 2004); Bonnie Schwartz, "Student Rioters Battle Police," *Ohio State Lantern*, 30 April 1970; "Students Push Health Care Reform," *Cardinal Points* (SUNY Plattsburgh), 14 March 1972.

5. Heather Munro Prescott, *Student Bodies: The Influence of Student Health Services in American Society & Medicine* (University of Michigan Press, 2007), 144; Kelly Morrow, *Sex and the Student Body: Knowledge, Equality, and the Sexual Revolution, 1960 to 1973* (Dissertation, University of North Carolina at Chapel Hill, 2012), 111–12 fn28, 113, 151, 195–97; "Students Push Health Care Reform," *Cardinal Points* (SUNY Plattsburgh), 14 March 1972; Sunni Ali Ber, "Sex Counseling," *South End* (Wayne State), 30 October 1972; Joanne Thiel, "Health Clinic Provides Aid," *Guardian* (Wright State), 13 October 1971; Jerry Stilkind, "Towson State to Help Girls Curb Births," *Sun* (Baltimore), 17 November 1970.

6. Kelly Morrow, *Sex and the Student Body: Knowledge, Equality, and the Sexual Revolution, 1960 to 1973* (Dissertation, University of North Carolina at Chapel Hill, 2012), 151.

7. Vickie Eslinger, phone interview by author, 16 February 2022; Marshall Swanson, "Abortions . . . Referral Agency Stops Butchering," *Gamecock* (University of South Carolina),

22 October 1973; Jeanne Manegold, "Abortion-Birth Control Referral Service," *Northwest Passage* 5(4) (May 24-June 5, 1971), 12; Margaret W. Bridwell and Louis W. Tinnin, "Abortion Referral in a Large College Health Service," *Journal of American Medical Women's Association* 27(8) (August 1972): 420–21; Peter J. Berman, Anne W. Davis, E. Lakin Phillips, "George Washington University Volunteer Hotline, A Descriptive Study," *Psychological Reports* 33 (1973): 364–66; Kelly Morrow, *Sex and the Student Body: Knowledge, Equality, and the Sexual Revolution, 1960 to 1973* (Dissertation, University of North Carolina at Chapel Hill, 2012), 238; Jerry Stilkind, "Towson State to Help Girls Curb Births," *Sun* (Baltimore), 17 November 1970.

8. Kelly Morrow, *Sex and the Student Body: Knowledge, Equality, and the Sexual Revolution, 1960 to 1973* (Dissertation, University of North Carolina at Chapel Hill, 2012), 127, 196, 199; Katarina Keane, *Second-Wave Feminism in the American South, 1965–1980* (Dissertation, University of Maryland, College Park, 2009), 179–80; Kelly Morrow, *Sex and the Student Body: Knowledge, Equality, and the Sexual Revolution, 1960 to 1973* (Dissertation, University of North Carolina at Chapel Hill, 2012), 194–96.

9. Karen Carnabucci, "Newest Contraceptives Change Old Morality," *Daily Collegian*, 11 October 1971; Heather Munro Prescott, *Student Bodies: The Influence of Student Health Services in American Society & Medicine* (University of Michigan Press, 2007), 110, 152, 157–59; Kelly Morrow, *Sex and the Student Body*, 110.

10. Kelly Morrow, *Sex and the Student Body*, 110–13; Heather Munro Prescott, *Student Bodies: The Influence of Student Health Services in American Society & Medicine* (University of Michigan Press, 2007), 110, 152, 157–59. AAUW and all quotations found in Prescott.

11. The standards were based, in part, on the group's study: "Campus 1970: Where Do Women Stand?." "AAUW Standards for Women in Higher Education," Section I, D. 1 and 2, in Standards in Higher Education Committee, 1967–1972, Box 1, Folder 12, Mabelle G. McCullough papers, University of Minnesota Archives; "AAUW Gives Guidelines for Academic Equality," *Times Herald* (Port Huron, Michigan), 26 September 1971; "Book Prices, Curfews Hit in SGA Poll," *Auburn Plainsman*, 13 November 1970; "UA Coeds and Abortion," *Crimson White* (University of Alabama), 9 August 1971; Joseph W. Maxwell, "College Students' Attitudes Toward Abortion," *Family Coordinator* 19(3) (July 1970): 247–52; Kelly Morrow, *Sex and the Student Body*, 112, fn 28.

12. Kelly Morrow, *Sex and the Student Body: Knowledge, Equality, and the Sexual Revolution, 1960 to 1973* (Dissertation, University of North Carolina at Chapel Hill, 2012), 226.

13. Student Committee on Human Sexuality at Yale University, *The Student Guide to Sex on Campus* (Signet, 1970); Anne Gardiner Perkins, *Yale Needs Women: How the First Group of Girls Rewrote the Rules of an Ivy League Giant* (Sourcebooks, 2019), 203–4; Kelly Morrow, *Sex and the Student Body: Knowledge, Equality, and the Sexual Revolution, 1960 to 1973* (Dissertation, University of North Carolina at Chapel Hill, 2012), 109–15; Judy Klemesrud, "Yale Students Have Own 'Masters and Johnson,'" *New York Times*, 28 April 1971; Philip M. Sarrel and Lorna J. Sarrel, "Birth Control Services and Sex Counseling at Yale," *Family Planning Perspectives* 3(3) (July 1971): 33.

14. Margaret Homans, email interview by author, 9 June 2020; Anne Gardiner Perkins, *Yale Needs Women: How the First Group of Girls Rewrote the Rules of an Ivy League Giant* (Sourcebooks, 2019), 204.

15. Margaret Homans, email interview by author, 9 June 2020; Henry Walker, "Abortion Laws Attacked," *Yale Daily News*, 28 January 1971; Dr. Virginia Stuermer biography, Yale School of Medicine, https://medicine.yale.edu/profile/115777/; Dr. Marshall Holley obituary, published in the *New Haven Register*, 6 and 7 June 2010, https://www.legacy.com/us/obituaries/nhregister/name/marshall-holley-obituary?pid=146983638 (all accessed 24 June 2022).

Students at Michigan State University volunteered with Lansing's Family Planning Clinic as part of their field study. They were majoring in Family Ecology, Social Work, and Education and doing referral services for adoption and abortion ("Family Planning Clinic Involves MSU Students," *State News*, 16 May 1972.) Judy Kunofsky described volunteering with Los Angeles Planned Parenthood that served UCLA students (email with author 7 February 2022).

16. Margaret Homans, email interview by author, 9 June 2020; Kelly Morrow, *Sex and the Student Body: Knowledge, Equality, and the Sexual Revolution, 1960 to 1973* (Dissertation, University of North Carolina at Chapel Hill, 2012), 105.

17. Chris Taaffe, "Birth Control Service to Give Telephone Info," *Flat Hat*, 12 February 1971

18. Chris Taaffe, "Birth Control Service to Give Telephone Info," *Flat Hat*, 12 February 1971; Bill Sizemore, "Flat Hat 'Obscenities' Spark Continuing Controversy," "Obscenity Is in the Eye of the Editor," "Texts of Complaints," and "Hyphenate Obscenities," *Flat Hat*, 26 February 1971; Ellen Griffith Spears, phone interview by author, 8 June 2022; Chris Faia, phone interview by author, 20 June 2022; Winn Legerton, phone interview by author, 16 February 2022.

19. Tom Mainor, phone interview by author, 8 March 2022; Ellen Griffith Spears, phone interview by author, 8 June 2022; Chris Faia, phone interview by author, 20 June 2022; Winn Legerton, phone interview by author, 16 February 2022.

20. Dorothy Riddle, phone interview by author, 12 April 2022; Ellen Griffith Spears, phone interview by author, 8 June 2022; Chris Faia, phone interview by author, 20 June 2022; Winn Legerton, phone interview by author, 16 February 2022. Larry Diehl, "Liberal Abortion Laws Urged," *Flat Hat*, 11 December 1970; Winn Legerton, "Legerton Responds to Catholic Criticism," *Flat Hat*, 12 March 1971.

The Women's Liberation Movement group at the University of Texas—Austin received $250 from the Student Senate to help them purchase a thousand copies of the McGill *Birth Control Handbook*. The following week, the Regents, angry over the appropriation of funds for an abortion loan (see Chapter 2), took some control of the student budget ("Booklet Available on Birth Control," *Prospector*, 10 June 1971; "Regents Change U.T. Austin Tax," *Prospector*, 17 June 1971).

21. Jane D Brown, phone interview by author, 11 and 12 June 2020; Jane D. Brown, "Abortion Dilemma: A Personal Experience," *Kentucky Kernel*, 18 January 1971.

22. Jane D. Brown, "Abortion Dilemma: A Personal Experience," *Kentucky Kernel*, 18 January 1971; Jane D. Brown, "Abortion Ruling Takes Us Back to the Future,"

Local Reporter, 27 June 2022, https://thelocalreporter.press/scotus-ruling-sends-womens-reproductive-rights-back-to-the-future/ (accessed 9 July 2022); Jane D Brown, phone interview by author, 11 and 12 June 2020.

23. Deborah Ross, Laura Peck, and Peg Spear, phone interview by author, 30 October 2020; Paula Glantz, "Abortion Group Gives Referrals," *Cornell Daily Sun*, 22 October 1971; Paula Glantz, "Abortion Referral Project May Increase Its Service" and ad for Women's Abortion Project listing hours, phone number, and address, *Cornell Daily Sun*, 11 November 1971; Jane Danowitz and Paula Glantz, "Cornellians Seek Abortion in NYC," *Cornell Daily Sun*, 20 April 1972.

24. Deborah Ross, Laura Peck, and Peg Spear, phone interview by author, 30 October 2020; Susan H. Metzger, "Sun Spotlight: A Guide to Abortion," *Cornell Daily Sun*, 10 March 1971; "C.U. Full-Time Sex Counselor Now Available," *Cornell Daily Sun*, 8 November 1971; Jane Danowitz and Paula Glantz, "Cornellians Seek Abortion in NYC," *Cornell Daily Sun*, 20 April 1972; Katherine Parkin, "The Women's National Abortion Action Coalition & the Abortion Tribunals, 1971–1972," *Journal of Family History*, June 2022.

25. Margaret W. Bridwell and Louis W. Tinnin, "Abortion Referral in a Large College Health Service," *Journal of American Medical Women's Association* 27(8) (August 1972): 420–21; Peter J. Berman, Anne W. Davis, E. Lakin Phillips, "George Washington University Volunteer Hotline, A Descriptive Study," *Psychological Reports* 33 (1973): 364–66; "On Campus: Abortion—The Academic Angle," *Mademoiselle*, 1970.

26. Jay Lawrence, "Infirmary Doctors Serve as Abortion Consultants, Would Prefer Prevention," *Emory Wheel*, 9 March 1971.

27. "Infirmary Addition: Gynecologist Joins Staff," *URI Beacon*, 23 September 1970; "Solomon Expected to Retract Abortion Statements Today," *URI Beacon*, 20 November 1970; "Social Worker Here to Counsel Unwed Mothers, *A Good 5c Cigar*, 24 March 1971; Patricia A. Lyons, "URI Personnel Voice Their Opinions on Abortions" and "Student Presses for Abortion Fund," in *A Good 5c Cigar*, 14 April 1971; "Social Worker Advises Pregnant URI Coeds," *A Good 5c Cigar*, 16 April 1971.

URI was not alone. In another example, in October 1971, Penn State University gynecologists also reported seeing ten to fifteen pregnant women every week, calculating that they saw two hundred pregnant women in fall 1970 (Karen Carnabucci, "Newest Contraceptives Change Old Morality," *Daily Collegian*, 11 October 1971).

28. "Foresight: Application for Recognition," April 1969, University of Colorado—Boulder, VSPA, Box 11, Folder 19; "On Campus: Abortion—The Academic Angle," *Mademoiselle*, 1970; Memo to Joint Finance Board from David Schoen of Birth Control Information Center, 1 February 1972, University of Colorado—Boulder, Joint Finance Board, Box 78, Birth Control Information Center.

Heather Munro Prescott noted that nationally "Male students played an important role in this contraceptive self-help movement" and that students were motivated by classmates dropping out due to pregnancy (*Student Bodies*, 146). Environmental concerns also motivated male activism for access to birth control and abortion. Overpopulation was part of the rhetoric of popular campus speaker Bill Baird. See, for example, Thomas Robertson, *The Malthusian Moment: Global Population Growth and the Birth of*

American Environmentalism (Rutgers University Press, 2012), 9–10; Alexandra Katta, "In the Shadow of the Population Bomb: The Campaign for Abortion Reform in Seattle, 1962–1970," MA Thesis, Western Washington University, 2012, 15–17, 24–25.

29. *The Boulder Birth Control Handbook* (1970) and letter from Takey Crist to David Schoen, 8 November 1971, Birth Control Information Center, University of Colorado—Boulder, Rare and Distinctive Collections, Box 5.2; Takey Crist and Lana Starnes, "Books in Review: Student Printing Presses Bring Birth Control Story to Colleges," *Family Planning Perspectives* 4(1) (January 1972): 60–61.

30. Abortion-Birth Control Referral Service, Accession No. 1930–003: Young Women's Christian Association, Special Collections, University of Washington; Jeanne Manegold, "Abortion-Birth Control Referral Service," *Northwest Passage* 5(4) (May 24–June 5, 1971), 12.

31. Abortion-Birth Control Referral Service, *Handbook for Operating an Abortion-Birth Control Referral Service* (Seattle, Washington), c. 1971, Jeanine Maland papers, Box 8.78, Special Collections and University Archive, UMass-Amherst; Department of Social and Health Services, *Abortions—1971* (Olympia, Washington: Division of Health Services, 1972). Katherine Saltzman, phone interview by author, 28 May 2020; Katherine Saltzman, *Abortion Referral & Counseling Service of Colorado,* Dissertation Project, School of Educational Change and Development, University of Northern Colorado, 1974. Project no longer held by UNCO, per archivist Jay Trask email, 2 June 2020.

Katherine Saltzman surveyed all family practice doctors and ob gyns in Northern Colorado by mail, asking "do you do abortion procedures, which ones, how much do you charge?" She used all that she learned to create the Abortion Referral and Counseling Service of Colorado in Denver. She described going to Seattle to learn from the Abortion-Birth Control Referral Service and taking the calls in her apartment: "I had a red phone with a flashing light—that was my abortion phone" (phone interview by author, 28 May 2020).

32. Lynn Hansen, Barbara Reskin, and Diana Gray, *How to Have Intercourse Without Being Screwed: A Guide to Birth Control, Abortion, and Venereal Disease* (ASUW Women's Commission, January 1972), 2nd printing.

33. "Free Help Idea Loses," *Spokane Chronicle*, 11 February 1972. Heather Munro Prescott points to University of California, Berkeley's health center as the earliest to attempt free abortions, after pressure from students, but budget cuts forced a dramatic increase in student health fees (*Student Bodies*, 160).

34. Philip H. Dougherty, "Advertising: Sale at *Reader's Digest*," *New York Times*, 4 December 1970; Cass Student Advertising, Incorporated v. National Educational Advertising Services, Inc. Volume: Reply Brief of Defendant-Appellant (May 14, 1976), 7–10, 15; Louis E. Ingelhart, *Freedom for the College Student Press: Court Cases and Related Decisions Defining the Campus Fourth Estate Boundaries* (Greenwood Press, 1985), 175–76.

35. ". . . Ad Row Roundup," *Chicago Tribune*, 14 July 1966; "More Than Just Student Battleground," *Advertising & Sales Promotion* 18 (July 1970): 46; Larry Makinson, "Abortion Referral Ads Will Continue, UB Editor Says," *Bridgeport Telegram*, 30 November 1970; Louis E. Ingelhart, *Freedom for the College Student Press: Court Cases and Related Decisions Defining the Campus Fourth Estate Boundaries* (Greenwood Press, 1985), 175.

36. "More Than Just Student Battleground," *Advertising & Sales Promotion* 18 (July 1970): 46; Dennis Eskow, "UA Paper's Abortion Ad Gets Results," *Tucson Citizen*, 4 May 1971; Pamela Swift, "Keeping Up . . . with Youth: The Trend," *Orlando Sentinel*, 5 December 1971; "Abortion Ads Aborted," *Campus Press Syllabus* (Commission on the Freedoms and Responsibilities of the College Student Press in America), Fall 1971.

The *Bigelow v. Virginia* (1972) lawsuit cited one for-profit abortion referral agency that "had an advertising budget of $1,000 a week and had carried advertisements in approximately 100 college newspapers throughout the country" (https://casetext.com/case/bigelow-v-commonwealth (accessed 14 June 2022).

37. Abortion Information Agency, Inc. ad, *Observer* (University of Notre Dame), 26 October 1970, 4; Bill Carter and John Knorr, "Abortive Thoughts," *Observer* (University of Notre Dame), 5 November 1970, 4; William A Sievert, "Student Newspapers Under Fire for Ads on Abortion Services," *Chronicle of Higher Education*, 22 February 1971, reprinted in *Chronicle* (Duke), 4 March 1971.

38. "How Not Like a Toothache," *Observer* (University of Notre Dame), 6 November 1970, 5–6; "A Forum on Abortion," *Scholastic* 112(10) (University of Notre Dame), 20 November 1970, 7, 12.

39. Abortion Information Agency, Inc. ad, *Scholastic* (University of Notre Dame), 30 October 1970, 2; "Why Talk About It?," 7; "A Forum on Abortion," 12; Julian Pleasants, "A Step Forward, a Step Back: Questions and Paradoxes," 13–15; Rudolph Gerber, "Protection Under the Law: Where the Fetus Should Stand," 16–18; Helen Williams, Carol Taylor, and Carolyn Gatz, "A Conflict of Rights: Some New Perspectives," 19–22; Elizabeth Poulson, "Abortion and Ecology," 23, all in *Scholastic* 112(10) (Notre Dame), 20 November 1970; Rev. Theodore M. Hesburg, "The Open Student," *Notre Dame Alumnus* 48(7), December 1970, 14–15.

Scholastic also ran a review of *The Birth Control Handbook*, "whose intent they applauded as to forward the liberation of oppressed people." It was titled, "From the Pope to the Pill" ("Abortion Ads Aborted," *Campus Press Syllabus* [Commission on the Freedoms and Responsibilities of the College Student Press in America], Fall 1971).

40. *Mountain Echo* (Emmitsburg, Maryland), 15 October 1971: Michael C. Keenan, Editor-in-Chief, "The Abortion Contortion," 18 October 1971; Michael C. Keenan, email interview by author, 22 June 2022.

41. Mount St. Mary's College was an all-male, Catholic college until 1972. *Mountain Echo* (Mount St. Mary's College, Emmitsburg, Maryland), 15 October 1971: Hal Lansche, "Echo Seized"; Ed Adams, "Faculty Mixed; Applaud and Appalled by Admin. Action"; 18 October 1971; "Newspaper Is Burned by MSM Dean," *Gettysburg* (Pennsylvania), 2 November 1971; Michael C. Keenan, email interview by author, 22 June 2022.

42. *Mountain Echo* (Mount St. Mary's College, Emmitsburg, Maryland), 18 October 1971: Hal Lansche, "Echo Seized"; Ed Adams, "Faculty Mixed; Applaud and Appalled by Admin. Action"; Michael C. Keenan, email interview by author, 22 June 2022.

43. Mark Silverman letter to Jack Bishop, 20 November 1970; Carolyn Hertz to Jack Bishop, 7 December and 15 December 1970, in civil_liberties_mass_box2_f20-1, Special Collections & University Archives, UMass Amherst Libraries. A lawyer retained by

the Student Senate advised the students of their violation of state statutes ("Abortion Ads Aborted," *Campus Press Syllabus* [Commission on the Freedoms and Responsibilities of the College Student Press in America], Fall 1971). For "Laws Against Chastity" or "Crimes Against Chastity," see Madalynn Deming Behrens, "'Guarding Innocence:' Age of Consent, Gender, & Progressivism," MA Thesis, University of Missouri-Columbia, 2016, 84–85, and Heather Munro Prescott, *Student Bodies*, 145.

44. "Abortion Ads Aborted," *Campus Press Syllabus* (Commission on the Freedoms and Responsibilities of the College Student Press in America), Fall 1971; *Sandspur* (Rollins College, Florida), 11 December 1970. That following April, a poll "How Rollins Students View the Population Problem," reported in the paper, found that 91 percent of the students polled answered "yes" to the question, "Should abortion be legalized?" *Sandspur* (Rollins College, Florida), 23 April 1971; Larry Makinson, "Abortion Referral Ads Will Continue, UB Editor Says," *Bridgeport Telegram*, 30 November 1970; "College Newspapers Told Abortion Ads Are Illegal," *Bridgeport Post*, 30 December 1970; Gail Fagen, "Says DI Ads Must Be Tasteful," *Daily Iowan*, 25 April 1972; Jerry Stilkind, "Towson State to Help Girls Curb Births," *Sun* (Baltimore), 17 November 1970.

45. "Editor's Note," *Skidmore News*, 12 November 1970; "Abortion Ad Discontinued; Davenport Outlines Services," *Lance* (St. Andrews College), 25 February 1971; "Abortion Policy," *Skidmore News*, 25 February 1971; "Why No Abortion Ads," *News Record* (University of Cincinnati), 28 April 1972; Letters to Editor re "Why No Abortion Ads," *News Record* (University of Cincinnati), 16 May 1972; "Ads and Editorials," *'Tonian* (Carleton College), 13 April 1972.

46. "Women's Lib Gives Abortion Info," *Daily Northwestern*, 30 April 1971.

47. Beth Bailey, *Sex in the Heartland*; Cathy Yarbourough and Suzanne Moore, "How Free Is the Collegiate Press," *Atlanta Constitution*, 6 January 1971; "Abortion Ad Ban Target of Lawsuit," *Tucson Daily Citizen*, 27 April 1972.

48. "Georgia Regents to Study Campus Newspaper's Ads," *Greenville News*, 10 December 1970; Marjorie C. Barnes, "The College Press: Freedom or Control?," MA Thesis (University of Wyoming, 1971), 1–3; "Abortion and Contraceptives Rapped," *Inkwell* (Armstrong State College, Massachusetts), 14 January 1971; "A New and Strained View of Freedom of the Press," *Jackson Sun* (Tennessee), 1 March 1971; "Paper Escapes Shutdown" and "Pregnant? Need Help?" ad, *Concordian*, 4 December 1970; Omar Olson, email interview by author, 26 June 2020.

49. Associated Press, "Abortion Ad Issue Hits Other Colleges," *Bismarck Tribune*, 11 December 1970; Greg Pinney, "Abortion Ads Called Not Clearly Illegal," *Star Tribune* (Minneapolis, Minnesota), 17 December 1970, 17; "Abortion Ads Cause Lock Out," *Bates Student* (Lewiston, Maine), 27 May 1971; Omar Olson, email interview by author, 26 June 2020.

50. "New Daily policy on Abortion Ads," *Daily Northwestern*, 10 January 1972; "Paper Canceling Ads for Abortion Referral Service," *Lincoln Star*, 10 March 1971.

51. Ken Cruickshank, "Abortion Ads Illegal in State; UofH Newspaper Ignores Ban," *Hartford Courant*, 23 March 1971.

52. Claudia Nunez-Eddy, "State v. New Times, Inc. (1973)," *The Embryo Project Encyclopedia*, https://embryo.asu.edu/pages/state-v-new-times-inc-1973; "Abortion

Outlook Optimistic" and "Abortion Ads Legal in S.C. Ruling Says," *State* (Columbia, South Carolina), 11 March 1971; Bill Bewster, "Woodahl Warns—No Abortion Ads," *Billings Gazette* (Montana), 16 January 1971; "Abortion Ad Stays," *State Press* (Arizona State University), 31 October 1971; Gilbert Lewthwaite, "Abortion Backers, Foes Trade Legal Crossfire," *Baltimore Sun*, 9 November 1971; "Abortion Ad Ban Target of Lawsuit," *Tucson Daily Citizen*, 27 April 1972; "Court Overturns Abortion Ad Rule," *Arizona Republic* (Phoenix), 6 July 1973; Stephen Lemons, "Back to the Future: Remembering How New Times Helped Overturn AZ's Abortion Laws," FrontPage Confidential, https://frontpageconfidential.com/when-new-times-overturned-arizona-anti-abortion-law/.

53. "Jacobetti Hits Student Papers on Abortion Ads," *Escanaba Daily Press*, 28 April 1971; "K. Of C. Protesting Abortion Ads in U. Of M. Paper," *Evening Sun* (Baltimore, Maryland), 25 October 1971.

54. Mary Fran Lowe, "Abortion Ads May Bring Penalties," *Flat Hat*, 2 February 1971; Robert Sherrill, "Hogging the Constitution: Big Business & Its Bill of Rights," *Grand Street* 7(1) (Autumn 1987): 99–101; Jeffrey Bigelow, phone interview by author, 22 June 2022; Legal Information Institute, Jeffrey Cole Bigelow, Appellant, v. Commonwealth of Virginia, Cornell Law School, https://www.law.cornell.edu/supremecourt/text/421/809.

55. Abortion ad, *Virginia Weekly*, February 1971; "Abortion Rap," *Virginia Weekly*, May-June 1971; "Abortion Ads Bring Arrest," *Kingsport Times-News* (Tennessee), 16 May 1971; "Bigelow Fined," *News Leader* (Staunton, Virginia), 16 July 1971; Robert Sherrill, "Hogging the Constitution: Big Business & Its Bill of Rights," *Grand Street* 7(1) (Autumn 1987): 95–113; Matt Schudel, "John C. Lowe, Lawyer Who Sued to Have Women Admitted to U-Va., Dies at 80," *Washington Post*, 26 October 2017; *Bigelow v. Commonwealth* (1973): https://casetext.com/case/bigelow-v-commonwealth (accessed 14 June 2022); Jeffrey Bigelow, phone interview by author, 22 June 2022; Linda Cayton, "Court Halts Reporters, OK's Reporting," *Salemite* (Salem College, NC), 10 October 1972.

56. Blackmun in David L. Hudson Jr., "*Bigelow v. Virginia* (1975)," *The First Amendment Encyclopedia* (Middle Tennessee State University, 2009): https://www.mtsu.edu/first-amendment/article/194/bigelow-v-virginia (accessed 14 June 2022); Eric T. Singer, Constitutional Law-Freedom of the Press-Prohibition of Abortion Referral Service Advertising Held Unconstitutional , 61 *Cornell Law Review* 640 (1976): http://scholarship.law.cornell.edu/clr/vol61/iss4/7 (accessed 24 June 2022); David Sheridan, "Commercial Speech: The Supreme Court Sends Another Valentine to Advertisers, 25 *Buff.L. Rev.* 737 (1976). Blackmun also wrote the *Roe* decision in 1973. See also Slate's Slow Burn, Season 7, Episode 4, re Blackmun: https://slate.com/podcasts/slow-burn/s7/roe-v-wade/e4/harry-blackmun-roe-v-wade-abortion-supreme-court (accessed 23 June 2022).

57. "Uphold Right to Publish Abortion Ads," *Bee* (Danville, Virginia), 23 November 1971; Pat Nockett and Cynthia Shortman, "Readers Endorse Bullet Stand," *Bullet* (Mary Washington College, Virginia), 14 February 1972; Linda Cayton, "Court Halts Reporters, OKs Reporting," *Salemite* (Salem College, North Carolina), 10 October 1972; "College Papers Drop Suit on Abortion Ads," *Free Lance-Star* (Fredericksburg, Virginia), 5 July 1972; Pam Kamarik, "Mehrige Confirms Students' Rights to Publish Abortion Advertisements," *Flat Hat* (William & Mary), 3 December 1971.

Bill Royall, editor of Virginia Commonwealth University's *Commonwealth Times*, also ran an abortion ad in defiance of the law on January 6, 1972, and staff members "went to the state Capitol and passed out copies," but was not arrested (Fadel Allassan, "A CT Editor Challenged a pre-Roe v. Wade Abortion Law," *Commonwealth Times*, 24 April 2019; Linda Cayton, "Court Halts Reporters, OK's Reporting," *Salemite* (Salem College, NC), 10 October 1972.

58. "Florida Student to Drop Abortion Directory," *Sitka Daily Sentinel* (Alaska), 11 October 1971.

59. Tom Cornelison, "Abortion Ads Lead to Legal Questions," *Florida Alligator*, 15 January 1971; "Abortion Ads Okay at FAU," *Palm Beach Post*, 21 July 1971; Bob Burdick, "FAU Pupils Print Abortion Advice," *Miami Herald*, 8 October 1971; "Abortion Referrals in 2 Other Papers," *Palm Beach Post-Times*, 9 October 1971; Steve King, "Editorial," *Atlantic Sun*, 12 October 1971.

Connecticut had a similar pattern of independent and allied student responses, and games of chicken with the state's attorney general (Larry Makinson, "Abortion Referral Ads Will Continue, UB Editor Says," *Bridgeport Telegram*, 30 November 1970; Robert L. Sawyer, "UB Paper Halts Ads on Abortion," *Bridgeport Post*, 1 December 1970); "College Newspapers Told Abortion Ads Are Illegal," *Bridgeport Post*, 30 December 1970; *Daily Campus* 2 December 1970; Ken Cruickshank, "Abortion Ads Illegal in State; UofH Newspaper Ignores Ban," *Hartford Courant*, 23 March 1971).

60. "Hopes to Publish More Abortion Information," *Kokomo Tribune* (Indiana), 7 October 1971; "Abortion Data Out Awhile; College Editor Arrested," *Press and Sun-Bulletin* (Binghamton, New York), 7 October 1971; "Florida Student Editor to Drop Abortion Directory," *Daily Sitka Sentinel* (Alaska), 8 October 1971; "Jacksonville Student Paper Ran Abortion Ad," *Tampa Bay Times* (St. Petersburg), 8 October 1971; Associated Press, "Abortion Referrals in 2 Other Papers," *Palm Beach Post-Times*, 9 October 1971; "Student Editor Tests Law," *Editor & Publisher*, 30 October 1971; "Student Editor No Longer Helps Girls Find Abortionist," *Charlotte Observer*, 25 October 1971; Ron Sachs, phone interview by author, 24 July 2020; Louis E. Ingelhart, *Freedom for the College Student Press: Court Cases and Related Decisions Defining the Campus Fourth Estate Boundaries* (Greenwood Press, 1985), 170–71; Marian Jedreaux, "Sachs to Challenge Two Laws About Abortions Next Month," *Florida Alligator*, 25 January 1972.

Other notable cases centered on printers that refused to print the student paper. After the University of Wyoming administration threatened that it would be "violating state law," UW students included a copy of an abortion ad in each November 12 *Branding Iron*. The county attorney stated he would not prosecute the students for abortion advertising, and the *Branding Iron* ran the ad on the front page on December 12, 1971 ("BI Reprints Abortion Ad," *Branding Iron*, 12 December 1971. Florida State University's paper, *Flambeau*, ran a front-page promotion of a "list" of abortion information on page seven, which was left blank when the printer Steve Fox refused to print it (Hamp Carruth [Editor], 14 January 1972).

61. "Journalistic Society Will Support Sachs," *Tampa Bay Times* (St. Petersburg), 8 October 1971; Ron Sachs, phone interview by author, 24 July 2020.

62. Resolutions 71–144 (October 12, 1971); 72–119 (May 16, 1972); 72–129 (August 15, 1972), Student Body Resolutions of the University of Florida Student Senate, Special and Area Studies Collections, George A. Smathers Libraries, University of Florida, Gainesville, Florida; Marian Jedrusiak, "Sachs to Challenge Two Laws About Abortion Next Month," *Florida Alligator*, 15 November 1971.

63. Atlanta Cooperative News Project v. United States Postal Service, 350 F. Supp. 234 (1972), Sept. 29, 1972, United States District Court for the Northern District of Georgia Civ. A. No. 16538, 350 F. Supp. 234, https://cite.case.law/f-supp/350/234/; Nick Taylor, "Abortion Material Ruled Mailable," *Atlanta Constitution*, 30 September 1972, 2; Problem Pregnancy Counseling Service ad, *Great Speckled Bird* (Atlanta, Georgia), 26 October 1970; "Abortion," *Great Speckled Bird* (Atlanta, Georgia), 15 February 1971, 17; abortion ad, *Great Speckled Bird* (Atlanta, Georgia), 25 October 1971; Jane Marcellus, "Tennessee Republicans Turn to Mail Regulation to Restrict Abortion," *Washington Post*, 25 May 2022; Katarina Keane, *Second-Wave Feminism in the American South, 1965–1980*, Ph.D. diss., University of Maryland, College Park, 2009, 170–74; Linda Cayton, "Court Halts Reporters, OK's Reporting," *Salemite* (Salem College, NC), 10 October 1972.

64. "Abortion Service Started Student Discount Available," *Purdue Exponent*, 23 October 1970; Barbara Sutherland, "Abortion: A Coed's Only 'Feasible Solution' to Pregnancy," *Kentucky Kernel*, 2 November 1970; Abbe David Lowell, "Abortion Referral Agencies Thrive," *Columbia Daily Spectator*, 7 December 1970; Jane D. Brown, "Abortions: Enter the Middle Man," *Kentucky Kernel*, 20 January 1971; "Dear Sirs," *Ridge Runner* (University of North Carolina—Asheville), 2 March 1971; "How to Avoid Abortion Rip-Offs," *Journal* (University of North Carolina—Charlotte), 22 April 1971; "Abortion," *Emanon* (Sarah Lawrence College), 26 April 1971; "Abortion Rap," *Virginia Weekly*, May-June 1971; "Hang On to These Numbers—You May Need Them Someday," *Forum* (Westminster College, UT), 9 September 1971; "ZPG Opens Abortion Office," *Journal* (University of North Carolina—Charlotte), 27 September 1971; Philip H. Dougherty, "Advertising: Birth-Control Campaign Set," *New York Times*, 5 October 1971; Robin Elliott, "Advertising Family Planning," *Family Planning Perspectives* 3(4) (Oct. 1971): 65–67; Frederick P. McGehan, "Abortion-Referral Agencies Are Marking Up the Cost of Help," *Baltimore Sun*, 28 February 1972.

65. Karen Carnabucci, "Abortion Referral Services Aid Women in Area," *Daily Collegian* (Pennsylvania State), 12 October 1971; "Abortion Referral: Big Business," *Spectrum* (University of Buffalo), 26 April 1971; Lani Baldwin, "Davenport Outlines Abortion Service, Plans," *Lance* (St. Andrews College, North Carolina), 11 November 1971; Rev. Carl Boaz, "My Experience with Clergy Consultation Service in Dallas Texas," to the "NM [New Mexico] House Consumer and Public Affairs Committee," New Mexico Religious Coalition for Reproductive Choice, https://nmrcrc.org/clergy-notes-blog/my-experience-with-clergy-consultation-service-in-dallas-texas (accessed 17 June 2022); Susannah Heschel, "Birth Control and Abortion Clinics Set Up," *Trinity Tripod* (Hartford, Connecticut), 7 March 1972; "Clergy Offers Aid for Unwanted Pregnancies," *Skidmore News*, 19 February 1970; John Mann, "Planned Parenthood Increases Services," *Kentucky Kernel*, 4 December 1972; "Pregnancy Counseling," *People's Phone Book* (Boston, 1971): https://

www.masscult617.com/peoples-yellow-pages?lightbox=dataItem-k9300lgc9 (accessed 20 June 2022).

66. Philip H. Dougherty, "Advertising: Birth-Control Campaign Set," *New York Times*, 5 October 1971; Robin Elliott, "Advertising Family Planning," *Family Planning Perspectives* 3(4) (Oct. 1971): 65–67.

67. Judy Kunofsky email with author 7 February 2022.

While it was predominantly male, women played active roles in the organization. Two of the most visible leaders were Anne Nicol Gaylor of Wisconsin, who was a ZPG member and a founder of the "ZPG Abortion and Sterilization Service," and Joyce Tarnow of Florida, who was coordinator of the Miami ZPG chapter and a public supporter of abortion rights (Annie Laurie Gaylor, "My Mother Anne Nicol Gaylor: Feminist, Activist, Freethinker," *Progressive Magazine*, 22 June 2015, https://progressive.org/latest/mother-anne-nicol-gaylor-feminist-activist-freethinker/; Anne Nicol Gaylor, *Abortion Is a Blessing* (Psychological Dimensions, Inc., 1975); Molly Sinclair, "Abortion: Two Views on Lifting Florida Restraints," *Miami Herald*, 15 March 1972.

68. Prescott, *Student Bodies*, 148–50; "ZPG Confronts 'Over Population,'" *Yale Daily News*, 28 October 1969; Charley Johnson, "ZPG Discusses Contraceptives," *Concordian*, 23 October 1970; "ZPG Opens Abortion Office," *Carolina Journal* (Charlotte), 2 September 1971; John Hartzell, "Population Control Groups Build Following in State," *Appleton Post-Crescent* (Wisconsin), 3 November 1971; "ZPG Plans to Spread Message," *Morning Call* (Allentown, Pennsylvania), 16 September 1971; ZPG announcement, *Duke Chronicle*, 14 March 1972; Rick Northern, "Panel Discussion on Abortion: Lively Debate, No Final Answers," *Courier-Journal* (Louisville), 6 November 1970.

For example, ZPG gained recognition as a campus organization in 1970 and acted "as a free abortion referral service" at Northwestern University (*Daily*, 21 September 1971).

69. ZPG ad: *Review* (University of Delaware), 20 April 1972, 25 April 1972; *Skidmore News*, 20 April 1972, 25 April 1972, 5 October 1972.

70. ZPG ad: *Review* (University of Delaware), 2 May 1972; *Skidmore News*, 8 December 1972.

71. ZPG ad: *Review* (University of Delaware), 9 May 1972.

72. Barbara Sutherland, "Abortion: A Coed's Only 'Feasible Solution' to Pregnancy," *Kentucky Kernel* (University of Kentucky), 2 November 1970; Jane D Brown, phone interview by author, 11 and 12 June 2020.

Chapter 5

1. Anonymous woman interview with author, 2023; Christabelle Sethna and Marion Doull, "Accidental Tourists: Canadian Women, Abortion Tourism, and Travel," *Women's Studies* 41(4) (2012): 457–75; Christabelle Sethna and Gayle Davis, eds., *Abortion Across Borders: Transnational Travel and Access to Abortion Services* (Johns Hopkins University Press, 2019); Christabelle Sethna, et al., "Choice, Interrupted: Travel and Inequality of Access to Abortion Services since the 1960s," *Labour / Le Travail* (Spring 2013): 29–48; Agata Ignaciuk and Christabelle Sethna, "Charters for Choice: Abortion Travel, Abortion

Referral Networks and Spanish Women's Transnational Reproductive Agency, 1975–1985," *Gender & History* 32(2) (July 2020): 286–303; Leslie Reagan, "Abortion Travels: An International History," *Journal of Modern European History* 17(3) (2019): 337–52; It Couldn't Happen to Your Daughter," *San Bernardino County Sun*, 7 May 1972; anonymous, "When Abortion Was Legalized: One Woman's DC Experience," *Montgomery Spark*, February 1972; Sarah Elvins and Katherine Parkin, "The Business of Abortion: Referral Services, Cross-Border Consumption, and Canadian Women's Access to Abortion in New York State, 1970–1972," *Enterprise & Society* 2024: 1–21.

2. Phil Santora, "Abortion Rate Is Challenging the Birth Rate," *Daily News*, 22 November 1963. Tijuana spelled as Tiajuana in the original.

3. Judith Randal, "Abortion Laws Are Discriminatory," *Evening Star*, 19 August 1971; Elaine Morrissy, "How Does Abortion Score Now, Legally?," *Dayton Daily News*, 10 October 1971. For an example of women's power vis-à-vis the telephone, see Chapter 5: A Poison Squad of Whispering Women, in Kathleen Blee's *Women of the Klan* (University of California Press, 2008).

4. Carol Joffe, *Doctors of Conscience*, 42, 66, 90; *Dear Dr. Spencer* (documentary) (Icarus Films, 1998); Vincent J Genovese, *Angel of Ashland: Practicing Compassion and Testing Fate* (Prometheus Books, 2000), 55–56.

5. Myra McPherson, "Abortion Demand Increases After Ruling on Vague Law," *Asbury Park Press*, 3 March 1970; Jessie Nicodemus, "Abortion Mill Smashed in Clinton," *Journal Herald* (Dayton), 20 November 1961; Jane Brody, "Gold Star Mother Is Abortionist," *Roanoke Times*, 17 January 1968.

6. Jacqueline Thompson, "For Immediate Release," Rolla Crick Collection, Box 1, Folder 8, Oregon Historical Society Research Library; Douglass Perry, "Ruth Barnett, Portland's Foremost Abortionist," *Oregonian*, https://www.oregonlive.com/history/2022/05/ruth-barnett-portlands-foremost-abortionist-before-roe-v-wade-endured-arrests-lived-high-life.html (accessed 9 October 2023); "Abortionist 'Ma' Ramsey Dies in Fire," *Press-Telegram* (Long Beach), 13 February 1967; "Grandmother of Abortions Now in Oregon State Penitentiary," *World* (Coos Bay, Oregon), 14 February 1968. Florida reported the arrest of a 71-year-old "grandmotherly" Kathy Cole (*Miami News*, 10 May and 26 May 1967).

7. Ruth Youngblood, "2,000 Abortions a Year in Hawaii," *Shreveport Times*, 26 February 1970.

8. Virginia Lee Hodge, "Abortion in California," *Arizona Daily Star* (Tucson), 2 June 1971; Mary Melcher, *Pregnancy, Motherhood, and Choice in Twentieth-Century Arizona* (University of Arizona Press, 2012), 147; Jeff Tucker, "Young Girl's Journey to a Safe Abortion," *Atlanta Journal & Constitution*, 4 October 1970.

9. Ann Dee, "The Abortion Issue," *American-Statesman* (Austin), 23 May 1971; "To Obtain an Abortion," *Playboy*, September 1971, 77; David K. Johnson, *Buying Gay* (Columbia University Press, 2019); Mia Bay, *Traveling Black* (Belknap Press, 2021); Kate Sosin, "The Damron Address Book," *LA Magazine*, 25 June 2019, https://www.lamag.com/culturefiles/damron-address-book/; *Green Book*, New York Public Library, https://digitalcollections.nypl.org/collections/the-green-book#/?tab=about (accessed 26 July 2023).

The Association to Repeal Abortion Laws required any man coming into their San Francisco offices to get referral information to be accompanied by a woman, because they believed "the involvement of women is important in the act of repealing abortion laws" ("The List," Large Femina Pamphlets, H84723, Northwestern University).

10. Nancy Howell Lee, *The Search for an Abortionist* (University of Chicago Press, 1969), 5.

11. "Drive to Cuba via Overseas Highway and Caribbean Ferry from Key West" brochure, 1950s; Annette Ramirez de Arellano and Conrad Seipp, *Colonialism, Catholicism, and Contraception* (University of North Carolina Press, 1983), 144–47; 25–28; Rachel Hynson, *Sex and State Making Revolutionary Cuba, 1959–1968* Ph.D. diss., University of North Carolina, 2014, 25–28; Susan Brownmiller, *In Our Time: Memoir of a Revolution* (Random House, 2000), 103–4; Lawrence Lader, "A Guide to Abortion Laws in the United States," *Redbook*, June 1971; Yamila Azize-Vargas and Luis A Aviles, "Abortion in Puerto Rico: The Limits of Colonial Legality," *Reproductive Health Matters* 9 (May 1997): 56–57; "Island's Abortion 'Racket' Patronized by U.S. Women," *Montana Catholic Register*, 17 May 1963; Phil Santora, "Abortions in Puerto Rico Boom on Tourist-Patients," *Daily News*, 19 November 1963; Ellen Messer and Kathryn E. May, *Back Rooms: Voices from the Illegal Abortion Era* (Prometheus Books, 1994), 155–56; Patricia G. Miller, *The Worst of Times: Illegal Abortion* (HarperCollins, 1993); Jill Clayburgh, *The Choices We Made*, ed. Angela Bonavoglia, 54–55.

In the 1960s, Miami police reported that abortion was a bigger business than all gambling and prostitution combined. Cuban doctors also fled to Miami. Drawing on women nationally and from Canada, the city was home to thirty clinics, with one estimated to be "grossing $10,000 a day." The profits were so large because the procedures ran $1,000 each. The lowest reported estimate for abortion income was $20 million; the highest estimate was $90 million a year (Dick Nellius, "Miami Termed Abortion Capital," *Miami News*, 9 December 1962; Karl Wickstrom and Clarence Jones, "Abortion Big Business in Miami," *Miami Herald*, 18 March 1966; Karl Wickstrom, "How Rich Abortionists Coexist With Lawmen," *Miami Herald*, 8 January 1967).

12. Phil Santora, abortion series, *Daily News*, 19–22 November 1963; Constance Harris, "Toughest Abortion Laws No Bar to Women," *Chippewa Herald-Telegram* (Wisconsin), 9 June 1970; Deborah Robinson, in *Abortion Rap* by Diane Schulder and Florynce Kennedy (McGraw-Hill Book Company, 1971), 58; Abortion: Precept & Practice," *Time*, 13 July 1962; Al Dinhoffer, "Doctors Struggle to Police Abortion Racket," *San Juan Star*, 13 May 1963; Roy Lucas, "Federal Constitutional Limitations on the Enforcement and Administration of State Abortion Statutes," *North Carolina Law Review* 46(4) (June 1968); Susan Brownmiller, *In Our Time: Memoir of a Revolution* (Random House, 2000), 128–29; Rosa E. Marchand-Arias, "Clandestinaje Legal: El Aborto en Puerto Rico de 1937 a 1970," *Puerto Rico Health Sciences Journal* 17(1) (April 1998): 21; "Abortos Criminales," *El Mundo*, 18 January 1968. [translated into English, Google]

13. Al Dinhoffer, *San Juan Star*: "Apathy Underlies Legal Action Against Abortions," 10 May 1963 and "Doctors Struggle to Police Abortion Racket," 13 May 1963; Rosa E. Marchand-Arias, "Clandestinaje Legal: El Aborto en Puerto Rico de 1937 a 1970," *Puerto Rico Health Sciences Journal* 17(1) (April 1998): 15–26 [translated into English, Google]; Puerto Rican Abortions to Get Stiff Competition," *Evening Sun* (Hanover, Pennsylvania), 30 May 1970; Phil Santora, "San Juan Weekend: Abortions in Puerto Rico Boom on

Tourist-Patients," *Daily News*, 19 November 1963; Phil Santora, "Abortionists Have No Concern about Women's Health," *Daily News*, 21 November 1963.

14. Al Dinhoffer, "Legal, Moral Attitudes on Abortion Conflict," *San Juan Star*, 15 May 1963; Phil Santora, *Daily News*: "Abortions in Puerto Rico Boom on Tourist-Patients," 19 November 1963 and "Meet Abortion King, A Pig in Clover," 20 November 1963.

15. *Daily News*, 14 May 1965; *Mount Vernon Argus* (New York) 12 October 1970; "Get Happy," allmusic.com (accessed 11 July 2023); Marion Purcelli, "Sunny Puerto Rico Is Just Six Hours Away," *Chicago Tribune*, 29 December 1963; "An Airline Map of the United States and Puerto Rico Showing Principal Non-Stop Routes, 1965," Digital Public Library of America, https://dp.la/primary-source-sets/puerto-rican-migration-to-the-us/sources/1142 (accessed 11 July 2023).

16. Rosa E. Marchand-Arias, "Clandestinaje Legal: El Aborto en Puerto Rico de 1937 a 1970," *Puerto Rico Health Sciences Journal* 17(1) (April 1998): 19, 21–22, 4 [translated into English, Google]; Al Dinhoffer, "Abortion," *San Juan Star*, 8 May 1963; Harry F. Themal, "Delaware Law Limits Abortions," *Morning News* (Wilmington), 1 April 1969; Carole Joffe, *Doctors of Conscience*, 110–23.

17. Deborah Robinson in *Abortion Rap* by Diane Schulder and Florynce Kennedy (McGraw-Hill Book Company, 1971), 58–63.

18. Deborah Robinson, *Abortion Rap*, 64.

19. Lawrence Lader, *Abortion II: Making the Revolution* (Beacon Press, 1973), 42, 45–46; ; Rosa E. Marchand-Arias, "Clandestinaje Legal: El Aborto en Puerto Rico de 1937 a 1970," *Puerto Rico Health Sciences Journal* 17(1) (April 1998): 23 [translated into English, Google]; Peggy Ann Darbie, "'Illegal, but They Look the Other Way," *Courier-News* (New Jersey), 30 January 1970; "Abortion," *Parade Magazine*, 17 August 1969.

20. Phil Santora, "Abortions in Puerto Rico Boom on Tourist-Patients," *Daily News*, 19 November 1963; Rosa E. Marchand-Arias, "Clandestinaje Legal: El Aborto en Puerto Rico de 1937 a 1970," *Puerto Rico Health Sciences Journal* 17(1) (April 1998): 19, 21–2, 4 [translated into English, Google]; Al Dinhoffer, "Abortion," *San Juan Star*, 8 May 1963; Harry F. Themal, "Delaware Law Limits Abortions," *Morning News* (Wilmington), 1 April 1969); Carole Joffe, *Doctors of Conscience*, 110–23.

21. "N.Y. Abortion Services Data Sent to Lehigh Valley Physicians," *Morning Call* (Allentown, Pennsylvania), 19 September 1970.

22. "Report of the Committee on the Working of the Abortion Act: Volume I," April 1974 (Her Majesty's Stationery Office), Sections: 457–460; Christabelle Sethna, "From Heathrow Airport to Harley Street," *Abortion Across Borders*, ed. Christabelle Sethna and Gayle Davis (Johns Hopkins University Press, 2019), 46, 53–54.

23. "$1,250 Deal: London Trip & Abortion," *Daily News* (New York), 18 January 1970; Ellen Glascock, "Abortion," *Connecticut College Alumni Magazine* (Winter 1972), 6; Christabelle Sethna, "From Heathrow Airport to Harley Street," *Abortion Across Borders*, ed. Christabelle Sethna and Gayle Davis (Johns Hopkins University Press, 2019), 52–55.

24. Richard Shull: "TV Probes Mass Abortions in London," *Bergen Record*, 17 November 1969 and "Britain's New Boom: Abortion on Demand," *Indianapolis News*,

24 November 1969; "Abortion Planning Agency Deluged with Phone Calls," *Corpus Christi Caller*, 23 January 1970; Tom Cullen, "American Girls Hooked on British Abortion Deal," *Fort Myers News-Press*, 8 March 1970.

25. Myra Macpherson, "Washington's Abortion Law Falls," *Sacramento Bee*, 16 November 1969; Emma Brockes, "Gloria Steinem: 'If Men Could Get Pregnant, Abortion Would Be a Sacrament,'" *Guardian*, 17 October 2015; Dala McKinsey, "More Abortions Done Out of State Than in State," *Courier News* (Blytheville, Arkansas), 9 December 1971; Leslie Reagan, *When Abortion*, 230.

One woman was surprised that the Midwestern women she talked with in Mexico, when they were all recovering from their abortions, were all "soundly against legalizing abortion" in the United States (Becca Andrews, "On a Desperate Journey to Ciudad Juárez—and the Costly, Dangerous Reality of Abortion in 1968," *Literary Hub*, 4 November 2022, https://lithub.com/on-a-journey-to-ciudad-juarez-and-what-abortion-looked-like-in-1968/ (accessed 14 August 2023).

26. "$1,250 Deal: London Trip & Abortion," *Daily News* (New York), 18 January 1970; Colin Frost, "'Pirates' Hijack Women," *Tampa Bay Times*, 7 February 1970; Tom Cullen, "American Girls Hooked on British Abortion Deal," *Fort Myers News-Press*, 8 March 1970; Christabelle Sethna, "From Heathrow Airport to Harley Street," *Abortion Across Borders*, ed. by Christabelle Sethna and Gayle Davis (Johns Hopkins University Press, 2019), 54 –55.

27. Leslie J. Reagan, "Crossing the Border for Abortions: California Activists, Mexican Clinics, and the Creation of a Feminist Health Agency in the 1960s," *Feminist Studies* 26(2) (Summer, 2000): 323–48; Lina-Maria Murillo, *Fighting for Control: Power, Reproductive Care, and Race in the U.S-Mexico Borderlands* (University of North Carolina Press, 2025); Alicia Gutierrez-Romine, *From Back Alley to the Border* (University of Nebraska Press, 2020); Peggy Bendet, "Japan Is Promoting Population Control," *Honolulu Star-Bulletin*, 12 December 1968.

28. Tom Mainor, phone interview by author, 8 March 2022; Joffe, *Doctors of Conscience*, 112–14; Robin G. Henderson, "Abortion: A Crisis of Self-Determination," *Chronicle* (University of Utah), 27 May 1969; Miroslava Chavez-Garcia, "From 'Tough Love' to 'Street Fight': Garrett Hardin and Cordelia S. May's Battle for Population Control and Eugenics at the Turn of the Millennium," *Revista Brasileira de Historia* 43 (94) (Sep-Dec 2023).

29. William C. Harrison, "California Abortion Law Problem," *Santa Cruz Sentinel*, 13 June 1967; Pat Hunter, "Local Physicians Polled on Opinions," *Honolulu Star-Bulletin*, 23 February 1969; Beverly Creamer, "House Uncertain on Abortion Law," *Honolulu Star-Bulletin*, 5 February 1970; Sheila Raskin in *Abortion Rap* by Diane Schulder and Florynce Kennedy (McGraw-Hill Book Company, 1971), 76–82.

30. Frank Jenkins, "In the News," *Herald and News* (Klamath Falls, Oregon), 4 April 1962; Tiana Norgren, *Abortion Before Birth Control: The Politics of Reproduction in Postwar Japan* (Princeton University Press, 2001), 57; Peggy Bendet, "Japan Is Promoting Population Control," *Honolulu Star-Bulletin*, 12 December 1968; Susan Matthews, "The Forgotten Story of Shirley Wheeler," slate.com, 1 June 2022, https://slate.com/news-and-politics/2022/06/roe-supreme-court-abortion-ruling-slow-burn-podcast.html.

31. Tiana Norgren, *Abortion Before Birth Control: The Politics of Reproduction in Postwar Japan* (Princeton University Press, 2001), 57, 183fn38; Tama Yasuko and Scott O'Bryan, "The Logic of Abortion: Japanese Debates on the Legitimacy of Abortion as Seen in Post–World War II Newspapers," *U.S.-Japan Women's Journal*. English Supplement 7 (1994):18; Joffe, *Doctors*, 114; Cassandra Tate, "Abortion Reform in Washington State," historylink.org, 23 February 2003, https://www.historylink.org/File/5313; Society for Humane Abortion, "'Rush' Procedure for Going to Japan" in *Before Roe v. Wade* by Linda Greenhouse and Reva B. Siegel (2014), 8–11, https://documents.law.yale.edu/sites/default/files/beforeroe2nded_1.pdf; Alexis Cheung, "At 16, My Mom Flew to Japan Alone to Have an Abortion," *Cut*, 6 February 2017, https://www.thecut.com/2017/02/at-16-my-mom-flew-to-japan-alone-to-have-an-abortion.html; Rosa Campbell, "What an Archive of Testimonials Tells Us About Abortion Before Roe," Lithub.com, 3 June 2022, https://lithub.com/what-an-archive-of-testimonials-tells-us-about-abortion-before-roe/ (all accessed 22 July 2023); "Japan Is Abortion Paradise," *Asahi shinbun*, 7 March 1967, title translated by Google and Deepl, 24 July 2023.

32. "Bank of Tokyo of California" (San Francisco), Society for Human Abortion Collection, MC289, Box 2 Folder 27, Schlesinger Library; William C. Harrison, "California Abortion Law Problem," *Santa Cruz Sentinel*, 13 June 1967; Robert L. Jackson, "Japanese Press LBJ on Pacific Air Routes," *Honolulu Advertiser*, 19 December 1968; Allen Nacheman, "Abortion in Japan Possible?," *Statesman* (Salem, Oregon), 22 May 1969; Thomas W. Bush, "Bank of Tokyo Shows It's Not Bound by Tradition," *LA Times*, 6 June 1969; Kathy Gautier, "Some Travel Agencies Arrange Abortions," *Honolulu Star-Bulletin*, 20 June 1969; "'Rush' Procedure for Going to Japan," Society for Human Abortion Collection, MC289, Box 4, Folder 73, Schlesinger Library and in *Before Roe v. Wade: Voices That Shaped the Abortion Debate Before the Supreme Court's Ruling* by Linda Greenhouse and Reva B. Siegel (Yale Law School, 2012), 8–11; Leslie Reagan, *When Abortion Was a Crime: Women, Medicine, and Law in the United States, 1867–1973* (University of California Press, 1997), 224.

Helen Hardacre discovered that in the early 1970s Hawai'ian women participated in the *mitzuko* ceremonies in Japan (*Marketing the Menacing Fetus in Japan* [University of California Press, 1997], 79). With thanks to Jeff Smith and Bill Ashbaugh for their insights into this phenomenon.

33. David Otis, "Abortion—Liberalized Laws, Guidance Sought," *San Bernardino County Sun*, 25 March 1968; Nancy Howell Lee, *The Search for an Abortionist* (University of Chicago Press, 1969), 85, 87; Lawrence Lader, *Abortion II* (Beacon Press, 1973), 27–28, 30–34; Alicia Gutierrez-Romine, *From Back Alley to the Border: Criminal Abortion in California, 1920–1969* (University of Nebraska Press, 2000); Leslie Reagan, "Crossing the Border for Abortions: California Activists, Mexican Clinics, and the Creation of a Feminist Health Agency in the 1960s," *Feminist Studies* 26(2) (Summer 2000); Lina-Maria Murillo, *Birth Control on the Border: Race, Gender, Religion, and Class in the Making of the Birth Control Movement, El Paso, Texas, 1936–1973*, Ph.D. Diss., University of Texas at El Paso, 2016; Leslie Reagan, "Abortion Travels: An International History," *Journal of Modern European History*, 2019; Lina-Maria Murillo, "*Espanta Cigüeñas*: Race and Abortion

in the US-Mexico Borderlands," *Signs: Journal of Women in Culture and Society* 48 (4) (Summer 2023).

34. William C. Harrison, "California Abortion Law Problem," *Santa Cruz Sentinel*, 13 June 1967; Anne Archer, *The Choices We Made*, ed. Angela Bonavoglia, 102; Association to Repeal Abortion Laws "The List," Large Femina Pamphlets, H84723, Northwestern University; Katherine Saltzman, phone interview by author, 28 May 2020; Caitlin Fendley, *Countdown To Zero: A History Of Grassroots Population Activism In The United States, 1968–1991* (Ph.D. Diss., Purdue, 2023), 210.

35. "A Guide to Mexico City," n.d., no author, SC Clergy Referral Service, 1970–1972, Louise Pettus Archives & Special Collections, Winthrop University.

36. Confidential, Mexico City, Mexico, 9 July 1970, SC Clergy Referral Service, 1970–1972, Louise Pettus Archives & Special Collections, Winthrop University.

37. Sam Newlund, "Suburban Man Arranges Abortions," *The Minneapolis Tribune*, 17 January 1970; Jim Klobuchar, "Matter of Life . . . and Life," *The Minneapolis Star*, 21 January 1970; Jerry Knight, "Abortions for Iowa Women," *Des Moines Sunday Register*, 26 July 1970; William Tome, "Mexico City: New Mecca for Abortions," *Oakland Tribune*, 24 August 1970; "Clergyman Here Counsels on Problem Pregnancies," *Sioux City Journal*, 23 August 1970; Lawrence Lader, *Abortion II* (Beacon Press, 1973), 50–51.

38. Beverly Koch, "Abortion Not So Hush-Hush Now," *Akron Beacon Journal*, 19 April 1970; Kay Homquist, "Abortion Quest Narrows," *Fort Worth Star-Telegram*, 26 July 1970; Jeff Tucker, "Young Girl's Journey to a Safe Abortion," *Atlanta Journal-Constitution*, 4 October 1970; "U of F Doctor Defends Open Dorms," *Miami Herald*, 20 May 1971.

39. Lucy Burke Meyer, "The Growing Dispute Over Abortion Laws," *Redwood City Tribune*, 7 February 1967; Jacquin Sanders, "Most Abortionists Sympathetic Toward Patients," *Press and Sun-Bulletin* (Binghamton), 7 June 1970; Middy Randerson, "For One, a Trip to the Border," *Corpus Christi Times*, 8 November 1970; Center for Disease Control, *Family Planning Evaluation. Abortion Surveillance Report—Legal Abortions, United States, Annual Summary, 1970* (US Dept. of Health, Education, and Welfare, 1970), 23.

40. "Juarez Abortions Hit U.S. Spotlight," *El Paso Herald-Post*, 18 October 1968; Mass Mailing for Dangerous Abortions" and "No 'Seal of Approval' for Ortega," *Medical World News* 9(41) (1968): 24–29; "Abortion Clinic Offered in Mexico," *Star* (Columbia, South Carolina), 24 August 1970; "Lina-Maria Murillo, "*Espanta Cigüeñas*: Race and Abortion in the US-Mexico Borderlands," *Signs: Journal of Women in Culture and Society* 48(4) (Summer 2023).

41. James C. Mohr, "Iowa's Abortion Battles of the Late 1960s and Early 1970s," *Annals of Iowa* 50(1), 63–89; Morgan, "Abortion Law as Safeguard," 22 January 1969; *Journal of the Kansas Medical Society* 69(4) (April 1968), 236; Robert Foley and James Foley, "Legalized Abortion Not Sex Lures, Youths State," *Lawrence Daily-Journal World*, 22 April 1970.

Beth Bailey's *Sex in the Heartland* captures the slow, quiet sexual revolution taking place in Kansas, and in particular reveals the significance of medical professionals like Dr. Dale Clinton, who distributed the birth control pill. Men like Clinton and Kermit Krantz believed in overpopulation and used their positions as medical doctors to combat it with birth control and abortion access (Harvard University Press, 1999), 108–113. Also, Beth Bailey, "Prescribing the Pill: Politics, Culture, and the Sexual Revolution in America's Heartland," *Journal of Social History* 30(4) (Summer 1997): 827–28.

42. "Doctor Disclaims Abortion," *Wichita Beacon*, 27 June 1968; "Daughter's Death Cause for Lawsuit," *Manhattanville Mercury*, 15 November 1968; Orville Scott, "More Liberal Abortion Law Near?," *Columbia Missourian*, 18 May 1969; Wayne Lee, "Kansas Won't Be Abortion Capital," *Olathe News*, 10 January 1970; Ted Blankenship, "Abortions to Be Legal July 1," *Wichita Eagle*, 20 April 1970; Jo Nelson, "Only 1 in 4 Local Hospitals Will Allow Liberalized Abortion" and Lynn Holt, "But KU Obstetrician Sees Law As a Right of Women," *Wichita Eagle*, 2 July 1970; "Blue Shield Will Pay Some Part of Abortion Fees," *Great Bend Tribune*, 2 July 1970; "Queues Forming for New York Abortions" and "Will Still Pay for Abortions," *Salina Journal*, 1 July 1970; Ray Morgan, "Abortion Law as Safeguard," *Kansas City Times*, 22 January 1969; James C. Mohr, "Iowa's Abortion Battles of the Late 1960s and Early 1970s," *Annals of Iowa* 50(1), 63–89.

43. Ray Morgan, "Abortion Law as Safeguard," *Kansas City Times*, 22 January 1969; James C. Mohr, "Iowa's Abortion Battles of the Late 1960s and Early 1970s," *Annals of Iowa* 50(1), 63–89.

44. Dr. Kermit Krantz testified in the second series of hearings on S.1 676 entitled "Population Crisis," held during the 2d session of the 89th Congress; Conwell Carlson, "A Doctor Urges Birth Control," *Kansas City Star*, 6 Nov 1962; Ray Morgan, "Abortion Law as Safeguard," *Kansas City Times*, 22 January 1969; "Change in Attitudes Sweeping States," *Kansas City Star* (Missouri), 4 August 1970; Laura Hockaday, "Friends Honor Med Ctr Professor," *Kansas City Star* (Missouri), 16 December 1990; William Moran Jr., "A Sourcebook on Population," *Population Bulletin* 25(5) (November 1969): 46.

45. Jane Lee, "No 'Abortion Mill' Seen Here Under Altered Policy," 26 June 1970; "Change in Attitudes Sweeping States," *Kansas City Star* (Missouri), 4 August 1970; David Redmon, "Query Abortion Legality," *Kansas City Times* (Missouri), 24 July 1971.

46. "Change in Attitudes Sweeping States," *Kansas City Star* (Missouri), 4 August 1970; David Redmon, "Query Abortion Legality," *Kansas City Times* (Missouri), 24 July 1971.

47. "Abortion Agency Opens State Offices," *Big Basin Herald* (Muldrow, Oklahoma), 19 August 1971; "Free Abortion Information Available to Oklahomans," *Andromeda* 1(6), Digital Collections—Oklahoma State Library—Underground Newspapers. Also, "Abortion Trip, Editor's Note," *Quad City Times*, 16 July 1972.

48. David Redmon, "Query Abortion Legality," *Kansas City Times* (Missouri), 24 July 1971; "Abortions in Kansas Affects Birth Rate," *Douglas County-Herald* (Ava, Missouri), 3 August 1972.

49. David Redmon, "Query Abortion Legality," *Kansas City Times* (Missouri), 24 July 1971; "Abortions in Kansas Affects Birth Rate," *Douglas County-Herald* (Ava, Missouri), 3 August 1972.

50. "Kansas Abortion Influx Dip," *Kansas City Star* (Missouri), 10 September 1972; Howard S Gitlow, "Abortion Services: Time for a Discussion of Marketing Policies," *Journal of Marketing* (April 1978): 74–75; Garrow, 323–27, Hoff, 182.

51. Grace Marie Prather, "Abortions Being Performed on Simplified Out-Patient Basis," *Albuquerque Journal*, 14 March 1971; Abortion ad, *Corpus Christi Caller-Times*, 18 May 1971; Howard S Gitlow, "Abortion Services: Time for a Discussion of Marketing Policies," *Journal of Marketing* (April 1978): 74–75; Garrow, 323–27, Hoff, 182; James C. Mohr, "Iowa's Abortion Battles of the Late 1960s and Early 1970s," *Annals of Iowa* 50(1), 63–89.

52. Alecia Long, *Great Southern Babylon* (Louisiana State University Press, 2004), 5; Henry Aurin, "Washington Is Becoming a Big Abortion Center," *Charlotte Observer*, 21 June 1971; Dorothy Marks, "Catholic Socialite Runs Abortion Clinic in D.C.," *Evening Sun* (Baltimore), 4 August 1971; Email correspondence from Nancy Gall-Clayton and Johanna Camenisch to Katherine Parkin, 17 June 2020; "Number of Abortions Increases in Georgia," *Macon News*, 18 April 1972; "Lexington Abortion Counseling," *Lexington Courier-Journal*, 1 August 1972; Katie Bernard, "She Had an Abortion Before Roe v. Wade," *Kansas City Star* (Missouri), 6 July 2022.

Even though Maryland legalized therapeutic abortions in 1968, doctors moved to reject applications from out-of-state women, to discourage access. A doctor at Johns Hopkins argued, "We can't be the abortionists for the East Coast. If Maryland becomes an abortion center no other state will do its share and invest the time and money we have to lower criminal abortion death rates." Prior to that ruling, about twenty percent of abortions were done for out-of-state women. Women from Maryland and Virginia comprised about one-third of D.C.'s abortion patients. ("Maryland Abortion Requests Skyrocket," *LaCrosse Tribune* (Wisconsin), 22 February 1969; "2 Hospitals Curb Abortions," *Evening Star* (D.C.), 22 February 1969; "Legal Abortions Increase to 743," *Evening Star* (D.C.), 22 May 1969; Margaret Gentry, "District of Columbia Abortion Rate Jumps," *Hattiesberg American*, 10 April 1972; Harvey Kabaker, "Rise in DC Abortions Continues in Early '72," *Evening Star*, 12 December 1972.

53. Crosby S. Noyes, "Abortion Is a Flourishing Racket Here," *Evening Star*, 8 May 1950; Jack Lait and Lee Mortimer, *Washington Confidential* (Crown Publishers, Inc., 1951), 89; Jocelyn Dingman, "Jet-Service Abortion," *Chatelaine*, June 1970, 4; Katherine Parkin, "The Women's National Abortion Action Coalition & the Abortion Tribunals, 1971–1972," *Journal of Family History* 47(4) 2022: 367–400; "Illegal Operations Still Taking Toll," *Kansas City Star*, 2 August 1970; Don Kirkman, "Abortions Now in Three Plus Hours," *Birmingham Post-Herald*, 30 July 1971; Carol Joffe, *Doctors of Conscience*, 60; Washington Women's Liberation, 20 October 1969 and National Organization of Women, "Abortion Counseling Information," revised April 1969, washingtonareaspark.com, https://washingtonareaspark.com/wp-content/uploads/2021/11/1969-10-20-Womens-Liberation-Bullewtin-2.pdf (accessed 15 July 2023).

Many places had this kind of identity at different points in history. Madeleine Ware, Cara Delay, and Beth Sundstrom revealed how Charleston, South Carolina, was the place to go for area women in the 1960s "because the medical university was there." One woman said, "Residents and interns would perform what we would call 'No-Tell Motel abortions' . . . and I mean, they would pick up $2000 on a weekend . . . there'd be girls coming from all over the place down here because it was quiet, it was discreet, and hopefully there were no complications" ("Abortion and Black Women's Health Networks in South Carolina, 1940–1970," *Gender & History* 32(3) (October 2020): 646–47).

54. Louise Cook, "Abortion No Longer a Dirty Word," *Evening Journal* (Wilmington, Delaware), 20 March 1970; "Abortion Go-Betweens Profit from Unnecessary Service," *Evening Sun* (Baltimore), 28 February 1972.

55. Dorothy Marks, "A Catholic Runs Abortion Clinic," *San Francisco Examiner*, 12 July 1971; Dorothy Marks, "Socialite Runs Abortion Clinic," *Times-Tribune* (Scranton, Pennsylvania), 12 July 1971; Don Kirkman, "New Abortion Facility (Preterm) Is Speedy, Inexpensive," *Memphis Press-Scimitar*, 19 July 1971.

56. Carole Joffe, *Doctors of Conscience: The Struggle to Provide Abortion Before and After* Roe v. Wade (Beacon Press, 1995), 8, 18–19, 147–51; Don Kirkman, "Abortions Now in Three Plus Hours," *Birmingham Post-Herald*, 30 July 1971; Lucy Matson, "Clinic Workers Strike for Your Health," *Science for the People Magazine* 9(3) (May-June 1977), 20.

57. Henry Aurin, "Washington Is Becoming a Big Abortion Center," *Charlotte Observer*, 21 June 1971; "Two-Thirds of Washington, D.C. Abortion Clinics Users Are White," *Jet*, 21 October 1971; Margaret Gentry, "Washington Moving into the Abortion Ranks," *Enterprise-Journal* (McComb, Mississippi), 10 April 1972; Nicholas Blatchford, "Our Town: 'You All Are Very Sincere,'" *Evening Star*, 9 November 1972.

58. Ralph Dighton, "Fewer Legal Abortions Than Predicted," *Honolulu Star-Bulletin*, 18 September 1968; Martin Smith, "1967 Abortion Law Is Having Impact," *Sacramento Bee*, 16 November 1969; Gil Davis, "Medical Men Feel Need for Liberalized Abortion Law," *Chula Vista Star-News*, 22 March 1970; "Liberal Laws Have Snags," *Daily News-Record* (Harrisburg, Virginia), 3 June 1970.

59. Martin Smith, "1967 Abortion Law Is Having Impact," *Sacramento Bee*, 16 November 1969; "Gov. to Attack Welfare Costs," *Valley Times* (North Hollywood, California), 26 February 1970; "Abortions for Teens Show Sharp Increase," *Sacramento Bee*, 2 June 1970; Lou Cannon, "The Leader He Was, the Leader He Wasn't," *Washington Post*, 26 April 1980.

60. Paul Corcoran, "Telephone Rings All Day," *Enquirer and News*, 30 July 1970; "Abortion Restrictions Killed, *Telegram-Tribune* (San Luis Obispo County, California), 8 June 1971; "New Laws Increasing California Abortion Rate," *Hanford Sentinel* (California), 6 August 1971; E. W. Jacson et al., "Therapeutic Abortions in California," *Western Journal of Medicine* 115(1) (July 1971): 31; George Langmyhr, "The Role of Planned Parenthood-World Population in Abortion," *Clinical Obstetrics & Gynecology* 14 (1971): 1192.

61. Edmund W. Overstreet, "Logistic Problems of Legal Abortion," *American Journal of Public Health* 61(3) (March 1971), 496–99; Edmund W. Overstreet, "Role of Female Sterilization in Population Control," *American Journal of Obstetrics and Gynecology* 101(3) (1 June 1968): 351–57; Matthew Connelly, *Fatal Misconceptions*, 162; Linda Gordon, "The Politics of Population"; "Edmund Overstreet," *University of California: In Memoriam, 1986*, David Krogh, Editor. Overstreet is listed in Osborne's 1974 American Eugenics Society list, American Philosophical Society.

62. "San Francisco Legal Center Opens," *Reno Gazette-Journal*, 12 May 1971; "Ways to Lower Costs of Legal Abortions Sought," *Daily Independent* (San Rafael, California), 14 May 1971; Kenneth Braddick, "Abortion Is One Answer to Unwanted Pregnancy,"

Sacramento Bee, 31 December 1972; Health and Welfare agency press release, "Abortion Rate in California Drops," 25 May 1973, Abortion (I12). November, 1962–1974, MS Women and Law: Section II: Politics. The National Women's History Project. Women's Studies Archive; George Langmyhr, "The Role of Planned Parenthood-World Population in Abortion," *Clinical Obstetrics & Gynecology* 14 (1971): 1192.

63. "Cut-Rate Clinic Slated," *Corpus Christi Caller-Times*, 4 September 1971; Moody Watten, "The Business of Abortion," *San Francisco Examiner*, 27 February 1972.

64. "Free Abortion Clinic Opens in Los Angeles," *Peninsula Times-Tribune* (Palo Alto, California), 17 March 1970; "Hang On to These Numbers—You May Need Them Someday," *Forum* (Westminster College, Utah), 9 September 1971.

65. Michael S. Goldstein, "Creating and Controlling the Medical Market: Abortion in Los Angeles After Liberalization," *Social Problems* 31(5) (Summer 1984): 515–19.

66. Marilyn Schwartz, "Abortion Flight: Lonely Journey," *Green Bay Press-Gazette*, 16 April 1972; "Abortion Capital Title Shifts from Bay City to Los Angeles Area," *Sacramento Bee*, 15 November 1972.

67. Phoenix Service Sends 25 women to California Weekly for Abortions," *State Press* (Arizona State University), 21 October 1971; Paul Recer, "Texas Abortions Are Resulting in Profits for Calif.," *Fort Worth Star-Telegram*, 2 June 1972; Jonathan Beaty, "They're Flying to California: Abortion's Only Air Fare Away," *Columbian* (Vancouver, Washington), 27 August 1972 and "Out-of-Towners Seeking Abortion Skip Red Tape," *Clarion-Ledger* (Jackson, Mississippi), 5 July 1972; "California Abortion Rate Expected to Level Off," *Reno Gazette-Journal* (26 September 1972); House of Representatives, "Out-of-State Abortions," *Extension of Remarks*, 21 February 1973, 4985.

68. Michael S. Goldstein, "Creating and Controlling the Medical Market: Abortion in Los Angeles After Liberalization," *Social Problems* 31(5) (Summer 1984): 521–25.

The takeover of failing hospitals happened quietly and behind the scenes. No one who imagined building a hospital devoted to abortion in the late 1960s, like famed doctor Milan Vuitch's proposed two-hundred-bed hospital in Silver Spring, Maryland, met with success (William Taaffe, "Vuitch's Hospital Plan Draws Fire at Hearing," *Evening Star*, 6 December 1969). Arlene Carmen and Howard Moody, leaders of the CCS, "fantasized about setting up an 'abortion ship' just outside the three-mile limit under a foreign (Japanese) flag" (Howard Moody and Arlene Carmen, *Abortion Counseling and Social Change from Illegal Act to Medical Practice: The Story of the Clergy Consultation Service on Abortion* [Judson Press, 1973], 67).

69. Michael S. Goldstein, "Creating and Controlling the Medical Market: Abortion in Los Angeles after Liberalization," *Social Problems* 31(5) (Summer 1984): 521–25; Anne Taylor Fleming, "Confessions of an Abortion Groupie," *LA*, 12 August 1972.

70. Lynn Sherr, "Troubles Strike Abortion Reform," *The Times* (Shreveport, Louisiana) 27 September 1970; Jonathan Beaty, "Out-of-Towners Seeking Abortion Skip Red Tape," *Clarion-Ledger* (Jackson, Mississippi), 5 July 1972; Doreen Bierbrier, Letter to Editor, *Tulare Advance-Register* (California), 14 September 1972; "Abortion," *Newsweek*, 5 February 1973.

71. Anne Taylor Fleming, "Confessions of an Abortion Groupie" and "They Call Me, Mr. Abortion," *LA*, 12 August 1972; "Abortion," *Newsweek*, 13 November 1972 and 5 February 1973.

72. Anne Taylor Fleming, "They Call Me, Mr. Abortion," *LA*, 12 August 1972; "Mr. Abortion," *Newsweek*, 12 November 1972.

73. "At 81, Feminist Gloria Steinem Finds Herself Free of the 'Demands of Gender,'" npr .org, 26 October 2015, https://www.npr.org/2015/10/26/451862822/at-81-feminist-gloria -steinem-finds-herself-free-of-the-demands-of-gender#:~:text=I%20had%20been%20doing %20all,I%20really%20was%20desperate; Leslie Reagan, *When Abortion Was a Crime*, 229–30; Mim Sharman in *Abortion Rap; To Find a Man* (Rastar Films, 1972).

74. Nancy Howell Lee, *The Search for an Abortionist* (University of Chicago Press, 1969), 59–77.

75. Daniel Abbott et al., *An Investigation of Women Seeking Abortions Through the Three Abortion Referral Agencies in Phoenix*, Master of Social Work Thesis, Arizona State University, 1972, 45–46, 63.

76. Nancy Howell Lee, *The Search for an Abortionist* (University of Chicago Press, 1969), 92–96.

77. *Doctors of Conscience*, 53–69.

78. Dick Nellius, "Miami Called 'Abortion Capital,'" *Miami News*, 9 December 1962; "Queen of the Abortion Capital Goes to Prison," *Tacoma News Tribune*, 16 February 1968; "Strong Safeguards Cited in Abortions," *Columbus Ledger*, 4 March 1968; "Catholics Fear Kansas to Be Abortion Capital, *Wichita Eagle*, 23 January 1969.

Chapter 6

1. New York state legislation did not require women to have the permission of their husbands, and clinics did not ask for it, but public hospitals sometimes did. Nationally, hospitals before and after *Roe* required the written signature of the husband before doing an abortion "to protect it from possible lawsuits by husbands who object to abortions" ("Married Woman Denied Legal Abortion," *Sarasota Herald Tribune*, 18 March 1971; K. B. Levitz, "Consent Provisions in Abortion Statutes," *Florida State University Law Review* 1(4) (Fall 1973): 645–62); Katherine Parkin, "No Husband, No Abortion: Married Women's Abortion Rights," in author's possession.

2. John Sibley, "New York Hospital Officials Pledge 'Safe' Abortions," *Edmonton Journal* (Alberta, Canada), 4 May 1970; Linda Greenhouse, "After July 1, an abortion should be as simple to have as a tonsillectomy, but–," *New York Times*, 28 June 1970; Bob Kuttner and Nanette Rainone (producers), *Abortion: What Now?*, recorded on: 30 June 1970, Broadcast on: WBAI, 1 July 1970; Peter Kihss, "Abortion Demand Expected to Rise," *New York Times*, 5 July 1970. In an unintended twist, the new law took effect in the buildup to a holiday weekend, so even getting referral information from Planned Parenthood had to wait until the following Monday.

3. Lael Scott, "The Urban Strategist: Legal Abortions, Ready or Not," *New York Magazine*, 25 May 1970, 64; Linda Greenhouse, "After July 1, an abortion should be as simple to have as a tonsillectomy, but–," *New York Times*, 28 June 1970; Jean Pakter and Frieda Nelson, "Abortion in New York City: The First Nine Months," *Family Planning Perspectives* 3(3) (July 1971): 5.

4. Linda Greenhouse, "After July 1, an abortion should be as simple to have as a tonsillectomy, but–," *New York Times*, 28 June 1970.

5. Jean Pakter and Frieda Nelson, "Abortion in New York City: The First Nine Months," *Family Planning Perspectives* 3(3) (July 1971): 5; Susan Edmiston, "A Report on the Abortion Capital of the Country, *New York Times*, 11 April 1971; Linda Greenhouse, "After July 1, an abortion should be as simple to have as a tonsillectomy, but–," *New York Times*, 28 June 1970; Johanna Schoen, *Abortion After Roe*, 25; Katherine Parkin, "'Joy Turned to Sorrow': Stillborns in Howard County, Indiana, 1890–1940," *Journal of Family History* 45(1) (2020); 64–87.

The clinics, too, collected data and reflected on their experience, with the Wickersham Women's Medical Center creating a "research division" and H. Hale Harvey and Barbara Y. E. Pyle researching and reporting "On the Healthiness of Four Thousand Abortions in a Free-Standing Abortion Service" to the public hearing in New York City in October 1970 (Wickersham, "Announcement," 5 April 1971; NY Clinics printed material, Schlesinger).

6. "Medicine: Abortion in New York," *Time*, 7 September 1970; Susan Reverby, "Abortion Reform: The Battle Lines Are Drawn," *Health/PAC Bulletin*, December 1970, 2; Jean Pakter and Frieda Nelson, "Abortion in New York City: The First Nine Months," *Family Planning Perspectives* 3(3) (July 1971): 5.

7. John Pennington, "Abortion," *Atlanta Journal and Constitution Magazine*, 30 January 1972.

8. Earl Wilson, "Last Night: 1970 Brought Bitter-Sweet Humor," *Morning Call* (Allentown, Pennsylvania), 2 January 1971; Sally Ann Morrison, Wickersham Women's Medical Center to Counselor, 3 December 1971, NARAL, NYC clinics, Schlesinger; Gordon Chase, New York City Health Services Administrator, Remarks to National Association for Repeal of Abortion Laws, Detroit, Michigan, 7 October 1972, 2–3, MSS423, Box 3, Folder 4, Wisconsin Historical Society; Jean Pakter and Frieda Nelson, "Abortion in New York City: The First Nine Months," *Family Planning Perspectives* 3(3) (July 1971): 12.

9. Gwendolyn Adams, "Processes and Facilities Available for Steering-School Females to an Abortion Clinic in Selected Area: Westchester," Hunter College MA Social Work Thesis, 1973; Lael Scott, "The Urban Strategist: Legal Abortions, Ready or Not," *New York Magazine*, 25 May 1970; Henriette Leith, "Abortion Comes Simple," *BG News* (Bowling Green, Ohio), 14 May 1971; Edward C. Burks, "New York City's Population Loss 442,000 Since 1970, Is Slackening," *New York Times*, 5 September 1977; Resident Population in Nassau County, NY (1970–1972), Federal Reserve Economic Data: https://fred.stlouisfed.org/series/NYNASS9POP; Number of Inhabitants 1970, Government Census, https://www2.census.gov/library/publications/decennial/1970/population-volume-1/1970a_v1pas2-04.pdf (all accessed 14 October 2023).

10. Art Spikol, "Across the Border and into the Mill," *Boston*, July 1970; "Concerned Collegians Against Abortion Abuse": *News Record* (University of Cincinnati), 4 December 1970; *Michigan Daily* (University of Michigan) and *Pipe Dream* (SUNY-Binghamton), 8 December 1970; *Current* (University of Missouri, St. Louis), 10 December 1970; and *Old Gold and Black* (Wake Forest University), 11 December 1970; Hollis Ingraham and Robert Longood, "Abortion in New York State Since July 1970," *Clinical Obstetrics and Gynecology*

14(1) (March 1971): 5–24. (October 197), Table 12, Induced Abortions by Recorded County and Place of Residence Recorded in Upstate New York, July, 1970–June, 1971; Gordon Chase, New York City Health Services Administrator, Remarks to National Association for Repeal of Abortion Laws, Detroit, Michigan, 7 October 1972, 8, MSS423, Box 3, Folder 4, Wisconsin Historical Society.

11. Email correspondence from Nancy Gall-Clayton and Johanna Camenisch to Katherine Parkin, 17 June 2020; Gretchen Ewing, "Area Women See Manhattan Abortion Clinic's Setup," *Morning Call* (Allentown, Pennsylvania), 15 March 1972; Joan Valles, "'Lousiest Form of Contraception,'" *Daily Item* (Port Chester, New York), 25 August 1972; Adele Gittler, "A C-T Exclusive: Inside an Abortion Clinic," *Sunday Chronicle Telegram* (Elyria, Ohio), 4 February 1973; Abortion Rights Association, *Listing of Selected New York State Abortion Clinics*, Second Printing—June 1972, Duke University; Johanna Schoen, *Abortion After Roe*, 33.

12. Hope Spencer, "Abortion Clinics: An Evaluation," *New York*, 24 July 1972.

A CCS director in Missouri described yellow ribbons used to designate women so the flight attendants could recognize them. For more on Missouri clergy referring women for abortions, see Doris Andrea Dirks and Patricia A. Relf, *To Offer Compassion: A History of the Clergy Consultation Service on Abortion* (University of Wisconsin Press, 2017), 114–15, 145; Becca Andrews, "How an Underground Network of Ministers and Rabbis Helped Women Get Abortions Before *Roe*," 3 October 2022, *New Republic*.

13. Hope Spencer, "Abortion Clinics: An Evaluation," *New York*, 24 July 1972.

14. Lynn Rosellini, "Abortions-Only Clinic is Flourishing on LI," *Newsday* (Nassau edition, New York), 19 October 1970; Nadine Cohodas, "Abortions on L.I.—A Progress Report," *New York Times*, 27 February 1972; Marilyn Duncan, "Abortion: The Right to Choose—Reasons Are Varied for Desires to Terminate Pregnancies," *Commercial Appeal* (Memphis, Tennessee), 16 April 1972; Marilyn Duncan, "Eastern Clinics Offer Multiple Services," *Commercial Appeal* (Memphis, Tennessee), 17 April 1972; email correspondence from Nancy Gall-Clayton and Johanna Camenisch to Katherine Parkin, 17 June 2020.

Frances Kissling, who was the director at Pelham Medical Center, noted that referral groups "frequently demanded that for every ten paying patients the clinic perform one free abortion" (Johanna Schoen, *Abortion After Roe*, 34).

15. Kathy O'Toole, "Mommas-To-Be Flock into Town," *Democrat and Chronicle* (Rochester), 28 June 1970; Howie Kurtz, "Erie Medical: Modern Abortion Clinic Geared to the Individual," *Spectrum* (SUNY-Buffalo), 18 October 1972; Sabra Moore, *Openings: A Memoir from the Women's Art Movement, New York City 1970–1992*, 15; Johanna Schoen, "Living Through Some Giant Change: The Establishment of Abortion Services," *American Journal of Public Health*, 17 January 2013; Don Sloan, with Paula Hartz, *A Doctor's Perspective/A Woman's Dilemma* (Donald Fine, Inc., 1992), 55; Johanna Schoen, *Abortion After Roe*: 23, 33–35; Nathanson, *Aborting America*, 135.

16. Kathy O'Toole, "Mommas-To-Be Flock into Town," *Democrat and Chronicle* (Rochester), 28 June 1970; George Langmyhr, "The Role of Planned Parenthood—World Population in Abortion," *Clinical Obstetrics & Gynecology*, 14 (1970): 1191, 1195; Howie

Kurtz, "Erie Medical: Modern Abortion Clinic Geared to the Individual" and "Continuing Dilemma," *Spectrum* (SUNY-Buffalo), 18 October 1972; Planned Parenthood Federation, *A Tradition of Choice: Planned Parenthood at 75* (1991), 70.

Midwest businessmen also arranged and charged for air travel to fly consumers and doctors to New York; see Chapter 5 and Cynthia Gorney, "After Abortion Became Legal," *Washington Post*, 27 April 1989.

17. Theodore Jacobus, "The Perspective of a Physician," in *Abortion, Birthright and the Counselor* symposium (January 1972): 10–16, ED065810, files.eric.ed.gov.

18. Suzanne Swauren, "Around the Town," *Calgary Herald*, 17 April 1970; Roberta Squire, "I'm Married, Happy, and Went Through Hell for a Legal Abortion," *Maclean's*, October 1970, 51–52; Eleanor Wright Pelrine, *Abortion in Canada* (Toronto: New Press, 1971), 118; Jean Pakter, Donna O'Hare, Frieda Nelson, Martin Svigir, "'Two Years Experience in New York City with the Liberalized Abortion Law—Progress and Problems," *American Journal of Public Health* 63(6) (June 1973): 524–25; Beth Palmer, *Choices and Compromises: The Abortion Movement In Canada, 1969–1988*, Ph.D. Diss. (York University, 2012): 143; Sarah Elvins and Katherine Parkin, "The Business of Abortion: Referral Services, Cross-Border Consumption, and Canadian Women's Access to Abortion in New York State, 1970–1972," *Enterprise & Society* (2024): 1–21.

19. "Jet-Service Abortion," *Chatelaine*, June 1970, 4; Paul Kidd, "Canadians Pouring Over the Border to New York with One Thing in Mind: Legal Abortions," *Calgary Herald* (Alberta, Canada), 31 July 1970; Gerard McNeil, "Inequities Abound Says CMA of Abortion Law," *Lethbridge Herald* (Alberta, Canada), 26 October 1970; Mollie Gillen, "Your Replies to the Abortion Quiz," *Chatelaine*, March 1971, 23, 62–63; Iain Barrie, "'New York Abortion Flight Now Boarding," *Vancouver Sun* (Canada), 12 May 1971; Sheila Thomas, "Young Montreal Couple Gets $450 Abortion in New York," *Gazette* (Montreal), 19 November 1971.

20. The number of Canadian women going to Dr. Morgentaler, getting therapeutic abortions, and traveling to England all paled in comparison to the volume of those having abortions in the United States (S. N. Wadhera and C. R. Nair, "Trends in Legal Abortions and Abortion Rates in Canada, 1970–1980," in *Perspectives on Abortion*, ed. Paul Sachdev [Scarecrow Press, Inc., 1985]: 89–94).

21. Research on Canada drawn from Sarah Elvins and Katherine Parkin, "The Business of Abortion: Referral Services, Cross-Border Consumption, and Canadian Women's Access to Abortion in New York State, 1970–1972," *Enterprise & Society* (2024): 1–21; "New York Counts 500 Abortions," *Sault Star* (Sault St. Marie, Ontario, Canada), 2 July 1970; Monopoly game, *Varsity* (University of Toronto), 25 September 1970; Gerard McNeil, "Inequities Abound Says CMA of Abortion Law," *Lethbridge Herald* (Alberta, Canada), 26 October 1970; Abortion advertising: *Ottawa Journal*, 22 August 1970; *McGill Daily Caller*, 16 February 1971; *Varsity* (University of Toronto), 29 January 1971; Ze'ev Ionis, "New York Abortions," *McGill Daily Caller*, 3 March 1971; "'Paradise for Quebec Abortions,'" *North Country Catholic* (Ogdensburg, New York), 21 March 1971; Hollis Ingraham and Robert Longood, "Abortion in New York State Since July 1970," *Clinical Obstetrics and Gynecology* 14(1) (March 1971): 5–24.

22. Lucianne Goldberg, "Journey to a New York Abortion," *Chicago Today*, 28 March 1972; Johanna Schoen, *Abortion After Roe*, 34; Cynthia Gorney, "After Abortion Became Legal," *Washington Post*, 27 April 1989.

23. "Women's Referral Service Now Offers Abortions Legalized by New York's Recent Abortion Law," *Miami Gazette* (Waynesburg, Ohio), 6 January 1971; Lucianne Goldberg, "Journey to a New York Abortion," *Chicago Today*, 28 March 1972; Johanna Schoen, *Abortion After Roe*, 34; Doris Andrea Dirks and Patricia A. Relf, *To Offer Compassion: A History of the Clergy Consultation Service on Abortion* (University of Wisconsin Press, 2017), 70.

24. Ellen Glascock, phone interview by author, 16 June 2020; Brenda Woods, "It's the Decision That Can Change a Woman's Life: Abortion," *Daily News (New York)*, 19 November 1971.

25. Don Sloan, with Paula Hartz, *A Doctor's Perspective/A Woman's Dilemma* (Donald Fine, Inc., 1992), 52–54. Even in Westchester, a small clinic would see "one hundred women on a Saturday" (Frances Kissling interviewed by Rebecca Sharpless, 13–14 September 2002, Sophia Smith Collection, Smith College archive).

26. Frances Kissling interviewed by Rebecca Sharpless, 13–14 September 2002, Sophia Smith Collection, Smith College archive.

27. "Women's Referral Service Now Offers Abortions Legalized by New York's Recent Abortion Law," *Miami Gazette* (Waynesburg, Ohio), 6 January 1971; Women's Referral Services ad, *Maine Campus* (University of Maine), 18 February 1971; Libby Rubin, Eastern Women's Center Press Release: "New Abortion Clinic Opens on New York's East Side," NARAL: NY Clinics printed material, Schlesinger; Lucianne Goldberg, "Journey to a New York Abortion," *Chicago Today*, 28 March 1972; Howard Moody and Arlene Carmen, *Abortion Counseling and Social Change from Illegal Act to Medical Practice: The Story of the Clergy Consultation Service on Abortion* (Judson Press, 1973), 73; Cynthia Gorney, "After Abortion Became Legal," *Washington Post*, 27 April 1989; Doris Andrea Dirks and Patricia A. Relf, *To Offer Compassion: A History of the Clergy Consultation Service on Abortion* (University of Wisconsin Press, 2017), 134.

28. "Letter from Women's Referral Service to Planned Parenthood," n.d. and Letter from Dorn Leslie White, Pregnancy Counseling Service to Dear Doctor," 3 February 1971, NARAL-NY Clinics, Schlesinger; Johanna Schoen, *Abortion After Roe*, 34.

29. Frances Kissling interviewed by Rebecca Sharpless, 13–14 September 2002, Sophia Smith Collection, Smith College archive; Sabra Moore, "Staff Proposal," 1971, Sabra Moore NYC Women's Art Movement Collection, Barnard Archives & Special Collections.

30. Lael Scott, "The Urban Strategist: Legal Abortions, Ready or Not," *New York Magazine*, 25 May 1970, 71; Tom Tiede, "N.Y. Hospital Girds for Abortion Boom," *Orlando Sentinel*, 28 July 1970; One study counted thirty-seven proprietary hospitals providing abortions (Jean Pakter and Frieda Nelson, "Abortion in New York City: The First Nine Months," *Family Planning Perspectives* 3(3) (July 1971): 5, 7); Ellen Glascock, phone and email by author, 16 and 25 June 2020.

City health officials reported in April 1971 that an "increasing number of women who can afford to pay are beginning to include the municipal hospitals on their 'shopping lists,' because word of the service available there has begun to get around" (John Sibley, *New*

York Times, 6 April 1971). Some groups offered pregnant women a local address, so they could access abortions as a local. Sheila Doran noted that the Women's Abortion Project did this for "any woman who cannot get within her own hospital district or is afraid that someone might recognize her at the hospital" (Reverby interview; Sheila Doran in *Abortion: What Now?*, Bob Kuttner and Nanette Rainone (producers), Recorded on: 30 June 1970, Broadcast on: WBAI, 1 July 1970).

31. "Hospital's Abortion Offer is Decried, Defended," *American Medical News* 13 (1970): 12; "Ads Rapped in Journal of Medicine," *Deseret News* (Salt Lake City), 12 October 1970; "Abortion Solicitation Blasted," *Courier-Post* (Camden, New Jersey), 13 October 1970; "Crackdown on Abortion Hucksters," *Afro-American* (Baltimore), 24 October 1970.

32. Janet Chusmir, "It's 'Abortion for Sale' from New York Hospitals," *Miami Herald*, 20 August 1970.

33. Steffi Cooper, "N.Y. Abortion Clinic Solicits Orlando Area," *Orlando Sentinel*, 9 August 1970; Howard Eisenberg, "The Mad Scramble for Abortion Money," *Medical Economist* (4 January 1971): 219.

34. Howard Eisenberg, "The Mad Scramble for Abortion Money," *Medical Economist* (4 January 1971): 220; Stuart Auerbach, "Quickie Abortions Bringing Thousands to New York," *Morning News* (Wilmington, Delaware), 15 January 1971.

35. Steffi Cooper, "N.Y. Abortion Clinic Solicits Orlando Area," *Orlando Sentinel*, 9 August 1970; Janet Chusmir, "It's 'Abortion for Sale' from New York Hospitals," *Miami Herald*, 20 August 1970.

36. Janet Chusmir, "It's 'Abortion For Sale' from New York Hospitals," *Miami Herald*, 20 August 1970.

37. Ellen Glascock, phone and email interview by author, 16 and 25 June 2020; Howard Eisenberg, "The Mad Scramble for Abortion Money," *Medical Economist* (4 January 1971): 219.

38. Ellen Glascock, Class of 1967 notes, *Connecticut College Alumnae News*, Winter 1970, 47; Ellen L. Glascock, "Abortion," *Connecticut College Alumnae News*, Winter 1972, 6–9.

39. Lael Scott, "The Urban Strategist: Legal Abortions, Ready or Not," *New York Magazine*, 25 May 1970, 71; Peter Rims, "Abortions Begun in State Under Liberal New Law," *New York Times*, 2 July 1970; Tom Tiede, "N.Y. Hospital Girds for Abortion Boom," *Orlando Sentinel*, 28 July 1970; Susan Edmiston, "A Report on the Abortion Capital of the Country," *New York Times*, 11 April 1971.

40. Marta Robinet, "Abortion Profiteers: Medical 'Brokers' Who Offer Women a Referral Service," *Evening Bulletin* (Philadelphia), 10 November 1970; John Sibley, "A Hospital Owner Tells Inquiry He Has Abortion-Steering Unit," *New York Times*, 20 February 1971; Women's Pavilion ads: *Maine Campus*, University of Maine: 2 February 1971; 18 March 1971; 6 May 1971; *Statesman* (SUNY Stony Brook), 5 February 1971. The Women's Pavilion ad in the 8 February 1971 issue of *Virginia Weekly* was the basis for Bigelow v. Commonwealth of Virginia, 1972 (https://casetext.com/case/bigelow-v-commonwealth-1); Johanna Schoen, *Abortion After Roe*, 34; Carole King, *Tapestry* (1971, A&M).

41. Sheila Doran in *Abortion: What Now?*, Bob Kuttner and Nanette Rainone (producers), Recorded on: 30 June 1970, Broadcast on: WBAI, 1 July 1970; Pakter and Nelson,

"Abortion in New York City: The First Nine Months," *Family Planning Perspectives* 3(3) (July 1971): 6.

42. NARAL—Printed Materials, "New York-Clinics," PR-3, Box 4, Schlesinger Library.

43. Susan Reverby, "Abortion Reform: The Battle Lines Are Drawn," *Health/PAC Bulletin*, December 1970, 6; NARAL—Printed Materials, "New York-Clinics," PR-3, Box 4, Schlesinger Library; Susan Edmiston, "A Report on the Abortion Capital of the Country," *New York Times*, 11 April 1971; *To Find a Man* (Rastar Films, 1972); "After 12 Weeks," *Special 8-Page Handbook: A Critical Guide to New York Abortion Facilities* in *New York*, 24 July 1972, 36. According to Johanna Schoen, "saline abortion had become the second trimester method of choice" by 1970 (*Abortion After Roe*, 30–31).

44. NARAL—Printed Materials, "New York-Clinics," PR-3, Box 4, Schlesinger Library; Linda Greenhouse, "After July 1, an abortion should be as simple to have as a tonsillectomy, but–," *New York Times*, 28 June 1970; Sheila Doran in *Abortion: What Now?*, Bob Kuttner and Nanette Rainone (producers), Recorded on: 30 June 1970, Broadcast on: WBAI, 1 July 1970; Susan Edmiston, "A Report on the Abortion Capital of the Country," *New York Times*, 11 April 1971; Gordon Chase, New York City Health Services Administrator, Remarks to National Association for Repeal of Abortion Laws, Detroit Michigan, 7 October 1972, 3–4, MSS423, Box 3, Folder 4, Wisconsin Historical Society.

45. J. Joshua Kopelman and Gordon W. Douglas, "Abortions by Resident Physicians in a Municipal Hospital Center," *American Journal of Obstetrics and Gynecology* 11(5) (1 November 1971), 666, 670.

46. Susan Edmiston, "A Report on the Abortion Capital of the Country," *New York Times*, 11 April 1971.

47. Lael Scott, "The Urban Strategist: Legal Abortions, Ready or Not," *New York*, 25 May 1970, 68; "Medicine: Abortion in New York," *Time*, 7 September 1970; Hale Harvey and Barbara Y. E. Pyle, "On the Healthiness of Four Thousand Abortions in a Free-Standing Abortion Service," report to the public hearing in New York City in October 1970 (Schlesinger), 1; Susan Reverby, "Abortion Reform: The Battle Lines Are Drawn," *Health/PAC Bulletin*, December 1970, 6; Howard Eisenberg, "The Mad Scramble for Abortion Money," *Medical Economist* (4 January 1971); Abortion Part 2: hearings before the Subcommittee on Constitutional Amendments of the Committee on the Judiciary, United States Senate, Ninety-third Congress, second session (Government Printing Office 1974); Susan Edmiston, "A Report on the Abortion Capital of the Country," *New York Times*, 11 April 1971; Carol Joffe, *Doctors of Conscience*.

48. Lael Scott, "The Urban Strategist: Legal Abortions, Ready or Not," *New York*, 25 May 1970, 68; Alfred Moran in *Abortion: What Now?*, Bob Kuttner and Nanette Rainone (producers), Recorded on: 30 June 1970, Broadcast on: WBAI, 1 July 1970; "Medicine: Abortion in New York," *Time*, 7 September 1970; Hale Harvey and Barbara Y. E. Pyle, "On the Healthiness of Four Thousand Abortions in a Free-Standing Abortion Service," report to the public hearing in New York City in October 1970 (Schlesinger), 1; Carol Joffe, *Doctors of Conscience*.

49. After Carmen Rodriguez's death in the newly formed abortion clinic, a Lincoln doctor reported that her chart revealed she had a health condition and should not have had the procedure. Wanting to honor her life, the protestors, locked in a long-standing effort to

improve the hospital (condemned as a "butcher house"), added to their demands that the hospital not only provide financial compensation for wrongful death to her family, especially as she left behind two children, but also name the new abortion clinic for her (Barbara Ehrenreich, "Bronx Wants Community Control," *Health/PAC Bulletin*, September 1970, 12–14).

Nationally, records generally reflect a minuscule number of Puerto Ricans acquiring abortions, although the Centers for Disease Control and Prevention reporting in this period collapsed Puerto Ricans, Mexicans, and Cubans into the "White" category in 1971, so it is not easy to quantify their abortions ("Annual Summary, 1971," *Abortion Surveillance Report,* 1971), 13. Harriet Presser speculates that the small number of Puerto Ricans seeking abortions stemmed from the use of voluntary sterilization as a preferred birth control method, including women denied sterilization in New York City traveling to Puerto Rico to secure it. It was so well-known a procedure that it was known as *la operacion*, and an estimated one-third of Puerto Rican women had been sterilized. "If Puerto Ricans seek abortions in a somewhat smaller proportion than might be expected [vis-à-vis white and Black women], this may be attributable to the greater incidence of contraceptive sterilization among this population (e.g., 21 percent among NYC mothers on welfare)." Of those traveling to New York City in the first nine months of legalization, "Puerto Ricans comprised less than one percent of non residents seeking abortions in NYC" ("The Role of Sterilization in Controlling Puerto Rican Fertility," *Population Studies* 23(3) (Nov. 1969): 343–61). In 1970, Frances Beal was more critical, suspecting that "people are pressured" into sterilization, especially as a tool by the government "as a means of population control" for women on welfare (Frances Beal in *Abortion: What Now?*, Bob Kuttner and Nanette Rainone (producers), Recorded on: 30 June 1970, Broadcast on: WBAI, 1 July 1970); Martin Gansberg, "Abortion Death Reported by the City," *New York Times*, 21 July 1970; Harriet Presser, "Puerto Rico: Recent Trends in Fertility and Sterilization," *International Family Planning Perspectives* 6(1) (March 1980): 20–25; Iris Lopez, *Matters of Choice: Puerto Rican Women's Struggle for Reproductive Freedom* (Rutgers University Press, 2008).

50. "Medicine: Abortion in New York," *Time*, 7 September 1970; Susan Reverby, "Abortion Reform: The Battle Lines Are Drawn," *Health/PAC Bulletin*, December 1970, 3; NARAL—Printed Materials, "New York-Clinics," PR-3, Box 4, Schlesinger Library.

In the first two months, the Clearinghouse only scheduled 2,573 appointments (Gordon Chase, Health Services Administration, New York, NY, 7 February 1971, Press Release, 4, MSS423, Box 3, Folder 4, Wisconsin Historical Society).

51. Sheila Doran in *Abortion: What Now?*, Bob Kuttner and Nanette Rainone (producers), Recorded on: 30 June 1970, Broadcast on: WBAI, 1 July 1970; Susan Reverby, "Abortion Reform: The Battle Lines Are Drawn," *Health/PAC Bulletin*, December 1970, 3–5.

52. "Empire Roundup: Caught in the Squeeze" and "Bronx," *Health/PAC Bulletin*, October 1970, 1–2; "Aborted Abortions," *Health/PAC Bulletin*, November 1970, 14; Susan Reverby, "Abortion Reform: The Battle Lines Are Drawn," *Health/PAC Bulletin*, December 1970, 3.

53. Robert E. Hall, "Abortion: Physician and Hospital Attitudes," *American Journal of Public Health* 61(3) (March 1971): 518–19; Bellevue, NARAL—Printed Materials, "New York-Clinics," PR-3, Box 4, Schlesinger Library.

54. John Sibley, "New York Hospital Officials Pledge 'Safe' Abortions," *Edmonton Journal* (Alberta, Canada), 4 May 1970; Lael Scott, "The Urban Strategist: Legal Abortions, Ready or Not," *New York*, 25 May 1970; Jane D. Brown, "Changing Abortion Laws: Reform or Repeal," *Kentucky Kernel*, 21 January 1971; Sally Ann Morrison, Wickersham Women's Medical Center to Counselor, 3 December 1971, NARAL, NYC clinics, Schlesinger; Richard Hausknecht, "Free Standing Abortion Clinic: A New Phenomenon," *Bulletin of the New York Academy of Medicine* 49(11) (November 1973): 985–91; Joshua Wolff, *Ministers of a Higher Law: The Story of the Clergy Consultation Service on Abortion* (Amherst College thesis, 1998), 169–70; Johanna Schoen, *Abortion After Roe*, 38. Doris Andrea Dirks and Patricia A. Relf also note Pyle's significance in founding Women's Services and described the clinic's "visionary innovation in medical care" (*To Offer Compassion: A History of the Clergy Consultation Service on Abortion* [University of Wisconsin Press, 2017], 140, 143). The Judson Church Board minutes reflected on 24 March 1970 that "The Board considered a proposal from Howard Moody that the second floor of (Judson) House be renovated for use as an 'abortorium'" (Howard Moody and Arlene Carmen, *Abortion Counseling and Social Change from Illegal Act to Medical Practice: The Story of the Clergy Consultation Service on Abortion* [Judson Press, 1973], 71). Guttmacher had similarly reflected on the establishment of an "abortorium ward" at Johns Hopkins University Hospital (Alan F. Guttmacher and Harriet F. Pilpel, "Abortion and the Unwanted Child," *Family Planning Perspective* 2(2) (March 1970): 18–19).

55. Susan Edmiston, "A Report on the Abortion Capital of the Country," *New York Times*, 11 April 1971; Barbara Pyle and Erica Meola, "The Meola/Pyle Backstreets Interview," https://backstreets.com/pyle.html (accessed 1 October 2022); Howard Moody and Arlene Carmen, *Abortion Counseling and Social Change from Illegal Act to Medical Practice: The Story of the Clergy Consultation Service on Abortion* (Judson Press, 1973), 72, 81.

56. Merle Hoffman papers, Box CH-1 c.1, Duke University; Richard Hausknecht, "Free Standing Abortion Clinic: A New Phenomenon," *Bulletin of the New York Academy of Medicine* 49(11) (November 1973): 989–91; Alan Guttmacher, Visit—Flushing Women's Medical Center, 10 November 1972, NARAL—Printed Materials, "New York-Clinics," PR-3, Box 4, Schlesinger Library.

"Population stabilization" motivated Barbara Pyle; she developed *Captain Planet and the Planeteers* between 1990–1992, including S1.E21 Population Bomb (1991), and worked with the Population Media Center.

57. Hale Harvey and Barbara Y. E. Pyle, "On the Healthiness of Four Thousand Abortions in a Free-Standing Abortion Service," report to the public hearing in New York City in October 1970 (Schlesinger), 1; "Medicine: Abortion in New York," *Time*, 7 September 1970; Johanna Schoen, *Abortion After Roe*, 23–25; Doris Andrea Dirks and Patricia A. Relf, *To Offer Compassion: A History of the Clergy Consultation Service on Abortion* (University of Wisconsin Press, 2017), 132.

58. John Sibley, "New York Hospital Officials Pledge 'Safe' Abortions," *Edmonton Journal* (Alberta, Canada), 4 May 1970; Brenda Woods, "It's the Decision That Can Change a Woman's Life: Abortion," *Daily News*, 19 November 1971; Frances Addelson, "Therapeutic Abortion: A Social Work View," *American Journal of Obstetrics and Gynecology* 11 (7) (1 Dec 1971): 989; Joseph Rovinsky, "Abortion Recidivism: A Problem in

Preventive Medicine," *Obstetrics & Gynecology* 39(5) (May 1972): 649–59; Richard Hausknecht, "Free Standing Abortion Clinic: A New Phenomenon," *Bulletin of the New York Academy of Medicine* 49(11) (November 1973): 985–91; Sally Ann Morrison, Wickersham Women's Medical Center to Counselor, 3 December 1971, NARAL, NYC clinics, PR-3, Box 4, Schlesinger Library.

59. Alfred Moran in *Abortion: What Now?*, Bob Kuttner and Nanette Rainone (producers), Recorded on: 30 June 1970, Broadcast on: WBAI, 1 July 1970.

60. Howard Moody and Arlene Carmen, *Abortion Counseling and Social Change from Illegal Act to Medical Practice: The Story of the Clergy Consultation Service on Abortion* (Judson Press, 1973), 77–79.

61. John Sibley (NYT), "New York Hospital Officials Pledge 'Safe' Abortions," *Edmonton Journal* (Alberta, Canada), 1 May 1970; Hale Harvey and Barbara Y. F. Pyle, "On the Healthiness of Four Thousand Abortions in a Free-Standing Abortion Service," report to the public hearing in New York City in October 1970 (Schlesinger); Susan Edmiston, "A Report on the Abortion Capital of the Country," *New York Times*, 11 April 1971; Brenda Woods, "It's the Decision That Can Change a Woman's Life: Abortion," *Daily News*, 19 November 1971; Frances Addelson, "Therapeutic Abortion: A Social Work View," *American Journal of Obstetrics and Gynecology* 11 (7) (1 Dec 1971): 989; Sally Ann Morrison, Wickersham Women's Medical Center to Counselor, 3 December 1971, NARAL, NYC clinics, Schlesinger; Joseph Rovinsky, "Abortion Recidivism: A Problem in Preventive Medicine," *Obstetrics & Gynecology* 39(5) (May 1972): 649–59; Richard Hausknecht, "Free Standing Abortion Clinic: A New Phenomenon," *Bulletin of the New York Academy of Medicine* 49(11) (November 1973): 985–91; Bridgette Dunlap, "How Clergy Set the Standard for Abortion Care," *Atlantic*, 29 May 2016; Doris Andrea Dirks and Patricia A. Relf, *To Offer Compassion: A History of the Clergy Consultation Service on Abortion* (University of Wisconsin Press, 2017), 71.

62. Doris Andrea Dirks and Patricia A. Relf, *To Offer Compassion: A History of the Clergy Consultation Service on Abortion* (University of Wisconsin Press, 2017), 137–38, 140–41.

63. Doris Andrea Dirks and Patricia A. Relf, *To Offer Compassion: A History of the Clergy Consultation Service on Abortion* (University of Wisconsin Press, 2017), 141; Bernard Nathanson with Richard Ostling, *Aborting America*, 1979, 134, 141; Joshua Wolff, *Ministers of a Higher Law: The Story of the Clergy Consultation Service on Abortion* (Amherst College thesis, 1998), 192; Howard Moody and Arlene Carmen, *Abortion Counseling and Social Change from Illegal Act to Medical Practice: The Story of the Clergy Consultation Service on Abortion* (Judson Press, 1973), 77.

64. Howard Moody and Arlene Carmen, *Abortion Counseling and Social Change from Illegal Act to Medical Practice: The Story of the Clergy Consultation Service on Abortion* (Judson Press, 1973), 79–80; Joshua Wolff, *Ministers of a Higher Law: The Story of the Clergy Consultation Service on Abortion* (Amherst College thesis, 1998), 146; Doris Andrea Dirks and Patricia A. Relf, *To Offer Compassion: A History of the Clergy Consultation Service on Abortion* (University of Wisconsin Press, 2017), 64, 136; Sabra Moore, "Summary of Women Counselors," SC16B1F3–1970, Barnard Archives & Special Collections.

65. Howard Moody and Arlene Carmen, *Abortion Counseling and Social Change from Illegal Act to Medical Practice: The Story of the Clergy Consultation Service on Abortion* (Judson Press, 1973), 79–80; Joshua Wolff, *Ministers of a Higher Law: The Story of the Clergy Consultation Service on Abortion* (thesis, Amherst College, 1998), 146; Doris Andrea Dirks and Patricia A. Relf, *To Offer Compassion: A History of the Clergy Consultation Service on Abortion* (University of Wisconsin Press, 2017), 64, 136.

66. Joshua Wolff, *Ministers of a Higher Law: The Story of the Clergy Consultation Service on Abortion* (Amherst College thesis, 1998), 146.

67. Joshua Wolff, *Ministers of a Higher Law: The Story of the Clergy Consultation Service on Abortion* (Amherst College thesis, 1998), Sabra Moore, "Staff Proposal" and "Summary of Women Counselors," SC16B1F3–1970, Barnard Archives & Special Collections; Sabra Moore, *Openings* (New York: New Village Press, 2016), 15; Howard Moody and Arlene Carmen, *Abortion Counseling and Social Change from Illegal Act to Medical Practice: The Story of the Clergy Consultation Service on Abortion* (Judson Press, 1973), 79–81; Ronald Clark, "At Least 400 in Area Have Gone to N.Y. for Abortions," *Akron-Beacon Journal*, 26 November 1970; "The Week in Review: Abortion Counseling," *Sunday Courier and Press* (Evansville, Indiana), 13 June 1971; Cynthia Gorney, "After Abortion Became Legal," *Washington Post*, 27 April 1989.

68. Doris Andrea Dirks and Patricia A. Relf, *To Offer Compassion: A History of the Clergy Consultation Service on Abortion* (University of Wisconsin Press, 2017), 71, 144.

69. Abner I. Weisman, "To the Editor: Abortion Is Not the Answer," *JAMA* 217(11) (13 September 1971): 1553–54; Gordon Chase, New York City Health Services Administrator, Remarks to National Association for Repeal of Abortion Laws, Detroit Michigan, 7 October 1972, 2–3, MSS423, Box 3, Folder 4, Wisconsin Historical Society; Don Sloan, with Paula Hartz, *A Doctor's Perspective/A Woman's Dilemma* (Donald Fine, Inc., 1992), 55.

70. Susan Edmiston, "A Report on the Abortion Capital of the Country," *New York Times*, 11 April 1971; Sabra Moore, "Summary of Women Counselors," SC16B1F3–1970, Barnard Archives & Special Collections; Johanna Schoen, *Abortion After Roe*, 33.

71. Sabra Moore, *Openings*, 14.

72. Felicia Norortt, *The Transition from Female Midwives to Male Physicians in America from the Seventeenth Century Through the Twentieth Century*, Honors Thesis, Monmouth University, 2010, 1, 13; Amanda Banks, *Birth Chairs, Midwives, and Medicine* (University Press of Mississippi, 1999), 50; Judith Walzer Leavitt, "Under the Shadow of Maternity: American Women's Responses to Death and Debility Fears in Nineteenth-Century Childbirth," *Feminist Studies* 12(1) (Spring 1986), 145–46; Cornelia Hughes Dayton, "Taking the Trade: Abortion and Gender Relations in an Eighteenth-Century New England Village," *William & Mary Quarterly* 48(1) (January 1991): 19–49; Sabra Moore, *Openings: A Memoir from the Women's Art Movement, New York City 1970–1992* (New Village Press, 2016), 15; Don Sloan, with Paula Hartz, *A Doctor's Perspective/A Woman's Dilemma* (Donald Fine, Inc., 1992), 68.

73. Susan Edmiston, "A Report on the Abortion Capital of the Country," *New York Times*, 11 April 1971; Merle Hoffman, *Intimate Wars: The Life and Times of the Woman*

Who Brought Abortion from the Back Alley to the Boardroom (Feminist Press, 2012), 66–68; Doris Andrea Dirks and Patricia A. Relf, *To Offer Compassion: A History of the Clergy Consultation Service on Abortion* (University of Wisconsin Press, 2017), 137; Moore, *Openings*, 16–18; "Sabra Moore on Her Experience as an Abortion Counselor before Roe v. Wade," 5 April 2017, https://barnard.edu/news/sabra-moore-her-experience-abortion-counselor-roe-v-wade (accessed 1 October 2022).

74. Susan Edmiston, "A Report on the Abortion Capital of the Country," *New York Times*, 11 April 1971; Lucianne Goldberg, "Journey to a New York Abortion," *Chicago Today*, 28 March 1972; Merle Hoffman, *Intimate Wars: The Life and Times of the Woman Who Brought Abortion from the Back Alley to the Boardroom* (Feminist Press, 2012), 66–68; Moore, *Openings*; Sabra Moore, "Summary of Women Counselors," SC16B1F3–1970, Barnard Archives & Special Collections; "Sabra Moore on Her Experience as an Abortion Counselor before Roe v. Wade," 5 April 2017, https://barnard.edu/news/sabra-moore-her-experience-abortion-counselor-roe-v-wade (accessed 1 October 2022).

When they unionized, abortion clinics joined the 1199 SEIU, The National Health Care Workers' Union.

So, too, did the counselors endure sexual harassment, especially those who "worked in traditional settings" (Johanna Schoen, "Living Through Some Giant Change: The Establishment of Abortion Services," *American Journal of Public Health*, 17 January 2013). See also Julie Berebitsky, *Sex and the Office: A History of Gender, Power, and Desire* (Yale University Press, 2012).

Howard Moody and Arlene Carmen continued their attacks, claiming that they hired an employee to oversee care for patients, "not the labor problems of workers" or the "protection of medical and administrative personnel who goof off" (*Abortion Counseling and Social Change from Illegal Act to Medical Practice: The Story of the Clergy Consultation Service on Abortion* [Judson Press, 1973], 81.)

75. Susan Reverby, "Abortion Reform: The Battle Lines Are Drawn," *Health//PAC Bulletin*, December 1970, 6; Robert E. Hall, "Abortion: Physician and Hospital Attitudes," *American Journal of Public Health* 61(3) (March 1971): 517–18.

76. Barbara Rose, "The New York Abortion," *New York Magazine*, 29 May 1972; Don Sloan, with Paula Hartz, *A Doctor's Perspective/A Woman's Dilemma* (Donald Fine, Inc., 1992); Johanna Schoen, *Abortion After Roe*, 35–36.

77. Don Sloan, with Paula Hartz, *A Doctor's Perspective/A Woman's Dilemma* (Donald Fine, Inc., 1992); Johanna Schoen, *Abortion After Roe*, 36.

78. Robert E. Hall, "Abortion: Physician and Hospital Attitudes," *American Journal of Public Health* 61(3) (March 1971): 517–19; Sabra Moore, "Summary of Women Counselors," SC16B1F3–1970, Barnard Archives & Special Collections; Sabra Moore, *Openings: A Memoir from the Women's Art Movement, New York City 1970–1992* (New Village Press, 2016), 17; Johanna Schoen, "Living Through Some Giant Change: The Establishment of Abortion Services," *American Journal of Public Health*, 17 January 2013.

79. Susan Edmiston, "A Report on the Abortion Capital of the Country," *New York Times*, 11 April 1971; Merle Hoffman, *Intimate Wars: The Life and Times of the Woman Who Brought Abortion from the Back Alley to the Boardroom* (Feminist Press, 2012), 74–77;

Doris Andrea Dirks and Patricia A. Relf, *To Offer Compassion: A History of the Clergy Consultation Service on Abortion* (University of Wisconsin Press, 2017), 147–48.

80. Susan Edmiston, "A Report on the Abortion Capital of the Country," *New York Times*, 11 April 1971; Merle Hoffman, *Intimate Wars: The Life and Times of the Woman Who Brought Abortion from the Back Alley to the Boardroom* (Feminist Press, 2012), 74–77; Moore, *Openings*, 17.

81. Philip H. Addison, "The Impact of the Abortion Act 1967 in Great Britain," delivered to the Canadian Medical Association on June 11, 1969, *Medico-Legal Journal* 38(1) (1970): 17; Helen Hennessy, "Expert Cites Abortion Clinic Need," *Lansing State Journal*, 2 January 1971; Norman K. Brown et al., "How Do Nurses Feel About Euthanasia and Abortion?," *American Journal of Nursing* 71(7) (July 1971): 1413–16; Carol Joffe, *Doctors of Conscience: The Struggle to Provide Abortion Before and After Roe v. Wade* (Beacon Press, 1995), 123; Susan Edmiston, "A Report on the Abortion Capital of the Country, *New York Times*, 11 April 1971; Johanna Schoen, *Abortion After Roe* (University of North Carolina Press, 2015), 54; Abortion Part 2: Hearings Before the Subcommittee on Constitutional Amendments of the Committee on the Judiciary, United States Senate, Ninety-third Congress, second session (US Government Printing Office, 1974); Karissa Haugeberg, "Nursing and Hospital Abortions in the United States, 1967–1973," *Journal of the History of Medicine and Allied Sciences* 73(4) (2018): 430.

82. Enid Nemy, "Even Now, Helping With Abortions Is Traumatic Shock for Some Nurses," *New York Times*, 1 February 1972; Karissa Haugeberg, "Nursing and Hospital Abortions in the United States, 1967–1973," *Journal of the History of Medicine and Allied Sciences* 73(4) (2018): 412–36.

83. Karissa Haugeberg, "Nursing and Hospital Abortions in the United States, 1967–1973," *Journal of the History of Medicine and Allied Sciences* 73(4) (2018): 412–36.

84. Enid Nemy, "Even Now, Helping With Abortions Is Traumatic Shock for Some Nurses," *New York Times*, 1 February 1972.

85. Doris Andrea Dirks and Patricia A. Relf, *To Offer Compassion: A History of the Clergy Consultation Service on Abortion* (University of Wisconsin Press, 2017), 71.

86. Jean Pakter and Frieda Nelson, "Abortion in New York City: The First Nine Months," *Family Planning Perspectives* 3(3) (July 1971): 12.

87. Jean Pakter and Frieda Nelson, "Abortion in New York City: The First Nine Months," *Family Planning Perspectives* 3(3) (July 1971): 12.

Conclusion

1. Susan Brownmiller, *In Our Time: Memoir of a Revolution* (Random House, 2000), 68–70; Susan Brownmiller, "When an Abortionist Dies," *Village Voice*, 30 January 1969; Jason Nark, "Before Abortion was Legal, Women Flocked to Rural Pa. to See the 'Angel of Ashland,'" *Philadelphia Inquirer*, 5 May 2022.

2. "King of the Abortionists," *Newsweek*, 17 February 1969; "Accepted as Abortionist," *LA Times*, 17 March 1969.

Toward the end of his life, when each abortion likely cost \$100 to \$200, Spencer made the decision to rely on Harry Mace to bring women seeking abortions. Seemingly unbeknownst to him, Mace was pocketing hundreds of dollars from each woman (Vincent Genovese, *Angel of Ashland: Practicing Compassion and Tempting Fate* (Prometheus Books, 2010), 115–16.

3. "Discusses Abortion in the City," *Manhattan Mercury*, 25 August 1972; Oral History Number: 164–001, Diane Sands interview of Anne Dunbar, 16 June 1981, Illegal Abortion in Montana Oral History Project, Archives and Special Collections, University of Montana; Diane Sands, "Using Oral History to Chart the Course of Illegal Abortions in Montana," *Frontiers: A Journal of Women Studies* 7(1) (1983): 32–37; Theresa Johnson, "Dr. Sadie," *Missoulian*, 11 June 1989; Barbara LaBoe, "Roadmap to Her Roots," *Montana Standard*, 11 May 2003; "'She Really Believed in Families': The Medical Career of Sadie Lindeberg," montanawomenshistory.org, 25 September 2014.

4. David Cohen and Krysten Connon, *Living in the Crosshairs: The Untold Stories of Anti-Abortion Terrorism* (Oxford University Press, 2015); "Recent Cases on Violence Against Reproductive Health Care Providers," Civil Rights Division of the Department of Justice, https://www.justice.gov/crt/recent-cases-violence-against-reproductive-health-care-providers (accessed 15 October 2023).

5. Susan Brownmiller, "When an Abortionist Dies," *Village Voice*, 30 January 1969; Nanette Davis, *The Abortion Market: Transactions in a Risk Commodity*, Michigan State University, Ph.D. Diss., 1973, ii.

6. Sabrina Talukder, "Project 2025's Distortion of a Reconstruction-Era Law Could Enact a National Abortion Ban," 13 June 2024, https://www.americanprogress.org/article/project-2025s-distortion-of-a-reconstruction-era-law-could-enact-a-national-abortion-ban/; Pew Research Center, "Public Opinion on Abortion," 13 May 2024, https://www.pewresearch.org/religion/fact-sheet/public-opinion-on-abortion/ (both accessed 8 December 2024).

INDEX

Page numbers in italics refer to figures.

Index

Index

ACKNOWLEDGMENTS

THIS BOOK BEGAN at the start of the Covid-19 pandemic. I was nervous to take on an abortion project in the political climate, but the evidence I found compelled the book forward. I had never interviewed people for my historical work, but quickly discovered in my quest that many of those I was reading about in the archives would share their story with me. I am grateful to everyone who took time to talk with me by phone, Zoom, and email, and to those who mailed me materials from their files.

More than that, I am grateful for the bravery and conviction of those who tried to secure reproductive justice for all more than fifty years ago. It has been devastating to watch as the protections of *Roe* got chipped away to the extent that even before *Dobbs* most American women had lost access to safe, legal abortions they could afford in close proximity. Even the promise of mifepristone, which has become the most common abortion method, remains contested, elusive, and expensive. From the origins of the movement in the 1960s to the present day, individuals, groups, and organizations have heroically come forward, and this work is indebted to them.

I am appreciative, too, of all the librarians, archivists, and student workers across the country who so generously assisted me with this project. Those of you who went into work only one day a week during the lockdown and used your time to help me find materials. Those who digitized materials because I could not travel, painstakingly going through college newspapers and other archival files. And even those who did not find materials still shared their enthusiasm and support for the project. All of this sustained me, not only with the precious evidence I needed, but with the shared endeavor of unearthing and valuing this history, especially as we were working in isolation. Thank you. To my own library at Monmouth University, a special thanks to Sherri Xie in Interlibrary Loan who helped me hunt up primary and secondary sources across the country.

When I brought this project to Bob Lockhart, he offered not just enthusiasm for the vision, but much-needed support of me. Having worked together over more than twenty years and now with three books, I am grateful for your incredible ability to meet me where I am and push me to do even more. You helped me to move it forward with good humor and patience as I worked through many unexpected elements. Thank you, and thank you to Gigi Lamm, Noreen O'Connor-Abel, Jon Dertien, and to the whole Penn Press team for another incredible production. Thanks also to Lisa DeBoer, who did a great job with the index.

To the historians and other scholars whom I relied on, I am indebted to your excellent work. Your scholarship not only informed my own, it inspired it. By asking important questions and helping us understand this often shrouded past, you helped guide my work.

My cherished colleagues at Monmouth University held me close and cheered me on. I am so lucky to work with such kind, generous colleagues in the Department of History and Anthropology, and across campus. Thanks especially to Julius Adekunle, Mel Bryzcki, Ken Campbell, Manuel Chávez, Nica Davidov, Chris DeRosa, Corey Dzenko, Hillary DelPrete, Maureen Dorment, Bill Gorman, Brian and Susan Greenberg, Adam Heinrich, Andi Hope, Susan Marshall, Fred McKitrick, Brooke Nappi, Matt O'Brien, Tom Pearson, Mike Phillips-Anderson, Maryanne Rhett, Karen Schmelzkopf and Dan Baker, Deanna Shoemaker, Rich Veit, Kurt Wagner, Hettie Williams, and Melissa Ziobro. I am also indebted to my students, some of whom read this work in draft form and Emily Homer, Joshua Chanley, Andy Dione, Paige Harrington, Killian Mann, Lincoln Pereira, and Derek Rose who helped with research. Thanks especially to Shannon Whartnaby, who did both. I am grateful, too, for financial support of this project from Monmouth University, including a sabbatical, a summer fellowship, Creativity and Research grants, and the financial resources of my endowed chair. All the support sustained me in a truly meaningful way. Thank you.

This book brought me tremendous joy in the midst of personal heartache. Two of my best friends died. Without the loving support of Trish Maloney and Julie Berebitsky, I might not have taken on the project, and I cherished being able to share my latest discoveries and insights with them. They loved to laugh and they loved to learn, and I miss them terribly. My family also persevered through trying circumstances, and I am so grateful to my loving friends, family, and colleagues who supported me through those difficult days and nights.

Thank you to the friends who cheered me on through it all—Samantha Francois, Alexandra Friedrich and Marcus Oebbecke, Annie Gill, Arlene Eskilson, Jennifer Tobey, Liza Gardner, Ed Timke, Sarah Elvins, Stacie Taranto, Woody Register, Margaret Marsh, and the UAP crew (Celia Feinstein, Jimmy and Dianne Lemanowicz, Robin Levine, Kathy Miller, Lisa Sonneborn). There is nothing better than sharing a meal and a good story with Nancy Banks; thank you for sustaining me as I worked on this project and for your loving friendship. Here's to another forty years of bombing around.

Esther and Joe DeRosa have so generously supported this project and me with their love. I am grateful, too, to Jon and Amelia, Ben and Katelyn, Joyce and Peter, Thomas and Alena, Joseph, Samantha and Tommy, and Matt, for your encouragement. Thank you. My mother, Marilyn Parkin, was unfailingly supportive through it all. She encouraged me when it was hard and celebrated when it came together. At one point when I was overwhelmed by piles, she dove in and created order. I loved sharing the journey with her and learned so much along the way. Thank you for listening as I marveled at an interview, thrilled at something I'd learned, or contemplated how the hell I was going to fix something in the manuscript. I cherished our evening walks. Thank you.

My family sometimes joked that the best present for me would be a great piece of abortion market evidence, but the truth is that they were the best gift. Chris, Quinn, and Vivian celebrated each unearthed discovery, laughed at outrageous anecdotes, and admired my eBay treasures. I was grateful to have you as a sounding board and appreciate deeply your commitment to this work and your love of me. I love you.